Islamic Insurance Products

Mohd Ma'Sum Billah

Islamic Insurance Products

Exploring Takaful Principles, Instruments and Structures

palgrave
macmillan

Mohd Ma'Sum Billah
Professor of Finance, Insurance, Fintech and Investment
Islamic Economics Institute
King Abdulaziz University
Jaddah, Kingdom of Saudi Arabia

ISBN 978-3-030-17680-8 ISBN 978-3-030-17681-5 (eBook)
https://doi.org/10.1007/978-3-030-17681-5

This Palgrave Macmillan imprint is published by the registered company Springer Nature Switzerland AG
The registered company address is: Gewerbestrasse 11, 6330 Cham, Switzerland

This book is dedicated to the remembrance of my most beloved parents, Allamah Mufti Nur Mohammad (r) and Ustazah Akhtarun Nisa' (r), who have nourished me with their love and wisdom. May Allah (swt) *shower them with His Love and Mercy and grant them Jannat al-Ferdaus Nuzulah. I would also like to dedicate this book to my wife Dr Khamsiah Nawawi and children Dr Ahmad Mu'izz Billah, Ahmad Mu'azz Billah, Ahmad Muniff Billah and Akhtarun Naba' Billah for their continuous support and sacrifices. May all be blessed with Muwaddau Wa Rahmah, Qurratu A'yun and Mardhaati Allah (swt) in the life and the next.*

This book is also dedicated to the Ummah *and the whole of humanity.*

The original version of the book was revised: The Front Matter has been revised to correct the 'Foreword' author signature to 'Tuanku Syed Faizuddin Putra'. The correction to the book is available at https://doi.org/10.1007/978-3-030-17681-5

Foreword

ROYAL MESSAGE FROM HIS ROYAL HIGHNESS THE CROWN PRINCE OF PERLIS DYTM TUANKU SYED FAIZUDDIN PUTRA JAMALULLAIL AS THE PRESIDENT OF THE PERLIS ISLAMIC RELIGIOUS AND MALAY CUSTOMS COUNCIL (MAIPs).

بسم الله الرحمن الرحيم

Assalamualaikum Warahmatullahi Wabarakatuh "Raja Berdaulat, Rakyat Berilmu, Negeri Sejahtera, Perlis Maju".

All praises to Allah Subhanahu Wa Ta'ala, blessings to our beloved Muhammad Salallahualaihi Wasallam, his companions and his followers.

Alhamdulillah, I am very grateful to Allah Subhanahu Wa Ta'ala for this opportunity to convey a message in this book *Takaful and Re-takaful Products.*

Among the contemporary Muslim nations, Malaysia has in less than 25 years succeeded in moving from a developing economy to a developed one. This has been achieved through the modernization of the country's most important economic sectors such as energy, transport and communications and by the development of industrial zones and tax incentives for investors in exporting industries.

For the fifth consecutive year, Malaysia leads the Thomson Reuters' Global Islamic Economic Indicator. Malaysia enjoys a top rank in *Halal* food and Islamic finance, despite having less engaged assets than many other countries. This impressive performance reflects Malaysia's robust Islamic economic environment including *Takaful* and *Re-Takaful* industries, based on a strong state support and encouragement to maximize market opportunities.

Prof Dr Mohd Ma'Sum Billah is a Malaysian globally renowned Islamic finance scholar from King Abdulaziz University, Kingdom of Saudi Arabia, whose initiative has led to this unique and specialized book, *Takaful and Re-Takaful Products.* I am confident that this title is timely in benefiting the contemporary Islamic financial environment and particularly the *Takaful, Re-Takaful* and risk management sectors by special treatment with products and services in the global reality.

Therefore, it is a great pleasure and immense pride to write this foreword for the "*Takaful and Re-Takaful Products*". The book will undoubtedly contribute to the development of the global *Takaful* industry in particular, *Insya Allah.*

Thank You.

HRH TUANKU SYED FAIZUDDIN PUTRA IBNI TUANKU SYED SIRAJUDDIN JAMALULLAIL, D.K., S.P.M.P., P.A.T THE RAJA MUDA/ THE CROWN PRINCE OF PERLIS Istana Arau, Arau, Perlis

DYTM RAJA MUDA PERLIS Istana Arau, 02600 Arau, Perlis, Malaysia.

Preface

In the first years of the twenty-first century it is clear that the Islamic banking, finance and *Takaful* industries have grown to secure a significance position in the global sound economic environment with an estimated USD 2.4 trillion of assets and an 18% annual growth rate. Despite such a success in the field of Islamic financial there is no corresponding published knowledge in these areas, and in particular covering *Takaful* and *Re-takaful* in English. Thus the relevant communities in academic, industry and public service are not well served.

This book is therefore, a timely contribution to awareness of *takaful* and *re-takaful* products and their structures applicable in the contemporary socio-economic reality. *Takaful* and *Re-takaful Products* gives specialized treatment of Shari'ah-compliant *takaful* and *re-takaful* product solutions as practised and applicable in today's economy.

The book is divided into five parts with specialized products and issues in forty-one different chapters besides an introduction, a bibliography and an index. Part I provides an overview of *Takaful* and *Re-takaful*, which consists of three chapters addressing different core issues. Chapter 1 gives an overview of *takaful* products. Chapter 2 provides a paradigm of *re-takaful* products applicable today. Chapter 3 focuses on governing principles and policies facilitate *takaful and re-takaful* products and services.

Part II focuses on general *takaful* products, describing sixteen different classes of general *takaful* over the same number of chapters. Chapter 4 analyses the general *takaful* scheme *or* short-term *takaful* policies and their structures in general. Chapter 5 covers the motor *takaful* scheme, its policies, rulings, mechanisms and application. Chapter 6 presents a paradigm of the accident *takaful* scheme and its applied solutions. Chapter 7 covers the fire *takaful* scheme and its operational structure. Chapter 8 deals with practical experiences in fire *takaful* schemes. Chapter 9 provides a short-term medical *takaful* plan with empirical examples. Chapter 10 explores a model of health *takaful-rider plan* for a better healthcare. Chapter 11 discusses the group *takaful* plan as practised in Malaysia and some other jurisdictions. Chapter 12 describes the group *takaful* plan for healthcare with its operational structure. Chapter 13 contributes a model of pilgrimage (*hajj*) *takaful* plan as practiced in Malaysia. Chapter 14 analyses the *Hajj Badal* (substitute *Hajj*) *takaful* scheme and its practical mechanisms. Chapter 15 provides a comprehensive analysis of the *Ziarah* (visit) *takaful* scheme and its model structure. *Chapter 16* reveals the model of the group Islamic cash-line *takaful* scheme. Chapter 17 discusses the *Sukuk takaful* model, its essence and practical structure. Chapter 18 analyses the model of online *takaful* business to protect all levels of business operators against catastrophe. Chapter 19 covers the digital currency or cryptocurrency *takaful* model, its operational mechanisms and structures.

Part III deals with different classes of *Family Takaful* (Islamic life insurance) products. In its fifteen chapters it covers different classes of *Family Takaful* products. Chapter 20 gives a preview of the Islamic life insurance model with Shari'ah justification. Chapter 21 covers the *Family Takaful* (long-term) scheme and its structure. Chapter 22 describes a model of personal accident family *takaful* scheme with applied mechanisms. Chapter 23 discusses the critical illness *takaful* scheme. Chapter 24 covers group students' *takaful* plan to protect students from unpredicted catastrophe. Chapter 25 focuses on the education *takaful* plan to open up a higher education opportunities. Chapter 26 covers the senior citizen *takaful* plan. Chapter 27 provides a comprehensive analysis of the endowment *takaful* plan (*takaful Ma'asyi*). Chapter 28 describes a model of foreign workers' takaful plan. Chapter 29 discusses the mortgage *takaful* scheme. Chapter 30 covers the breast cancer *takaful* scheme (*takaful Hawa*) as practised in Malaysia. Chapter 31 covers the pregnancy *takaful* (*takaful wiladah*) plan. Chapter 32 shows a model of saving *takaful* (*takaful mesra)* plan. Chapter 33 deals with the unit trust *takaful* scheme to protect small investors against unpredicted risks. Chapter 34 covers the online *family takaful* business and its structural model.

Part IV focuses on *re-takaful* products, covering four different classes of *re-takaful* products over four chapters. Chapter 35 contributes with a model structure of *re-takaful products* and their underlying mechanisms.

Chapter 36 describes *re-takaful* product structure with an empirical treatment. Chapter 37 discusses the management mechanisms of *re-takaful* funds within the *Maqasid al-Shari'ah.* Chapter 38 deals with the investment procedures, mechanisms and structures of *re-takaful* funds.

Part V deals with Claim and Damages in *Takaful* and *Re-takaful* practices. It covers the three core issues of claim and damages in *takaful* and *re-takaful* practices. Chapter 39 focuses on claim procedures applicable in general *takaful* schemes. Chapter 40 covers claim procedures for *Family takaful* (Islamic life insurance) schemes. Chapter 41 discusses the Shari'ah framework and application of quantum damages in *takaful* practices by complying with the rules of *Maqasid al-Shari'ah.*

The concept of *takaful* and *re-takaful* products is at an early stage, yet there is yet no comprehensive work dedicated to the subject that offers empirical solutions for use as a reliable reference for continuing academic or industrial research. Thus, *Takaful* and *Re-takaful Products* can be seen as a pioneer in the field, a guide to academia, researchers, practitioners, decision-makers, programmers, professionals, promoters and students for their future research and development of furtherance niche products. If the book contains shortcomings we will be glad to hear from readers so that we can improve future editions.

Jaddah, Kingdom of Saudi Arabia — Mohd Ma'Sum Billah

Acknowledgements

There is no strength and power except in *Allah (swt)*, To Him comes the praise, the Savant, the Wise, the Omniscient, the most beautiful names belong to Him. May the blessing of Allah (swt) and peace be upon *Muhammad (saw)* and all the Prophets (*aws*) from the first to the last.

First of all, I would humbly like to acknowledge King Abdulaziz University, Kingdom of Saudi Arabia, and its prestigious wing Islamic Economics Institute for supporting us with every facility in research, academic, human capital and professional development activities outreaching the global *Ummah*. It is also a great honour for me to humbly acknowledge His Excellency Professor Dr. Abdulrahman Obaid AI-Youbi, the President of King Abdulaziz University, Professor Dr. Yousef Abdul Aziz Al Turki, the Vice President of King Abdulaziz University, Dr. Abdullah Qurban Turkistani, the Dean of the Islamic Economics Institute (IEI), King Abdulaziz University (KAU), Dr. Mohammad A. Naseef (Vice Dean, IEI-KAU), Dr. Marwan G. A. Andejani (Vice Dean, IEI-KAU), Dr. Hasan Mohammad Makhethi (Vice Dean, IEI-KAU), Dr. Maha Alandejani (Vice Dean, IEI, KAU), Dr. Faisal Mahmoud Atbani (Head, Department of

Insurance, IEI-KAU), Dr. Adnan M.A. Al-Khiary (Head, Department of Finance, IEI-KAU) and Dr. Albara Abdullah Abulaban (Head Department of Economics) for their continuous supports and encouragements towards dynamic professional development, excellent academic contributions and specialized advance scientific research activities. Humble acknowledgement is also extended to my respected fellow-colleagues from the IEI, King Abdulaziz University, including Dr. Yousef Abdullah Basodan (Associate Professor of Accounting, FEA-KAU), Dr. Ibrahim M.S. Abolola, Dr. Omar Hafiz, Prof Dr. Abdulrahim Al-Saati, Sheikh Dr. Ali Ahmed Al-Nadwi, Prof Abdul Azim Islahi, Dr. Ahmed Mahdi Belouafi, Dr. Fadul AbdulKarim Al-Bashir, Dr. Abdul Razzaq Belabes, Dr. Hichem Salem Hamza and my talented colleague Mr. Mohammed Alabdulraheem, Lecturer (Islamic banking and finance), IEI-KAU. Further acknowledgement is extended to Bank Negara Malaysia, ACIG Saudi Arabia, ARIL, Takaful Nasional Bhd, Takaful Malaysia Bhd, Takaful Ikhlas Bhd, MNRB Malaysia, Maybank Takaful, Takaful Etiqa, Bank Islam, Bank Mu'amalat, RHB, CIMB, HSBC, Standard Chartered, IBFIM, other universities, industries and professional firms including Dr. Ammar Bin Hassan (Malaysian Politician) and my research assistant Hafiz Akram bin Mohd Ghani whose direct and indirect supports with knowledge, experiences and resources are whole-heartedly recorded.

Mohd Ma'Sum Billah

Contents

Part I An Overview of *Takaful* and *Re-takaful* 1

1 An Overview of Takaful Products 3

2 Re-takaful Products in a Nutshell 29

3 Governing Principles of *Takaful* and *Re-takaful* Products 47

Part II General *Takaful* Products 65

4 Preview of General *Takaful* 67

5 Motor *Takaful* 75

6 Accident *Takaful* 97

7 Fire *Takaful* Plan 103

8 Experience in Fire *Takaful* 113

9 Medical *Takaful* Plan 123

10 Health *Takaful* Rider Plan 147

11 Group *Takaful* Plan 159

12 Group *Takaful* Plan for Health Care 167

13 Pilgrimage (Hajj) *Takaful* 181

14 Hajj Badal (Substitute Hajj) *Takaful* 189

15 Ziarah (Visit) *Takaful* 199

16 Group Islamic Cashline *Takaful* 211

17 *Sukuk* Takaful Plan 221

18 Online Takaful Business 227

19 Digital Currency Takaful 237

Part III Family *Takaful* Products 245

20 Preview of Islamic Life Insurance Products 247

21 Family *Takaful* Plan 271

22 Personal Accident *Takaful* 283

23 Critical Illness *Takaful* 295

24 Group Students' Takaful Plan 305

25 Education *Takaful* 313

26 Senior Citizen Takaful 321

27 Endowment (Ma'asyi) Takaful 325

28 Foreign Worker Takaful 331

29 Mortgage Takaful 343

30 Breast Cancer Takaful (Takaful Hawa) 355

31 Pregnancy Takaful (Takaful Wiladah) 367

32 Saving Takaful (Takaful Mesra) 377

33 Unit Trust Takaful 387

34 Online Family *Takaful* 395

Part IV *Re-takaful* Products 405

35 *Re-takaful* Products 407

36 Structure of *Re-takaful* Products 417

37 Management of the *Re-takaful* Fund 423

38 Investment of *Re-takaful* Funds 435

Part V Claim and Quantum 443

39 Claims Procedure in General *Takaful* 445

40 Claims Procedure in Family *Takaful* 457

41 Quantum of Damages in *Takaful* 473

Correction to: Islamic Insurance Products C1

Index 501

About the Author

Mohd Ma'Sum Billah, DBA, PhD, MCL, MMB, LLB (hons), is Professor of finance, insurance, fintech and investment, Islamic Economics Institute, King Abdul Aziz University, Kingdom of Saudi Arabia. Billah has been serving and contributing both academic as well as corporate industries for more than 20 years with management, teaching, research, solution proving and sharing of strategic and technical thoughts towards the advancement of Islamic finance and insurance (*Takaful*) besides *Halal* standard. He has published 32 books and chapters in books apart from more than 200 articles in journals and social media. He has been presenting in more than 300 conferences, seminars, executive workshops and industrial trainings in different parts of the world. In addition, he had also been affiliated with corporate, academic and financial industries including central banks, international corporate organizations, governments and NGOs in his capacity as a member in boards, advisor, strategic decision maker, transformer and reformer with strategic solutions. Among the areas of his interest and contributions are Islamic finance, insurance (*Takaful*), crowd-funding, investment, capital market (*Sukuk*), social finance, petroleum finance, trade, fin-tech and cryptocurrency models and standards.

List of Figures

Fig. 2.1	Structure of *Re-Takaful*. (Source: Author's own)	32
Fig. 2.2	*Re-Takaful* structure. (Source: Author's own collection)	39
Fig. 2.3	Joint guarantee. (Source: Author's own collection)	42
Fig. 2.4	Tabarru'. (Source: Author's own collection)	43
Fig. 2.5	Example of Re-takaful flow chart operation. (Source: Author's own collection)	44
Fig. 4.1	Organisation of the General *Takaful* contract. (Source: Author's own collection)	68
Fig. 5.1	Claim. (Source: Author's own collection)	80
Fig. 7.1	The distribution of profit ratio for Fire *Takaful* plan. (Source: Author's own collection)	109
Fig. 8.1	Distribution of profit ratio for the Fire *Takaful* plan. (Source: Author's own collection)	116
Fig. 8.2	Premium rating on buildings. (Source: Author's own collection)	117
Fig. 8.3	Claims procedure. (Source: Author's own collection)	118
Fig. 9.1	The Health *Takaful* Plan. (Source: Author's own collection)	124
Fig. 9.2	Scope of coverage. (Source: Author's own collection)	125
Fig. 9.3	Maturity periods of Health *Takaful* Plan. (Source: Author's own collection)	126
Fig. 10.1	The product. (Source: Author's own collection)	149
Fig. 10.2	The product. (Source: Author's own collection)	150
Fig. 10.3	Claim procedures. (Source: Author's own collection)	154
Fig. 10.4	PRIA of family *Takaful*. (Source: Author's own collection)	155
Fig. 12.1	Practicalities. (Source: Author's collection from TMB)	177
Fig. 12.2	Practicalities. (Source: Author's collection from TMB)	177
Fig. 12.3	Experiences. (Source: Author's collection from TMB)	178

Fig. 15.1	Participant. (Source: Author's collection from TMB)	201
Fig. 18.1	Functional structure. (Source: Author's collection)	230
Fig. 19.1	Digital currency receiver *Takaful* model. (Source: Author's own)	240
Fig. 19.2	Digital currency user *Takaful* model. (Source: Author's own)	242
Fig. 21.1	Process of the Family *Takaful* scheme. (Source: Author's own)	274
Fig. 23.1	The product structure. (Source: Author's collection TI)	300
Fig. 24.1	Scope of coverage. (Source: Author's collection)	308
Fig. 28.1	The experience of Takaful Nasional of the product. (Source: Author's collection)	339
Fig. 30.1	Cancellation. (Source: Author's collection from TMB)	363
Fig. 30.2	Experience. (Source: Author's collection from TMB)	364
Fig. 30.3	Experience. (Source: Author's collection from TMB)	365
Fig. 30.4	Experience. (Source: Author's collection from TMB)	365
Fig. 31.1	Funeral expenses. (Source: Author's collection from TMB)	374
Fig. 31.2	Funeral expenses. (Source: Author's collection from TMB)	375
Fig. 32.1	Takaful Mesra Niche. (Source: Author's collection from TNB)	379
Fig. 32.2	Application. (Source: Author's collection from TNB)	384
Fig. 33.1	Mechanisms of unit trust *Takaful*. (Source: Author's collection)	393
Fig. 35.1	Structure. (Source: Author's collection)	410
Fig. 37.1	*Re-Takaful* fund. (Source: Author's collection)	431
Fig. 37.2	*Re-Takaful* fund. (Source: Author's collection)	431
Fig. 40.1	The flow of contribution. (Source: Author's collection)	467
Fig. 40.2	Claim process practiced by *Takaful* Malaysia. (Source: Author's collection)	470
Fig. 41.1	Benefits may be awarded under *Takaful* against bodily injury or accidental death. (Source: Author's own)	494

List of Tables

Table 2.1	*Re-Takaful* versus reinsurance	33
Table 5.1	Types of vehicle	85
Table 5.2	Types of motorcycle	91
Table 9.1	Package A (with savings)	141
Table 9.2	Package B (without saving)	141
Table 10.1	Gross contribution rate (Per RM 10 daily hospital benefit)	151
Table 12.1	Type of package	172
Table 13.1	Compensation category	185
Table 13.2	Benefits	186
Table 14.1	A study on pilgrims after pilgrimage	195
Table 14.2	Changes between repeat pilgrimage and life improvement of pilgrims	196
Table 18.1	*Takaful* products	231
Table 21.1	Special circumstances	276
Table 22.1	Personal Accident *Takaful* (PA)	288
Table 22.2	Group Personal Accident *Takaful* Scheme (GPA)	288
Table 22.3	Group Personal Accident *Takaful* (short period)	289
Table 24.1	Benefits schedule	308
Table 25.1	Payment procedure: *Tabarru'* percentage into PSA (www.takaful-malaysia.com)	316
Table 25.2	Payment procedure: Fatwa complied by SAC (http://www.islamic-insurance.com/fatawa.html)	317
Table 27.1	Product package	328
Table 28.1	Rational outlook	332
Table 30.1	Contributions (p.a.)	357
Table 30.2	Additional payment	358
Table 30.3	Benefits	359

Table 31.1	Schedule payment of *Takaful* benefits	371
Table 32.1	Niche of Takaful Mesra	378
Table 32.2	Takaful Mesra Niche	379
Table 32.3	Takaful Mesra Niche	380
Table 34.1	Family *Takaful*	398
Table 34.2	General *Takaful*	399
Table 35.1	Performance and size of *Re-takaful* industry	413
Table 35.2	Performance and size of *Re-takaful* industry	414
Table 40.1	Central idea	458
Table 40.2	Documents for *Takaful* National Malaysia Berhad claims	461
Table 40.3	Statistics for death and permanent total disability claims for *Takaful* Malaysia for 2001	468
Table 40.4	*Tabarru'* Rates for PSA by *Takaful* Malaysia	469
Table 41.1	Beneficiaries of *al-Diyāh* (Bloodwit) against bodily injury or death	482
Table 41.2	Damages: *Al-Diyāh* versus *Takaful*	487
Table 41.3	Example of benefits for accidental death and permanent disablement in *Takaful*	488

Introduction

In the first years of the twenty-first century it is clear that the Islamic banking, finance and *Takaful* industries have grown to secure a significance position in the global sound economic environment with an estimated USD 2.4 trillion of assets and an 18% annual growth rate. Despite such success in the Islamic financial industries, dissemination of knowledge on these areas has not been correspondingly widespread. Therefore to date there are very few works available in the area of *Takaful* and *Re-takaful* in English. In addition, there is no comprehensive encyclopedia or databank on *Takaful* and *Re-takaful* with exclusive information available for academia, the relevant industries or general public, to be updated with a data on the global *Takaful* and *Re-takaful* industries.

Therefore, it is timely to produce a comprehensive encyclopedia with detailed information on *Takaful* and *Re-takaful* bringing benefits to the Muslim community from the resurgence of Islamic finance. Hence, by the blessing of Allah (swt), this manuscript has been humbly produced to provide updated information on the *Takaful* and *Re-takaful* industries across different parts of the globe.

The manuscript derives partly from earlier works and findings of the principal author, though with significant updates. It comprises of eight parts with different aspects of *Takaful* and *Re-takaful* besides a preface and an introduction and a list of references, glossary and index. Part I provides an outline and the conceptual frameworks of *Takaful* and *Re-takaful*. Part II continues with several aspects of regulatory frameworks governing *Takaful and Re-takaful* industries. Part III provides analysis of *Takaful* and conventional insurance practices. Part IV contributes a practical scenario of *Takaful* in the contemporary economic environment. Part V provides a *Shari'ah* alternative life insurance (family Takaful) model. Part VI contributes a comprehensive understanding of *Retakaful* business. Part VII analyses contemporary issues of *Takaful* implementation. Part VIII, the final part, provides a databank of *Takaful* and *Re-takaful* that might be useful to researchers, academia as well as industry experts.

Finally, it is hoped that this humble work may contribute possible benefits for researchers, academia, *Takaful* and *Re-takaful* practitioners, bankers, financiers, regulators, decision makers, marketers, students and members of the public who have an interest in the field of *Takaful*, *Re-takaful*, mutual fund, risk management and financial industries. The authors recognize that the book may contain shortcomings, which are solely the responsibility of the authors; but they will be very grateful to hear of such anomalies so that they can in the future improve the text and thereby offer even greater benefits to the *Ummah*, Ensha Allah (swt).

PART I

An Overview of *Takaful* and *Re-takaful*

CHAPTER 1

An Overview of Takaful Products

1.1 Introduction

Takaful (Islamic insurance) is a financial transaction of mutual co-operation between two parties with the aim of providing financial security for one of them against unexpected material risk. In a *Takaful* transaction, the party called the participant (insured) pays a particular amount of money known as a contribution (premium) to another, who is known as the *Takaful* operator (insurer), with mutual agreement that the operator is under legal obligation to provide the participant with financial security against unexpected loss or damage caused to the subject of the policy should such arise within the agreed period of the policy. However, in *Takaful* life policies, where the loss does not occur to the subject in question within the specified period, the participant is entitled to the entirety of any contributions paid to the participant's account together with the share of profits made out of the cumulated paid contributions from that same, based on the principles of *Al-Mudharabah* financing technique. In this transaction, both the *Takaful* operator and the participant help each other for the sake of financial protection.

It is acknowledged that the idea for this chapter has been shared with the author's other related research works, for the common benefit of academia, regulators, researchers as well as industries.

Mohd Ma'Sum Billah, *Islamic Insurance Products*,
https://doi.org/10.1007/978-3-030-17681-5_1

Such co-operation is in line with the Qur'anic doctrine of mutual co-operation as Allah (swt) commanded:

> co-operate you one another in righteousness and piety. (Qur'an, 5:3)

Under Shari'ah, the commandment to practice mutual co-operation is not an absolute. There is, in other words, a limitation to it, as Allah (swt) has further prohibited mankind from co-operating in any manner that involves sinful elements:

> and do not co-operate in sin and rancor. (Ibid.)

Based on the above verse of the Qur'an, it is submitted that the practice of *Takaful* contract and business will only be in harmony with the Islamic concept of mutual co-operation should the transaction be based on the principles of *Al-Mudharabah*, which is permissible in the eyes of Allah (swt) and is carried out with the noble and sincere intention to ensure the participant with financial security against unexpected future material risk. Hence, in order for a *Takaful* transaction to be valid and enforceable, it should be free from unlawful elements, such as usury, fraud and so on (Billah 1993).

This research, however, seeks to provide a conceptual framework for Islamic insurance and also the scenario of governing principles that regulate *Takaful* and *Re-takaful* products on the ground today.

1.2 The *Takaful* Niche

- Islamic insurance differs from conventional insurance. This is because an Islamic insurance policy must operate based on the concept of *Al-Mudharabah*, a profit-sharing scheme, and must be free from elements illegal under Shari'ah. Scholars who are not in favour of legalising this sort of insurance must have based their opinions and judgments on conventional insurance practices, which certainly involve a few unlawful elements in the eyes of the Shari'ah.
- A *Takaful* contract binds the insurer only on a unilateral basis, so that the insurer is under obligation to provide compensation against the loss to the subject of the policy, while the insured will not be forced if he does not want to continue payment of the premiums. Yet it is necessary for the insured to continue payment of premiums in

order to claim any benefits from the policy. If the insured discontinues payments, the paid premium should not be forfeited.

- An Islamic model of insurance is based on the fundamental principles of mutual co-operation and solidarity, as ordained by Allah (swt) to this effect:
- "Sustain a mutual co-operation among yourselves in the righteousness and piety" (Qur'an, at 5:2).
- A Shari'ah-based insurance policy does not involve the unlawful element of usury (*Riba*), but is based on the profit-sharing financing technique of *Al-Mudharabah*, whereby the insured pays premiums to the insurer (insurance company) who will run a business with such accumulated monies, while the profits arising from such transactions will be shared by both the insurer and the insured (Rashid 1993).
- In the case of an Islamic life insurance policy, some claim that such practice is prohibited in Islam, relying on the fact that the insurer and the insured, in this case, are trying to determine life or death, as claimed by the Muslim Brotherhood in 1941 (Klingmuller n.d.). However, such criticism was proven to be groundless.
- In an Islamic model of life insurance, however, the nominee(s) is not an absolute beneficiary(s), but a mere trustee who is under obligation to receive the benefits over the policy and distribute them among the legal heirs of the deceased in accordance with the principles of *Mirath* (inheritance) and *Wasiyah* (bequest) (Billah 1993).
- In an Islamic insurance transaction, an agent is working for the company. Hence, it is posited here that an agent should also have a certain share in profits of the business carried out by the company as their salary. The agent, therefore, should not be paid out of the insured premiums.
- In an Islamic life insurance policy, if the insured passes away any time before the maturity then the beneficiary(s) is expected to claim from the policy the total paid premiums, a share of the profits and any dividends made over the paid premiums, which are all based on *Al-Mudharabah* financing technique, plus an additional sum of donation from the company taken out of its charitable fund upon considering the financial status of the beneficiary(s) (Billah n.d.). But if the insured sustains his life upon maturity of the policy, the insured is entitled to claim from the insurer the total paid premiums and also a share of the profits and dividends accordingly.

- In the case of general *Takaful*, it is to be mutually understood by both the insurer and the insured that the insured's payment of premiums will be given out as a donation based on the principle of *Tabarru'* (Rashid n.d.) (donation or contribution) whereby the insured cannot legally claim back the premium if there is no loss on the agreed subject. However, if loss or damage occurs to the subject within the policy period, the insurer is unilaterally bound to pay the agreed compensation to the insured for that particular loss or damage.
- The person who claims the benefits over a policy must have an insurable interest on the subject matter.
- The parties involved in a *Takaful* policy must have legal capacity to enter into contract.

1.3 Socio-economic Foundation of *Takaful*

Takaful possesses certain fundamental characteristics upon which an insurance contract is to be validated. Those fundamental characteristics can mainly be classified into four categories, as follows.

*1.3.1 Sincerity (***Ikhlas***)*

Every transaction and dealing should always be done with sincerity and pure intention in order to achieve the desired result from Allah (swt). He (swt) says:

> And they have been commanded no more than this, to worship Allah (swt), offering him sincere devotion. (Qur'an, at 98:5)

This has been enhanced by the tradition of the Prophet (saw) as follows:

> Narrated by Omar Ibn Khattab (R) the Holy Prophet (saw) said: The validity of the actions depend on intention and therefore every man shall have but that which he intended. (Bukhari and Muslim)

Moreover, the parties to the insurance contact must have the sincerity not simply for gain, but to be bound by that transaction based on the principles of mutual co-operation, solidarity and brotherhood with the intention of rescuing one of them from unexpected losses and damages.

This is because Allah (swt) never looks at any material gains but rather at the sincerity of the heart. The Holy Prophet (saw) stated words to this effect:

> Narrated by Abu Huraira (R) the Holy Prophet (saw) said: Verily Allah (swt) never look at your physical shape nor at your appearance but considers sincerity in your hearts. (Ali, Maulana Syed Muhammad et al. 1990)

What is more, in an insurance transaction the parties must undertake to put their trust and faith in Allah (swt) (Shafi, Mawlana Mufti Mohd n.d.) in order to get His (swt) protection from any unpredicted loss. This is because an insurer formally undertakes only to compensate the insured against a loss or damage, though he (i.e. the insurer) is not liable to guarantee ultimate protection. This is because Allah (swt) is the one who has power of protection over all in the universe. He (swt) indicates this as follows:

> To Him belongs the domination of the heaven and the earth: to give life and death: and He has power over all things. (Qur'an at 57:2)

1.3.2 Shari'ah Principles

A *Takaful* business in the eyes of Islamic discipline will not be valid should any aspect of it contravene Shari'ah principles. The Takaful Act (Malaysia) 1984 (and the Islamic Financial Services Act 2013) rules that a Shari'ah-based insurance is enforceable if its "aims and operations do not involve any element which is not approved by the Shari'ah" (Takaful Act (Malaysia), 1984). Therefore, it is a prerequisite for the validity of an insurance contract that no aspect of it should contravene any expressed or implied Shari'ah sanctions. It is also to be clarified here that Islam is the only system of life recommended by Allah (swt) (Qur'an, at 3:19) and, therefore, it is logical for any transaction (including insurance) to conform with the Divine rules and regulations. Any transaction that fails to be practised in line with such Divine will thus be rendered invalid. Allah (swt) says:

> If anyone desires any system other than Islam never will it be recognised by Allah (swt). (Ibid.)

1.3.3 *Moral Attributes*

A *Takaful* contract and practice must also conform with moral sanctions. Those moral sanctions and values are itemised as follows:

- The principle of *utmost good faith*: In a *Takaful* contract, the parties should observe the principles of utmost good faith, honesty, disclosure and truthfulness. This principle could be justified by the following verse of the Qur'an:

> Do not misappropriate your property among yourselves in vanities. (Qur'an, at 4:29)

- The parties involved in a *Takaful* contract should not be greedy in gaining something but should purify their purposes and aims based on the principle of mutual co-operation in protecting one from an unexpected disaster or loss. This is in line with Divine sanction:

> help ye one another in righteousness and piety. (Ibid.)

1.3.4 *Elements of a* Takaful *Contract*

It is suggested that the following elements should be available in a Shari'ah-based *Takaful* transaction:

- The parties to the contract must have legal capacity (The Takaful Act (Malaysia) 1984);
- The availability of insurable interest (Rashid n.d.); indemnity clause: The *Takaful* operator is unilaterally bound to compensate the insured for the loss to the agreed subject;
- The payments of premiums by the insured as a consideration in the contract;
- Mutual consent by both parties. This requirement has been justified by the Qur'anic sanction:

> Do not misappropriate your property among yourselves in vanities, but let there be amongst you traffic and trade by mutual good-will. (Qur'an, at 4:29)

- An offer and an acceptance is to be expressed in formal agreement between the insurer and the insured, in which the terms and conditions being set out are subject to the doctrine of *Uberrimae Fidei*, and of course in compliance with the Shari'ah principles (Sudan n.d.).
- Specification of the period for the agreed policies which are to be contained in the agreement.
- A contract that is *Takaful* should be enacted based on the principles of *Riba* but should operate along the lines of *Al-Mudharabah* financing technique (Shafi, Maulana Mufti Muhammad n.d.), whereby both parties will enjoy a share of any profits and dividends made over the paid premiums and company's policies.

1.4 Rational Outlook

A *Takaful* policy does not signify a change for a material gain nor does it override the power and determination of Allah (swt) in one's life, death or destiny. But it aims at being pleasing to Allah (swt) through the concept of mutual help and co-operation, with the goal of providing material assistance against unexpected future damage, loss or peril. After all, Allah (swt) does not prohibit one from making effort in overcoming difficulties or obstacles in life. Here are some of the basic purposes of having a *Takaful* policy:

- A *Takaful* policy will enable certain helpless people to be rescued from unexpected future material risk which may lead to hardship in those unfortunate lives. The Holy Prophet (saw) advised the *Ummah* to come forward in relieving one's hardship. He (saw) said the following:

> Narrated by Abu Huraira (R) from Holy Prophet (saw) saying that: whosoever removes a worldly hardship from a believer Allah (swt) will remove from him one of the hardship of the hereafter; Whosoever alleviates the needy person, Allah (swt) will alleviate from him in this world and the next. (Ibrahim Ezzeddin et al. IIFSO 1985)

- A *Takaful* policy contributes towards the reduction of poverty in society while ensuring a comfortable life for the poor. It is universal in nature that anyone might become poor resulting from the occurrence of material loss or damage. Such material poverty could be solved should one have an insurance policy, insuring him/her against such damage or loss. An insurance policy hence guarantees the insured a comfortable life or material security against unexpected loss or risk. Allah (swt), indeed, encourages people to seek a better life in the world and in the hereafter. He (swt) says to the effect:

> Our Lord, give us comfortable life in both the world and the hereafter. (Qur'an, at ch. 2:201)

- Having a *Takaful* policy may ensure a development of mutual co-operation and the spirit of brotherhood as well as cultivating solidarity. The rationale behind the establishment of such insurance is further highlighted by the Takaful Act (Malaysia) 1984 (Islamic Financial Services Act 2013), which reads as follows:

> It is a scheme based on brotherhood, solidarity and mutual assistance which provides mutual financial aid and assistance to the participants in case of need whereby the participants mutually agreed to contributed for the purpose. (Takaful Act (Malaysia, 1984))

For example, the insured in a policy pays regular premiums to the insurer (*Takaful* company) which enables the insurer to invest and make profits, while the insurer undertakes to provide material assistance for the insured in the case of unexpected loss, damage or peril. Such financial co-operation could certainly strengthen brotherhood among the parties to the policy in achieving economic progress and independence. Here, the practice of mutual co-operation is of course recommended by Allah (swt):

> maintain a mutual co-operation among yourselves in righteousness and piety. (Ibid.)

- A *Takaful* policy contributes towards producing a society with self-reliance. Such an insurance policy materially protects the insured from unexpected tragedy, loss or damage. However, availability of this material protection will ensure that the insured will not be dependent on others' assistance and help in difficulties. Allah (swt) in this respect always intends to facilitate and make life easy and comfortable for all. He (swt) says:

Allah (swt) intends an easy life for you while he does not want you to be in difficulties. (Ibid.)

- A *Takaful* policy is based on the principles of *Al-Mudharabah* financing technique whereby the parties involved share the profits with an agreed portion, simultaneously avoiding the consumption of *Riba*. An interest-based transaction, on the other hand, always leads to unfairness in a commercial society. The practice of *Riba* is prohibited not only by Allah (swt) in the Qur'an, it has also been prohibited in other faiths and traditions as well. Aristotle, for instance, rejected the concept of interest, while Cato, in rejecting such practice, equated interest consumption to homicide in 340 BC. Lex Genucia declared in Rome that interest consumption was unlawful. According to the teachings of Judaism, interest was considered as unfair and unfriendly appropriation. In AD 1311, Pope Clement announced that all transactions involving usury were prohibited and, hence, he declared that all secular legislations in favour of such practice were null and void (Pervez, Imtias Ahmad, 1995). As far as Islam is concerned, Allah (swt) has prohibited the consumption of *Riba* for the obvious reason of its unfairness. The Holy Prophet (saw) said to the effect:

O ye who believe! Do not eat usury, doubled and multiplied. (Qur'an, at 3:130)

The *Al-Mudharabah* financing technique is, however, considered by Islamic jurists to represent a fair and just transaction and hence presents fair commercial dealing for the community as the best alternative to unfair interest-based transactions (Shafi, Mawlana Mufti Muhammad n.d.).

- The case of an Islamic life insurance policy has often been misunderstood by Muslim scholars as a transaction determining one's life and destiny (Klingmuller n.d.). Such a misconception is of course groundless. This is because a life insurance policy is a transaction for welfare aimed at compensating and providing material protection for, inter alia, the unfortunate offspring, who may have been left helpless upon the death of the deceased (policy holder or the insured). The Holy Prophet (saw) also advises people to provide for their offspring's material protection:

Narrated by Amir bin Saad bin Abi Waqqas (R), The Holy Prophet (saw) said: Verily it better for you to leave your offspring wealthy than to leave them poor asking others for help. (Khan, Muhammad Muhsin n.d.)

- An Islamic life insurance policy guarantees future material security for the widow and other dependants of the deceased (assured). The Holy Prophet (saw) encouraged people to strive towards ensuring security for widows and the poor in society.

Narrated by Safwan bin Salim (R), the Holy Prophet (saw) said: The one who looks after and works for a widow and for a poor person, is like a warrior fighting for the cause of Allah (swt), or like a person who fasts during the day and prays through the night. (Ibid.)

- An Islamic life policy guarantees future material protection for, *inter alia*, orphans and it is again justified by a tradition of the Holy Prophet (saw). He (saw) advised people to provide security for orphans for the purpose of getting great significance in the hereafter.

Narrated by Sahal bin Saad (R), the Holy Prophet (saw) said: I and the person who looks after an orphan and provides for him security will be in paradise like this. (Ibid.)

- Finally, an Islamic insurance policy also has its own hidden rationale in the sense that it generally insures security for someone from unexpected risk and this may encourage every individual in society to involve themselves in any lawful transaction without hesitation or fear of facing possible future loss or damage. Allah (swt) has always encouraged people to be involved in any lawful trade. He (swt) says:

Allah (swt) permitted trade and transaction while prohibiting usury. (Qur'an, at 2:275)

1.5 Argument for and Against *Takaful*/Insurance

The *Ulama* have mixed views on the validity of insurance. Generally, the views of Muslims scholars may be divided into three classes, viz.:

- Insurance practice is entirely lawful provided that it is free from element of usury. Among the Ulama sharing this viewpoint are Shaikh Mohammad Abduh (Vardict, Mankabady n.d.), the Hanafi lawyer Shaikh Ibn Abidin (Kling Muller n.d.), Mohammad Taqi Amini, Shaikh Mahmud Ahmad, Mustafa Ahmad Zarqa, Syed Mohammad Sadeeq al-Ruhani, Ibrahim Tahawi, Ahmad Taha Al-Sanusi, Yusuf Musa, Mohammad Al Bahi, Ali Al-Khafif, Zafar Shahidi, Mohammad Nejatullah Siddiqi, Mohammad Muslehudin, M.A. Manna, Ali Jalamuddin Awad (Siddiqi, M.N. n.d.) as well as Ayatullah Khomeni (Khomeni, Ayatullah, *Tawzih al-Masaill* 1979).
- The second group accepts general insurance practice but objects to Islamic life insurance policy as it involves the elements of gambling *(Maisir)* and uncertainty (*Gharar*), as well as contrasting with the principles of *Mirath* and *Wasiyah*. The Muslim scholars belonging to this group decided this view in a seminar held in Morocco on 6 May 1972 (Mankabady n.d.). Among these are Abdur Rahman Isa, Ahmad Ibrahim, Shaikh Shawkat Ali Khan, Mohd. Musa, Mufti Mohammad Bakheet, Mohammad Abu Zuhra (Siddiqi n.d.), Shaikh al-Azhar Shaikh Jaid al-Haq Ali Jaid al-Haq (Al-Iqtisadul Islami, July 1995) the Muslim Brotherhood, which published its views in 1941 (Kling Muller n.d.) and the Muslim World League Conference in 1965 (Rashid, n.d.).
- The third group clearly and totally rejects any practice of insurance policy or business on the grounds that it involves the elements of *Riba*, *Maisir* and *Gharar*, which are strictly prohibited by Shari'ah. Among the Islamic scholars who are in favour of the third view are Mustafa Zaid, Abdullah al-Qalqeeli, Jalal Mustafa al-Sayyad and Shawkat Ali Khan (Siddiqi, M.N. n.d.).
- We have seen how Muslim scholars in particular and Muslims in general have objected to the validity of insurance policy and practice. In my efforts to justify the validity of insurance practice, please allow me to highlight the misconceptions that have surrounded the very idea of insurance as well as its operations, which may have urged some Muslim scholars to such rejection. Finally, I would also like to refute these misconceptions in my sincere and humble attempts to prove that insurance practice may become valid in the eyes of the Shari'ah.

1.6 Misconceptions

- An Islamic insurance policy contains the element of riba (Shafi, Mawlana Mufti Mohd n.d.). Hence, any transaction that involves *Riba* is void ab initio. Allah (swt) has clearly forbidden *Riba*-based transaction in the following verse:

Allah (swt) permitted trade while He prohibited *Riba*. (Qur'an at ch. 2:275)

- This is because it contains an element of betting, as the insured, in an Islamic insurance policy, hopes to get the opportunity for material gain and hence this is similar to betting. This view had been developed unanimously by some *Ulama* (Conference held in Mecca in Sha'ban, 1398H).
- It also contains the element of *Gharar*, which means uncertainty in either the object or the subject matter of a transaction. Any transaction involving the element of *Gharar* is void ab initio under Shari'ah. The Holy Prophet (saw) prohibited any transaction involving the element of *Gharar* in the following tradition:

The Holy Prophet (saw) prohibited transaction by *Gharar*. (Dr. Saad, Faruq, Darul afaq al-Jadidah, Bairut, 1985)

- Further, it contains the element of *Maisir* which has been strictly prohibited by Allah (swt) in the Qur'an (ch. 2:219). A transaction involving gambling is such that the gambler pays a certain amount of money in which the gambler hopes for material gain. Hence, it was argued that an insurance policy has the elements of *Maisir* in that the insured pays the premiums with the hope for a chance of material gain with a large amount of money. Therefore, such a transaction is alleged to involve the unlawful element of *Maisir*. Thus, it is not permissible. As Allah (swt) prohibited *Maisir* in the following sanction:

They ask you concerning the wine and gambling. Say: In them is great sin. (Ibid.)

- There is also no express authority from the Divine principles justifying the validity of the practice of insurance. Hence, it has been argued that any transaction or dealing that is inconsistent with the Qur'an and the Sunnah or Tradition of the Holy Prophet (saw) should be held as void. Allah (swt) has indicated this to the effect:

> if anyone desires a system other than Islam never will it be accepted from him. (Id., at ch. 3:85)

- It is contrary to the principle of *Tawakkul*. In an Islamic insurance policy, the insured puts trust in the insurer to protect him against unexpected loss instead of putting his trust in almighty Allah (swt). Such practice is against the principle of *Tawakkul*, according to which every believer is obliged to put his own trust (*Tawakkul*) in Allah (swt) only. Allah (swt) says:

> but in Allah (swt) put your trust if you have faith. (Ibid., at ch. 5:26)

- It is contrary to the principles of *Mirath* and *Wasiyah*. This is because in an Islamic life insurance policy the nominee(s) is (are) an absolute beneficiary(s) over the policy after the demise of the insured, in which case the nominee(s) deprives the heirs of the deceased from their legal rights based on the principles of *Mirath* and *Wasiyah* (Billah, M. Masum n.d.).
- Some Muslims and even some Islamic scholars claim that to have a life insurance policy means to insure one's life against death and that such practice is unlawful. Among those who support this opinion are Shaikh Al-Azhar Shaikh Zad al-Haqq Ali Zad al-Haqq (Al-Iqtisadul Islami, supra), the publication of Muslim Brotherhood of 1914 (Kling Muller n.d.), the unanimous decision of the Muslim scholars in a seminar held in Morocco on 6 May 1972 (Mankabady n.d.) and also the verdict of the Supreme Islamic Court in Egypt on 27 December 1926 (Al-Sanhuri 1968). The above view is mainly based on the grounds that no one can insure one's life or death but Almighty Allah (swt) who is the all-powerful Cherisher and Sustainer of the whole universe. Allah (swt) justifies this like so:

> Verily the knowledge of hour is with Allah (swt). It is He who sends down rain, and He who knows what is in the wombs nor does anyone know what it is that he will earn tomorrow, nor does anyone know in what land he is to die. Verily with Allah (swt) is full knowledge and He is acquainted (with all things). (Qur'an, at 31:34)

- An Islamic insurance policy counts towards insuring one's wealth and property. In the light of the Shari'ah, a transaction that guarantees protection of another's property is said to be invalid except in three situations: fear of unjust enrichment; fear of losing one's property; and fear of one's property being destroyed or perishing. This view was upheld by Shaikh al-Azhar Zal al-Haqq in denying the validity of a life insurance policy (*Al-Iqtisadul Islami*, *op. cit.*, at 60).
- An Islamic life insurance contract involves unlawful elements. A contract that is based on unlawful elements is not binding, as the Holy Prophet (saw) said in one Tradition:

> Muslims are bound by their conditions except the condition which prohibits the lawful one or the one which permits the unlawful one. (Shaikh Jad al-Haqq in Al-Iqtisadul Islami n.d.)

Finally, the Shaikh al-Azhar Zad al-Haqq Ali Zadal-Haqq in a recent fatwa session advised the Muslim Ummah against practising the taking out of life insurance policies as this involves unlawful elements and a Muslim should not make money or profit through unlawful means (see Al-Iqtisadul Islami).

1.7 Response to the Misconceptions

- An Islamic model of an insurance policy does not involve the element of *Riba* because it is practised based on the *Al-Mudharabah* financing technique (Shafi, Mawlana Mufti Muhammad n.d.) in which both the insurer and the insured share the profits and dividends made out over the paid premiums in agreed proportion. Such a transaction is based on mutual agreement between parties and, therefore, the Shari'ah Supervisory Board in Sudan held that such a transaction does not contravene the Shari'ah nor does it contain any unlawful element (*Rules of the Supervisory Board*, Sudan). Moreover, it is further justified by the Divine principle of mutual transaction, as Allah (swt) says to the effect:

> O ye who believe! do not misappropriate your property among yourselves in vanities, but let there be among you traffic and trade by mutual good will. (Qur'an, at 4:29)

- An Islamic insurance policy does not supersede the will of Allah (swt). In such a policy, particularly in a life insurance policy, it is not the aim to insure and determine one's life or death nor does one intend to determine the future material fortunes of one's dependants. A life insurance policy also does not connote the idea of the insured trying to protect his life from death, against the will of Allah (swt). Nor does an insurance policy mean that the insured is determining his future financial capacity. A policy, be it general or life, simply means that both the insurer and the insured, in a contract of insurance, mutually agree to work for compensation of or security against an unexpected tragedy. Such a concept is of course in line with the Islamic principles whereby Islam encourages the *Ummah* to strive hard in overcoming difficulties in their lives. As the Prophet (saw) said:

> Narrated by Abu Huraira (R) the Holy Prophet (saw) said: Whosoever removes a worldly grief from a mu'min, Allah (swt) will take away from him one of the griefs of the hereafter. Whosoever alleviates a needy person, Allah (swt) will alleviate from him in both the world and the hereafter. (Sahih Muslim in an Nawawi)

- In an Islamic insurance policy, the insured is not putting his own trust (*Tawakkul*) on the insurer for future protection; rather, it is a mere mutual transaction whereby both parties agree to work for the welfare or protection of the insured against an unexpected occurrence of loss or damage. This is of course in line with the Divine principle of mutual co-operation as Allah (swt) commanded:

> Do mutual co-operation one another in righteousness and piety. (Qur'an, at 5:3)

- An Islamic insurance policy does not involve gambling or betting. Mustafa Al-Zarqa maintains that the gambler in a transaction of gambling or betting is always hoping for a chance of material gain, in the spirit of defeating each other rather than co-operating (Al-Zarqa, Mustafa, *Nizam al-Tameen*, *Muassasatul Risalah*, Beirut, 1984). In contrast, the parties in a contract of insurance are bound together in a manner of mutual co-operation and good-will in providing material security for the orphans (For justification, see in *Sahih al-Bukhari*, *op. cit.*, Vol. 8, No. 34, at 23) widows (Id., at no. 35) and other dependents (*loc. cit.*) as well as one's own self against an unexpected future loss, damage or peril.

- An Islamic insurance contract also does not involve *Gharar*. In an insurance policy generally, the subject matter is the property against which the risk is presumed to potentially occur in the future. The subject matter of the insurance contract is thus definite. Similarly, the subject of a life insurance policy is the life of the insured, which is also definite in the sense that the insured has been given life by Allah (swt) and will one day die by the will of Allah (swt) too. Such occurrence of life or death is of course certain as Allah (swt) says:

Every soul shall have a test of death. (Qur'an, at 3:185)

Therefore, the allegation that Islamic insurance policy involves the element of *Gharar*, thus making it invalid, is groundless.

- Some believe that an Islamic insurance policy cannot be justified as something that expresses Divine sanction, and that hence it is unlawful. In responding to this misconception, there are a couple of Divine provisions in the Qur'an and the Tradition or Sunnah of the Holy Prophet (saw) approving the principles of mutual co-operation (Id., at 5:3) and *Al-Mudharabah* financing technique (Shafi, Mawlana Mufti Mohammad n.d.). Thus, both Divine elements mentioned above are contained in a Shari'ah-based insurance policy. Moreover, the idea of insurance policy and practice originated from the traditional doctrine of *al-Aqila*, which was later approved by the Holy Prophet (saw) in one of his verdicts on a dispute between two women from the Hudhail tribe (Ibn. Asir n.d.). The case in which the Holy Prophet (saw) gave the above judgment can clearly be observed in the below Tradition:

Narrated by Abu Huraira (R) that two women from Hudhail tribe fought with each other and one of them flung a stone at the opponent, killing her and what was in her womb; the case was brought to the Prophet (saw) in which he gave verdict that the *dyat* (bloodwit) of her unborn child is a male or female slave of the best quality and he also decided that the vicarious liability of the *dyat* on behalf of the slain is to be rendered to her paternal relatives while the Prophet (saw) made her son and those who were with them her heirs.[1]

The same doctrine of *al-Aqila* was subsequently approved by the second caliph Sayyedana Umar (R), who even practised it mandatorily in some cases (Gibb n.d.). Thus, it is baseless to allege that insurance policy and practice have no basis for justification.

- Some argue that the practice of Islamic insurance is contrary to the Islamic principle of *Tawakkul* (putting trust in Allah (swt)). It is admitted here that the insurer and the insured, in such a policy, mutually agree to take an initiative for the protection of the insured against an unexpected risk, loss or damage on the subject in question, but they ultimately still put their trust in almighty Allah (SWT) who is the sole Cherisher and Sustainer of the whole universe. In fact, the initiative that is taken by both parties does not deviate from the principle of *Tawakkul*, as such an initiative is only an effort made to the best of their ability to overcome future unexpected difficulties and nothing more. Indeed, in accordance with *Tawakkul*, man is asked to strive to the best of their ability in performing a particular act or job before putting one's trust in Allah (swt). The Holy Prophet (saw) gave a paradigm of *Tawakkul* in the following Tradition:

> The Holy Prophet (saw) told a Bedouin Arab who left his camel untied, trusting to the will of Allah (swt), tie the camel first then leave it to the will of Allah (swt). (Sunan al-Tirmizi, op. cit., No. 2517 at 668)

Therefore, it is concluded here that the practice of insurance does not contravene the Islamic principle of *Tawakkul.*

- An Islamic life insurance policy does not contravene the principles of *Mirath* and *Wasiyah*. In a life insurance policy, the nominee(s) is nothing more than a trustee, as held by the supreme court of Pakistan in the case of ([1974] PLD 185 (SC)), who is under an obligation to

[1] For the text, see *Sahih al-Muslim* (Tahqiq) Mohd. Nasiruddin al-Albani, Laznatu Ihya al-*Sunnah*, Ashare, Arabi, Asyuf (n.d.), *Kitab Tahreem al-Dimaa' wa Zitnil Qisas al al-Diyyat*, No. 1032, at 274. Also see *Sahih al-Bukhari, Kitab al-Diyyat*, Bab *Janeen al-Marat*, No. 6395. For a translation see *Sahih al Muslim* (translation English), Siddiqi, A. Hamid, Darul arabia, Lebanon, 1978, Vol. 3, No. 4:68, at 905.

receive the benefits over the policy on behalf of the heirs of the deceased (assured) and distribute these benefits among the heirs of the deceased in accordance with the Islamic principles of *Mirath* and *Wasiyah*.

Hence, the nominee(s) here is not an absolute beneficiary(s) but a mere trustee and the nominee(s) may only receive a portion of the benefits if he or she is one of the legal heirs of the deceased.

1.8 Further Justifications

Besides the grounds that have already been mentioned in justifying the ideas and practices of taking out an insurance policy, there are some additional grounds that could well justify insurance—as follows:

- An Islamic insurance transaction is quite similar to the principle of *Wadiyah*, whereby two parties engage themselves in an agreement in which one of them deposits money with the other as a trust or *Amanah* for the purpose of safekeeping (Al-Zubaidi, Mohammad, *Tajul Aris*, Vol. 2, Kuwait, 1967). Likewise, such methods of dealing also exist in a contract of insurance, as the insured deposits money to the insurer for future safety. The governing principles of *Wadiyah* have been developed from the Qur'an. Allah (swt) says to the effect:

> Verily, Allah (swt) commands you to render back your trust to those to whom they are due. (Qur'an, at ch. 4:58)

- Any transaction originated from ancient custom or *Urf* is permissible so long as such custom is not in contravention of any of the Divine principles enshrined in the Qur'an and the Sunnah of the Prophet (saw). Islam in this matter has always been flexible in accepting any custom or *Urf* of the people which may be convenient for society, but of course with the condition that such custom is in line with the Shari'ah. The justification of *Urf* is indicated in the following Hadith:

> Whatever Muslims see good it is appreciated by Allah (swt). (Qudama, Ibn, Raudatul Nadhir, n.d.)

An Islamic insurance contract was thus originated from the ancient Arab doctrine of *al-Aqila*, which had been approved by the Prophet (saw) (Gibb n.d.), hence making the custom and at the same time the practice of insurance is justified as a legal entity (*The Mejelle* n.d.).

- The origin of every transaction is permissible unless an authority proves it invalid. This principle has been laid down by Ibn Nazim in the following maxim:

The origin in everything is lawful unless an authority proves one unlawful. (Suyuti, Al-Imam Jalaluddin Abd. Rahman, Al-Ashbah Wa-al-Nazair, Darul Kutub al-Alamiyyah, Lebanon 1983)

In an Islamic insurance contract, the fundamental aspects—such as its origin being from the ancient Arab custom of *al-Aqila*, its objective being mutual co-operation justified by the Qur'an at 5:3, its operation being based on *Al-Mudharabah* financing technique for the purpose of public interest relying on the doctrine of *Masalih al-Murasalah*—must all have been highly approved of and justified by the Shari'ah. Hence, it is only logical and natural to hold such practice of insurance policy valid.

- Any transaction in which the parties undertake to fulfil their respective lawful obligations is naturally valid and binding for both parties. This is because the Shari'ah has emphasised the performance or undertakings of promises. The Prophet (saw) once said in one of his traditions:

Muslims are bound by their conditions except the one which prohibits the permitted one or permits the prohibited one. (At Tirmizi, as quoted by Shaikh Jad-al-Haq n.d.)

This is further justified in the Qur'an:

O ye who believe! fulfil your promises. (Qur'an, at 5:1)

The terms and conditions required in a contract of insurance between two parties are lawful and hence binding. The school of Maliki made a remark on the practice of insurance contracts when it said that this is a binding promise and hence permissible in the eyes of the Shari'ah (Hadagha n.d.).

- The practice of Islamic insurance is also actually based on, inter alia, the doctrine of public interest or Masalih al-Mursalah—for the purpose of eliminating hardship from one's life, while taking the initiative to look after the welfare of the poor who may have suffered resulting from an occurrence of loss or damage. It is thus justified in the Qur'an that Allah (swt) always wishes a good and convenient life for His creatures, one where they do not have to face any difficulty:

> Allah (SWT) intends [an] easy life for you while He does not want to put you to difficulties. (Qur'an, at 2:185)

- An Islamic insurance policy does not signify an opportunity for the insured to hope for a chance for material gain. In fact, it is a transaction whereby the insured takes the initiative, to the best their one's ability, to be compensated in the event of unexpected loss, damage or peril. Such compensation and indemnity is to be mutually agreed by both the insurer and the insured. This further signifies the element of co-operation between both parties in the contract of insurance. The principle of mutuality is justified in the Shari'ah. As Allah (swt) says:

> Maintain a mutual co-operation among yourselves in righteousness and piety. (Id., at 5:2)

- An Islamic insurance contract also operates for the purpose of necessity. Any transaction operating along the lines of necessity is permissible as justified in the maxim:

> Necessity makes forbidden things canonically harmless. (Nazim, Ibn n.d.)

Hence, an Islamic life insurance policy also operates based on the principle of necessity in providing material protection for the unfortunate widow, offspring and so forth in the event of the death of the assured. Islam again justifies such an approach. The prophet (saw) advised in one of his traditions:

Narrated by Saad bin Abi Waqqas (R): The Holy Prophet (saw) said: It is better for you to leave your offspring wealthy than to leave them poor asking others for help. (Sahih al-Bukhari, op. cit., at Vol. 8, No. 725 at 477)

The Holy Prophet again spoke thus:

Narrated by Safwan bin Salim (R), the Holy Prophet (saw) said: The one who looks after and works for a widow and for a poor person is like a warrior fighting for the cause of Allah (swt) or like a person who fasts during the day and prays overnight. (Id., at 35 at 23)

- An Islamic insurance policy involves an element of donation or *Sadaqah*. For instance, the insured in a general policy pays regular premiums for the purpose of compensation in case of unexpected loss or damage occurring to a particular subject. However, if there is no occurrence of loss, then the premiums will be considered as *Tabarru'* (Rashid n.d.) in general insurance, which means that these premiums will be non-refundable. Meanwhile in a life insurance policy, the assured pays regular premium like a gift for the welfare of his dependants and at the same time the assured pays a certain amount as a donation to a charitable fund for the beneficiary(s) of the assured as an addition to the paid premiums and share of profits (Billah, M. Masum n.d.). The Holy Prophet (saw) also used to accept donations (Al-Sanani, Mohammad, *Subul al-Salam*, Egypt, 1987). Thus, a transaction-like insurance contract that involves the element of donation could be held lawful.

The nature of an Islamic life insurance policy is similar to that of a retirement pension scheme. Al-Zarqa and Al-Alwan apparently discovered that all contemporaneous Islamic scholars unanimously agreed on the lawfulness and validity of a retirement pension scheme (Al-Zarqa, *op. cit.*, at 62; also Al-Alwan, Abdullah, 1987).

Adil Salahi accepted the fact that all scholars of Islamic Jurisprudence had approved the idea of a pension scheme for the reason of ensuring material security for the subscriber himself as well as his family in cases of difficulty or death (Salahi, Adil, Nov. 1995).

- Salahi went on to defend the validity of life insurance, relying on the approval of all Islamic scholars for the pension scheme, and posed the question of why should family security should be rendered lawful in a pension scheme and unlawful in a life insurance policy when their method of operations are practically the same (ibid.). It was also inferred that the reason why all Ulama accepted the idea of a retirement pension is that it was widely accepted during the time of Omar (R). Hence, it is submitted that a life insurance policy is similar to that of pension scheme and therefore should be held valid.

Indeed, based on the abovementioned arguments, it is submitted and asserted that an insurance policy that is based on the Islamic principle of *Al-Mudharabah* is valid and enforceable. It is also observed that the arguments forwarded by Islamic scholars opposing the idea and validity of insurance are entirely rebuttable.

The purpose of having an insurance policy is to provide indemnity against unexpected loss, peril or any form or risk.

As far as the fundamentals of a contract of insurance under the Common Law are concerned, and these determine its legality and validity, there are the legal capacity of the parties to the contract, consideration (i.e. the payments of premiums) for the subject of the insurance contract and the insurable interest of the beneficiary. Finally, the parties to a contract of insurance must also abide by the doctrine of *Uberrimae Fidei*.

The sources of an insurance policy under the Common Law are the relevant Acts of Parliament, customs, judicial precedents as well as relevant literature on insurance such as in books, articles and so on.

As far as the view on the validity of an insurance policy under the Common Law is concerned, it is found that there is no variance of views among Common Law scholars or jurists. However, prior to the development of insurance policy and practice, the people of the primitive society used to object to the practice of insurance-based transaction for the reason that they lived in a tribal society in which they were used to being well protected by their tribes and families against any risk or peril (Clayton, Rehman Afzalur, n.d.). So, they did not feel a necessity for insurance.

1.9 Conclusion

In Islam, insurance policy and practice originated from customs practised by ancient Arabs tribe before the rise of Islam in the form of the doctrine of al-Aqila, which was subsequently approved by the Prophet Mohammad (SAW) during his lifetime in one of his decisions given against a woman from the Hudhail tribe. Later, such insurance transactions gradually came to be practised and were even made mandatory in some cases during the reign of the second Caliph, Saydina Omar (R) (Gibb n.d.).

It is further concluded that *Takaful* policies and transactions practised based on mutual co-operation and good-will are those where the parties involved in any contract of *Takaful* look after each other's welfare. Islamic scholars may no longer be confused by the multiplicity of views as regards the validity of the idea and operation of insurance, but rather seek to invent an alternative model of insurance (as opposed to the conventional one) for the benefit and betterment of the present Ummah.

References

1. Ali, A. Y. (n.d.), The Holy Qur'an, Text and Translation.
2. *Al-Mudharabah* is one of the financial techniques found in Islamic partnership dealings between two or more parties whereby one party provides capital while the other offers a service or skill in a particular business, both sharing profits accordingly. Today's Islamic banks and Islamic insurance companies have been operating based on the principle of *Al-Mudharabah*, which is an alternative to the interest-based transaction. In other words, *Al-Mudharabah* is a complete, interest-free profit- and loss-sharing transaction.
3. Billah, M. M. (1993), "Life Insurance? An Islamic View", *Arab Law Quarterly*, 8:4, P. 317.
4. Rashid, S.K. (1993), Islamization of Insurance – A Religio – Legal Experiment in Malaysia, Religion and Law Review, Vol. 2, No. 1, P. 26.
5. Bukhari and Muslim, (agreed), Kitabul Iman.
6. Sahih Muslim, compiled in An Nawari, Riyadhussalihin (trans) Ali, Maulana Syed Muhammad et al. (1990), Riadussaliheen, Vol. 1, Bangladesh Islamic Centre, Dhaka, No. 7 at 5.
7. Takaful Act (Malaysia), 1984 at S. 2.(Repealed by the Islamic Financial Services Act 2013).
8. The Holy Qur'an, at 3:19, "The System of Allah (SWT) is Islam (Submission to His Will)".

9. One of the legal capacities is, *inter alia*, the majority of the Takaful Act (Malaysia) 1984, which at S 64 rules that a person involved in a contract of insurance must be at least 18 years old.
10. The Rules of Shari'ah Supervisory Board, Faisal Islamic Bank Sudan Publications, English Series (5), Sudan n.d. at 12.
11. Sahih Muslim, as compiled in Nawawi Forty Hadith, (trans. Eng.) Ibrahim Ezzeddin et al., IIFSO 1985, No. 36 at 114 f.
12. Takaful Act (Malaysia), 1984 S. 2. (Repealed by the Islamic Financial Services Act 2013).
13. Pervez, Imtias Ahjmad, "The Financial Instrument Used by Islamic Bank" in New Horizon, No. 45, No. 1995 at 3.
14. Sahih Bukhari (trans. Eng.) Khan, Muhammad Muhsin, Kazi Publication, Lahore, 1979, Vol. 8, No. 725, at 477 f.
15. Siddiqi, M.N., 'Muslim Economic Thinking: A Survey of Contemporary Literature", in Studies in Islamic Economics (ed) Khurshid Ahmad, The Islamic Foundation, UK, 1980, at 265–315.
16. Khomeni, Ayatullah, Tawzih al-Masaill, 1979, Problem No. 2863–65 as cited in Amin, S.H. Islamic Law in the Contemporary World, Glasgow, 1985 at 79.
17. Al-Iqtisadul Islami, July 1995 at 60.
18. The Conference was held in Cairo in 1965.
19. The decision was made in a judicial conference held in Mecca in Sha'ban, 1398H.
20. Anas, Imam Malik bin al-Muatta, compiled by Dr. Saad, Faruq, Darul afaq al-Jadidah, Bairut, 1985 at Baiul Garar, No. 63, at 554.
21. Al-Sanhuri, Civil Law, Vol. 7, 1964 at 1088 (Arabic), as cited in Mankabady, op. cit., at 201.
22. Al-Zarqa, Mustafa, Nizam al-Tameen, Muassasatul Risalah, Beirut, 1984 at 46
23. Ibn. Asir, An Nihayat Garibil Hadith., Vol. 3, at 45.
24. Sahih al-Muslim, (Tahqiq) Mohd. Nasiruddin al-Albani, Laznatu Ihya al-Sunnah, Ashare, Arabi, Asyuf (n.d.), Kitab Tahreem al-Dimaa' wa Zitnil Qisas al al-Diyyat, No. 1032, at 274. Also see Sahih al-Bukhari, Kitab al-Diyyat, Bab Janeen al-Marat, No. 6395. For translation see Sahih al Muslim (translation English), Siddiqi, A. Hamid, Darul arabia, Lebanon, 1978, Vol. 3, No. 4:68, at 905
25. [1974] PLD 185 (SC).
26. Al-Zubaidi, Mohammad, Tajul Aris, Vol. 2, Kuwait, 1967, at 591.
27. Qudama, Ibn, Raudatul Nadhir (n.d.) at 85.
28. The Mejelle, op. cit., at arts. 36, 40 and 45.
29. Suyuti, Al-Imam Jalaluddin Abd. Rahman, Al-Ashbah Wa-al-Nazair., Darul Kutub al-Alamiyyah, Lebanon 1983, at 60.

30. Al-Sanani, Mohammad, Subul al-Salam, Egypt, 1987, Vol. 1–3 at 90.
31. Al-Zarqa, op. cit. at 62; and also Al-Alwan, Abdullah, Hukum al-Islam fi Tameen, Darul Islam, Egypt, 1987, at 13.
32. Salahi, Adil, "Is Life Insurance Haram?" in New Horizon, Islamic Banking and Insurance, No. 45, Nov. 1995 at 12.

CHAPTER 2

Re-takaful Products in a Nutshell

2.1 Introduction

The challenges posed by both neo-modern and postmodern society and their secular cultures are very far reaching. The impact can be felt in every facet of life, be it religious, political, social or economic. Following the rapid and strangulating development of the economies of large western powers, including the insurance sector, most developing economies—especially in the Muslim world—feel a pressing need to readjust their economies in order to meet the rapid development and high rates of economic growth taking place in these developing economies. The Muslim world, among others, needs to access large and open markets among the different Muslim countries in order also to achieve a high rate of economic growth. A survey of recent Muslim scholarship on western theories and epistemologies reveals an attempt to understand the western legacy for modern society so as to liberate Muslim societies from secular and foreign control. This aims to ensure that political, economic and other preoccupations of Muslims do not become mere worldly distractions from their care and development for the hereafter. Islam is concerned both with material

It should be acknowledged that the idea for this chapter/product has derived significantly from the practices/experiences/thoughts of Bank Negara, ARIL, MNRB, Takaful Malaysia, Takaful Ikhlas, Takaful Nasional, Etiqa Takaful, IBFIM, IIUM, MII (Malaysia) and others.

Mohd Ma'Sum Billah, *Islamic Insurance Products*,
https://doi.org/10.1007/978-3-030-17681-5_2

and spiritual advancement. The Islamic worldview can therefore never be compared to any other worldview.

It is against this background that current Muslim scholarship in the field of finance and economics in general should be viewed. It is an attempt at the total Islamisation of the banking and financial sector so as to free the Muslim world from the dominant Western civilizational and ideological value-laden economic, financial and banking principles. Presently, most of the Muslim world, as with developing nations, has under-developed economies that suffer enormously under the yoke of western economic and financial interest-based systems. One key area of modern financing where the Muslim world needs a form of economic co-operation in order to confront the challenges posed by the western interest-based financial system is in *Re-Takaful* business, which forms the focus of this chapter. It is pertinent that in spite of the abundance of human and natural resources in the Muslim world, *Takaful* and *Re-Takaful* business and the entire Muslim economic sector can still not compete with conglomerate companies such as the American Insurance Group. Though the insurance business in principle was accepted by Islam right from the time of the Prophet, when He instituted what can be regarded as *ma'qil al-ijtima'* or social insurance between the *Muhajirun* (Muslims who migrated from Mecca) and the *Ansar* (Muslims who welcomed the emigrants in Medina), the insurance business has undergone a lot of developments and innovations since then (M. O. A. Abdul 1982). In view of the Islamic acceptance of insurance in principle as well as the necessity of insurance schemes in our complex society, there is a need to undertake continuous research into the modern concept of insurance as a whole so as to bring it into harmony with the rulings and requirements of the Shari'ah. The need to abide by Islamic teachings, guided by Muslim historical heritage and current global insurance and reinsurance indexes, cannot be over-emphasised. This work is therefore an attempt to examine an aspect of the insurance system in Islam known as the Re-*Takaful* business.

2.2 *Re-Takaful* Product

Re-Takaful or Islamic reinsurance is essentially about handling risk. It is a risk aversion method in which the *Takaful* ceding company resorts to either a conventional reinsurer or a *Re-Takaful* operator to reinsure original insured risks against an undesirable future situation if the risk insured were over and above the normal underwriting or claim. Thus, a *Takaful* ceding company may, based on limited financial resources, hedge against possible incapability to meet all *Takaful* reinsurance protection from a financially capable reinsurer, which will take over the coverage of the large proportion of the risk.[1]

Fathi Lashin, a member of the Shari'ah Supervisory Board of the Dubai Islamic Bank stated that *Re-Takaful* does not, in principle, differ from *Takaful* operations. The Shari'ah principles applying to *Takaful* apply to *Re-Takaful* operations as well. The difference, if any, is that in the *Re-Takaful* operations, the participants are *Takaful* operators instead of individual participants. It is argued that the current practice of the insurance business has shown that a *Takaful* ceding company cannot do without *Re-Takaful* facility. Therefore, there is a need for *Takaful* operators to split risks by way of establishing *Re-Takaful* operators. By doing so, they share their risks with *Re-Takaful* companies. The *Re-Takaful* operator, on the other hand, assumes the responsibility of managing and investing the premiums of *Takaful* operators on the basis of profit and loss sharing.[2]

According to Billah, conceptually the function of reinsurance is not against the principles of Shari'ah. However, the operations of conventional reinsurance companies are not in compliance with the rules and practices of the Shari'ah as evidenced by Resolution No. (9) concerning insurance and reinsurance of the Islamic Fiqh Academy which states:

> "The Islamic Fiqh Academy, emanating from the Organisation of Islamic Cooperation (OIC), meeting in its Second Session in Jeddah, Kingdom of Saudi Arabia, from 10 to 16 Rabiul Thani, 1406 H (28th December 1985);
>
> And after reviewing the presentations made by the participating scholars during the Session on the subject of Insurance and Reinsurance".
>
> And after discussing the same;
>
> And after closely examining all types and forms of insurance and deeply examining the basic principles upon which they are founded and their goal and objectives;

[1] Al-Jamal, Garib, al-Ta'min al Tijari wa al-Badiil al Islami (Cairo:Dar al I'tisam, n.d.), pp. 340–344; al-Khafif,'Ali Muhammad, al-Ta'min, a paper presented at the 2nd Conference of the Academy of Islamic Research, Cairo, 1965. Quoted from Mohammed Burhan Arbouna, "The Operation of *Re-Takaful* (Islamic Reinsurance) Protection", Journal IIUM, pp. 336.

[2] Lashin, Fathi, "Sigha Muqaddama li-al-Sharikat Ta'min wa I'adat al-Ta'min fi al-Islam", Bayt al-Tamwil al Kuwaiti. '*Amal al-Nadwa al-fiqhiyya al-Thaniya*, 28–31 May, pp. 95–122. Quoted from Mohammed Burhan Arbouna, "The Operation of *Re-Takaful* (Islamic Reinsurance) Protection", Journal IIUM, pp. 336.

And having looked into what has been issued by the Fiqh Academies and other edifying institution in this regard; (Ma'sum Billah, n.d.)

2.3 Parties to *Re-Takaful* Contracts

There are always two parties involved in *Re-Takaful* operations:

- the insured (ceding company), that is, the direct insurer, which desires to relieve itself of part of the risks. This party is termed the *Takaful* operator;
- the insurer, that is, the company that accepts that portion of the risk which is reinsured. This party is known as the *Re-Takaful* operator.

As mentioned earlier, the competitiveness of the *Re-Takaful* market is dependent on the competitiveness of the direct *Takaful* market. Thus, *Re-Takaful* operators cannot operate without the operation of *Takaful* operators. In addition, the Shari'ah laws leading the process of *Takaful* also apply generally to the *Re-Takaful* operator.

2.4 Objectives of *Re-Takaful* Products

Re-Takaful is designed "to enhance *Takaful* activity by distributing risks. It is mainly for covering large risks and large accumulation of risks subject to common loss". The aim is to ensure that *Takaful* funds are managed so as to meet the indemnity obligations of the insured and reinsured and to assure the continuity of *Takaful* operations (Fig. 2.1 and Table 2.1). This means that *Re-Takaful* gives underwriting capacity to the *Takaful* ceding company. Thus, the objectives of *Re-Takaful* can be summarised as:

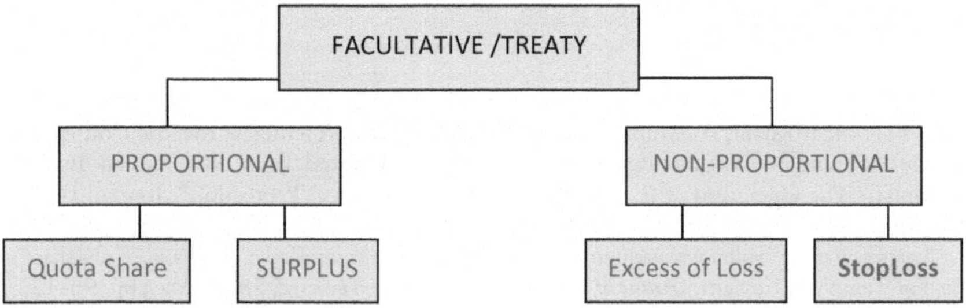

Fig. 2.1 Structure of *Re-Takaful*. (Source: Author's own)

Table 2.1 *Re-Takaful* versus reinsurance

Issuers	Re-Takaful	*Reinsurance*
Riba and *Gharar*	*Re-Takaful* operation does not earn commission as profit or interest, because this commission is subject to *Riba* and dilutes the purpose of setting up a *Takaful* operation. The *Re-Takaful* operation is dependent on actual expenses spent by the *Takaful* operator in the process of *Re-Takaful*	Conventional reinsurance operations are subject to *Riba* and *Gharar*, which are not in line with Shari'ah principles. For instance, this applies to any reinsurance commission that the direct insurance company earns from the reinsurance treaty. This is because this commission is framed in such a way that renders the commission *ribawi* and implicates it in a high degree of *Gharar*
Principle of insurable interest	According to Islamic laws pertaining to insurable interest, that is, holding specific financial interest in the subject matter of the insurance as a cardinal principle of the legality of the *Re-Takaful* contract, the reinsured party does not get an insurable interest or is not able to reinsure the property of the original insured party without permission from the policyholder. However, because the *Re-Takaful* operation is based on the *Al-Mudharabah* principle, it vests a right to reinsure on the insurer because permission from the policyholder is automatically inherent in the contract of *Al-Mudharabah*	Insurable interest is vested in the reinsured party. The fact that the reinsured party has issued a policy and assumed liability for its original insured party has been held to give it insurable interest sufficient to enable it to reinsure. The point is that although the reinsured party (direct insurance company) has no actual legal interest in the property—the subject matter of the original insurance policy—it has assumed responsibility in regard to it, and has therefore put itself into a position, recognised by law, in which it would be prejudiced by its loss (Arbouna, M. B. n.d.)

Source: Author's own collection

- Protecting the *Takaful* operator from the threat of insolvency, underwriting and interests of participants, forging co-operation among the participants and investing the accumulated funds in an Islamic way;
- Providing underwriting flexibility and further consolidating the financial stability of the *Takaful* operator in order to compete with conventional insurance companies in accepting risks. This means *Re-Takaful* "build a very close continuing business interest in common

between the *Takaful* ceding company and the reinsurer because they are both at risk";

- It may allow the *Takaful* operator to utilise the retained deposit reserves of the *Re-Takaful* fund in the interests of its clients without paying interest as part of a process of making the reinsurance industry an interest-free business.

The methods that apply in *Re-Takaful* also apply to reinsurance. In Fig. 2.1 above chart, facultative reinsurance means the reinsurance of individual risks by offer and acceptance wherein the reinsurer retains the 'faculty' to accept or reject each risk offered. Then, this is divided into two: proportional and non-proportional. Under proportional we have a quota share and also a surplus, where quota share is the basic form of participating treaty whereby the reinsurer accepts a stated percentage of each and every risk within a defined category of business on a pro rata basis. Participation in each risk is fixed and certain. Surplus is the excess of assets over liabilities. Statutory surplus is an insurer's or reinsurer's capital as determined under statutory accounting rules. Surplus determines an insurer's or reinsurer's capacity to write business.

On the other hand, non-proportional methods consist of excess of loss and stop loss. Excess of loss is a form of reinsurance under which recoveries are available when a given loss exceeds the cedant's retention as defined in the agreement. Stop loss is a form of reinsurance under which the reinsurer pays some or all of a cedant's aggregate retained losses in excess of a predetermined dollar amount or in excess of a percentage of the premium.

2.5 Shari'ah Requirements of *Re-Takaful*

In view of the above and the context of the *Re-Takaful* business, it is proposed that the same Shari'ah rulings and requirements governing the *Takaful* business should also govern the *Re-Takaful* business. Both the *Takaful* business and the *Re-Takaful* business in Islam are part of the same business operation: they are both concerned with the management of risks, with one insuring against risk and the other reinsuring against it. In line with the resolutions of Muslim jurists, *Re-Takaful* business should therefore be based on the principle of mutuality and co-operation. Contrary to conventional contracts, the Islamic contract of mutual co-operation is founded on shared responsibility, charity and indemnity. Islam supports the insurance or *Takaful* companies coming together to co-operate among themselves for the joint sharing of losses and risks. In conformity with the contract of mutual co-operation, the *Takaful* companies will help one another with a defined fund from a joint donation or *Tabarru'* to pay defined damages and losses based on an agreed scheme.

Takaful companies and operators generate a defined fund from joint donations so as to eliminate the element of uncertainty in the *Re-Takaful* business. It will be used to assist any *Takaful* company that requires compensation against loss without obtaining any benefit or gain at the expense of other *Takaful* operators or companies. This therefore eliminates uncertainty both in the pooling together of joint donations and the compensation of any *Takaful* operator (*Takaful* (Islamic Insurance), Concept and Operational System, 1996). The Re-takaful business is also based on the Islamic principle of *Al-Mudharabah* (profit sharing). According to this principle, Re-takaful operators serve as the *mudarib* and accept the premium or, in this case, the joint donations from the *Takaful* operators known as *ra's al-mal*, which should be invested in Shari'ah-compliant shares, bonds and other money market instruments. The clients, investors and providers of the joint donation, in this case the *Takaful* operators, are termed the *rabbul-mal*. This principle of *Al-Mudharabah* is applied as an alternative to the interest-based reinsurance contract (A.R.I. Doi, 1984).

Re-takaful operators assume the role of the entrepreneurs or the *mudarib* and they must specify under the *Al-Mudharabah* contract how any profits that accrue from Re-takaful business investments will be shared. A certain portion of the profits generated from the investments in Shari'ah-compliant shares, bonds and other money market instruments can also be accumulated to the defined funds. This relocation will enable the Re-takaful operators to pay contributors who suffer losses or damages. In order to protect the smooth running of the Re-takaful business investments and to ensure that the Shari'ah is always observed, there is need for a Shari'ah board in each Re-takaful company to monitor its operations. Central banks and the Shari'ah boards or councils can be used to regulate these operations, as done in Malaysia (*Takaful (Islamic Insurance)* op. cit).

2.6 Principles of Re-takaful

2.6.1 Principles of Contract ('Aqd)

In Islam, *'Aqd* is a very important element and must be present in all business transactions. An offer and acceptance (*sighah*) will render the particular transaction valid and both parties who have entered the contract are then bound by it. For an insurance policy, a person who enters the contract must fulfil some requirements such as legal capacities of the parties, subject matter, insurable interest, *ijab* (offer) and *qabul* (acceptance) and *Uberrimae fidei* (Billah, Mohd. Mas'um, n.d.). Once a person has entered into a mutual contract, it is therefore an obligation for both parties to fulfil the contract, as Allah (swt) has commanded:

> O ye believe! Fulfil your agreement. (Qur'an 5:1)

2.6.2 Principles of Liability

A person who buys an insurance policy from an insurance company is ready to transfer part of the risk to the insurer. Insurers are willing to undertake such risk and are willing to compensate for any losses that may occur to the policyholder. An insurance policy will mainly cover losses that occur from accident, fire, flood, death, disaster, business burglary, property and others similar losses. In this situation, the concept of *al-Aqila* is pertinent: in ancient Arab tribes, and as approved by the Prophet (saw), if a person was killed by another person from a different tribe either mistakenly or negligently, this would bring liability to members of his tribe to pay blood money to the heirs of the slain.

2.6.3 Principles of Wakalah *(Agencies)*

Application of the *Wakalah* principle in insurance (Takaful) is also important where the insurer (Takaful operator) will appoint a designated agent to deal with the insured or other customers. The main intention of this appointment is to ensure that the transactions and dealings between insurer and policyholder become more efficient and effective. The governing principles for the agents and brokers are laid down in the *mejelle* as follows:

> *Wakalah* is when someone puts his business on another and makes him stand in his own place in respect of that business.

2.6.4 Principles of Daman (Guarantee)

The Principles of Daman have always been practised in Takaful where insurers are willing to undertake the risk from the insured and where the insurer promises to provide material security against any unexpected loss or disaster that may arise in the future and is willing to compensate for any such losses that may occur.

2.6.5 *Principles of Mudharabah*

The *Al-Mudharabah* concept is widely used in Takaful as an alternative to interest-based securities (Rosly, Saiful Azhar 1996). In practice, conventional insurance companies will invest in long-term bonds or stocks of companies which may or may not be involved in non-permissible activities such as gambling, production of alcoholic beverages or interest-based banking. However, the operation of Takaful exists under Shari'ah principles. It is based on *Al-Mudharabah* and *Musharakah* principles. The Takaful operator acts as a *mudarib* will receive a sum of investment from sahib ul mal or rabbul-mal (capital provider) through the payment of premiums. With this sum of investment, the *mudarib* will conduct investments in productive industry using their skills and knowledge. At the end of the day, when Takaful receive return (profit) from the investment, the Takaful operator will distribute the profit to the capital provider based on the proportions that they agreed before.

2.6.6 *Tabarru'*

A certain proportion of a client's payment instalments known as premiums is relocated to a *Tabarru'* account to repay his fellow participants who might suffer from a defined loss. Thus, each client is able to fulfil his obligation of mutual help and joint guarantee. In the same vein, a *Re-Takaful* company requires the *Takaful* company to pay a certain percentage of their premium to them, which shall be used for partial coverage of their risk in case the *Takaful* company could not cover such risk.

2.7 The Corporate Paradigm of Re-takaful

The reinsurance or *Re-Takaful* operation is a company-to-company relationship and is basically about handling risk where the agreement is between the *Takaful* operator and the *Re-Takaful* operator. Thus, the original policyholders are not party to the reinsurance agreement. Nonetheless, the insured party may want to know that a professional and reliable reinsurer is administering the original policy since this concerns its security. But the insured party has not and cannot have any direct interest in the reinsurance contract. On the other hand, some legal scholars have emphasised that the contract of *Re-Takaful* should stay between the *Takaful* operator and *Re-Takaful* operator, whereas the original policyholders of the *Takaful* fund are not involved in the contract in any way. Therefore, the operational and legal relationship of the *Re-Takaful* and *Takaful* operators may be summarised like so:

- The *Re-Takaful* operator assumes responsibility to invest the fund on the basis of *Al-Mudharabah* and shares the profits with *Takaful* operators by mobilising premiums or contributions of *Takaful* companies;
- The profit earned will be distributed between the *Re-Takaful* operator and *Takaful* operators according to the percentages that have been drawn up in the agreement certificates issued;
- If any damages occur, the *Re-Takaful* operator indemnifies the defined risks and settles the expenses of the process of *Takaful* from the gross premiums, reserves and profits from investment;
- If there is surplus, this should be proportionately accredited into the *Takaful* operators' account;
- In the event of insolvency of the *Takaful* operators, the *Re-Takaful* operator should provide a loan from the *Re-Takaful* shareholder's fund by which the *Takaful* operator settles claims and incoming premiums which will cover the loan.

2.8 Operational Mechanisms

Al-Mudharabah contracts are applied to *Takaful* and *Re-Takaful* operations as an alternative to interest-based securities in which the conventional insurance system invests any surplus funds. This account is referred to as a participant account. Clients are investors and are referred to as *rabbul-mal*, while *Takaful* operators assume the role of entrepreneur and are referred to as *mudarib*. They would invest the pool of funds into Shari'ah-compliant investments and specify how the expected profits shall be shared among the clients. The same goes for *Re-Takaful*. Mutual help among clients or investors in *Takaful* operations is observed through the concept of *Tabarru'*, which means to donate, contribute or to give away. In Islam, mutual help and co-operation are ethical values that are promoted among believers. In *Surah al-Maidah*, Allah commands believers as follows:

> Help one another in carrying out righteousness and piety, but help not one another in sin and bitterness: Lo! Fear Allah for Allah is very severe and strict in punishment. (Surah al-Maidah, verse 2)

Asean *Re-Takaful* International Ltd. (ARIL) is the first *Re-Takaful* company under *Takaful* Malaysia Berhad to have been established. The operations of this company are based totally on *Re-Takaful* business. The charts in Fig. 2.2 show the overall framework that being applied by ARIL for *Re-Takaful* operations. It can be concluded that this company has its own methods for establishing business and that it has obtained income from three main sources: returns on investments of shareholders, profit from the general *Re-Takaful* fund and profit from family *Re-Takaful* funds.

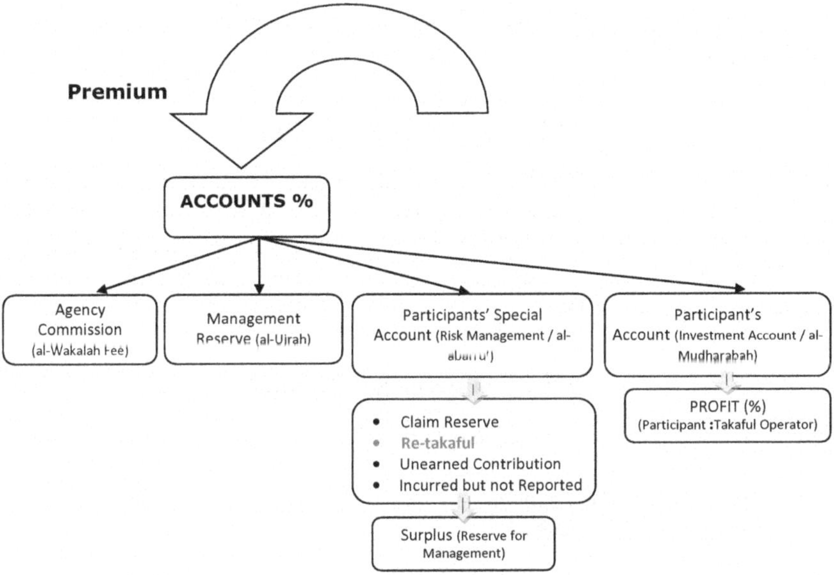

Fig. 2.2 *Re-Takaful* structure. (Source: Author's own collection)

2.9 General Re-takaful Products

2.9.1 Fire and Property Re-Takaful

Fire/property *Re-Takaful* normally covers or protects the policyholder's property from damage or loss due to fire, lightning, explosion (domestic) or any other related dangers. Additional coverage is extended to any damages caused by:

- riot, strike or malicious damage
- explosion
- impact damage
- bursting or overflowing of water tanks or pipes
- earthquake or volcanic eruption
- flood
- aircraft damage
- windstorm.

This fire/property *Re-Takaful* policy covers buildings and/or machines, stocks and also the householders themselves.

2.9.2 Accident Re-Takaful

This offers cover for miscellaneous accidents occurring to individuals, for instance on the way to the workplace or while traveling, as well as cover for drivers and also passengers where the scope of coverage includes medical expenses, suffering from physical or mental disability either temporary or permanent and also death.

2.9.3 Marine Re-Takaful

There are two types of marine *Re-Takaful*:

- marine cargo *Re-Takaful*
- marine hull *Re-Takaful*.

2.9.4 Automobile Re-Takaful

This offers cover for private cars or motorcycles as well as commercial transport.

2.9.5 Engineering Re-Takaful

Engineering *Re-Takaful* normally covers loss of profit due to machinery breakdown, boiler and pressure vessel, erection all risk, storage tanks and others.

2.9.6 Special Risks Re-Takaful

Special risks coverage Re-*Takaful* scheme.

2.10 Operational Mechanisms of General Re-takaful Protection

Takaful operators can establish a *Re-Takaful* scheme on two bases. The first basis is co-operation and the second is solidarity. This is because *Re-Takaful* operations are needed to strengthen the *Takaful* sector and since the relations between this sort of reinsurance and conventional reinsurance may raise doubts about the genuineness of Islamic insurance as a whole, a co-operative form of reinsurance is pertinent to meeting this need. Therefore, in this situation, to strengthen the function of the *Takaful* operation, co-operative Islamic reinsurance mechanisms have to be developed. In doing so, the mechanisms below might function as guidelines:

- All *Takaful* operators must give a portion of money as donation-based premiums to establish a *Re-Takaful* fund.
- This payment shall be equal to the defined risks of each *Takaful* operator. The money may be paid in advance and be submitted to a company purposely established to manage the fund or presented to a professionally capable and reliable fund manager for investment purposes in the interests of all contributing parties.
- The person or individual who manages the fund will be paid on the basis of *ijarah* (hire contract) or according to the rules of profit and loss sharing (*Al-Mudharabah*). This manager is responsible for compensating any *Takaful* operator who faces financial difficulties in meeting their original obligation.
- *Takaful* operators may also defer payment of their premium instead of giving advanced payment of contributions but with a pledge to settle their financial obligations at a later date. In this case, the estab-

lished company or professional manager of the *Re-Takaful* fund must accept the pledge. In addition, in the case of danger, the *Re-Takaful* manager must indemnify the losses suffered by a *Takaful* operator and subsequently recoup their expenses from each *Takaful* operator according to the agreement.

- Initially, the mechanisms of the *Re-Takaful* operation above may face impediments. If any immediate extraordinary loss occurs which has to be paid off according to the *Re-Takaful* agreement, this will threaten the perpetuity of the fund. For instance, a *Re-Takaful* operator may issue a reinsurance policy to operate within a certain period and the reinsured risk may arise a few days after the inception of the agreement. But the *Re-Takaful* operator may not have accumulated sufficient funds to settle the claim of the *Takaful* operators. In such a case, to solve the problem, this situation could be resolved by resorting to Islamic banks for *qard al-hassan* (interest-free loan) to serve as a deposit reserve, or *Ihtiyati madfu'*, for the *Takaful* operator. This fund will be part of the *Re-Takaful* portfolio and be invested in the interests of all participants. If there are immediate extraordinary losses arising, the covering of such losses would be met by this reserve.

2.11 Basis of Operations

A portion of claims can be settled by A as it is a *Re-Takaful* company, by using funds gathered from each Takaful operator, B, C, D and E (Fig. 2.3).

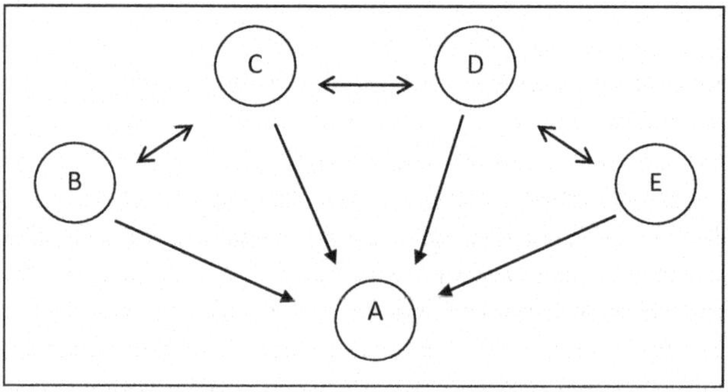

Fig. 2.3 Joint guarantee. (Source: Author's own collection)

2.11.1 Mutually Agreed Participation

The participation of each Takaful operator under one *Re-Takaful* company is mutually agreed. With these binding conditions, each of Takaful operators is willing to help each other in event of any difficulties.

2.11.2 Tabarru'

- Each Takaful operator, B, C, D and E will contribute some percentage to the *Re-Takaful* company, A.
- A will invest some portion of the total insured into profitable investment.
- Profit from the investment will then be distributed to the Takaful operators according to their portion of contribution to the *Re-Takaful* company (Fig. 2.4).

The diagram in Fig. 2.5 shows an example of a *Re-Takaful* flow chart operation, which was taken from ARIL. First, the company invests RM 1,000,000 from a *Re-Takaful* Fund. Let us say that the investment brings a profit of RM 100,000 to the company; this profit will be added back into the *Re-Takaful* fund. Now the company has RM 1,100,000 in the *Re-Takaful* fund. This amount of money will be used for operational costs of *Re-Takaful* to pay for claims up to RM 500,000 and also a reserve of RM 300,000. Then, the surplus profit of RM 300,000 will be divided between the *Re-Takaful* company and the cedants, which are the *Takaful* operators. The *Re-Takaful* company will get 60% of the profit which is RM 180,000 and *Takaful* operators will get 40% from the surplus profits, that is RM 120,000.

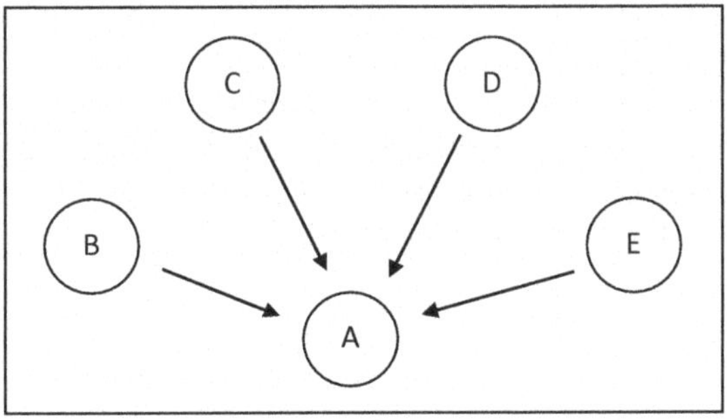

Fig. 2.4 Tabarru'. (Source: Author's own collection)

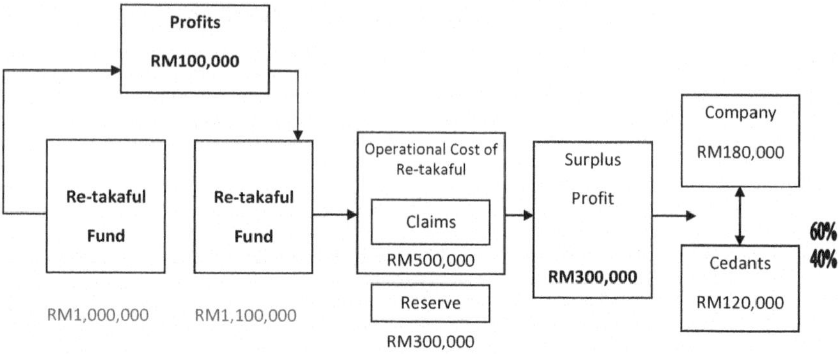

Fig. 2.5 Example of Re-takaful flow chart operation. (Source: Author's own collection)

2.12 Conclusion

The challenges posed by modernity and secular culture to Islam in general and financing and economic aspects thereof in particular and the wider implications of all this in the Muslim world have been discussed in this chapter. There is a significant discrepancy between Islamic concepts of insurance and reinsurance, known as *Takaful* and Re-takaful business or industry, and the western or conventional insurance and reinsurance industry. There is also a total disparity between the Islamic principles that govern any *Takaful* and Re-takaful contract and the principles of contract in western or conventional insurance and reinsurance.

While Islamic principles are based on divine and ethical values, western or conventional principles are based on human or mere normative values. This accounts for the different ways the two industries generate, control and utilise funds. It also links to the manner in which the two systems approach the issue of surplus profits, such as through ownership and application. For the *Takaful* and Re-takaful business or industry, there are principles of interest-free financing, profit- and risk-sharing rates and avoidance of speculative risks.

References

1. M. O. A. Abdul (1982), *The Historical Origin Of Islam, Lagos*, Islamic Publication Bureau.
2. Al-Jamal, Garib, al-Ta'min al Tijari wa al-Badiil al Islami (Cairo: Dar al I'tisam, n.d.), pp. 340–344; al-Khafif,'Ali Muhammad, al-Ta'min, a paper presented at the 2nd Conference of the Academy of Islamic Research, Cairo, 1965. Quoted from Mohammed Burhan Arbouna, "The Operation of *Re-Takaful* (Islamic Reinsurance) Protection", Journal IIUM, pp. 336.
3. Lashin, Fathi, "Sigha Muqaddama li-al-Sharikat Ta'min wa I'adat al-Ta'min fi al-Islam", Bayt al-Tamwil al Kuwaiti. *'Amal al-Nadwa al-fiqhiyya al-Thaniya*, 28–31 May, pp. 95–122. Quoted from Mohammed Burhan Arbouna, "The Operation of *Re-Takaful* (Islamic Reinsurance) Protection", Journal IIUM, pp. 336
4. Billah, M. M. (2003), Principles and Practices of *Takaful* and *Re-Takaful*, Manual of FIN 4030 IIUM
5. Mohammed Burhan Arbouna, "The Operation of *Re-Takaful* (Islamic Reinsurance) Protection", Journal IIUM, P. 336.
6. *Takaful* (Islamic Insurance), Concept and Operational System, 1996, p. 8.
7. The principles of al-mudarabah in A.R.I. Doi, Shari'ah the Islamic Law, Lagos: Taha Publishers, 1984.
8. Billah, M. M. (2002), *Manual of Principles and Practices of Takaful and Re-Takaful*. Department of Business Administration, Kulliyyah of Economic and Management Sciences, International Islamic University Malaysia.
9. Qur'an 5:1.
10. Rosly, S. A. (1996), "Islamic Insurance: *Takaful*", Business-Focus. *The Sun*
11. Qur'an, al-Maidah: 2.

CHAPTER 3

Governing Principles of *Takaful* and *Re-takaful* Products

3.1 Introduction

The primary objective of insurance is to facilitate co-operation between two parties, in which one party offers to protect the other party against unexpected peril. In such a scenario, the parties agree that one party will pay a particular premium to the other party, who undertakes to compensate the former (Hughes, James Langhlin, 1990) in consideration of the paid premium(s) against an accidental loss or injury, which might happen to the subject matter of the contract. In an insurance contract, the party who pays the premium(s) is called the insured or the policyholder, and the other party, who undertakes to compensate against the risk, is known as the insurer. The contract itself is often referred to as the policy. The payment made by the insured is identified as the premium, while the event insured against is usually termed the risk (ibid.).

The governing principles of insurance under Common Law are based on the principles of case laws and positive laws (statutes), while their operations are based on the principles of usury or interest.

The central idea of insurance under Islamic law is that it is a mutual financial transaction between two parties, in which one provides material

It is acknowledged that, the idea of this chapter has been shared with author's other research works for the common benefit of academia, regulators, researchers and industries.

Mohd Ma'Sum Billah, *Islamic Insurance Products*,
https://doi.org/10.1007/978-3-030-17681-5_3

security for the other against a defined risk. In an insurance policy, the operator provides compensation against an unexpected loss or damage, if any was to occur, but in a case where the risk does not transpire to the subject matter of the policy within the agreed period, the insured participant, upon the maturity of the policy should be[1] entitled to the whole amount (in a life policy) and a bonus (after deductions or charges[2] in general policies) of the paid contributions, together with a share of profits made over and above the paid contributions based on the principles of *Al-Mudharabah*.[3] In such a transaction, both the operator and the participant help each other to obtain financial security.

As far as the general idea and principles of insurance contracts are concerned, there are some differences between Common Law and Islamic Law. In this chapter, an analysis is made of the general ideas and principles of insurance contracts and aspects of possible conflicts between Common Law and Islamic Law.[4]

3.2 Governing Principles of *Takaful* and *Re-Takaful* Products

An insurance practice under Islamic teachings possesses certain fundamental characteristics upon which an insurance contract is to be held valid. Those fundamental characteristics can mainly be classified into four categories.

[1] The suggestion is made relying on the logical fact that an insurance contract under Islamic law operates on the basis of the principle of *Al-Mudharabah* (profit and loss sharing). Hence, the benefits (over and above the policy) should also be disbursed according to this profit- and loss-sharing technique. It is sincerely believed that this suggestion could work well in an equitable nature.

[2] Since a general policy is only for a short period, in an effort to be fair to the insured, the insurer has to deduct the service charges (for the management of the company) including the percentage for the charitable account from the paid-premiums according to the company's financial policy.

[3] Mudharabah is a mutual financing technique in Islamic commercial law in which two or more parties agree that one will provide capital while the other may offer a service or skill in a particular business in view of sharing the profits and losses accordingly. Today's Islamic banks and insurance companies operate on the basis of *Al-Mudharabah*, which is an alternative to interest-based transactions.

[4] The Islamic part is based on (with possible revision) one of my unpublished manuscripts entitled "Islamic Insurance: Its Original Sketch and Development Scenario."

3.2.1 General Principles

The general sources of Islamic Law begin with the Qur'an and the Sunnah or the Traditions of the Holy Prophet (saw). These two are regarded as the principal sources of Islamic Law. Other secondary sources of Islamic law indeed should strictly be based on these two primary sources. This has been indicated in the following Divine injunction:

> O you who believe! Obey Allah (swt) and obey the Prophet (saw) and those charged with authority among you. If you differ in anything among yourselves, refer it to Allah and His Messenger, if you do believe in Allah (swt) and the Last Day: That is best, and most suitable for final determination. (Qur'an, Surah an-Nisa, 4:59)

3.2.2 The Qur'an

There are five hundred verses in the Qur'an that deal with legal sanctions (in I doi, Abdur Rahman, 1984). There are indeed a number of Divine injunctions in the Qur'an, which justify the validity of an insurance contract. The contract of insurance contains the elements of mutual cooperation (See Qur'an, Surah al-Maidah, 5:2). It is a binding promise, which binds both the insurer and the insured based on the general principle of contract (Qur'an, Surah al-Maidah, 5:1). It also contains the elements of alleviation of hardships and provision of material security and assistance for those who face unexpected risk and peril, and ensure for them a comfortable life (Qur'an, Surah al-Baqarah, 2:201). All these elements of a contract of insurance are justified by the Qur'anic principles. Thus, the Qur'an is the principal guidance to provide an instrumental justification for the application of insurance contract, as the Qur'an offers plain statements and guidance for humankind in order for them to be successful in both worlds. This is indicated in the following *ayat* of the Qur'an:

> it is a plain statement to man, a guidance and instruction to those who fear Allah (swt). (Qur'an, Surah al-Imran, 3:138)

The above provisions render an opportunity for humankind to practice, inter alia, insurance policy so long as one does not violate the Divine sanctions either directly or indirectly.

3.2.3 The Sunnah

The Sunnah of the Holy Prophet (saw) are a second source of Islamic law immediately after the Qur'an (Qur'an, Surah An-Nisa, 4:59). Apropos the justification of an insurance contract and practice, there are indeed numerous traditions justifying the validity and permissibility of its concept and practices. For instance, an insurance policy embodies the concept of Tawakkul, whereby one should strive hard in overcoming one's unexpected future risk or peril before leaving one's fate and destiny in the hands of Allah (swt). Such a concept has been justified in one of the traditions of the Holy Prophet (saw), which reads:

> Narrated by Anas bin Malik, the Holy Prophet (saw) told a Bedouin Arab who left his camel untied trusting to the will of Allah (swt): Tie the camel first and then leave it to Allah (swt). (Cagri yayinlari Istanbul, 1981)

Moreover, an insurance policy aims at protecting the insured from future material constraints upon the occurrence of a particular unexpected risk. Such an idea of protection for those who are in need is justified by the following hadith of the Holy Prophet (saw):

> Narrated by Abu Huraira, the Holy Prophet (saw) said: whosoever removes a worldly hardship from a believer, Allah (swt) will remove from him one of the hardships of the day of judgment. Whosoever alleviates from one, Allah (swt) will alleviate his lot in this world and the next. (Sahih al-Muslim (Arabic), Kitab al-Birr, No. Hadith 59)

There are also other essential aspects of an insurance contract justified by the Sunnah, such as the fact that an insurance policy originated from the ancient Arab custom of *al-Aqila*, which was approved by the Holy Prophet (saw) during his time (see in Gibb, *Shorter Encyclopedia of Islam, op. cit.*, p. 29). Moreover, a life insurance policy aims at providing, in advance, material security for the offspring of the deceased (assured) and this is also justified by one of the Traditions of the Holy Prophet (saw) as follows:

> Narrated by Amir bin Saad bin Abi Waqqas, The Holy Prophet (saw) said verily it is better for you to leave your offspring wealthy than to leave them poor asking others for help. (See Sahih al-Bukhari, Kitab al-Diyat, op. cit., Vol. 8, No. 725, p. 478)

Insurance originated from the doctrine of *al-Aqila*. During the later stage of the period of the second Caliph, Sayyidina Umar, the Caliph directed that, in the various districts of the state, lists of Muslim brothers-in-arms should be drawn up. The people whose names were contained in those lists owed each other mutual assistance or co-operation and had to contribute to the payment of *al-Diyah* (bloodwit) for manslaughter committed by one of their members of their own tribe (See in Gibb, *Shorter Encyclopedia of Islam*, *op. cit.*, p. 29f). This was how Sayyidina Umar developed the practices of the doctrine of *al-Aqila*.

3.2.4 *Ijtihad*

The idea, meaning and legal characteristics of an insurance policy as practiced in the world of today, had first been discovered by the famous Hanafi lawyer Ibn Abidin (1784–1836), probably in early nineteenth century. The ruling of Ibn Abidin is therefore quoted as follows (*Raddu al-Mukhtar*, n.d.):

> And from our noting, the question about which a large number of inquiries are being made, is a lsoans were danditis that, when merchants charter ship-owned by the subject(s) of belligerent state, then, together with the charges for the ship, another amount is separately paid to the same or another subject of the belligerent state. This payment is known as *Sukra*, or insurance premium. (Anwar Ahmad Meenai, n.d.)

From the above rulings of Ibn Abidin, it is understood that a merchant used to charter a ship from the respective shipowner with a mutual understanding that the charterer would pay an additional amount known as *Sukra* (a premium in today's parlance) in which, if the ship faced any form of risk, the owner, in consideration of the *Sukra*, would provide a reasonable indemnity for the loss suffered by the merchant (charterer). The *Sukra* used to be collected by a nominated agent on behalf of the principal (shipowner) and he (agent) would also settle the indemnity (claimed by the merchant) on the owner's behalf.

Thus, these rulings could be a basis to justify the Islamic insurance (*Takaful*) practice of today's world. For example, in *Takaful*, the participants resemble the merchant in the above ruling and contributions paid by the participants resemble *Sukra*, while the indemnity provided against the risk is similar to the indemnification in *Takaful* practice. Moreover, the mutual understanding held between the merchant and the shipowner is like a *Takaful* policy agreement between the participants and the operator.

3.2.5 Al-Masalehal-Mursalah

The insurance contracts we see today are not exactly the same as those practised during the time of the Holy Prophet (saw). However, life, necessity and the status of human beings have changed with the passing of time and the necessity to take out insurance arose to suit the changing environment, in the sense that there is an urgent need to find a way of providing material security for those who are suffering in the society due to unexpected loss, damage or peril. Hence, insurance is necessary for the public interest so that the victim can be rescued from any unexpected risk. And thus, it is justified by the doctrine of *al-Masalehal-Mursalah*. Even though, the practice of insurance could also be based on the said doctrine, its validity is still subject to compliance with the divine principles laid down in the Qur'an and the Sunnah of the Holy Prophet (saw). The significance of an insurance practice based on the doctrine of *al-Masalehal-Mursalah* is, inter alia, to ensure a comfortable life, which is also a wish of Allah (swt) as evident in the following *ayat*:

> Allah (swt) intends every facility for you; He does not want to put you to difficulties. (Qur'an, Surah al-Baqarah, 2:185)

3.2.6 Al-'Urf

'Urf means custom, practice or usage of the community. An *'Urf* could also be used as a justification of a particular matter provided that, an *'Urf* does not contravene any divine sanction. The initial idea of Islamic insurance practices originated from the Arab's tribal custom known as *al-Aqila*, which was approved by the Holy Prophet (saw) in a dispute between two women from the Huzail tribe.[5] Hence, it is clear that the *'Urf* of *al-Aqila* practised by the ancient Arab tribes, and approved by the Holy Prophet (saw) could stand as a valid justification for the insurance.

[5] See *"al-'Aqila"*, in Gibb, *op. cit.*, p. 29.

3.2.7 Al-Fiqh

There are provisions in the *Fiqh* that deal with the practices of insurance. For instance, Sayyed Sabeq, in his book *Fiqhal-Sunnah*, under the section 'Shirkatut Tameen' discusses the validity of insurance contracts. An insurance contract is based on the general principles of *Al-Mudharabah*, Wakalah, *Sharikah* and so on, which have also been discussed in detail in his book (Sayyed as-Sabiq, n.d.). There are many other *Fiqh* sources,[6] which discuss either directly or indirectly, partly or wholly, the relevant aspects of insurance.

3.2.8 Sincerity

Every transaction and dealing should always be done with sincerity and pure intentions, in order to achieve the desired result from Allah (swt). He (swt) says:

> And they have been commanded no more than this, to worship Allah (swt), offering him sincere devotion. (Qur'an, Surah al-Bayyinah, 98:5)

A tradition of the Prophet (saw) adds:

> Narrated by Omar bin al-Khattab, the Holy Prophet (saw) said: The reward of deeds depends upon the intentions and every person will get the reward according to what he has intended.[7]

Moreover, the parties to the insurance contract must have the sincerity not to gain, but to be bound by that transaction based on the principles of mutual co-operation, solidarity and brotherhood towards rescuing one from unexpected losses and damages. This is because Allah (swt) never looks at material gains, but at the sincerity in the hearts of His creatures. The Holy Prophet (saw) said:

> Narrated by Abu Huraira, the Holy Prophet (saw) said: Verily Allah (swt) never look at your physical shape nor at your appearance but considers sincerity in your hearts.[8]

[6] The literature which focuses on the ruling of *Mudarabah, Musharakah, Wakalah* and *Wadiah* etc.

[7] *Bukhari* and *Muslim,* (agreed), *Kitab al-Wahi,* (trans. Eng.) Khan, M. Mohsin, *op. cit.* Vol. 1, No. 1, p. 1.

[8] *Sahih al-Muslim,* See An-Nawawi, *Riyadhussalihin,* (trans by) Ali, Maulana Syed Muhammad et al., *Riadussaliheen,* Vol. 1 Bangladesh Islamic Centre, Dhaka, 1990, No. 7, p. 5.

This is even more to in an insurance transaction whereby the undertaking parties must put all their trust and faith in Allah (swt) (Shafi, Mawlana Mufti Mohd., *Bimae Zindegi*, n.d.) in order to get His (swt) protection from the consequential unpredicted loss. This is because, an operator, in principle, undertakes only to compensate the insured against loss or damage. The operator is not liable to guarantee ultimate protection. This is because Allah (swt) is the One, who has the absolute power of protection over all in the universe.

> To Him belongs the dominion of the heaven and the earth: to give life and death: And He has power over all things. (Qur'an, Surah al-Hadid, 57:2)

3.3 Absolute Shari'ah Principles

An insurance business in the eyes of Islam is not valid should any of its aspects contravene any Shari'ah principle. The *Takaful* Act (Malaysia) 1984 prescribes that an insurance policy is enforceable if its

> aims and operations do not involve any element which is not approved by the Shari'ah. (*Takaful* Act (Malaysia), 1984)

Therefore, it is a prerequisite for the validity of a *Takaful* contract that none of its aspects contravene any express or implied Shari'ah sanction. Islam is the system of life recognised by Allah (swt) (Qur'an, Surah al-Imran:19) and, therefore, it is necessary for any transaction (including that of insurance) to be in conformity with the Divine rules and regulations. Any transaction that fails to be practised in conformity with such Divine rules and regulations will therefore become invalid. Allah (swt) says:

> If anyone desires any religion other than Islam never will it be recognised by Allah (swt). (Qur'an, Surah al-Imran:85)

3.4 Moral Attributes

An insurance contract and practice must also conform with moral sanctions. For example, in an Islamic insurance contract the parties should observe the principles of utmost good faith, honesty, disclosure and truthfulness. These principles could be justified by the following sanction of the Qur'an. Allah (swt) commands:

> Do not misappropriate your property among yourselves in vanities. (Qur'an, Surah an-Nisa, 4:29)

The parties involved in an insurance contract should not be greedy to gain something, but should build their purposes and aims based on the principle of mutual co-operation in rescuing a person from an unexpected disaster or loss. This is in line with following sanction:

> co-operate with one another in righteousness and piety. (Qur'an, Surah al-Maidah, 5:2)

3.5 Al-'Aqd (Contract)

It is suggested that the following elements should be available in a Shari'ah-based insurance transaction.

The parties to the contract must have legal capacities. The legal capacities are, inter alia, the age of majority (18 years) (Charles, Hamilton, n.d.), sanity and medical fitness. The party expected to obtain benefits from a policy must have an insurable interest (Rashid, S. K., n.d.) in the subject matter of the policy. The parties are bound by a unilateral contract, whereby the insurer is unilaterally responsible to indemnify the insured for an unexpected loss on the agreed subject matter. A participant must pay the first contribution. The subsequent payments of contributions are not an obligation, but necessary in order to enable the policyholder to make a claim on the policy. For the validity of a policy, the contract must be concluded by mutual consent of both the operator and the participant. Such requirement has been justified by the Qur'anic sanction:

> Do not misappropriate your property among yourselves in vanities, but let there be amongst you traffic and trade by mutual good-will. (Qur'an, Surah an-Nisa, 4:29)

A policy should be concluded by an offer and an acceptance, with a formal agreement between the insurer and the insured, in which the terms and conditions are put forward based on the doctrine of utmost good faith and in compliance with the Shari'ah principles (Sudan, n.d.). The period for each policy should be determined and recorded in the agreement before the signing of the contract.

3.6 Acts of Parliament

There are several Shari'ah-based insurance companies established and operating today in the contemporary world, for example, in Malaysia, Sudan, Brunei, Qatar and Saudi Arabia, to name a few. These Islamic insurance companies have been established and operate along the lines of the Shari'ah-based enactment and regulations approved by the parliaments of the respective countries. A clear example among such enactments and regulations is the *Takaful* Act (Malaysia) 1984 (Act 312) (*the Islamic Financial Services Act* 2013), which is one of the Acts of Parliament aimed at controlling insurance practices in Malaysia based on Shari'ah principles.

3.7 Rules of the Shari'ah Supervisory Board

Behind every Shari'ah-based insurance company, there is a council or board called the Shari'ah Supervisory Board. This Supervisory Board functions as the supervisor of the Islamic Insurance activities run by that particular company, to ensure that all these insurance activities operate in accordance with the Divine principles. For instance, the Malaysian *Takaful* Operation is supervised by a Shari'ah Supervisory Council by virtue of Section 8 (5) (b) of the *Takaful* Act 1984. In Sudan, moreover, there is a Shari'ah Supervisory Board, which supervises, inter alia, insurance business in the country and it also passed the rules of the Shari'ah Supervisory Board published by the Faisal Islamic Bank of Sudan (n.d.).

3.8 Precedents

Precedents could also play a role as one of the sources of insurance law and practice. Some Islamic scholars have given particular decisions on several issues of insurance policy and practice. These may be useful to regulate Islamic insurance practices. For instance, the opinion given by Ibn 'Abidin later became a precedent, which influenced Muftis in advising the governmental departments and various bodies on insurance matters (Mankabadi, Shamir, n.d.). Mufti Muhammad 'Abduh said on many occasions that insurance policy and practices are valid (Muhammad al-Sayyid al-Dusuqi, n.d.). Besides the precedents set by these independent Islamic scholars, there is also another type of precedent set by the contemporary courts relevant to insurance practices.[9] Such precedents could also be considered as a valid source of insurance law.

3.9 Unanimous Decision of the Islamic Scholars

There have been numerous conferences on Islamic insurance held worldwide in which Muslim scholars have unanimously agreed on the validity of various insurance practices. Some of those conferences are listed as follows:

> The Islamic Fiqh Week held in Damascus from 1st–6th April in 1961 (ibid.); the seminar held in Morocco on 6 May 1972, which upheld the validity of insurance business with the exception of life insurance business (Mankabadi, n.d.); the Second Conference on Muslim Scholars held in Cairo in 1965 (Hadagha, n.d.); the Symposium on Islamic Jurisprudence held in Libya from 6 to 11 May 1972 (ibid.); the First International Conference on Islamic Economics held in Makkah from 21 to 26 February 1976 (ibid.); the Islamic Conference held in Mecca in October, 1976 (Shawky, Muhammad, n.d.); the First International Summit on Islamic Insurance held in Dubai on 11 November 1996; and the Labuan International Summit on *Takaful* (Islamic insurance) held in Labuan, Malaysia, on 19–20 June 1997.

3.10 Principles of Liability

An insurance policy covers losses arising from the death, accident, disaster and other losses to human life, property or business. The insurer (insurance company) undertakes in the policy to compensate against the losses to the agreed subject matter. Such undertaking is considered as vicarious liability. For instance, in the case of ***al-Aqila*** practised in the ancient Arab tribes and approved by the Holy Prophet (saw), if a person was killed by another from a different tribe either mistakenly or negligently, this would bring a liability to the members of his tribe to pay bloodwit to the heirs of the slain (Uddin M. Musleh, n.d.).

Moreover, the rights and obligations in an insurance policy mainly arise from the law of contract and tort. For example, in a case of a motor accident, the operator (insurance company) is liable on behalf of the person

[9] Among the cases, the decision of *Amtul Habib vs Musarrat Parven* (1974) PLD 185 (SC) in which it was held that the nominee in a policy shall not be regarded as an absolute beneficiary but a mere trustee.

who causes that accident (i.e. the insured) to compensate the victim. Here, the operator is bound by the terms stipulated in the proposal to pay that compensation, under the principles of vicarious liability under the law of tort.

3.11 Principle of Utmost Good Faith

In an insurance contract, for the enforcement of the policy, the parties involved in it should have good faith. Therefore, as for non-disclosure of material facts, involvement of a fraudulent act, misrepresentations or false statements are all elements, which could invalidate a policy of insurance, Allah (swt) says:

> Do not misappropriate your property among yourselves in vanities, but let there be amongst you traffic and trade by mutual good-will. (Qur'an, Surah an-Nisa, 4:29)

3.12 Principles of Mirath and Wasiyah

In a life policy, the assured (Muslim) appoints a nominee, who must not be an absolute beneficiary. This decision was given in the fatwa on Succession and Will by the National Council for Muslim Religious Affairs, Malaysia, in 1974 ([1974] 1 MLJ X) and also in *Amtul Habib v Musarrat Parveen* in 1974 ([1974] PLD 185). In both fatwa and the following decision, it was ruled that a nominee in a life insurance policy of a Muslim is a mere trustee, who receives benefits from the policy and distributes them among the heirs of the deceased, in accordance with the principles of *Mirath* and *Wasiyah* (Billah, M. Masum, n.d.). The above fatwa and the case recently gained statutory weight in the Malaysian Insurance Act 1996, which came in force on 1 January 1997. S167 (1) states:

> A nominee, other than a nominee under subsection 166(1), shall receive the policy moneys payable on the death of the policy owner as an executor and not solely as a beneficiary and any payment to the nominee shall form part of the estate of the deceased policy owner and be subject to his debts and the licensed insurer shall be discharged from liability in respect of the policy monies paid.

In the light of this provision, it is concluded that the nominee in a policy nominated by a Muslim policyholder should be treated as a mere executor and not as an absolute beneficiary of the policy.

3.13 Principles of Wakalah (Agencies)

The appointment of the agent by the insurer and the broker by the insured are of utmost importance. In fact, such appointments are widely practised for the purpose of making the transaction and dealings between the insurer and the insured more effective. The governing principles for the agents and brokers are laid down in the *mejelle* as follows:

> *Wakalat* is for someone to put business of his on another and to make him stand in his own place in respect of that business. (C.R., n.d.)

3.14 Principles of Daman (Guarantee)

In an insurance policy, the insurer undertakes to provide material security for the insured against unexpected future loss, damage or risk. The idea of such guarantee is justified by the principles of *Daman* or guarantee under Islamic law.[10] In *Fiqh*, insurance can only be classed under Daman, which is governed by some essential conditions. Among them, the guarantor can only take upon himself a liability, which has fallen or may possibly fall upon a person or property (Yusuf, SM., 1977). Thus, Daman or guarantee may only be payable to the victim if the victim dies to his legal heirs, according to their respective shares in inheritance.[11]

3.15 Principles of Al-Mudharabah and Al-Musharakah

The operation of an insurance policy under Shari'ah is in fact, based on the principles of *Al-Mudharabah* financing scheme, which is an alternative to the contemporary interest-based transaction (Shafi, Mawlana Mufti Muhammad, n.d.). In such financing, one person provides the capital, while the other

[10] The Principle of *'al-Daman'* is highlighted in detail in Hamilton, Charles, *The Hedaya*, *op. cit*, Vol. II, pp. 318 *ff.*

[11] See, Government of Pakistan, Council of Islamic Ideology, *Offences against Human Body, (Enforcement of Qisas and Diyat) Draft Ordinance*, 1981, at S.94.

party contributes business skills, and both parties mutually agree to share the profits accordingly.[12] However, an insurance policy is a transaction wherein both parties agree that the participant pays regular contributions and the operator invests the accumulated contributions in a lawful business, in which both the insured and the operator share the profits in an agreed portion. At the same time, the insurer also undertakes to provide the insured with compensation (in consideration of the paid contributions) against an unexpected future loss or damage occurring on the subject matter of the policy. This is how the principles of *Al-Mudharabah* financing operate in an insurance policy.

An insurance policy also operates on the basis of the principle of *Al-Musharakah*, as both the operator and the participants are partners in the policy run by the insurance company.[13]

3.16 Principles of Rights and Obligations

An insurance policy is based on the principles of rights and obligations arising from humanity and nature. For instance, it is logical and natural for every person in a society to feel obliged to provide material security and protection as a right for themselves, their property, family, for the poor and helpless widows, and for children against unexpected perils and dangers. Such a natural obligation and right could well be justified by the following Sunnah of the Holy Prophet (saw):

> Narrated by Saad bin Abi Waqas, the Holy Prophet (saw) said … it is better for you to leave your offspring wealthy than to leave them poor asking others for help.[14]

The Holy Prophet (saw) had also emphasised the importance of providing material security for widows and poor dependents in the following Tradition:

> Narrated by Safwan bin Salim, the Holy Prophet (saw) said: The one who looks after and works for a widow and a poor person, is like a warrior fighting for Allah's cause or like a person who fasts during the day and prays all the night. (Id, Kitabul Adab, No. 35, p. 23).

[12] See *Mudharabah Companies and Mudharabah bond Control Ordinance* 1980 (The Gazette of Pakistan, extra, June 26, 1980, part 1) Article 2(2).

[13] For further detail, on *"Mudharabah"* see Niazi, *op. cit.*, at 227ff and for *"Sharikah,"* see p. 420 *f.*

[14] *Sahih al-Bukhari, Kitabul Adab, op. cit.*, Vol. 8, No. 725, p. 477 f.

3.17 Principles of Humanitarian Law

It is one of the purposes of humanitarian law to inculcate mutual understanding in the community, to protect one against unexpected loss, damage or other forms of risk or hardship. Hence, an insurance policy contributes towards alleviating hardships from a person arising from unexpected material risks, which is of course within the scope of the principles of humanitarian law. This has been justified in the following Tradition of the Holy Prophet (saw), which reads:

> Narrated by Abu Huraira, [...] the Holy Prophet (saw) said [...] whosoever removes a worldly grief from a believer, Allah (swt) will remove from him one of the grieves of the day of judgment. Whosoever alleviates grieves from a needy person, Allah (swt) will alleviate from him in this world and the next. (Sahih al-Muslim, Kitab al-Birr, 59)

3.18 Principles of Mutual Co-operation

In a policy, both the operator and the participant mutually agree to lawful co-operation, in which the participant provides capital (through the payments of contributions) to the operator (insurance company), enabling the insurer to invest the accumulated contributions in a lawful business (on the basis of *Al-Mudharabah*). Meanwhile, the insurer, in return for the payments of the contributions, mutually agrees to compensate the insured in the occurrence of an unexpected loss or damage or risk on the subject matter. Such mutual co-operation among the parties in an insurance policy is justified by the Divine principles of mutual co-operation, solidarity and brotherhood (The *Takaful* Act (Malaysia) 1984). Allah (swt) commanded:

> co-operate you one another in righteousness and piety (Qur'an, Surah al-Maidah, 5:3)

References

1. Ali. A. Y. (n.d.), The Holy Qur'an, Text and Translation.
2. 'Insurance' in Hughes, James Langhlin, The New Educator Encyclopedia, Akashdee Publishing House Delhi, 1990, Vol. V, p. 1813.

3. The suggestion is made relying on the logical fact that an insurance contract under Islamic law operates on the basis of the principle of mudharabah (profit and loss sharing). Hence, the benefits (over and above the policy) should also be disbursed according to this profit and loss sharing technique. It is sincerely believed that this suggestion could work well in an equitable nature.
4. Since a general policy is for a short period, in an effort to be fair to the insurer, the insurer has to deduct the service charges (for the management of the company) including the percentage for the charitable account from the paid-premiums according to the company's financial policy.
5. Mudharabah is a mutual financing technique in Islamic commercial law in which two or more parties agree that one will provide capital while the other may offer a service or skill in a particular business in view of sharing the profits and losses accordingly. Today's Islamic banks and insurance companies operate on the basis of mudharabah, which is an alternative to interest based transactions.
6. The Islamic part is based on (with possible revision) one of my unpublished manuscripts entitled "Islamic Insurance: Its Original Sketch and Development Scenario".
7. Al-Suyuti, Itqan fi Ulumel Qur'an, as cited in I doi, Abdur Rahman, Shari'ah: The Islamic Law, A.S. Noodeen, Kuala Lumpur, 1984, p. 36.
8. Sunanat Tirmizi, Vol. 4, Cagri yayinlari Istanbul, 1981 in Kitab-ul Sifatul Qiyamah wa ar-Rakaik al-Wara, Bab 60, No. 2517, p. 668.
9. Sahih al-Muslim (Arabic), Kitab al-Birr, No. Hadith 59.
10. Raddu al-Mukhtar, Bab al-Musta'min, Vol. 3, at p. 345.
11. Sayyed as-Sabiq, Fiqh al-Sunnah, Darul Kitab al-Arabi, Lebanon, 1971, Vol. 3.
12. The literature, which focuses on the ruling of mudarabah, musharakah, Wakalah and Wadiah etc.
13. Bukhari and Muslim, (agreed), Kitab al-Wahi, (trans. Eng.) Khan, M. Mohsin, Vol. 1, No. 1, P. 1.
14. Sahih al-Muslim, See An-Nawawi, Riyadhussalihin, (trans by) Ali, Maulana Syed Muhammad et al., Riadussaliheen, Vol. 1 Bangladesh Islamic Centre, Dhaka, 1990, No. 7, p. 5.
15. *Takaful* Act (Malaysia), 1984 at S 2.
16. al-Qur'an, Surah al-Imran:19 "The religion before Allah (swt) is only Islam (Submission to His Will)".
17. One of the legal capacities is, inter alia, the age of majority. The Hedaya, set the age of majority is 15 years regardless of sex. (This opinion is according to the majority of the fuqaha); See Charles, Hamilton, The Hedaya, Vol. III, op. cit. p. 529.
18. The Rules of Shari'ah Supervisory Board, Faisal, Islamic Bank Sudan Publications, English Series (5), Sudan. n.d., p. 12.

19. The *Takaful* Act (Malaysia) 1984 at S. 8 (5)(b), Repealed by the Islamic Financial Services Act 2013.
20. Among the cases, the decision of Amtul Habib vs Musarrat Parven (1974) PLD 185 (SC) in which it was held that the nominee in a policy shall not be regarded as an absolute beneficiary but a mere trustee.
21. Shawky, Muhammad, Al-Islam wat Tameen, p. 14.
22. For example, See Uddin M. Musleh, Concept of Civil Liability in Islam and the Law of Torts, Islamic Publication Ltd. Lahore, 1982 at 62, See also Niazi Liaqat Ali Khan, Islamic Law of Tort, Research Cell Dayal Singh Trust Library, Lahore, 1988, p. 339.
23. al-Qur'an, Surah an-Nisa, 4:29.
24. [1974] 1 MLJ X.
25. [1974] PLD 185.
26. Mejelle al-Ahkam al-Adiyah by Tyser (trans.), C.R., The Mejelle, Law Publishing Company, Lahore n.d. art 1449.
27. Yusuf, SM., Economic Justice in Islam, Sh. Muhammad Ashraf, Lahore, 1977, pp. 92–93.
28. Government of Pakistan, Council of Islamic Ideology, Offences against Human Body, (Enforcement of Qisas and Diyat) Draft Ordinance, 1981, at S.94.
29. Mudharabah Companies and Mudharabah Bond Control Ordinance 1980 (The Gazette of Pakistan, extra, June 26, 1980, part 1) Article 2(2).
30. For further details on mudharabah see Niazi, op. cit., at 227ff and for "Sharikah," see p. 420 f.
31. Sahih al-Muslim, Kitab al-Birr, 59.
32. The *Takaful* Act (Malaysia) 1984, S. 2.

PART II

General *Takaful* Products

CHAPTER 4

Preview of General *Takaful*

4.1 Introduction

Takaful comes from the word *kafala* which means responsibility to help or to take care of one's needs. The word *Takaful* itself means shared responsibility. Muslim jurists generally accept that the concept of Takaful does not contradict the Shari'ah as the essence of insurance could be seen in the system of mutual help in relation to the custom of blood money under Arab tribal customs. The teaching of Islam encompasses the essence of peace, economic well-being and development of Muslims at all levels. The principle of compensation and group responsibility was accepted by Islam and the Holy Prophet. Takaful practices can be seen in the practices of *al-Aqila*, even before the rise of Islam. This practice was further developed after the rise of Islam to be in accordance with Shari'ah regulations. There are four *Takaful* operators providing Takaful services in Malaysia. They are *Takaful* Malaysia, *Takaful* Nasional, *Takaful* Maybank and *Takaful* Ikhlas. These four companies generally provide the same sort of services. The two Takaful schemes are General *Takaful* and Family *Takaful*. General *Takaful* is a scheme that provides protection for the short term.

It is acknowledged that the ideas in this chapter/product have been significantly contributed to by the practices/experiences/thoughts of Bank Negara, *Takaful* Malaysia, *Takaful* Ikhlas, *Takaful* Nasional, Etiqa *Takaful*, IBFIM, IIUM, MII and others (Malaysia).

Mohd Ma'Sum Billah, *Islamic Insurance Products*,
https://doi.org/10.1007/978-3-030-17681-5_4

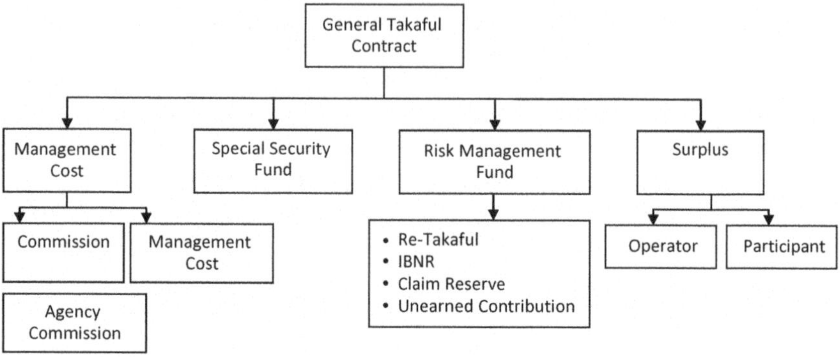

Fig. 4.1 Organisation of the General *Takaful* contract. (Source: Author's own collection)

It is designed to meet the needs for protection against material losses or damage inflicted upon property. Some of the policies under the General Takaful are Motor Takaful, Fire Takaful and Accident Takaful. A General *Takaful* contract is based on the principles of *Al-Mudharabah* and *Tabarru'*. The basic organisation of General *Takaful* is illustrated in Fig. 4.1.

The contributions of the participants under the contract of General *Takaful* are divided into four classes. They are Management Costs, Special Security Fund, Risk Management Costs and Surplus. A certain percentage of the contributions will be allocated for each of the classes according to the contract. Management costs are further divided into agency commission and management costs of administration. A special security fund is a liquidity or solvency margin as advancement in facing any circumstances. This is still under consideration and will be implemented soon. Risk management cost is also known as a *Tabarru'* fund, which cannot be claimed back by the participant. This fund is classified into Re-takaful, incurred but not claimed, claim reserve and unearned contributions. Finally, there are the underwriters' surplus, which is divided into operator and participant.

The Takaful operator will collect the contributions paid by the participant and distribute them accordingly. The contributions will be credited to two accounts. A smaller portion will be credited in Participant Account (PA), while the bigger portion will be credited to the Participant Special Account (PSA). The amount allocated under PA is invested and the profit is shared according to *Al-Mudharabah* between the operator and participant. This amount will be received by the participant whether risk is encountered within the policy period or not. Under the PSA, the contribution will be further distributed into the four funds mentioned above. This account is credited under the concept of *Tabarru'* and cannot be claimed back unless the participant has incurred losses or damage within the policy period.

4.2 An Overview

Takaful as a system of Islamic insurance is based on mutual cooperation for the good of the society at large. For *Takaful* business to prosper and be managed properly, it is necessary to enable the authority to regulate and supervise its operations accordingly. Therefore, a form of legislative framework is essential for the authority to exercise its supervisory function both in terms of business operations as well as Shari'ah compliance. For instance, the operation of *Takaful* business in Malaysia is licensed and regulated. In underlining with Islamic principles, every *Takaful* operator should establish their own religious supervisory council to advise the company on the operations of its Takaful business. These religious supervisory councils are unique entities found only in Islamic banks and financial institutions. They play an important role in Islamic financial institution. Therefore, in respect to this we can see that in Section 8.3(a), the *Takaful* Act 1984 states that:

> A Religious Supervisory Council, whose members would made up of Muslim religious scholars in the country, shall be established to advise the Company on the operations of its Takaful business in order to ensure that they do not involve any element which is not approved by Religion of Islam.

Let us take *Takaful* Malaysia Bhd as an example. In the Memorandum of Understanding and Articles of Association stated that

> all business of the company will be transacted in accordance with Islamic principles, rules and practices.

Basically, there are two types of Takaful business;

- Family *Takaful*
- General *Takaful*

Both types of business must be governed by Islamic principles. The products from both types of business must go through Shari'ah screening by Shari'ah Supervisory Council before entering into the market. For the purposes of this chapter, we just concentrate on General *Takaful* business operations.

4.3 Framework of General *Takaful* Products

Most scholars who support the opinion that insurance is permissible said that insurance is a modem contract and there is no injunction (*nass*) regarding it. If there is no injunction, then it is allowed (*mubah*). They base their argument on the established legal maxim that "the original legal position on any matter is permissibility until there is evidence prohibiting it" (Azman Ismail n.d.). This is based on the Qur'an verses as follows:

> We have subjugated to you all that is in the heavens and the earth. (Qur'an, 45:13)

According to the scholars, this verse shows that in principle we are permitted to use the resources of the universe. This universe is described as an adornment of Allah. This is stated in the Qur'an.

> Who has forbidden the adornment of Allah which He has brought forth for His bondsmen, and the good things of His providing? (Qur'an, 7:32)

The scholars further claim that Takaful is a contract that brings *maslahah* to the insured. For example, without Takaful, a family will suffer a huge burden after someone's death. A *Takaful* contract is not a contract of exchange but falls under the concept of *Tabarru'* and as assistance and guarantee by the insurer to the insured. The beneficiary in Takaful is a trustee who is in charge of collecting the claim when the policyholder encounters risk. He is responsible for distributing the amount to the heir according to the principle of *Faraid*. The contract of Takaful is based on the Divine virtues of co-operation, mutual help, shared responsibility, benefit, brotherhood and solidarity. In order to achieve this, the motives of Takaful should be to bring equality to all. The main objective is to help each other in times of misfortune.

4.4 Shari'ah Rulings

The primary objectives of the Islamic Shari'ah can be described according to the definition given by al-Ghazali and Ibn al-Qayyim (Datuk Syed Othman Alhabshi 1995).

> The very objectives of the Shari'ah are to promote the welfare of the people, which lies in safeguarding their faith, their life, their intellect, their posterity and their wealth. Whatever ensures the safeguarding of these five serves public interest and is desirable. (Al-Ghazali)

> The basis of the Shari'ah is wisdom and welfare of the people in this world as well as the Hereafter. This welfare lies in complete justice, mercy, well-being and wisdom. Anything that departs from justice to oppression, from mercy to harshness, from welfare to misery and from wisdom to folly, has nothing to do with the Shari'ah. (Ibn al-Qayyim)

Based on the above definitions, it is clear that Islam is a comprehensive religion. From this statement, we can conclude that the basic operation of Takaful business is approved by Shari'ah because the main objective of Takaful business is to provide financial security against a defined risk. As far *Takaful* is concerned, there are three elements presents in the operation that make *Takaful* different from conventional insurance. Therefore, the Shari'ah Supervisory Council has played its role in confirming the business is free from the following elements:

- *Gharar*
- *Maisir*
- *Riba*.

4.4.1 Gharar

This term means unknown or uncertain factors that may occur in a transaction. It is the basis of gambling and hence prohibited. This may be witnessed from the following hadith:

> Abu Hurairah reported that the Holy Prophet forbade *Gharar* sales (indeterminate, doubtful and speculative transactions or the sale of unpossessed things). Ibn Umar and Ibn Abbas repeated this hadith.

4.4.2 *Maisir*

This refers to gambling that arises as a consequence of the presence of *Gharar*. The element of *Maisir* is usually associated with life insurance. However, in the case of life insurance under *Takaful*, the parties in a contract are bound together the manner of mutual co-operation and goodwill, providing material security for the orphans, widows, other dependants as well as one's own self against unexpected future loss, damage or peril (Billah n.d.). This evidence can be seen through the following hadith:

> Narrated by Saad b. Abi Waqqas (r.a.) [...]: it is better for you to leave you off-spring wealthy than to leave them poor, asking others for help.

4.4.3 *Riba*

Riba is perhaps the only way to convince Muslims that life insurance of *Takaful* is permissible because the basis operation of Takaful business is reliant on the concepts of *Tabarru'* and *Al-Mudharabah. Tabarru'* refers to the sharing and co-operative relationship among policyholders, while *Al-Mudharabah* is the profit-sharing contract between the Takaful operator and participants.

> O ye who believe devour not *Riba*, doubled and multiplied but fear Allah that ye may prosper. (Qur'an, 3:130)

4.5 Problems and Issues

Some of the problems faced are due to misunderstandings by some ulama that a practice of Takaful is prohibited completely without considering it mechanism. According to them, Takaful contains elements of *Gharar*, *Maisir* and *Riba*. First, the outcome of the contract is uncertain because neither does the participant nor the operator know whether the risk will happen. Uncertainty also exists because the operator does not know the exact amount that will be received before the risk occurs. The timeframe of the policy is also not known. Second, there is the element of *Maisir*. This is because if the risk take places then participant will win, but if the risk does not happen then the operator will win. Furthermore, the source of the money is also not known. Thirdly, there is the element of *Riba*. The differences in the amount and quantity shows that *Riba* exists in the practices of Takaful. All these allegations have been refuted, as discussed above. Through the true teachings of Islam and the guidance from the

Qur'an and the Sunnah we can see that the practices of Takaful are recommended in Islam.

Besides the above issues, there are also other problems created by policyholders. Participants sometimes fail to understand the cover provided by the operator. For example, in the case of fire Takaful the items in a house which are not registered will not be covered. Participants sometimes request full coverage and create problems that tarnish the reputation of the Takaful operator. There is also another example whereby after further investigation the fire is discovered to have been caused by, for example, the son of the policyholder while he was playing. The operator does not provide cover in such case because the cause of fire was not natural. Misunderstandings have arisen between the Takaful operator and policyholder which result in a dispute.

Sometimes the participant does not provide all the information required. When accidents happen and the Takaful operator finds that the information provided is not complete, then the contract is rendered void. In these situations, the participant is not compensated for the loss encountered. Beside all these issues, a common problem faced is deferred payment of contributions. It is difficult to track all customers who delay payment and requires extra work on the operator's part.

4.6 Conclusion

The emergence of many Takaful operators and policies should not be seen as a way to make material gains or to overpower the determination and will of Allah (swt). In contrast, it aims at achieving the pleasure of Allah through the principles and concepts of mutual help and co-operation. The purpose is only to provide material assistance to those who face hardship because of unexpected risk. The prophet himself advised the Arab who left his camel untied to tie his camel and then left it to the will of Allah (swt). This shows that effort should be taken to minimise risk.

References

1. Billah, M. M. (2003), Manual of Principles & Practices of *Takaful* and *Re-Takaful*, IIUM, Malaysia.
2. *General Takaful Models*, *Takaful* Malaysia, *Takaful* Nasional, *Takaful* Ikhlas and others.
3. Ismail, A. (n.d.), "Insurance and Shari'ah", *Nidaul Islam*.
4. Syed Othman Alhabshi (1995) Islamic Fund in Malaysia.

CHAPTER 5

Motor *Takaful*

5.1 Introduction

In our daily life, we always face the risk of possible mishap, disaster and calamity befalling our life or property. As a Muslim, we must strongly believe that anything happen to us is *Qada'* and *Qadar* came from Allah and we must face it with patience. Hence, a Muslim is obliged to make efforts to avoid any kind of disaster and catastrophe that might endanger his life or property. Therefore, he has to seek ways to reduce the burden of himself of his family if this sort of misfortune occurs.

Insurance practice is the most popular method to ensure one's material security or that property is insured against risk. However, some Muslims are disinclined to accept insurance because they believe that it involves *Riba*. In response to this, Islamic scholars have analysed the operation of insurance and eliminated the illegal elements in conventional insurance; they have then suggested the *Takaful* is the best insurance to substitute for the conventional approach. *Takaful* or Islamic insurance is policy of mutual co-operation, solidarity and brotherhood in which the participants

It is acknowledged that, the idea of this chapter/product is significantly contributed by the practices/experiences/thoughts of Bank Negara, *Takaful* Malaysia, *Takaful* Ikhlas, *Takaful* Nasional, Etiqa *Takaful*, IBFIM, IIUM, MII and others (Malaysia).

Mohd Ma'Sum Billah, *Islamic Insurance Products*,
https://doi.org/10.1007/978-3-030-17681-5_5

share responsibility with the insurer against losses. They are expected to contribute to the fund (*Tabarru'*) with good intentions to help each other. Allah commands such mutual co-operation as in the following verse:

> And do co-operate ye one another with righteousness and piety.[2]

Nowadays, people can seek protection against risk through various types of Takaful product. At present, there are two types of Takaful products, Family *Takaful* schemes and General *Takaful* schemes. Family *Takaful* is a kind of life insurance, which is based on Shari'ah principles. While General *Takaful* Schemes are divided into various types, such as fire, miscellaneous and accident, marine, engineering and motor Takaful. This chapter will focus on the Motor *Takaful* Scheme in order to understand its operation. Almost everybody has a vehicle and need to seek protection of material security on their vehicles and life as well.

5.2 Motor *Takaful* Scheme

Motor insurance policy is a policy that provides coverage for a vehicle and the owner or any other person connected to the vehicle. This type of policy is a mandatory requirement for all vehicle owners in Malaysia, since they cannot have their vehicle road taxed without registering it to a motor insurance policy. *Takaful* Malaysia also provides this type of policy, which called the Motor *Takaful* Scheme. In *Takaful* Malaysia at present, the Motor *Takaful* Scheme represents a sizeable portfolio of the General *Takaful* business of the company. The main objective of this policy is to facilitate or ease the burden of the policyholder by helping them through financially in case of mishap and avoiding unlawful element as in conventional insurance practices such as *Riba* (interest), *Gharar* (uncertainty) and *Maisir* (gambling).

5.2.1 Contract of Motor Takaful *Scheme*

This policy uses the concept of *Al-Mudharabah* and *Tabarru'*. Mudharabah is the commercial profit-sharing contract between the providers of fund for business venture and the entrepreneur. This concept is used in a Participant Account (PA), while *Tabarru'* is used in Participant Special Accounts (PSA). *Tabarru'* is a consideration of participants where they agree to donate some amount to help other participants who have faced accident or disaster.

5.2.2 Procedure for Application

Filling the Proposal and Declaration Form → Underwriting Process → Aqad
↓
Takaful Certificate

A person or a corporate body may participate in the Motor *Takaful* Scheme easily as the procedure is very simple. First, a person or a proposer only has to complete the Proposal and Declaration Form, which contains the main material aspect of the risk and also contains brief details of the cover available under the company's standard certificate for the class of cover. This form must be completed and returned to the company for evaluation. Upon receiving the form, company's underwriter will arrange the terms and conditions of the cover and its price, at levels, which reflect the degree of risks, which the case brings to the General *Takaful* fund by way of potential frequency, and potential severity of loss. The underwriter also must ensure that the proposer had the capacity to contract and its compliance with Shari'ah Law. All this is called the underwriting process. When everything is deemed valid, there will be an *aqad* between the proposer and *Takaful* Company. This *aqad* will be recorded in a document called a Takaful certificate.

5.2.3 Scope of Cover

This policy covers two major types of vehicle, which are private cars and private motorcycles. In addition, it covers commercial vehicles; however, it is for selected corporate clients on accommodation basis only. In general, motor Takaful policy covers:

Private Third Party
Under this type of coverage, there are two types of indemnity; first is the indemnity of a participant or his authorised driver against any liability which may attach to him in consequence of any third party being injured/death by the use of his vehicle and the other indemnity is indemnity for liability in respect of damage to properties belonging to a third party in consequence of the use of the vehicle covered.

Private Comprehensive
This type of coverage also covers the two listed above, indemnity to the participant or his authorised driver and indemnity for liability in respect of damage to properties belonging thereto and it also has another indemnity, which is indemnity for the participant for the loss or damage to the vehicle or its spare parts. The loss or damage must be arising from events such as accidental collision or overturning, collision or overturning caused by mechanical breakdown, collision or overturning caused by wear and tear, impact damage caused by falling objects (not resulting from flood, typhoon, hurricane, storm, tempest, volcanic eruption, earthquake, landslide, landslip or other convulsion of nature), fire explosion or lightning, burglary, housebreaking or theft, malicious act, whilst in transit (including its loading and unloading by road, rail, inland waterway, direct sea route across the straits between the island of Penang and the mainland).

The *Takaful* operator will cover the death or injury of the passenger by an endorsement, which covers:

- *Legal liability to passenger*—liability of the driver to the passenger when something happens during the journey. For example, an accident happened, the passenger got injured.
- *Legal Liability of passenger*—liability of the passenger in the driver's car. For example, if a passenger opens the door of the car, then causes a person (such as a motorcycle rider) to break the door and become injured. He may claim against the car driver. Endorsement will impose an additional charge.

5.2.4 Premium

A premium is the contribution paid by a participant to the *Takaful* Company. This premium is paid based on type of vehicle. Normally, a *Takaful* premium is 50% more than in conventional insurance because its cover is more comprehensive. For a *Takaful* Company such as *Takaful* Nasional and *Takaful* IKRAM, they use the PIAM (Persatuan Insurans Am Malaysia) rate.

This rate is a recognised rate determined by PIAM. The column "Code" refers to type of vehicle, for example the code 01 for car might refer to vans and 4WD vehicles. The column "Rate" is a rate given by PIAM to that type of vehicle, for example a rate of 25% for a motorcycle might be refer to motorcycles above 501cc. That rate is the percentage or premium that the participant in that Motor *Takaful* has to pay every year. *Takaful* Malaysia Berhad uses tables calculated by actuaries to determine the contributions that participants have to pay.

For the first time, a policyholder (third party) for motorcar or motorcycle has to pay contributions, which are calculated based on the market value of the vehicle. For example, in the case of *Takaful* Malaysia Berhad, if the car's market value is RM 25,000 and has no policy insurance beforehand, then the participant has to pay premiums of RM 1323 per year. This contribution will become less year on year. *Takaful* Malaysia Berhad uses tables that calculate by actuaries to determine the contribution that participants have to pay. Under the Section 25 of the *Takaful* Act 1984, and regulation on "Assumption of Risks and Collection of Contribution" it is prescribed that the contribution for Motor *Takaful* Scheme must to be paid fully and settled before acceptance. This called Cash Before Cover. It means that full payment must be received from the date of cover. No payment means no coverage.

5.2.5 Claims

Type of Claim

Claims can be categorised into three major types: motor vehicle damage claims, fire claims and personal accident claims.

Related Documents

In the event of loss, necessary action should be taken. Part of this is notification of loss, which must be accompanied and substantiated by the following documents:

- claim form
- police report
- copy of registration card
- copy of driving license of the driver at the material time of accident
- copy of identity card (driver and participant)
- Repairer's estimate and copy of Road Tax Disc.

For theft, the documents needed are:

- claim form
- police report
- original registration card
- original Takaful certificate
- sets of keys and original MV 3 duly signed
- letter from finance company showing amount outstanding or their release letter (if the motor vehicle under financing or loan)
- copy of participant's identity card.

Claim Procedure
If there is any mishap, the policyholder must make a claim to *Takaful* Malaysia to get the benefit of insurance. The policyholder must complete certain procedures in order to make a claim. These are applicable to all types of claim, as mentioned above. Firstly, Notification of Loss where he must lodge a police reports within 24 hours of the mishap. Then, within 14 days he must go to any branch of the *Takaful* company where he registered his vehicle and fill out a preliminary loss advice (PLA) form. Third step, he must send a copy of the PLA together with all the other supporting documents to the Claims Department as soon as possible. The supporting documents needed in order to make a claim are different depending on the mishap in question (Fig. 5.1).

The policyholder or claimant must make sure he has sent his car to the panel workshop after he has sent all the documents to the Claims Department. Second, checking scope refers to where the covering branch will check some important matters before proceeding with processing the claim. Some of the matters herein pertain to whether the loss or subject matter is covered under the certificate, if the damage occurred within the

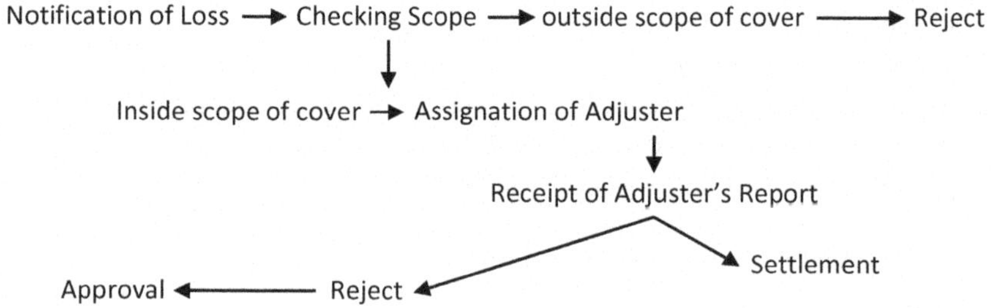

Fig. 5.1 Claim. (Source: Author's own collection)

period of *Takaful*, what is the cause of the loss and is the risk covered under the certificate, and has the *Takaful* contribution been paid. From these questions, the branch will decide whether the mishap is within the scope of cover or outside it. If, for example, the mishap falls within the scope of cover, the branch will assign an adjuster within two days of receipt of the supporting documents; then the branch must ensure that the adjuster's report be submitted within seven working days.

The loss adjuster is usually assigned by the company's panel of adjusters. If the mishap is outside the scope of cover, the participant or claimant will be informed of the rejection in writing within 21 days. Upon receiving the adjuster's report, the relevant branch will ensure that the adjuster did not recommend that the claim should be repudiated or rejected. There have also been cases where the claim is rejected or repudiated after receiving the adjuster's report, if after investigation the adjuster found out that there is something not valid within the claim. If this happens, the claim is rejected and participant or claimant will be informed in writing. If there is no recommendation of rejection from the adjuster, the branch will make sure of the loss figure and if it is over or above the prescribed limit, the claim must be immediately submitted to Claims Department, together with all relevant documents for a decision. The claim must be decided within seven days from receipt of the report. After the claim has been approved, a copy of approval letter and the supporting documents will be sent to the Claims Department. Upon receiving the final bill and discharge voucher, all of these documents are to be submitted to the Claim Departments for settlement payment.

5.2.6 Benefit

Benefit can be divided into three categories. First is benefit from a claim. Benefit from a claim is the money a company is paid after the approval of a claim. Normally, this benefit is taken from the PSA which operates under *Tabarru'* and also from the PA which operates under the concept of *Al-Mudharabah*. But there is a minimum rate for the claim. For example, in the certificate it stated that the minimum rate is RM 2, and then if the claim is not more than the minimum rate, this policy is not covered. Second, there is benefit from an unclaimed policy. The contract of Motor Takaful is treated as *Tabarru'*, which consist of four accounts: Re-takaful, Incurred But Not Recorded, Claim Reserve and Unearned *Takaful* Contribution. In case of no claim being made within the policy period, the participant will be given the amount reserved in the Unearned *Takaful* Contribution account only. Lastly, there is benefit from surplus. At the end of period of *Takaful*, if there is a net surplus in the company's General *Takaful* Fund, the same shall be shared between the participant and the company in accordance with the principles of *Al-Mudharabah* in the proportions of 40% to the participant and 60% to the company, as set out in the proposal and declaration.

5.3 Motor *Takaful* for Private Cars

5.3.1 Conditions Applied to the Whole Type of Contract

- Duty of Disclosure

In the registration period, the participant must disclose all information needed fully and faithfully. If the participant fails to do so, the agreement or certificate is rejected.

- Accidents and Claims Procedures
  - The participant must notify in writing with the full details as soon as possible after an event which may become the subject of a claim and all accidents must be reported to the police as required by Law.
  - The participant must also inform the *Takaful* company immediately if there is a writ, summons and process from other parties, and any impending prosecution inquest or fatal inquiry. The participant is also required to co-operate with the *Takaful* company in order to settle the claim.
  - No negotiation, admission or rejection of any claim may be entered into without the prior written consent of the *Takaful* company.
  - The *Takaful* company shall have full discretion in the conduct, defence and settlement of any claim
  - No repairs may be authorised to the participant's vehicle without prior written consent of the *Takaful* company.
  - If the participant's vehicle is involved in an accident and gives rise to a claim, the vehicle must be removed to *Takaful* company's approved repairer for repairs. Failure to do so would be a breach

of contract and the *Takaful* company has the right to decline liability under section A of the Certificate for Motor *Takaful* for Private Cars.

- Cancellation

Under cancellation, both parties can cancel the contract by giving 14 days written notice. So, if the participant decides to cancel the contract, he can do so at any time by giving 14 days written notice to *Takaful* company. The *Takaful* company also can cancel the contract by giving 14 days' written notice by registered post to participant's last-known address. In case of cancellation, the participant shall be entitled to a pro-rata refund of the unexpired contributions.

- Other *Takaful* or Insurance

Participant must give written notice if he has any other *Takaful* or insurance company covering his vehicle. If at any time any claim arises under the Certificate for Motor *Takaful* for Private Cars, or if there is any other existing certificate covering the same loss, damage or liability, then the *Takaful* Company shall only pay its proportion of any loss damage compensation costs or expenses.

- Subrogation

The *Takaful* company shall be entitled if they desire to take over conduct at their own expense in the participant's settlement of any claim for indemnity or damages and they shall have absolute discretion in the conduct of any proceedings and in the settlement of any claim and the participant shall give all such information and assistance as they may require.

- Arbitration Clause

All differences arising out of the Certificate for Motor *Takaful* (Private Car) shall be referred to an arbitrator who shall be appointed in writing by participant and the *Takaful* company. If both parties are unable to agree on who is to be the arbitrator within one month, then both parties must appoint an arbitrator each who shall proceed to hear the differences, together with an umpire to be appointed by both arbitrators. However, it is provided that any disclaimer of liability by the *Takaful* company for any claim must be referred to an arbitrator within 12 calendar months of the date of disclaimer.

- Replacement Parts

In the event of loss damage to the motor vehicle or its accessories or spare parts necessitating the supply of a part not obtained from stocks held in the country in which the motor vehicle is held for repair or in the event of the company needing to pay in cash the amount of the loss or damage, the liability if the company in respect of any such parts shall be limited to:

- the price quoted in the latest catalogue or price list issued by the manufacturer or his agent for the country in which the vehicle is held for repair

OR

- if no catalogue or price list exists, the price last obtaining at the manufacturer's work plus the reasonable costs of transportation to the country in which the vehicle is held for repair and also the amount of the relative import duties

AND

- the reasonable costs of fitting such part/s.

- Other Matters

The Certificate for Motor *Takaful* (Private Car) will only be effective if:

- any person claiming protection has complied with all its terms, conditions, endorsements, clauses or warranties;
- the participant has taken all reasonable precautions to maintain his vehicle in good condition;
- the participant has taken all reasonable precautions to safeguard his vehicle from loss or damage.

5.4 Types of Vehicle

Under the Motor *Takaful* Scheme, there are several types of private car covered (Table 5.1).

5.4.1 Coverage

Based on Certificate for Motor *Takaful* (Private Car) section A and section B, this scheme covers loss or damage to a vehicle and liability to third parties.

Loss or Damage to a Vehicle
The Motor *Takaful* scheme will cover three things under loss or damage to a vehicle. First, if it is damaged or lost in the following circumstances:

- accidental collision or overturning
- collision or overturning caused by mechanical breakdown
- collision or overturning caused by falling objects provided no flood, typhoon, storm, tempest, volcanic eruption, earthquake, landslide, landslip or when another convulsion of nature is involved
- fire, explosion or lightning
- burglary, housebreaking or theft
- a malicious act
- when in transit (including its loading and unloading) by road, rail, inland waterway and direct sea route over the straits between the island of Penang and the mainland.

Table 5.1 Types of vehicle

Code	*Type*
A	Vehicle with engine capacity less than 1400 cc
B	Vehicle with engine capacity between 1401 and 1650 cc
C	Vehicle with engine capacity between 1651 and 2200 cc
D	Vehicle with engine capacity between 2201 and 3050 cc
E	Vehicle with engine capacity between 3051 cc
F	Vans and 4WD vehicles

Source: Author's own collection

Second, this scheme will also cover the basis of settlement where they have an option to

- pay the cost of repairs to the vehicle;
- pay in cash the amount of the loss or damage to vehicle; or
- reinstate or replace the vehicle.

Under the basis of settlement, the *Takaful* company is also required to pay the maximum amount, which is the market value of the vehicle at the time of the loss, OR the sum covered in the certificate, OR whichever one is lower. In some cases, the cost of loss or damage at the time of event is greater than its market value; then participant is considered as being his own insurer and he has to pay the difference or remaining balance of the proportion of the loss or damage. This situation only applies when market value at the time of the loss exceeds the value covered by at least 10%. There are several ways to determine the market value of the vehicle:

- in the event of a dispute by the head office of the franchise-holder and this value being equal to the cost of purchasing a replacement vehicle of the same make, model and age of the vehicle at the time of loss;
- if there is no franchise-holder, the market value is determine by a loss adjuster licensed under the Insurance Act 1963 and its subsequent legislation agreed to by both the *Takaful* company and the participant.

Third, under this section the scheme also covers transportation of a damaged vehicle where the *Takaful* company will pay up to RM 20,000 as towing charges for taking the vehicle to either the nearest repairer, or towing the vehicle by returning it to the participant's residence, or towing it to a secure place for it to be put in a garage, provided the vehicle has been damaged by circumstances described earlier in this section.

These are all cases that would be covered by Motor *Takaful* Scheme for Private Cars. However, there are still some exceptions to the scheme, where if some exceptional cases happen the company would not be liable to pay. Such cases are:

- consequential losses of any nature
- loss of use of the vehicle

- depreciation, wear and tear, rust and corrosion, mechanical or electrical breakdown, failures or breakages to the vehicle, except breakage of windscreen or windows
- damage to the vehicle's tyres unless the vehicle is damaged at the same time
- any loss or damage caused by or attributed to the act of cheating or criminal breach of trust by any person within the meaning of the definition of the offence of cheating or criminal breach of trust set out in the Penal Code.

Liability to Third Parties
For this liability, the *Takaful* company will pay an amount which the participant or the participant's authorised driver are legally liable to pay, including an amount that will include the claimant's costs and expenses, for two cases:

- death or bodily injury to any person except those specifically excluded under Exceptions to Liability to Third Party (to be explained later);
- damage to property as a result of an accident arising due to use of the vehicle.

For the two cases outlined above, the *Takaful* company would only cover such eventualities if either the participant or the participant's authorised driver follows all terms and condition of the certificate that the participant is subject to. The liability of the *Takaful* company for death or bodily injury of any person is unlimited while their liability for the second case is limited to RM 3 million only, if a claim on these two cases arises in one event. In case of death, the *Takaful* company will indemnify that person's legal representatives only and they will pay up to maximum of RM 2,000,00 for defence of any charge, including the charge of causing death by driving the motor vehicle.

From all of this coverage, there are still some cases of exception for the *Takaful* company in terms of its liability to a third party. These are:

- death or bodily injury to any passenger being carried for hire or reward
- death or bodily injury to any person where such death or injury arises out of and in the course of the employment of such person by the participant or by the participant's authorised driver

- damage to property belonging to or in the custody of or control of or held in trust by the participant or his authorised driver or any member of participant's household
- liability to any person who is a member of the participant's household or the participant's authorised driver, who is a passenger in the vehicle unless he/she is being carried by reason of or in the pursuance of a contract of employment
- any claims brought against any person in any country in courts outside Malaysia, the Republic of Singapore or Negara Brunei Darussalam
- all legal costs and expenses that are not incurred in or recoverable in Malaysia, the Republic of Singapore and Negara Brunei Darussalam
- participants not less than 18 or more than 65 years of age at the time of such injury
- death or injury directly or indirectly, wholly or in part resulting from intentional self-injury, suicide or attempted physical defect or infirmity or an accident occurring while the participant is under the influence of intoxicating liquor or drugs.

5.5 Motor *Takaful* for Motorcycles

5.5.1 Conditions Applied to the Whole Certificate

There are ten conditions need to be understood by all parties, the participant and also the *Takaful* company.

The Contract
Both parties must read and understand the contract clearly and if there is anything ambiguous they must speak out.

Notice to Be Made in Writing
If there is any notice or communication from the participant, it must be sent to the company in writing.

Security and Maintenance of the Vehicle
The participant must ensure the security of the vehicle from loss or damage and also must maintain the vehicle in good condition, and the company may have free and full access at any time to examine the vehicle or

any part of the vehicle or the driver or any employee of the participant. If there is an accident or breakdown, the vehicle should not be left unattended without proper precautions taken to secure the vehicle from loss or further damage.

Notices of Claim

In case of accident or breakdown, the participant must give notice together with all particulars to the *Takaful* company as soon as possible and also every writ, summons, letter or claim received must be sent the *Takaful* company immediately. Participants must also have knowledge of any impending prosecution, inquest or fatal inquiry in connection with the event. In case of theft, the participant must immediately lodge a police report and co-operate with the *Takaful* company in order to find the thief.

Claim Under Damage of Property

If there is damage to property, the *Takaful* company will pay full amount of the company's liability; unfortunately, the company will not be liable for any damage of property as result of illegal actions taken by the participant.

Cancellation of Contract

The *Takaful* company could cancel the contract at any time, but the company must give seven days' notice by registered letter to participant using participant's last known address. The participant also has the right to cancel the contract at any time by giving seven days' notice to the *Takaful* company. As a result of the cancellation, the participant is entitled to a pro-rata refund of the unexpired contributions but there is a condition for the participant to cancel the contract. If he has made a claim within the period of *Takaful*, he is therefore not entitled to the pro rata refund.

Rateable Proportion

If the participant had registered the vehicle under other *Takaful* fund with another *Takaful* company—for example if a person has registered his motorcycle with *Takaful* Malaysia and he also registers the same motorcycle to another *Takaful* Company such as *Takaful* Nasional—then in case anything happens, *Takaful* Malaysia would only be liable to pay its rateable proportion.

Arbitration

Arbitration is needed when any differences arise out of the contract. The arbitrator will be appointed in writing by both parties and if both parties cannot agree to choose a single arbitrator, then each party must appoint their arbitrator within one calendar month. To settle differences, both arbitrators would appoint an umpire who will sit together with them and be a head in the meeting.

Conditions Precedent to Liability

The due observance and fulfilment of the terms of the contract as they relate to anything to be done or not to be done by the participant and the truth of the statements and answers in the proposal shall be conditions precedent to any liability of the company to make any payment under this contract.

Replacement Parts

In the event of loss damage to the vehicle or its accessories or spare parts necessitating the supply of a part stocks which is not within the country in which the vehicle is held for repair or in the event of the company having to pay in cash the amount of the loss or damage, the liability of the company shall be limited to:

- the price quoted in the latest catalogue or price list issued by the manufacturer or his agent for the country in which the vehicle is held for repair

OR

- if no catalogue or price list exists, the price last obtaining at the manufacturer's work plus the reasonable cost of transportation to the country in which the vehicle is held for repair and also the amount of the relative import duties

AND

- the reasonable cost of fitting such parts.

5.6 Types of Motorcycle

Under Motor *Takaful* (Motorcycle), there are five types of motorcycle covered (Table 5.2):

5.6.1 *Coverage*

As with Motor *Takaful* for Private Cars, Motor *Takaful* for Motorcycles also covers loss or damage and legal liability to third parties.

Loss or Damage

Under this coverage, the *Takaful* company may indemnify the participant against loss and damage to the vehicle and its accessories and spare parts if one the following occurs:

- accident collision or overturning consequent upon mechanical breakdown or consequence upon wear and tear;
- fire, external explosion, self-ignition by lightning;
- burglary, housebreaking or theft;
- malicious act;
- when in transit (including its loading and unloading) by road, rail, inland waterway and direct sea route over the straits between the island of Penang and the mainland;
- impact damage caused by a falling object, provided no convulsion of nature is involved.

For payment, the *Takaful* company has three choices:

- pay the cost of repairs to the vehicle;

Table 5.2 Types of motorcycle

Code	*Type of vehicle*
A	Below 110 cc
B	111–225 cc
C	226–350 cc
D	351–500 cc
E	Above 551 cc

Source: Author's own collection

- pay in cash the amount of the loss or damage to vehicle; or
- reinstate or replace the vehicle.

Though the liability of the company of loss or damage of vehicle cannot exceed the value of the parts lost or damaged and reasonable price of fitting it, in the case of vehicle breakdown the company would only be liable for reasonable cost of protection and removal to the nearest repairers and delivery within the country where the vehicle is found. However, there are two conditions need to be fulfilled for the company to be liable for the cost of repairs. If one of these conditions is not valid, then the company will not be liable for the loss or damage. The conditions are:

- the estimated cost of repairs does not exceed the authorised repair limit;
- a detailed estimate of the cost is sent to the company without delay.

Under this coverage, there are some other cases considered as exceptions to company liability:

- consequential loss, depreciation, wear and tear mechanical or electrical or electronic breakdown, equipment or computer malfunction failure or breakages;
- damage to tyres, unless the vehicle is damaged at the same time;
- loss or damage to accessories or spare parts by burglary, housebreaking or theft, unless the vehicle is stolen at the same time;
- any loss or damage caused by or attributed to the act of cheating by any person;
- any loss or damage caused by or attributed to an act of criminal breach of trust by any person.

Legal Liability to Third Parties

The *Takaful* company will indemnify the participant in the event of an accident caused by the use of the vehicle or in connection of loading and unloading of the vehicle against all sums including claimant's costs and expenses to which the participant might be liable to in respect of:

- death or bodily injured to any person
- damage to property.

The *Takaful* Company will also indemnify any authorised driver of the vehicle, provided that they fulfil the requirements stated in the contract.

In case of death, the company will only indemnify the dead person's personal representatives provided that their representative fulfil the requirements stated in the contract, and if in the case of accident the company needs to indemnify more than one person, then it is limited to its liability as stated in the contract only.

Nevertheless, the *Takaful* company is given two options regarding indemnification:

- to arrange for the representative at any inquest or fatal inquiry in respect of any death which may be the subject of indemnify.
- undertake the defence of proceedings in any court of law in respect of any act or alleged offence causing or relating to any event which may be the subject of indemnification.

Among the coverage under liability to third parties, there are some cases in which the *Takaful* company would not be liable. Those cases are:

- death or bodily injury or damage caused beyond limit of any carriageway;
- death or bodily injury of any person in the employment of the participant;
- death or bodily injury to any person (other than passenger carried for reason of or in purposes of employment) being carried by the vehicle at the same time as the occurrence of the event.
- damage to property belonging to the participant or held in trust by or in custody or control of the participant or any member of the participant's household or being conveyed by the vehicle;
- compensation for damages in respect of judgement not in the first instance delivered or obtained from a court of competent jurisdiction within Malaysia, Republic of Singapore or Negara Brunei Darussalam;
- costs and expenses of legal action recovered by any claimant from the participant which are not incurred in and recoverable in Malaysia, Republic of Singapore or Negara Brunei Darussalam.

5.7 Motor *Takaful* Scheme for Commercial Vehicles

5.7.1 Criteria for Selection of Corporation to Be Covered

This scheme is not available to all corporations. The *Takaful* company will verify whether a corporation is suitable for the scheme based on the following criteria:

- the main or core activity of the participant is not transport
- all other *Takaful* requirements of the participant are placed with the company of which its total Takaful contribution exceeds the motor contribution
- good claims record for the past three years
- good and sound housekeeping, particularly in relation to the maintenance and management of vehicles.

5.7.2 Conditions Applied to All Types of Contract

There are several conditions that need to be fulfilled in order to make the contract valid. Those conditions are the same as the conditions for other contracts.

- notices to be made in writing
- security and maintenance of the vehicle
- claims: notices and consent
- claim under damage of property
- cancellation of contract
- rateable proportion
- arbitration
- conditions precedent to liability
- replacement parts

5.7.3 Coverage

As with the other policies, Motor *Takaful* for Commercial Vehicles also covers loss or damage and liability to third parties.

5.7.4 Loss or Damage

The *Takaful* company would only liable to indemnify participant against loss or damage to the vehicle and its accessories and spare parts under several situation, which are exactly the same as those outlined for other sorts of vehicle in Sect. 5.6.1.1. above.

It may also be the case that at the time of the event, the cost of loss or damage of vehicle is greater than its market value, as explained in Sect. 5.3. If this situation occurs, the participant is consider as being his own insurer and he has to pay the difference or remaining balance of the proportion of the loss or damage. This situation only applies when the market value at the time of the loss exceeds the value covered by more than 10%. The way of determining the market value is just the same as for Motor *Takaful* for Private Cars. As with all the coverage explained above, this scheme also has an exception in several cases, where company would not be liable to pay:

- consequential loss, depreciation, wear and tear, mechanical or electrical breakdowns, failures or breakages
- damage cause by overloading or strain
- damage by explosion of any boiler forming part of attached to or on the vehicle
- damage to tyres, unless the vehicle is damaged at the same time
- any loss or damage caused by or attributed to the act of cheating by any person.

Liability to Third Parties

Cover for liability to third parties is just the same as Motor *Takaful* for Motorcycles, as outlined in Sect. 5.6.1.2.

Similar to the coverage for loss or damage to vehicle, coverage for liability to third parties also has several exceptions where company would not pay if certain situation occurs. These are also as stated in Sect. 5.6.1.2, with the further exceptions of:

- damage to any bridge or to any road caused by the vibration or by any weight of the vehicle or of the load carried by the vehicle;
- damage to property caused by sparks or ashes from the vehicle if steam driven;
- damage to property or death or bodily injury caused by the explosion of a boiler forming part of or attached to the vehicle.

5.8 Conclusion

The emergence of Islamic insurance or the Takaful system provides people with an alternative to the conventional system. The effort to research and develop Islamic insurance practices and products should be appreciated. *Takaful* is the best way to insure the material or one's life security against risks of catastrophes or disaster. The elements of co-operation, solidarity and brotherhood in Takaful should be inculcated into Muslims specifically, and also into the public in general. The tremendous development of family and general Takaful schemes should be revealed to the people, showing the special characteristics of the product and how it competes with conventional ones. In Malaysia, although there are many Takaful companies offering various products, there are still many Muslims who buy conventional policies. A good example is motor insurance. *Takaful* operators have provided motor Takaful schemes, with special coverage to the public. However, there are still people, especially Muslims, who purchase conventional policies to seek security for their vehicles. It is true that the contributions that must be paid to the Takaful company are much higher than with conventional insurance, but they must be aware that the Takaful company provides greater coverage for their losses. In addition, their operation is legal under Shari'ah as it does not contain the elements of *Riba*, uncertainty and gambling. Muslims have to know that these prohibited elements will have a bad effect on other people and will lead to the hellfire. Consciousness of the illegality of conventional insurance is not really observed. Therefore, people have to be made aware of this situation and of the Takaful operators and their products. It is the duty of a person who knows about the existence of Takaful to promote the Takaful system in Malaysia to the public.

References

1. Ali, A. Y. (n.d.), The Holy Qur'an, Text and Translation.
2. *Motor Takaful Plan*, *Takaful* Malaysia.

CHAPTER 6

Accident *Takaful*

6.1 Introduction

This chapter discusses accident policy under *Takaful*, Shari'ah rulings regarding this topic and further recommendations. In *Takaful*, basically there are two main types of insurance. The first is life insurance, also known as Family *Takaful*. The other one is General Insurance. An Islamic *Takaful* transaction is a policy of mutual co-operation, solidarity and brotherhood against unpredicted risk or catastrophe, in which the parties are expected to contribute genuinely. In Life Insurance there is a PA and Participant Special Account (PSA), while in General Insurance there is no PA only PSA. Compared to conventional insurance, *Takaful* policies have a right to use their own rates. Basically, other conventional insurance agencies follow the Persatuan Insurans Am Malaysia (PIAM) standard. For example, under PIAM, air condition, radio, glass and spot rim are not covered by PIAM but under *Takaful* it will be covered. This chapter will discuss these issues further to deepen the understanding of the reader.

It is acknowledged that the ideas in this chapter/product have been significantly contributed to by the practices /experiences/thoughts of Bank Negara, Takaful Malaysia, Takaful Ikhlas, Takaful Nasional, Etiqa Takaful, IBFIM, IIUM, MII and others (Malaysia).

Mohd Ma'Sum Billah, *Islamic Insurance Products*,
https://doi.org/10.1007/978-3-030-17681-5_6

6.2 Central Ideas

Takaful is an Islamic insurance aid which based on policy of mutual operation, solidarity and brotherhood against unpredicted risk or catastrophe, in which the parties involved are expected to contribute genuinely (Billah 2002). As an insurance aid, Takaful covers many risks such as subjective risk, objective risk, pure and defined risk, speculative risk, risk of certain happenings, risk caused deliberately and other permissible risks which can be insured in an Islamic perspective. An accident can be defined as unpleasant event that happens unexpectedly and leads to damage or injury. Normally, an accident is always viewed as motor vehicle accident (i.e. traffic accident) but there are many other situations can be called as an accident, for example a broken leg after falling from a tree or on slippery surface, or suffering from an unpredicted disease. In Takaful accident policy, insurance is separated into two categories: life insurance and general insurance.

6.2.1 Life Insurance

Life insurance is the conventional insurance term for what in Takaful insurance is known as Family *Takaful*. Family *Takaful* is cover for people (i.e. life). The insurance is not meant to insure one's life but to help or to give financial benefits to helpless people in society. Family Takaful plan provides cover to any individual participant who wishes to save a sum of money for his dependants should he die prematurely or as contingency saving if he is to survive. It is also so as to be financially prepared if he suffer from illness or tragedy or becomes invalid. An individual who participates in a family Takaful plan is required to pay Takaful instalments regularly to the given company. The amount of the instalments is at the discretion of the individual. A participant may choose to pay the Takaful instalments either in the interval of monthly, quarterly, bi-annually or annually. Any instalment paid will be credited into family Takaful fund. The fund is divided into two accounts which are Participant Account (PA) and Participant Special Account (PSA). A substantial proportion of the instalment will be credited into PA, and the remaining balance will be credited into PSA account as a donation (*Tabarru'*) for the purpose of joint guarantee and share responsibility among participants. Rate of *Tabarru'* varies for each individual, where the proportion made is based on the age of participant and the period of Takaful of the plan chosen.

The instalments made by participants will be invested by the company in line with Shari'ah and not contrary to any Islamic ruling. Any surplus from the investment will be shared in accordance to the principles of *Al-Mudharabah* based on certain ratio as mutually agreed between the company and the participants (30:70). In the event of death before the maturity of the Takaful plan, the participant's heirs will receive the total amount of Takaful instalment paid by the late participant due to due date of payment of the instalments and his share in the profit from investment in the PA account. In a PSA account, his heirs will receive the outstanding amount of Takaful instalments paid by the deceased, and calculation start from the date of death to the date of maturity of his Takaful plan.

In the case of maturity, where the participant survives until maturity date, the participant will get the total amount of the Takaful instalments paid and his share of profit from the investment in his PA account. In a PSA account, the participant will receive some of the surplus made and the surplus will be distributed according to the terms and the age of participant. To decide whether to issue a family Takaful certificate—under what terms and conditions, rate and classification, the company has to look several factors such as age, gender and medical condition. Age is the main factor, as expected future morality is highly correlated with age. Age is also a key factor in determining the *Tabarru'* rate an individual is to be charged for family Takaful plan. Gender is included because of probability of death of females are generally less compared to male and, as a result, the majority of Takaful operators charge a lower rate and higher annuity rates for females compared to males. Medical aspects cover physical condition, personal history, family history, financial status and occupation.

6.2.2 General Insurance

General insurance in Takaful is meant to cover things and to help and compensate any participant who incurs loss or damages. Participants of general Takaful are tied along the lines of *Al-Mudharabah* principles with the company. Since the company (operator) is applying *Al-Mudharabah* principles which mean loss and profit sharing, the participant's money will be invested and any surplus gained will be distributed between the company and the participant based on an agreed ratio (60:40). Participants also contribute some money to the company as *Tabarru'* (donation).

Tabarru' is for helping participants who suffer from loss or damage and for management activities of the insurance company (General *Takaful* Business).

In General *Takaful*, only one account exist, the PSA. The account is treated on the basis of *Tabarru'*. For example, the insurance company invests RM 500,000 of participants' money and from the investment, profit gained is 15%, which is RM 75,000. RM 75,000 of surplus will be divided into 60:40 ratio (60% of RM 75,000, RM 45,000 goes to the company-operator and 40% from RM 75,000 will be distributed evenly between participants). Under General *Takaful*, there are various schemes that are grouped into several classes such as five Takaful schemes, which are the fire Takaful scheme, the motor Takaful scheme, the accident/miscellaneous Takaful scheme, the marine Takaful scheme and the engineering Takaful scheme. Each scheme has its own divisions. For instance, under the miscellaneous and accident scheme, personal accident, group personal accident, burglary and equipment all risks are several divisions thereof.

The premium varies depending on what is being insured. For instance, in car insurance, the premium is different from one policy to another according to the no-claims bonus/no-claims discount (NCB/NCD), value of car, CC of car and type of car. NCB or NCD is a bonus or discount given to a participant who has not claimed for any damage of the car or who has been free from accident. For the first year, a 25% discount will be given, in the second year 30%, third year 38.33% and in the fourth year 45%, with a maximum discount of 55% for more than five years with no claims. If any claim is made by the participant, the percentage will be started at zero. NCB will be paid to participants by reducing next year's premium. Loss and damage will only be borne by the Takaful company if loss is more than 2% from the total amount of insured things. *Takaful* determines its own rate of claim, and it is different from conventional insurance company thus, where the conventional rate is standardised and the rates are determined by PIAM. For commercial vehicles, Takaful covers the entire parts of the insured vehicle, including accessories, sport rim, tyres and others but this sort of policy is not practised in conventional insurance where accessories are excluded if any damaged occurs. Furthermore, a conventional insurance company will not cover a missing car; however, the Takaful company has the policy to cover it.

6.3 Shari'ah Rulings

Basically, one's life cannot be exchanged or be valued in cents and dollars because our life belongs to Allah (swt). It is Him who gives us life and it is Him who will take it back. We as a human who are responsible to take care of it so that our life will be more meaningful and worthwhile. That is while, by having a Family *Takaful* or what is also known as an Islamic insurance policy, it does not mean that one has insured one's life but rather it is a transaction that brings benefits to those who are in need and are helpless. A Shari'ah-justified insurance policy thus has reasons of its own to exist.

First, by having an insurance policy, it will protect certain groups of people such as the orphans and the widows from unexpected future difficulties that will result in more difficulties for them. According to the Holy Prophet (saw), he advised the ummah to protect one from any form of difficulties and hardship when he said:

> Whosoever removes a worldly grief from a believer Allah (swt) will removes from him one of the griefs of the Day of Judgement. Whosoever alleviates a needy person Allah (swt) will alleviate from him and the next.

Second, it also enables us to move towards ensuring a self-reliant society without difficulties. This way, we as humans living in different kinds of society will be able to live in a good and stable condition. As in line with the Qur'anic verse (in Sahih al-Bukhary), Allah (swt) says:

> Allah (swt) intends easy life for all of you while he does not want you to be in difficulties.

Furthermore, it is intended to provide a material safeguard for offspring, as in the saying of the Holy Prophet (saw):

> it is better for your offspring [to leave them] wealthy than to leave them poor, asking others for help.

6.4 Conclusion

Under the *Takaful* system, it is the *Takaful* Act that deals with the rate of the claim, whereas for the conventional system is based on the PIAM system. Therefore, to make the system more reliable, it is more systematic if both systems follow the PIAM system. It is also suggested that the *Takaful* operator should impose and give reasonable rates of changes and annuity to the participant regardless of anyone's sex. This is because it is clear that it is groundless for the *Takaful* operator to assess life expectancy and discriminate against males and females through imposing or giving higher or lower rates of charges and annuity respectively on family *Takaful* practices. Moreover, this is an important role for the agent and the broker as the promoters of the insurance practices among the societies at large. This is so as to make *Takaful* operations popular with their societies, and to attract people to the practices of *Takaful*. Furthermore, *Takaful* operations should in practice recognise licensed agents and brokers who may specifically work for the development of *Takaful* operations.

As a conclusion, *Takaful* is the best Islamic insurance because Islamic insurance policies operate based on the concept of *Al-Mudharabah*, a profit-sharing scheme which is free from elements which are illegal in the eyes of Shari'ah. The nature of the principles of *Takaful* are fundamentally different from the principles of conventional insurance. An Islamic insurance transaction is a policy of mutual co-operation, solidarity and brotherhood against unpredicted risk or catastrophe. The operation of *Takaful* is in line with Shari'ah principles. Besides, the operation of *Takaful* is generally based on the governing principle of *Al-Mudharabah*, which is an alternative to the interest-based financing technique as adopted by conventional insurance practices.

The main objectives of *Takaful* are not only to gain a profit but at the same time help the needy. An insurance policy will enable certain helpless people to be rescued from unexpected future material risks and contribute towards the reduction of poverty in society while ensuring a comfortable life for the poor. As discussed, there are two account which are involved in this *Takaful*: PA and PSA. Every Muslim in Malaysia should choose *Takaful* insurance to cover and protect their life.

References

1. Ali, A. Y. (n.d.), The Holy Qur'an, Text and Translation.
2. *Accident Takaful Plan*, *Takaful* Malaysia, *Takaful* Nasional, *Takaful* Ikhlas and others.
3. Billah, M. M. (2002), *Manual of Principles & Practices of Takaful & Re-Takaful*, International Islamic University Malaysia.
4. The Islamic Financial services Act 2013.
5. *Takaful Malaysia* (Product Operational Model).
6. *Takaful Ikhlas* (Product Operational Model).

CHAPTER 7

Fire *Takaful* Plan

7.1 Introduction

The Fire *Takaful* plan is an Islamic insurance policy that offers general schemes that operate in line with Shari'ah. The Fire *Takaful* plan is the basic cover provided by the *Takaful* companies in the event of any loss or damage by fire, lightning and explosion to the property concerned. It is also a way to ensure complete coverage for one's assets. This Fire *Takaful* plan is very much similar to the fire insurance policy offered by conventional insurance companies. Under the Fire Takaful plan, additional coverage (similarly provided by conventional insurance companies) for the following can be obtained for loss or damage:

- by strike, riot or civil commotion
- by flood, typhoon, hurricane or earthquake
- by aircraft and other aerial devices and articles dropped therefrom
- in consequence of earthquake and volcanic eruption
- in consequence of hurricane, cyclone, typhoon, windstorm and flood
- caused by explosion

It is acknowledged that, the idea of this chapter/product is significantly contributed by the practices /experiences/thoughts of Bank Negara, Takaful Malaysia, Takaful Ikhlas, Takaful Nasional, Etiqa Takaful, IBFIM, IIUM, MII and others (Malaysia).

Mohd Ma'Sum Billah, *Islamic Insurance Products*,
https://doi.org/10.1007/978-3-030-17681-5_7

- caused by impact by any road vehicles into horses and cattle
- by fire to the electrical appliances and installation arising from over-running excessive pressure
- caused by bush
- caused by subsidence and heave of the site on which the building stands
- directly caused by smoke due to a sudden unusual and faulty operation of any heating or cooking unit.

The above additional coverage is used to cover properties other than private dwellings. The Takaful companies provide a similar coverage for private dwellings, called House Owner Takaful. This covers:

- fire, lightning, thunderbolt, subterranean fire
- explosion
- aircraft and other aerial devices and articles drooped therefrom
- impact with any of the buildings by any road vehicles, horses and cattle not belonging to or under the control of the participant or any member of the family
- theft but only if accompanied by actual forcible and violent breaking into or out of a building
- hurricane, cyclone, typhoon, windstorm subject to the following excess clause
- earthquake, volcanic eruption subject to the following excess clause
- flood but excluding loss or damage caused by subsidence or landslip; subject to the following excess clause.

Fire *Takaful* schemes are offered to individual, corporation, financial institution, business or industry to protect their property and interests from disaster that are covered under this scheme. There are four types of coverage on offer:

- Basic Fire Takaful scheme
- House Owner Takaful scheme
- Household Takaful scheme
- Special House Owner Takaful scheme.

7.1.1 House Owner Takaful Scheme

This scheme provides a wide range of coverage and offers comprehensive protection aimed at the private dwelling in the event of fire covered under the scheme.

7.1.2 Householder Takaful Scheme

This scheme provides coverage against any losses or damages from fire to household goods, personal belongings and other property specified in the respective policies.

7.1.3 Basic Fire Takaful Scheme

This scheme provides basic coverage for properties, including private or commercial buildings in current existence or under construction against physical losses or damages from fire, lightning or explosion.

7.1.4 Fire Takaful *for Squatter Houses*

This scheme provides coverage for home that made from wood in the event of fire, lightning and storm. However, this scheme will not cover for home which is still under the duration of payment, squatter's house and any house (*rumah desa*) which is located less than 20 feet from another.

Assets covered under this Fire Takaful plan are:

- buildings and/or machines
- stocks
- householders.

Any claim or compensation under this Fire Takaful plan will be based on the actual market value during the fire. Some further information is needed for this coverage amount, such as:

- location of building
- structure of building
- type of building
- occupation of building.

As mentioned above, the Fire Takaful plan provides cover for material damage to the property covered. However, losses are not confined to the actual property lost or damaged but also to business if it is interrupted and this would result in loss of income and therefore profit. In other to cover this loss, the Takaful operators provide consequential loss cover.

The consequential loss provides for losses in respect of:

- gross profit following reduction in turnover
- increase in cost of working (expenses necessarily and reasonably incurred for the sole purpose of avoiding or diminishing the reduction in turnover).

7.2 Scope of Cover

The basic cover provided under terms and conditions of the contract as detailed in the Fire *Takaful* certificate are loss or damage due to or arising from fire, lightning or domestic gas explosion. The certificate may also be extended to include other dangers, as mentioned below.

7.2.1 *Determination of Sum Covered*

Building and/or Plant and Machinery
Indemnity under an ordinary Fire *Takaful* certificate is limited to the actual value at the time of the occurrence of fire—in other words, depreciation will be taken into consideration and generally the amount of claims payable will be as per prevailing market value.

Therefore, it is always advisable that cover be affected on a 'reinstatement value' basis. On this basis, the actual reconstruction and/or replacement value of the subject matter covered such as building and/or its contents (except for stock) can be made. Should under-coverage exist, that is, when the sum covered is less than the actual reconstruction cost/value or replacement value, the participant will have to bear a proportionate share of the loss, and this means the 'average clause' will be applied. Such under-coverage is also applicable on an 'indemnity' basis.

7.2.2 *Stock*

The indemnity value of compensation in case of loss is based on the prevailing current market value payable by the participant and not the selling price. Discounts should be made in view that the participant would usually enjoy similar discounts from his supplier when the damaged goods are replaced by new stock. Deductions may have to be made against depreciation of stock through age, and particularly for goods that have become out of fashion or obsolete. 'Declaration basis' cover on stock may not be issued without prior approval of the manager, Underwriting Department, General *Takaful* Division.

7.3 Principal Certificate Exclusions

This certificate does not cover loss and/or damage arising from:

- perils unless it is extended and additional Takaful contribution paid
- loss by theft during and after occurrence of fire
- war and civil commotion
- radioactive contamination
- arson by participant themselves
- collapse of building
- the building covered and/or containing the properties covered is unoccupied and remains so for a period of more than 30 consecutive days.

7.4 Shari'ah Rulings

- Muslims have practiced the concept of *Takaful* since the beginning of Islam. It could be seen in the system of mutual help in relation to the custom of blood money by the Arab tribes. Muslim jurists generally accepted that the concept of insurance does not contradict with the Shari'ah. In fact, Islam and the Prophet accepted the principle of compensation and group responsibility. Muslim jurists acknowledge that the basis of shared responsibility in the system of *al-aqila* as practised between Muslims of *Meccah* (*Mujahirin*) and *Medinah* (*Ansar*) laid the foundation of mutual insurance. Hadith of the Prophet (saw) narrated by Abu Hurairah:

> Two women from Bani Huzail clashed when one of them hit the other with a stone which killed one of them and the baby in the victim's womb. The heirs of the victim brought an action to the Prophet who later give a judgement that the compensation for the foetus should be a male or female slave, while the compensation for the killed woman would be blood money (*al-aqila*) which must be paid by the *aqila* of the killer.

- *Takaful* is based on the Islamic principles of mutual help and cooperation in good and virtuous acts. It is got together and mutually agreed to contribute to a fund. The fund will be used to compensate anyone who incurs losses, as is clear in the following verse:

> Help one another in furthering virtue and God consciousness (*taqwa*), and do not help one another in furthering evil and enmity. (al-Mai'dah: 2)

From the above verse, we know that the concept of *Takaful* means to unite a group of people so as to protect its members from any liability in the form of mutuality by sharing losses in common.

Hadith of Prophet (saw), reported by A. Tarmizi and Ibn Majah:

> The Prophet (saw) told the Bedouin Arab who left his camel untied to the will of Allah. The Prophet said, "Tie the camel and then leave it to the will of Allah."

Every Muslim believes that any disaster that befall is "Qadha and Qadar" from Allah. The teaching of Islam encompasses the essence of peace, economic well-being and imposes a duty on all Muslims to do their utmost to be prepared and to seek protection in their activities against disaster, as clearly stated in the above Hadith. The form of protection or cover a Muslim can benefit himself against the consequences of disaster is through *Takaful* services, which are under a general *Takaful* scheme.

This General *Takaful* scheme is designed to meet the needs for protection of both individuals and corporate bodies in relation to material loss or damage inflicted upon their property consequent upon a disaster.

- *Takaful* is similar to conventional insurance, which has its own specific procedures, but is still under the supervision of Bank Negara Malaysia. So, in order to meet the specific rules and requirements in accordance with Islamic business concepts, *Takaful* has developed its own specialised accounting system. The *Takaful* accounting system complies generally with the existing Malaysian Accounting Standard (MAS). The system applied is in accordance with Islamic requirements, as mentioned in the Qur'an:

> So establish weight with justice and fall not short in the balance. (al-Rahman: 9)

7.5 Practical Scenario

The *Takaful* operator will invest whatever amount of money has been paid by the insured. Then, the profit from the investment is divided to two types of account. The first account is the Participants' Account, where the profit will be distributed at the ratio 40:60. In the Fire *Takaful* plan, the ratio has been determined by the *Takaful* operator where this ratio is known as surplus that must be shared between the participants and the company. The other account is the Participants' Special Account where the money will be used to pay any participant who needs it. So, for example, a participant who has had a fire in his building or stock could claim from this fund (Fig. 7.1).

7.5.1 How to Value a Building and Its Premiums

Example
Company A wants to apply for a Fire *Takaful* plan, so the company needs to fill in the proposal and declaration form which is available at all branches

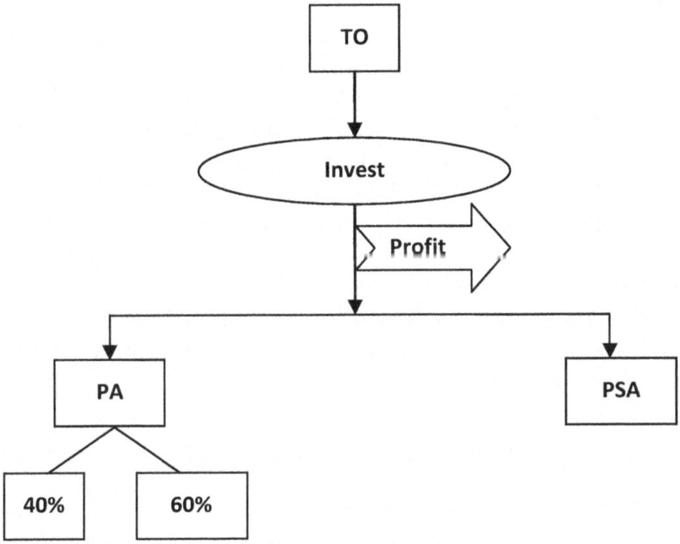

Fig. 7.1 The distribution of profit ratio for Fire *Takaful* plan. (Source: Author's own collection)

of *Takaful* Malaysia. Then, the *Takaful* operator will forward the application to headquarters under an underwriting department. Underwriting is the process of selection through which the *Takaful* underwriter determines which of the risks offered should be accepted, under what terms, conditions and rates. Headquarters will evaluate a sum of Fire *Takaful* plan to be paid by the company, based on observation of company's building—whether it has a portable extinguisher, hose reels and so on—the underwriting claim officer will issue certificate, debit note and quotation for the company.

7.6 Claims Procedure

Before any claim under property damage claim can be made, there are certain points that should be kept in mind by all participants:

- notification in *Takaful* certificate
- preliminary check
- registration of claim
- documentation and Proof of Loss
- claim settlement.

If Company A suffers damage by fire and wants to make a claim, the company has to bring all the required documents (i.e. police report, *Takaful* Certificate, etc.) to the *Takaful* operator. The *Takaful* operator will then forward the claim request by company A to the Claims Department at headquarters. A loss adjustor in the Claims Department is responsible for investigating the cause of fire damage. It is very important to know whether the claim made by Company A will be paid or not. The result of the observation will be reported back to the Claims Department. Then, the *Takaful* operator will be informed about claim's approval by the Claims Department. Lastly, Company A will get the amount claimed by the *Takaful* operator.

7.7 Recommendations

Generally, we agree with the principles applied in the Fire *Takaful* plan. However, we would like to suggest some ideas for further improvement to this scheme:

- Muslim society should give full support for the establishment of the *Takaful* company which is in line with Shari'ah. Besides, corporate sectors can also show their support by taking out a Fire *Takaful* plan to protect their buildings and stocks.
- *Rumah desa* Fire *Takaful* Plan provides protection to wooden houses from destruction by fire, storm and thunder. This Fire *Takaful* plan is specifically designed for rural areas such as villages and small towns.

It is further suggested that the *Takaful* company should expand its marketing strategy in order to advertise this Fire *Takaful* plan to villagers. It is because not many wooden houses have fire coverage. As villagers have little knowledge in *Takaful*, the *Takaful* operator should organise and conduct briefing on the plan. Another way would be for a *Takaful* operator to meet villagers by going from door to door and provide a special rate which is affordable for them.

7.8 Conclusion

The Fire *Takaful* plan offers many benefits to the public. It provides coverage in terms of mutual financial benefit in the event of material loss or subject matters covered in this scheme. It applies the principle of *Tabarru'* and *Al-Mudharabah* under General *Takaful* which is in line with Shari'ah principles. However, claims can be made by the participant on the *Tabarru'* account only for damages included under this scheme. Claims payment made based on mutual agreement by both parties (*Takaful* operator and the participant). It shows the difference between Fire *Takaful* plan and conventional fire insurance in term of its operation. In a conventional scheme there are three elements that contradict the rules and requirement of Shari'ah: *Riba*, *Maisir* and *Gharar*. Any transaction that involves these elements is considered void and prohibited.

References

1. Ali, A. Y. (n.d.), The Holy Qur'an, Text and Translation.
2. *Fire Takaful Plan*, *Takaful* Malaysia, *Takaful* Nasional, *Takaful* Ikhlas and others.

CHAPTER 8

Experience in Fire *Takaful*

8.1 Introduction

In our lives we cannot avoid encountering risks. As human beings, we are exposed to risks, disaster or catastrophe that can impact our life, property or business venture. Because of this matter, the principle of insurance has been practised. However, this involves *Riba* and other elements that are contrary to Shari'ah. Most insurance companies base their business on trade. Trading is permissible in Islam but *Riba* is prohibited. Insurance means a scenario where risks are shared so that the losses of a few are shouldered by many. However, the practices or mechanism used in such cases are not justified by Shari'ah. All the operations are in line with the man thought and customs.

Hence, *Takaful* is the best alternative to such practice. *Takaful* is derived from an Arabic word which means 'shared responsibility' or 'mutual cooperation for a noble cause'. In other words, it means financial security against a defined risk. *Takaful* can be divided into two parts: Family *Takaful* and General *Takaful*. Family *Takaful* is a long-term policy that is paid on a monthly or annual basis. It provides coverage and benefits

---

It is acknowledged that, the idea of this chapter/product is significantly contributed by the practices/experiences/thoughts of Bank Negara, *Takaful* Malaysia, *Takaful* Ikhlas, *Takaful* Nasional, Etiqa *Takaful*, IBFIM, IIUM, MII and others (Malaysia).

Mohd Ma'Sum Billah, *Islamic Insurance Products*,
https://doi.org/10.1007/978-3-030-17681-5_8

if something was to happen. Meanwhile, General *Takaful* is a short-term policy, normally for one-year period. Both Family and General *Takaful* consist of two accounts which are *Al-Mudharabah* and *Al-Tabarru'*. *Al-Mudharabah* means profit sharing and it is known as a Participant's Account. The contribution received from the participant will be kept in a fund and invested in the Islamic investment and at the end of the period of Takaful, the profit (if any) will be shared with the participants provided there has been no claim made by the participant. The profit-sharing ratio will be made known to the participant up front and agreed by both parties.

Al-Tabarru' is a charity account which is also known as Participants' Special Account. *Tabarru'* means that the participant agrees to donate his contribution to the fund to a mission to help other participants in Takaful covered under the various Takaful schemes when needed. In this chapter, we will discuss in particular the Fire Takaful plan, one of the General Takaful products offered by *Takaful* Malaysia.

8.2 Fire *Takaful*, the Product

This Takaful plan offers basic protection from risk to a participant's property. The main objective of the plan is to help them in facing their burden through the supporting of financial mechanisms. This plan offers protection to participants in the event of fire, lighting strike or explosion. It also covers:

- loss directly caused by aircraft
- earthquake and volcanic eruption
- loss due to hurricane, typhoon, cyclone or flood
- fire due to the electrical appliances and installation arising from over-running excessive pressure, short-circuiting, self-heating or leakage of electricity
- bush fire
- fire due to smoke.

The coverage mentioned above is for a property other than a private dwelling. For a private dwelling (house owners), its covers:

- fire, lightning, thunderbolt
- explosion
- aircraft damages and debris being dropped onto the property
- theft.

Takaful Malaysia is now offering long-term house owner Takaful and also a policy for private dwellings. Under this plan, a house owner who obtains a loan or financing from an institution may take Takaful cover up to the period of repayment of the loan or financing. Fire Takaful plans are not only offered to individuals, but also to corporations, financial institutions, business and industry in order to protect their property from any risk. The assets that are covered under the Fire Takaful plan are buildings and machines, stocks and householders. There are four types of coverage offered under this scheme:

- basic Fire Takaful
- house owner Takaful
- household Takaful
- special owner Takaful.

8.2.1 Basic Fire **Takaful** *Scheme*

Provides basic coverage for properties, including private or commercial buildings that already exist or are still under construction.

8.2.2 House Owner **Takaful** *Scheme*

This scheme provides a wide range of coverage and offers comprehensive protection to the private dwelling if any fire occurs.

8.2.3 Household **Takaful** *Scheme*

Coverage for household goods, personal belongings and other aspects of the property against any losses or damage from fire.

8.2.4 Special Owner **Takaful** *Scheme*

Under this scheme, there is also offered a Takaful plan for houses made from wood known as the *Takaful* plan for *Kebakaran Rumah Desa*. The purpose of this scheme is to provide coverage for homes made from wood in the event of fire, lightning or storm.

Even though the Takaful company provides lots of coverage, there are certain conditions that will not be covered:

- loss due to theft during and after occurrence of fire
- war

- radioactive contamination
- loss when the participant intentionally sets fire their property in order to claim from the Takaful company
- collapse of building.

8.3 Distribution of Profit Ratio for the Fire *Takaful* Plan

The insured will contribute an amount of money and Takaful operator will invest that money. The insured party will be known as a participant after contributing their money. Then, any profit from the investment is divided into two types of account. The first account is the Participant Account, where the profit will be distributed to the ratio 40:60. In the Fire Takaful plan, the ratio has been determined by the Takaful operator where this ratio is known as surplus that must be shared between participants to the company. The amount of 40% will be allocated to the participant and the other 60% to the *Takaful* operator. Meanwhile, in the Participants' Special Account the money will be used to pay needy participants. A participant who has suffered fire to his building or stock may claim from this fund (Fig. 8.1).

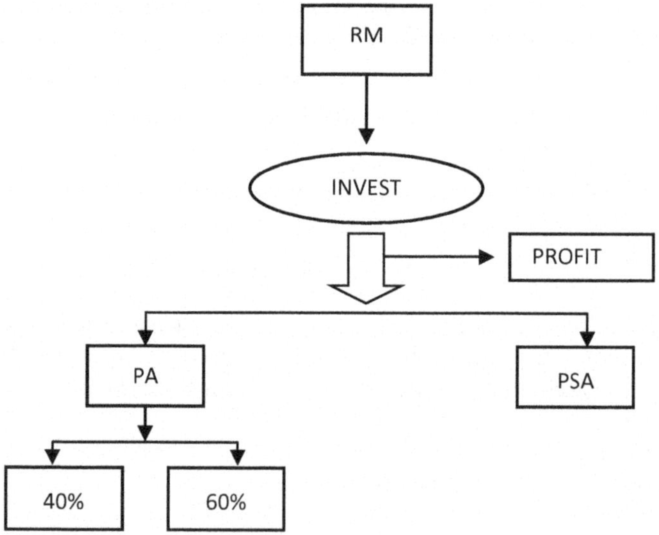

Fig. 8.1 Distribution of profit ratio for the Fire *Takaful* plan. (Source: Author's own collection)

8.4 Premium Rating on Buildings

When a participant wants to purchase a Fire Takaful plan, an evaluation of their building will be made. For example, Company A wants to apply for a Fire *Takaful* plan, so the company needs to fill in the proposal and declaration form which is available at all branches of *Takaful*. Then, the *Takaful* operator will forward the application to headquarters under an underwriting department. Underwriting is the process of selection through which the Takaful underwriter determines which of the risks offered should be accepted, and under what terms, conditions and rates. The headquarters will evaluate the sum of Fire *Takaful* plan needing to be paid by the company. This evaluation will be based on observation of the company buildings, such as its provision of portable fire extinguisher, hose reels and many more aspects. The underwriting claim officer will then issue a certificate, debit note and quotation to the company (Fig. 8.2).

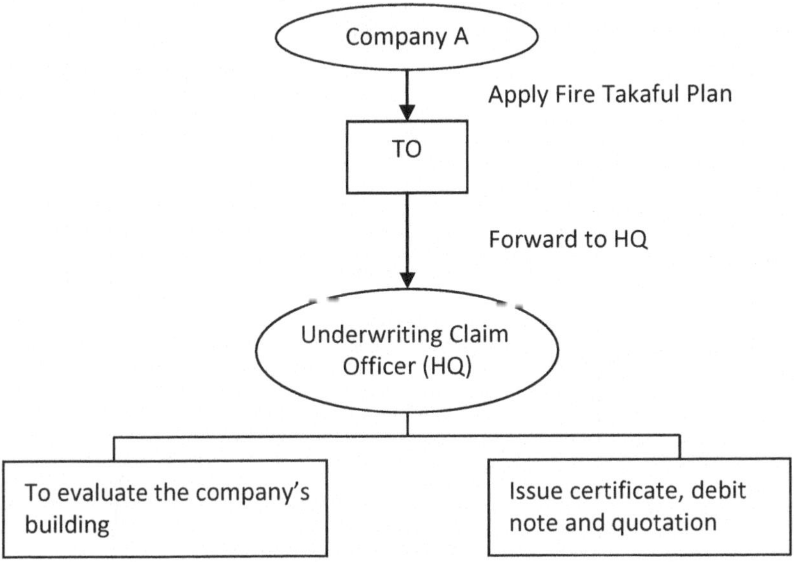

Fig. 8.2 Premium rating on buildings. (Source: Author's own collection)

8.5 Claims Procedure

There are certain points that should be kept in mind by the participant when claiming for damages caused by fire, lightning or explosion at the property concerned (Fig. 8.3). The points are:

- notification on *Takaful* certificate
- preliminary check
- registration of claim
- documentation and proof of loss
- claim settlement.

An example of the claims procedure is shown above. When Company A's building is damaged by fire and the company wants to make a claim, the company has to bring all the required documents (police report, *Takaful* certificate etc.) to the *Takaful* operator. After that, the *Takaful* operator will forward the claim requested by the company to Claims Department at headquarters. A loss adjustor at the Claims Department is responsible for observing and investigating the cause of fire damages. It is very important to know whether the claim made by Company A will be approved or not. The result of the observation will be reported back to the

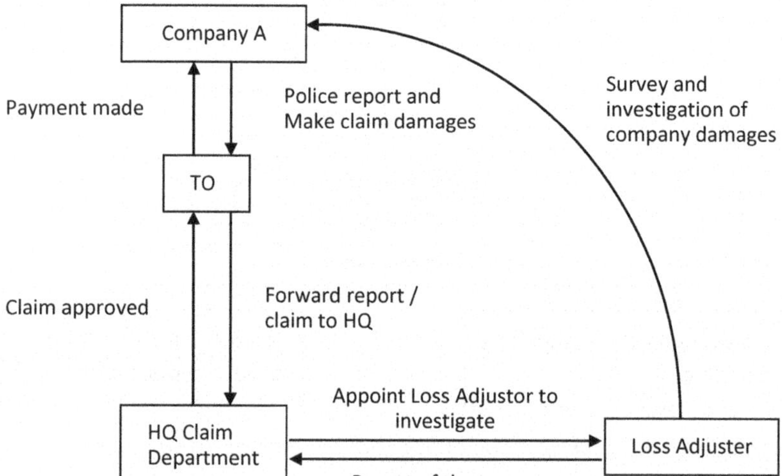

Fig. 8.3 Claims procedure. (Source: Author's own collection)

Claims Department. Then, the *Takaful* operator will be informed about the claim's approval by the Claims Department. Finally, Company A will receive the amount of the claim which has been made by the *Takaful* operator.

8.6 Governing Principles

8.6.1 Mutual Cooperation

> Help you one another in righteousness and piety, but help you no one another in sin and rancour: fear God: for God is strict in punishment. (Al-Maidah: 2)

> Such in true are believers: they have grades of dignity with their Lord, and forgiveness and generous sustenance. (Al-Anfal: 4)

Mutual cooperation is a really important aspect of the *Takaful* concept. This clearly shown in the Family Takaful scheme. Participants will contribute to the fund and whenever there is person who is in need, a contribution from this will help them. Whatever has thus been given as a donation cannot be taken back. As applies in the Family Takaful scheme, the concept of *Tabarru'* is operative here. This fund only can be given to those who are in need, and any participant who has donated is considered a donor; they cannot take their donation back.

8.6.2 Free from Prohibited Element

> But Allah hath permitted trade and forbidden usury. (Al-Baqarah: 275)

> They ask thee concerning wine and gambling, saying: "In them is great sin, and some profit, for men but the sin is greater than the profit." They ask thee how much they are to spend, saying: "What is beyond your needs." Thus doth God make clear to you His Signs: in order that ye may consider. (Al-Baqarah: 219)

In order to enjoin what is right and forbid what is wrong, the Takaful product can be the best alternative to conventional insurance products, because the practice of this latter sort of insurance company is not in line with Shari'ah principles—due to the involvement of *Gharar*, *Riba*, *Maisir* and so forth.

8.6.3 Distribution of Wealth

> From what is left by parents and those nearest related there is a share for men and a share for women, whether the property be small or large—a determinate share. (An-Nisa: 7)

In Family Takaful, the distribution of wealth is carried out according to Shari'ah principles. If the policyholder dies, the trustee should distribute the wealth or donation that they get to the beneficiaries according to certain percentages.

8.6.4 Trust

> Allah commands you to render back your trusts to those whom they are due: and when you judge between man and man, that you judge with justice, verily how excellent is He teaching which He giveth you! For God is He Who heareth and seeth all things. (al-Qur'an)

The Takaful operator is responsible for managing the wealth of the participant in an appropriate way. There is no interest charged by the Takaful operator to participants.

8.7 Recommendations

After completing this chapter on Fire *Takaful*, we would like to recommend that the Takaful company gives a brief explanation of the importance of Fire Takaful to society in general. This is because people do not see the benefit of Takaful and often think that it is a burden to donate an amount of money. Fire Takaful is especially important for those who live in rural areas and dwell in wooden houses. This scheme can provide protection to their property if any risk occurs such as fire, thunderstorm and so on. We would like to suggest that those who already have knowledge of these benefits of Takaful policy should support the Takaful company by sharing their knowledge with others.

8.8 Conclusion

The Fire *Takaful* plan has given many benefits to Muslim society such as financial coverage from any losses. It also apples the concepts of *Tabarru'* and *Al-Mudharabah*, which are in line with the Shari'ah principles and are not present within the conventional practice of insurance. As Takaful means mutual cooperation and shared responsibility, it is evident that the objective of the Takaful company is not only to gain profit but at the same time to help the needy. For Muslims, in order to seek the pleasure of Allah, we should enjoin what is right and forbid what is wrong.

References

1. Ali, A. Y. (n.d.), The Holy Qur'an, Text and Translation.
2. *Fire Takaful Practices*, *Takaful* Malaysia, *Takaful* Nasional, *Takaful* Ikhlas and others.

CHAPTER 9

Medical *Takaful* Plan

9.1 Introduction

The concept of *Takaful* comes from an Arabic word which means "guaranteeing each other." The concept of *Takaful* is similar to conventional insurance because the main aim is to help those who are at risk or are needy. However, in Islamic insurance—better known as *Takaful*—the Qur'an and Sunnah have provided the main guidance in practising it. *Takaful* practice is not prohibited in the Qur'an, as Islam prohibits various elements present in conventional insurance, and this is where it differs. The main reason is that *Takaful* practices are based on the Qur'an and Sunnah and so do not bring a burden to either the insurer or the insured. It is practised by mutual consent.

Takaful Malaysia acts as an operator to manage insurance transactions in the country. There are many products offered by *Takaful* Malaysia and one of them is the Health *Takaful* Plan. This plan was launched in 1995, 11 years after the establishment of *Takaful* Malaysia. The Health *Takaful* Plan was the second marketable product after Plan *Takaful* Siswa. The Health *Takaful* Plan is meant for medical purposes and covers 36 types of

It is acknowledged that, the idea of this chapter/product is significantly contributed by the practices /experiences/thoughts of Bank Negara, Takaful Malaysia, Takaful Ikhlas, Takaful Nasional, Etiqa Takaful, IBFIM, IIUM, MII and others (Malaysia).

Mohd Ma'Sum Billah, *Islamic Insurance Products*,
https://doi.org/10.1007/978-3-030-17681-5_9

illness. It was introduced to alleviate the burdens faced by people suffering from critical illness. As stipulated in the agreement, payment will be paid directly to the patient upon their eligibility being proved. The Health *Takaful* Plan will provide the best treatment and coverage for what the patient suffers. Further explanations of the Health *Takaful* Plan will be discussed in the next section, while examples of scenarios and practical applications come later.

9.2 Central Idea

The Health *Takaful* Plan is one of the policies provided by *Takaful* Malaysia. The Health *Takaful* Plan acts as a fund for its contributors, helping if they face an unexpected illness in the future. Contributors will be covered by this fund according to their contribution (Fig. 9.1).

There are two packages under Health *Takaful* Plan, Package A and Package B. Package A combines the benefit of saving and protection against 36 types of critical illnesses in addition to profit sharing or, in other words, *Al-Mudharabah*. Package B offers protection only against the 36 types of critical illness with a low rate of contribution aside from the profit-sharing (*Al-Mudharabah*) opportunity, according to it principles.

One advantage of the Health *Takaful* Plan is that contributors may have a flexibility in terms of payment. They have a choice to pay from RM 15 to 100. In addition, the Health *Takaful* Plan also will help pay for funeral expenses not only to the contributors, through their family members. After that, the participants also will benefit under *Al-Mudharabah* agreement. Finally, as part of the advantages for permanent disability, a monthly allowance will be given until the contributor reaches 65 years of age.

Participants in this plan must be between 18 and 55 years. This Health *Takaful* Plan gives basic coverage to these contributors as well as in the event of the 36 unexpected critical illnesses (Fig. 9.2). The basic coverage is thus:

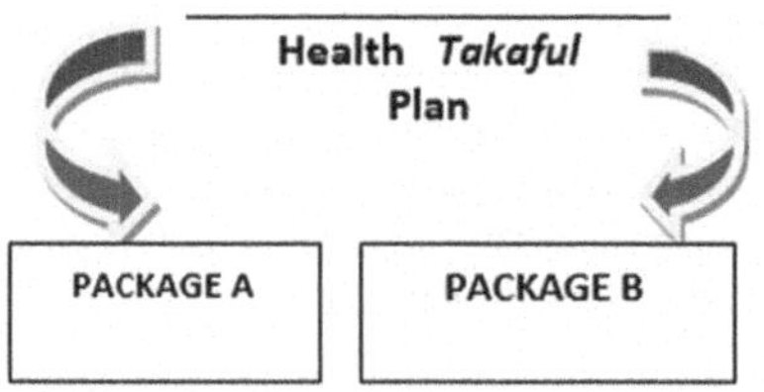

Fig. 9.1 The Health *Takaful* Plan. (Source: Author's own collection)

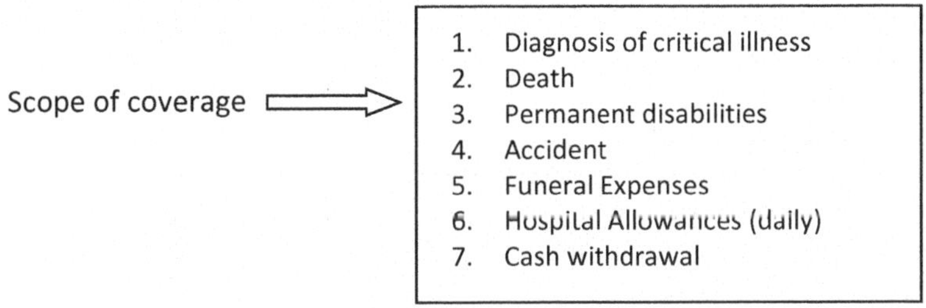

Fig. 9.2 Scope of coverage. (Source: Author's own collection)

There are 36 types of critical illness covered by the Health *Takaful* Plan:

- heart attack
- stroke
- coronary artery disease requiring surgery
- cancer
- kidney failure
- fulminant hepatitis
- major organ transplant
- paralysis
- multiple sclerosis
- pulmonary arterial hypertension
- blindness
- heart valve surgery
- deafness
- surgery to aorta
- loss of speech
- major burns
- Alzheimer's disease
- coma
- motor neurone disease
- AIDS due to blood transfusion
- Parkinson's disease
- chronic liver disease
- chronic lung disease
- head injury due to accident
- aplastic anaemia
- muscular dystrophy
- benign brain tumour

- encephalitis
- poliomyelitis
- brain surgery
- bacterial meningitis
- other serious coronary artery disease
- apallic syndrome
- AIDS due to occupation
- full-blown AIDS
- terminal illness.

The Health *Takaful* Plan does not cover pre-existing symptoms or any illness which commences within a period of 30 days from their certificate's effective date (Fig. 9.3).

There are three maturity periods for the Health *Takaful* Plan: 10 years, 15 years and 20 years, according to the option of the packages. The lowest contribution is RM 15 per month, and the highest is RM 100 per month depending of the package that has been chosen by the contributors. In order to participate in the Health *Takaful* Plan, they need to fill out the proposal and declaration forms that are free and available at any branches of *Takaful* Malaysia Berhad. The modes of payment are:

- bank standing order
- giro
- cheque or cash
- credit or charge card
- salary deduction
- ATM smart card.

Contributors have many choices for to make payments to *Takaful* Malaysia Berhad. Beside these six modes stated above, contributors also can make payments directly at the payment counter of any *Takaful* Malaysia branch.

Fig. 9.3 Maturity periods of Health *Takaful* Plan. (Source: Author's own collection)

9.3 Shari'ah Rulings

The differences between conventional insurance and Islamic insurance, which is known as *Takaful*, is in the way they operate. Conventional insurance is an exchange transaction under a buy and sell agreement, but this does not occur in *Takaful* where the holder of the insurance has full rights over it. Furthermore, the doctrine of *Takaful* basically operates based on Shari'ah principles of shared responsibility, mutual co-operation, solidarity and brotherhood. Before that, it is also stated in the Qur'an and Sunnah that Allah encourages people to do good deeds for others. For example, in Surah Al-Maidah (5:2), Allah (swt) says:

> Co-operate each other in doing good deeds but not help each other to commit sin and rancour. (Surah al-Maidah, 5:2)

In this *ayah*, Allah says that we need to help each other in doing good deeds but not help each other to commit sin and rancorous deeds. In *Takaful* there are rules and requirements of Shari'ah rulings that govern its operation. There are three important elements that make *Takaful* and conventional insurance different. The three elements which not be implemented under *Takaful* insurance are *Gharar*, *Maisir* and *Riba*. As far as Shari'ah is concerned, all products under *Takaful* as well as the Health *Takaful* Plan must not implement any these three elements in their operation.

Gharar means uncertain or unknown factors in the operation of both the life and general insurance policies. This element thus means that in the conventional insurance the policyholder or insured is not informed by the company as to the amount of compensation that the company will pay him. But in *Takaful* insurance the amount of compensation and how the *Takaful* operator (*Takaful* Malaysia Berhad) delivers it (the amount of compensation) will have been stated in the agreement according to a certain ratio.

For instance in Family *Takaful*, of which the Health *Takaful* Plan is one of the products, at the time of an agreement or contract being made the *Takaful* operator will state in what portion the compensation will be given to the policyholder and in what ratio that amount will be included in the *Tabarru'* fund. Also stated in the agreement is that only 36 types of critical illness will be covered by *Takaful* insurance. Another example pertaining to eligibility is that 36 illnesses that the contributors can get must not arise before he or she buys the scheme but only after that time. AIDS is one of the critical illnesses that the Health *Takaful* Plan will cover if the manner in which it has been contracted does contravene the tenets of Shari'ah, such as it being through the fault of a doctor or through blood donation. However, if a person becomes infected with HIV because of factors that are prohibited then they cannot be covered by the Health *Takaful* Plan. So, the way HIV is caught must certain which not over the line of the Shari'ah. It can be proved by the *ayah* before,

> but not help each other to commit sin and rancour. (Surah al-Maidah, 5:2)

Basically, *Maisir* or gambling arises as a consequence of the presence of *Gharar*, in particular in the case of life insurance. This can be illustrated in that when a policyholder dies before the end of the period of his insurance policy, after paying only part of the premium, then his dependants will receive a certain sum of money about which the policyholder in the first place has not been informed and has no knowledge of how and from where it is to be derived. But in *Takaful* insurance, when, say, a father who is the policyholder dies, the premium that he contributed will be given by that operator (the *Takaful* operator) to his nominee and the nominee has absolute authority to claim and divide it between the widow and the children according to *Faraid*. This also occurs in the Health *Takaful* Plan, as when, say, a father who was a contributor to the Health *Takaful* Plan dies then this plan will cover his funeral expenses and any profit that the operator gets goes to his nominee.

> Allah (swt) allow trade but prohibited *Riba*. (2:188) (Surah al-Baqarah, 2:188)

In conventional insurance, there is the practice *Riba* (interest) in investment activities—and this contradicts Shari'ah rulings. Looking at the above basic characteristics, the jurists resolved that the system of insurance that falls within the confines of an Islamic framework should be founded on the concepts of *Takaful* and *tijari*. Furthermore, in the *Takaful* application, the premium that had been contributed by the policyholder under Family *Takaful* will be divided into Participant's Account and Participants' Special Account. Participant's Account will be actioned under *Al-Mudharabah* concept, whereas Participants' Special Account will be practised under *Al-Tabarru'* concept. Here, when it is included under a profit-sharing account or investment account, there is not instance of *Riba* in their application. This is because when the agreement is made between both parties the ratio at which the profit or loss will be divided between the Takaful operator and the policyholder is clearly stated.

Takaful Malaysia Berhad also owns the council that governs cases that deal with the Shari'ah, known as the Shari'ah Supervisory Council. Moreover, Jabatan Kemajuan Islam Malaysia also plays an important role in giving opinions about the Islamic insurance transactions. On 15 April 2000 (see Appendix), Jabatan Kemajuan Islam Malaysia sent a letter to *Takaful* Malaysia Berhad, stating that life insurance will be prohibited in Islam if the transaction includes *Gharar*, *Maisir* or *Riba*.

As mentioned before, Allah (swt) had guided all Muslim activities in the Qur'an and the Hadith. This also refers to the practices of the Islamic insurance or *Takaful*. There are many *ayat* in the Qur'an that can be related to *Takaful* operations, as well as specifically to the Health *Takaful* Plan. These *ayat* are:

> Our Lord! Give us good in this world. (Surah al-Baqarah, 2:201)
>
> From this first ayah, the word 'good' can be related to the health, which indirectly relates also with the Health *Takaful* Plan. From this by asking Allah to give us good in this world, we also must put our effort take care of our health and prepare for future risk or illness.
>
> To him belongs the dominion of the heavens and the earth: it is He Who gives Life and Death; and He has power over all things. (Surah al-Hadid, 57:2)
>
> 'Death' in this *ayah* means that Allah has given us a chance to protect ourselves and it is our responsibility as a servant and vicegerent of Allah. As far as the Health *Takaful* Plan is concerned, indirectly it protects our life in the future as well as securing us against unexpected critical illnesses.

9.4 Applications

Although the Health *Takaful* Plan is quite new when compared with other Family *Takaful* products, customer responses have been very encouraging. This is due to the advantages it provides to participants. Nowadays, there are so many unexpected diseases or critical illnesses that may happen due to unhealthy lifestyle or the technological changes linked to the improvement of our economy. People often do not take enough care to look out for chemicals and other substances in food that may affect their health. But people cannot run from the technological changes, which offer ways to lighten their burdens in life. For example, the use of high-tech machines help a great deal in performing everyday tasks. According to the officer we interviewed, people now realise the need of this plan in their life. They have become conscious to the benefits or advantages of the Health *Takaful* Plan. The improvement of their status in life and the increase in their income contribute to the growing awareness of the need of this plan. People are able to allocate certain amount of money to pay for this plan per month for their use in the future: only God knows what will happen in the future. Therefore, we are required to prepare for our own future. Let us say, in the 15 years from now we might have a critical heart attack. In such an eventuality, we will need a lot of money to pay for the expenses of our treatment and operations. Of course, at that time the Health *Takaful* Plan will provide coverage for all expenses incurred. We do not have to worry anymore about what will happen in the future because we have been assured by the Health *Takaful* Plan.

By becoming a participant in this plan, we will not only get coverage but will also get benefits for the hereafter. According to the Hadith, we must allocate our income into three portions: for our own use, for savings and for helping needy people. So, by joining this plan we have already fulfilled what the Sunnah of Rasulullah has asked. This is because part of the contributions made will be treated as a donation and will be given to the needy people in the plan.

9.5 Coverage Under the Health *Takaful* Plan

9.5.1 Diagnosis of Critical Illness

Coverage will be given to the contributors or participants diagnosed with a critical illness in any hospital or medical institution. They have to get an approval letter from the doctor in order to get coverage from this plan. Diagnosis is done in order to identify the disease or the critical illness after observing its signs.

9.5.2 Death

If the participant dies, payment by the company will be paid to the inheritors according to the contributions made by the participant. Inheritors will get full amount from the Participant's Account plus the RM 5000 contribution from the Khairat Kematian Fund (Funeral Expenses). No benefit shall be payable for a death occurring during the first 12 months due to illness or injury occurring before the commencement date of the policy.

9.5.3 Total and Permanent Disabilities

The Health *Takaful* Plan provides coverage to participants who face permanent disabilities, either caused by disease or injury. These will prevent the participant from engaging in any business or performing any work for compensation or profit. If the participant sustains permanent disability caused by any critical illnesses covered, he may choose either to receive critical illness benefit or permanent disability benefit. If the participant dies after the payment of permanent disability benefits, the company will pay the inheritors the death benefit less the total monthly instalment benefits paid. The company will not be liable for permanent disability occurring either directly or indirectly from any of the following causes:

- war, invasion, act of foreign enemies, hostilities, civil war, mutiny, civil commotion assuming military uprising, insurrection, rebellion, military or usurped power or any act of the participant acting on behalf of or in connection with any organisation actively directed towards the overthrow by force of any government or to the influencing of it by terrorism or violence;
- attempted suicide or self-inflicted injury whilst sane or insane;
- misuse of drug or alcohol;
- aviation, gliding or any other form of aerial flight other than as a pilot, cabin crew or fare paying passenger of a recognised airline or charter service;
- participation in or training for any dangerous or hazardous sport or competition or riding or driving in any form of race or competition;
- involvement in any underwater activity necessitating the use of artificial breathing apparatus;
- military or naval service in time of declared or undeclared war while under orders for war, such as operations or restoration of public order;

- injury caused by nuclear fission, nuclear fusion, nuclear weapons material or radioactive contamination;
- no benefit shall be payable if the participant is found to be infected by HIV;
- any other causes prohibited by Shari'ah.

9.5.4 Accident

If the participant dies caused in an accident, the company will pay the coverage additional to the benefits of death. If the participant sustains permanent disability caused by the events such as loss of a finger, loss of all sight or others, then the benefits of the permanent disability will be paid according to the percentage stated in the Schedule of Benefits.

9.5.5 Suicide

This is new coverage that will be provided under the *Health Takaful Plan* and under other *Takaful* Product. *Takaful* will pay the benefit to the beneficiaries of participants who commit the suicide. Further explanation will be discussed under basic coverage.

9.5.6 Funeral Expenses

The Health *Takaful* Plan gives coverage on the death of participants, a participants' husband or wife, participants' children and also parents. It provides coverage for the expenses of a funeral. Therefore, it will help to release the burden of the family. Besides that, the coverage includes expenses for the ceremony.

9.5.7 Hospital Daily Cash Allowances

The Health *Takaful* Plan provides hospital allowances to participants. When they have a disease, that is, a critical illness, they certainly need the best treatment available from hospitals or any other medical institution. So, the coverage provided by this plan will fulfil the need of participants. Sometimes the cost of treatment is too high, and so cannot be paid by them alone. Therefore, the Health *Takaful* Plan will play its role by paying for the participants or contributors. If the participant is warded in any hospital for more than one day, either caused by accident or any disease, they will be paid hospital allowances. This depends on how many days they are warded. The benefits will not be paid after 30 days they have been there. Hospital allowances are not confined to critical illness but also applicable to other types of disease. The coverage will be paid according to the participant's contribution in this plan.

9.5.8 Cash Withdrawal

Participants are given the option to withdraw their money from the Participant's Account. They can withdraw the money only 50% from two years to five years and 70% after five years' contributions. Those participants who are already made a claim for critical illness benefit are eligible to make a cash withdrawal from the Participant's Account. But it all depends on the maximum limit that has been stated by *Takaful* Malaysia.

9.6 Types of Critical Illness

There are 36 types of critical illness as far as the Heath *Takaful* Plan is concerned. It does not cover pre-existing symptoms or any illness which commences within a period of 30 days from certificate's effective date. Furthermore, any diseases directly or indirectly caused by ionising, radiation or contamination by radioactivity from any nuclear fuel will not be covered. Diseases arising from causes prohibited by the sheriff are also excepted from coverage. For example, suicide, drug abuse, alcohol and so forth. There follows definition of the various relevant critical illnesses.

9.6.1 Heart Attack

Heart attack means that the diagnosis of the death of a portion of a heart muscle as a result of inadequate blood supply to the relevant area as by symptoms such as prolonged chest pain, new electrocardiograph changes characteristic of myocardial infarction and by elevated levels of cardiac enzymes.

9.6.2 Stroke

Stroke means that that the diagnosis of a cerebrovascular incident producing permanent neurological sequelae lasting more than 24 hours caused by haemorrhage, infarction of brain tissue or an embolus from an extrannial source. Evidence of permanent neurological damage must be confirmed by a consultant neurologist at the earliest six weeks after the event and no claims can be admitted earlier.

9.6.3 *Coronary Artery Bypass Surgery*

This means the actual undergoing of coronary artery bypass surgery to correct stenosis or occlusion in the coronary arteries but excluding non-surgical techniques such as angioplasty, laser treatment or other non-surgical procedures.

9.6.4 *Cancer*

Cancer means the uncontrolled growth and spread of malignant cells and invasion of tissue as evidenced by definite histology and includes leukaemia but excludes non-invasive cancers in situ, papillary cancer of the bladder and all skin cancers except malignant melanomas. All cancers are excluded if the participant is HIV positive.

9.6.5 *Kidney Failure*

End-stage renal failure presenting chronic irreversible failure of both kidneys to function and causing either regular long-term peritoneal dialysis or haemodialysis or for a renal transplant to be carried out. The necessity of continuous dialysis treatment must be certified by a nephrologist's report.

9.6.6 *Fulminant Hepatitis*

This is a submassive to massive necrosis of the liver by the Hepatitis virus, leading precipitously to liver failure. The diagnosis in respect of the illness must be based on meeting of all the following criteria:

- rapidly decreasing liver size
- necrosis involving entire lobules leaving only a collapsed particular framework
- rapid deterioration of liver function tests
- deepening jaundice.

9.6.7 Major Organ Transplant

It means the actual undergoing as a recipient of the transplant of a heart, lung liver, kidney, pancreas or bone marrow.

9.6.8 Paralysis

Clinically certified complete and permanent loss of the use of two or more limbs through paralysis as a result of sickness or accident, except when such injury is self-inflicted.

9.6.9 Multiple Sclerosis

Unequivocal diagnosis of multiple sclerosis made by consultant neurologist with evidence of the typical symptoms of demyelination, persisting the neurological abnormalities and impairment of function during at least a continuous period of six months. Diagnosis will be based on confirmatory neurological investigations.

9.6.10 Primary Pulmonary Arterial Hypertension

This is established by clinical and laboratory investigations including echocardiography, cardiac catherisation and pulmonary angiography.

9.6.11 Blindness

Irreversible loss of sight in both eyes as a result of acute sickness or accident. Blindness must be certified by an ophthalmologist's report.

9.6.12 Heart Valve Surgery

The actual undergoing of open-heart surgery to replace cardiac valves as consequences of heart valve defects, except congenital malformation.

9.6.13 Deafness

Irreversible loss of hearing in both ears for all sounds as a result of acute sickness or accident. Medical evidence in form of audiometric and sound-threshold test must be provided.

9.6.14 *Aorta Surgery*

The actual undergoing of surgery for a disease of the aorta needing excision and surgical replacement of the diseased aorta with a graft. Excluded here are its branches and any traumatic injuries of the aorta.

9.6.15 *Loss of Speech*

Total and irrecoverable loss of the ability to speak, which must be established for a continuous period of 12 months.

9.6.16 *Alzheimer's Disease*

This means a presenile dementia condition caused by deterioration or loss of intellectual capacity as evidenced by the clinical state and accepted standardised questionnaires, tests or abnormal behaviour for Alzheimer's disease. This involves irreversible organic degenerative disorders resulting in significant reduction in mental and social function to perform independently three or more of the following activities of daily life:

> bathing, dressing, eating, ability to move in or out of bed or chair and voluntarily control bladder or bowel function, either with or without the use of mechanical equipment, special devices or other aids and adaptation in use for disabled persons.

9.6.17 *Major Burns*

Third-degree burns covering at least 20% of the body surface area.

9.6.18 *Coma*

Failure of cerebral function characterised by total unarousable unresponsiveness to all external stimuli, persisting continuously with the use of life-support system for a period of at least 96 hours and resulting in permanent neurological defect. Coma resulting directly from alcohol or drug abuse is excluded.

9.6.19 Terminal Illness

When the advent of death is highly probably within six months and medical opinion has rejected active therapy in favour of the relief of symptoms and supports of both patient and family. This decision must be confirmed by the company's medical advisor.

9.6.20 Motor Neurone Disease

Motor neurone disease of unknown aetiology is characterised by progressive degeneration of corticospinal tracts and anterior horn cells or bulbar efferent neurons. Claim shall only be admitted if the condition is confirmed by a consultant neurologist as progressive and resulting in irreversible damage to the nervous system.

9.6.21 HIV Infection from Blood Transfusion

The participant being infected by HIV:

- the infection is due to a blood transfusion received in Malaysia, Singapore, Brunei or Middle East;
- the company, on the advice of the medical advisor appointed by the company, is fully satisfied that the infection was due to a blood transfusion given as part of medical treatment;
- the infected participant is not a haemophiliac;
- the conditions must be life threatening and there exists no known cure;
- the infected participant is not a member of any high-risk group, such as homosexuals, intravenous drug users or prostitutes.

9.6.22 Parkinson's Disease

Progressive degenerative disease of the central nervous system as a result of pigment-containing neurons of the brain. Unequivocal diagnosis of Parkinson's disease by a consultant neurologist must take place, where the condition:

- cannot be controlled with medication;
- shows signs of progressive impairment

- daily life assessment confirms the inability of the participant to perform without assistance three or more of the following: bathing, dressing, using the lavatory, eating, ability to move in or out of a bed or chair.

Only idiopathic Parkinson's disease is covered. Drug-induced or toxic causes of Parkinsonism are excluded.

9.6.23 *Chronic Liver Disease*

End-stage liver failure as evidenced by all of the following:

- permanent jaundice
- ascites
- hepatic encephalopathy.

Liver disease due to alcohol or drug misuse is excluded.

9.6.24 *Chronic Lung Disease*

End-stage lung disease including interstitial lung disease, requiring extensive and permanent oxygen therapy as well as FEV 1 test result of less than one litre.

9.6.25 *Accidental Head Injury Resulting in Major Head Trauma*

This is an event that results in neurological deficit causing significant functional impairment lasting at least six weeks and which is considered to be permanent by a consultant neurologist.

9.6.26 *Aplastic Anaemia*

Bone marrow failure, which results in anaemia, neutropenia and thrombocytopenia requiring treatment with at least two of the following:

- transfusion
- marrow-stimulating agent
- immunosuppressive agents
- Bone marrow transplant.

9.6.27 Muscular Dystrophy

Hereditary muscular dystrophy confirmed by a consultant neurologist resulting in the inability to perform without assistance three or more of the following: bathing, dressing, using the lavatory, eating and ability to move in or out of the bed or chair.

9.6.28 Benign Brain Tumour

A life-threatening, non-cancerous tumour in the brain giving rise to characteristics symptoms of increased intracranial pressure such as papilloedema, mental symptoms, seizures and sensory impairment as confirmed by imaging studies such as CT scan or MRI.

9.6.29 Viral Encephalitis

Severe inflammation of the brain, resulting in significant complications lasting at least three months, and which in the opinion of consultant neurologist will result in serious permanent neurological deficit. Encephalitis resulting from HIV infection is excluded.

9.6.30 Poliomyelitis

Unequivocal diagnosis by consultant neurologist of infection by the Polio virus leading to paralytic disease as evidenced by impaired motor function or respiratory weakness. Cases not involving paralysis will not be eligible for benefits. Other causes of paralysis are specifically excluded.

9.6.31 Brain Surgery

Undergoing surgery to the brain during general anaesthesia during which a craniotomy is performed. Brain surgery following an accident is excluded.

9.6.32 Acute Bacterial Meningitis

A confirmed diagnosis of bacterial meningitis causing inflammation of the membranes of the spinal cord of the brain and resulting in permanent neurological deficit as proven to the satisfaction of the company by a consultant neurologist.

9.6.33 Other Serious Coronary Artery Disease

The narrowing of the lumen of at least three major arteries by a minimum of 75%, as proven by coronary arteriography carried out in Malaysia, Singapore or Brunei, regardless of whether any form of coronary artery surgery has been performed.

9.6.34 Apallic Syndrome

Universal necrosis of the brain cortex, with the brain stem remaining intact. A consultant neurologist must confirm. The condition has to be medically documented for at least one month.

9.6.35 Occupationally Acquired HIV Infection

The participant being infected by HIV unequivocally as a result of an accident occurring during the course of carrying out normal occupational duties within six months of the accident. Any accident giving rise to a potential claim must be reported to the company within 30 days of taking place and supported by a negative HIV test taken in Malaysia, Singapore or Brunei within seven days of the accident. Infection in any other manner is excluded.

9.6.36 Full-Blown Aids

Clinical manifestation of AIDS which must be supported by the results of a positive HIV antibody test and a confirmatory Western Blot Test. In addition, the participant must have a CD4 cell count of less than 200 and evidence of opportunistic infection and AIDS-related tumour.

Coverage for those of 36 types of critical illness shall be payable not more than once in the lifetime of the participant. If a valid claim has been made under this benefit, no future benefit shall be payable. If the participant is diagnosed to be suffering from more than one illness at the same time, only one benefit shall be payable.

9.7 Conditions of Participation

Participants to this plan must be in the age range of between 18 and 55 years old. There is no restriction for the non-Muslims to be the participants. Participants can choose one of three maturity periods provided by the plan. But the limit age of the participant must not exceed 65 years old at the maturity period.

9.8 Packages Available Under the Health *Takaful* Plan

There are two packages under Health *Takaful* Plan: Package A and Package B. Package A gives coverage and also the benefits of long-term saving which will be acquired on the maturity of the policy. Package B only gives coverage without the benefits of long-term saving. The purpose of this package is to provide coverage at the lowest possible cost. Tables 9.1 and 9.2 summarise the differences between Package A and Package B.

Table 9.1 Package A (with savings)

Scope of coverage	*Minimum contribution per month*	*Each additional RM 50*
Death	RM 20,000 + PA	RM 10,000
Critical Illness:		
After diagnosis	RM 10,000	RM 5000
Death after diagnosis	RM 10,000 + PA	RM 5000
Total and permanent disabilities	RM 100 a month + AP (until the age of 65 years old)	RM 50 a month
Accident	RM 40,000	RM 20,000
Hospital daily cash allowances	RM 100 a day (minimum 2 days, maximum 30 days)	RM 50 a day
Cash withdrawals		
After 2 years	50%	50%
After 5 years	70%	70%

Source: Author's own collection

Table 9.2 Package B (without saving)

Scope of coverage	*Minimum coverage*	*Each additional*
Critical Illness	RM 20,000 + PA	RM 10,000 a month
Total and permanent disability	RM 100 a month + PA (until 65 years old)	RM 50 a month
Accident	RM 40,000	RM 20,000
Death (funeral expenses)	RM 5000 + PA	RM 50 a day
Hospital daily cash allowances	RM 100 a day (min. 2 days, max. 30 days)	

(*continued*)

Table 9.2 (continued)

Monthly payment for minimum coverage RM 20,000				*Monthly payment for additional coverage RM 10,000*			
Age	*10*	*15*	*20*	*Age*	*10*	*15*	*20*
18–25	RM 15	RM 15	RM 15	18–25	RM 6	RM 6	RM 6
26–30	RM 15	RM 15	RM 15	26–30	RM 6	RM 7	RM 7
31–35	RM 15	RM 16	RM 17	31–35	RM 7	RM 7	RM 8
36–40	RM 17	RM 19	RM 21	36–40	RM 8	RM 8	RM 9
41–45	RM 21	RM 23	RM 26	41–45	RM 9	RM 9	RM 10
46–50	RM 25	RM 29	RM 33	46–50	RM 10	RM 11	RM 13
51–55	RM 15	RM 15	RM 15	51–55	RM 13	RM 14	RM 16
56–60	RM 15	RM 15	RM 15	56–60	RM 16	RM 1800	RM 21
61–65	RM 15	RM 15	RM 15	61–65	RM 21	RM 24	RM 28

Source: Author's own collection

9.9 *Takaful* Contributions

This plan can be paid monthly, quarterly or half yearly or to other schedules, as with other Family *Takaful* Plans. For Package A, the lowest contribution is RM 100 a month and it can be topped up by RM 50 a month. For example, the participant can contribute RM 100, RM 150, RM 200 and so on based on their ability. While for Package B, the minimum contribution is determined based on total amount of coverage. The minimum amount for coverage is RM 20,000. Additional amounts for coverage can be made in duplication of RM 10,000. For example, the participant can participate for the coverage amount of RM 20,000, RM 30,000, RM 40,000 and so on.

As discussed above, *Takaful* instalments payable under this plan will be divided into two accounts: the Participant's account and Special Participant's Account. The participant must agree to donate the portion of *Takaful* instalments and the profits as *Tabarru* for the purpose of solidarity, brotherhood and co-operation among participants. The money that is credited into the latter account will be used to pay the coverage for death, total and permanent disabilities or critical illness. Moreover, it will also be used to cover those who suffer an accident or who are admitted to any hospital or medical institution.

For package A, when there is no risk faced by the participant during the period, the money from Participant's Account will be returned to the participants with the profit from the investment. The investments based on the rulings of Shari'ah. Any profit generated from the investment of the Participant's Account shall be distributed in accordance with the principle of *Al-Mudharabah* in the following ratio:

- 70% shall be credited into the Participant's Account
- 30% shall be paid to the company.

The net surplus from Special Participant's Account will be shared in the proportion 50%, which shall be credited into the Participant's Account and 50% to the company. Table 9.2 shows the approximate returns after the maturity period based on monthly contributions. It also shows the coverage that will be given to participants.

9.10 Recommendations

In this chapter, our group would like to give some recommendations pertaining to the Health *Takaful* Plan in order to suit the requirement of the societies, such as the following.

9.10.1 Expansion of the Types of Critical Injuries

This is due to the changes in the environment nowadays, whereby some new infectious disease is always emerging. So, in order to solve this problem the Health *Takaful* Plan should update its information about newcomer diseases that can harm society. This means that they should not reserve their coverage only to the 36 types of critical injuries listed in the scheme.

9.10.2 Broaden the Coverage Scope

According to the Health *Takaful* Plan, the company only provides coverage to seven large areas:

- diagnosing critical illness
- death
- permanent disability
- accident

- funeral expenses
- hospital allowances
- cash withdrawal.

Our suggestion is to provide coverage for temporary disability too, because if we think of the opportunity cost incurred, the victim will lose their source of income at that particular period when the injuries took place. But the temporary disability that we suggest to be covered is at present only for the person who buys the policy, for which the maturity period is 20 years. So, in order to lighten the burden of the victim as well as his family, coverage should be expanded to a broader scope. The coverage should be terminated after the victim can continue to do his job as usual.

9.10.3 Longer the Duration of the Participation

In the Health *Takaful* Plan, the terms of participation according to the package provided are:

- 10 years
- 15 years
- 20 years

We believe that the duration of the package should be longer, to 25 years and 30 years, because some people want to have coverage for a long period. Usually, these types of people are those who want to be well prepared if any risk occurs in any time that they themselves did not even think they would face this type of risk or problem.

9.11 Conclusion

In conclusion, we can say that Health *Takaful* Plan is a good product for the health of the nations. It is good because it does cover 36 types of critical injuries that we need great sum of money to pay for the treatment of and other miscellaneous things related to those critical injuries if we were to act individually. In the Health *Takaful* Plan and other Takaful practices, people will co-operate in giving contributions in order to help each other. This means that by mutual co-operation, one's burden in facing the problem related to those injuries can be lightened. Moreover, profit in the Health *Takaful* Plan shall be shared according to the principle of

Al-Mudharabah. If a person joins the Takaful scheme, the claims can be made for a defined risk. This means that the person will not get any additional benefit from the fund if the contribution in it is made by a group of people. In this way, unfairness in claims can be avoided. When the situation is different, such as when the participant survives at the maturity of the policy, his claim shall be confined within the amount available in the Participant's Account. This practice is not the same as with conventional insurance, where the policyholder has a right to claim the whole amount named in the policy and, if the risk does not occur, the insured has a right to claim the policy value at the maturity period together with the interest, if any. This is one of the many differences in practices between ordinary insurance and the Takaful scheme. There are many further differences too, such as in the issues of benefits, bonuses, guarantees, commission investment, nomination, profits, premiums and many others. The Health *Takaful* Plan offers great benefits. It depends on the participant whether he or she wants to joint in this scheme after differentiating its pros and cons in light of conventional insurance practices.

References

1. Ali, A. Y. (n.d.), The Holy Qur'an, Text and Translation.
2. *Medical Takaful Plan*, *Takaful* Malaysia, *Takaful* Nasional, *Takaful* Ikhlas and others.

CHAPTER 10

Health *Takaful* Rider Plan

10.1 Introduction

One of Malaysian National Reinsurance Berhad's subsidiaries is *Takaful* Ikhlas Sdn. Bhd. (*Takaful* Ikhlas). Malaysian National Reinsurance Berhad is one of Malaysia's leading reinsurance companies and an established business on the main board of Kuala Lumpur Stock Exchange. *Takaful* Ikhlas operates under the Shari'ah principles and promote fairness and equity in all its business.

Takaful Ikhlas uses *Al-Wakalah* model despite also using the concept of *Al-Mudharabah*, which is applicable to *Takaful* Malaysia and *Takaful* Nasional. *Al-Wakalah* come from the Arabic word *Wakalah*, which means 'agent' or 'intermediaries.' In this concept, *Takaful* Ikhlas will act as an agent of the participant to conduct *Takaful* business on their behalf. In other words, *Al-Wakalah* is a form of representative relationship between an operator (*Takaful* Ikhlas) and participant (*Takaful* Ikhlas). *Takaful* Ikhlas uses agents or intermediaries as a means to serve customers better. This model involves two types of contract:

It is acknowledged that, the idea of this chapter/product is significantly contributed by the practices /experiences/thoughts of Bank Negara, Takaful Malaysia, Takaful Ikhlas, Takaful Nasional, Etiqa Takaful, IBFIM, IIUM, MII and others (Malaysia).

Mohd Ma'Sum Billah, *Islamic Insurance Products*,
https://doi.org/10.1007/978-3-030-17681-5_10

- *At-Tabarru'*, which means the participant agrees to give away or donate a predetermined percentage from his/her contribution to the fund to provide assistance to the members of the fund, and
- *Al-Wakalah*, which means that the participant authorised *Takaful* Ikhlas to conduct affairs of the fund on his/her behalf.

There are three components of *Takaful* Ikhlas model, which are Family *Takaful* Fund Pool, General *Takaful* Pool and Ta'awuni Account Pool (TAP). The Family *Takaful* Fund Pool consists of Personal Investment Account (PIA) and Personal Risk Investment Account (PRIA). The PIA is an account where the contribution from the participant is used for protection and investment, while the PRIA is where the contribution from the participant is used only for the protection of the participant and the family or, put simply, for the payment of benefits in case of emergency.

In the General *Takaful* Pool, there is only one account namely General Risk Investment Account, where part of the participant's contribution is credited in this account to provide any payment of benefits in the future. TAP basically consists of three major sub-accounts, which are Expense Fund, which comprises front- and back-end charges, the Risk Fund for benefits payment, and the Special Fund which acts in an emergency to sustain the Risk Fund.

There are several advantages of using this *Takaful* Ikhlas model:

- expenses are charged on a monthly basis, rather than yearly
- expectation of lower reserves allocation due to the yearly renewal
- profit distribution to participant is higher
- surplus is determined on a monthly basis
- the participant will receive better benefits payment upon any type of claims
- proper and easy maintenance of participant's account
- the Special Fund will act as back-up for any shortfall or deficit in the Risk Fund.

10.2 The Product

The Ikhlas Hospital Benefit *Takaful* Rider Plan is one of the products under *Takaful* Ikhlas. It is one of the components of the Ikhlas model under the Family *Takaful* fund pool, which is part of the Personal Risk Investment Fund (PRIA) (Fig. 10.1).

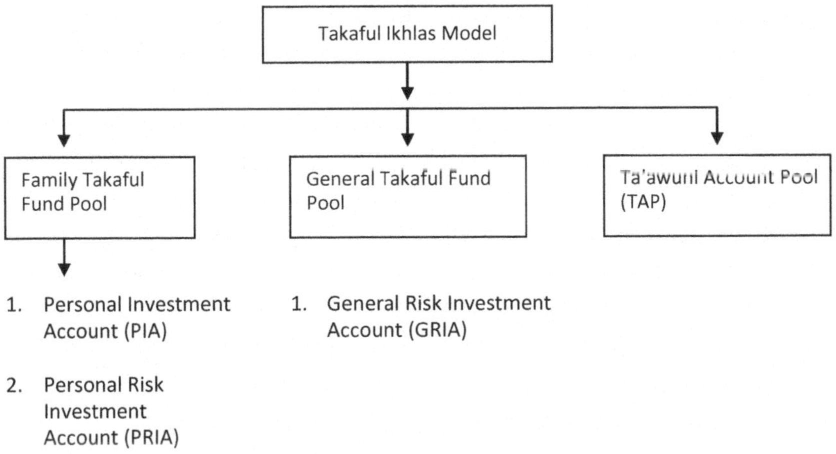

Fig. 10.1 The product. (Source: Author's own collection)

The PRIA is an account that only provides coverage for a participant who in need. Ikhlas Hospital Benefit *Takaful* Rider Plan is an individual *Takaful* Rider Plan that must be attached to any basic plan. For example, it can be attached to Ikhlas Savings *Takaful* or Ikhlas Education *Takaful*. It provides the participant with cash benefits should they be hospitalised for any reason. It is termed 'rider' because it cannot be a stand-alone policy and must have something to attach to. It is like an accessory or supplementary to any *Takaful* Basic Plan.

Hospital benefit only provides coverage for a participant who hospitalised due to illness or injury due to any cause for a minimum duration of three days. Only in this event will the benefits be payable and it is thus a trigger point for payment of benefits. Its objective is to provide the participant a facility to minimise their burden or to minimise their costs, so they do not have to pay for their medical expenses (Fig. 10.2).

For example, the participant is hospitalised for five days and the hospital bill is RM 500. He buys a policy for RM 10. Then, the benefit payable by *Takaful* Ikhlas for that participant is only RM 50 (RM 10 × 5 days) and not payable for all the medical expenses. In such a case, the maximum number of days of hospitalisation basically on any occasion or any event is 180 days per occasion or per event or 365 days. The policy will be terminated when the participant has used the maximum duration. Before the

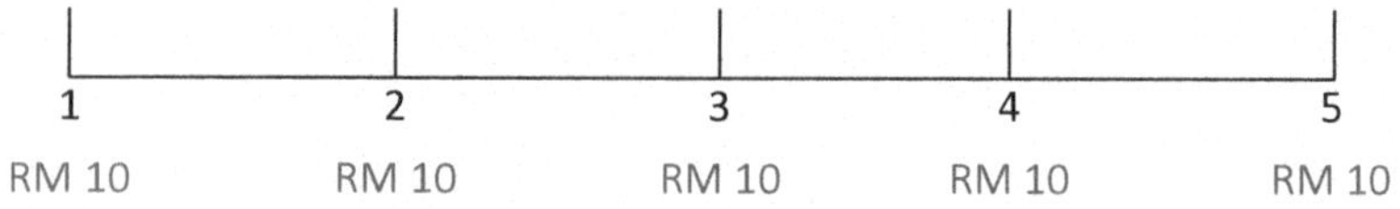

Fig. 10.2 The product. (Source: Author's own collection)

Takaful Ikhlas Sdn. Bhd. limit the duration up to 365 days, they have estimated through statistics that the average maximum number of days a person will be hospitalised is around four to five days.

The benefit payable for a participant is applicable for various types of diseases and causes. It is also applicable for any hospital, whether public or private. It is like an allowance for participant in order to lessen their burden or expenses. The Shari'ah concept that applicable for Ikhlas Hospital Benefit *Takaful* Rider Plan is:

> Help you one another in righteousness and piety, but help you not one another in sin and rancour. (Al-Maidah: 2)

Due to hospitalisation, the hospital benefit payable must fulfil these conditions:

- no hospitalisation benefit will be payable unless the hospitalisation takes place at least three months after the inception date of Hospital Benefits *Takaful* Rider Plan;
- this benefit excludes pre-existing conditions.

10.3 Contract

Generally, in any transaction, there will be a contract. Under this scheme, the underwriting issue is quite similar to other schemes offered by *Takaful* Ikhlas. Before any contract can be drawn up between the *Takaful* participant and the *Takaful* operator, the participant need to fulfil all conditions and requirements. They also must understand all the terms and conditions of the contract.

Minimum Entry Age	30 days old
Maximum Entry Age	65 years, age next birthday

Table 10.1 Gross contribution rate (Per RM 10 daily hospital benefit)

	Occupational Class			
	Class 1	*Class 2*	*Class 3*	*Class 4*
Gross rate	RM 12.40	RM 14.00	RM 15.50	RM 18.60

Source: Author's own collection

The minimum entry age for this scheme is 30 days old and the maximum entry age is 65 years old. For those aged less than one year, the final acceptance entry age will be defined as age one. They are qualified to enter into this scheme under their guardian's consideration. It is also to ensure that the chosen child is not suffering from any impediment and is in good health. The parents or guardians are responsible for paying the premiums and become the trustees of this policy.

The rate of contribution or premium varies between the occupational classes (Table 10.1).

The occupational class is classified in order to differentiate the physical risk between industries. The occupational class represents the occupation of the participant. The lower risk participants will be classified as class 1 and the higher risk individuals will be classified as class 4. For example, a participant who works in an office will be classified class 1. Participants who work in construction will be classified in class 4 because they face greater risks. The police and the army are considered class 2 or class 3 because they face average levels of risk.

Benefit Limit	
Minimum Coverage	RM 10 per day
Maximum Coverage	RM 200 per day

The benefit payable to the participant will be based on the *Takaful* policy that they have chosen. The minimum coverage payable is RM 10 per day and the maximum coverage is RM 200 per day.

Expiry age

- the end of policy term
- 65 years, age next birthday.

The Ikhlas Hospital Benefit *Takaful* Rider Plan will expire at the end of the policy term or when the participant reaches the age of 65.

Coverage Term	
Minimum Policy Term	5 years
Maximum Policy Term	Follows the expiry date of the basic plan

The participant can buy a policy at the minimum policy term of five years and maximum by following the policy terms of the basic plan. The maximum coverage term follows the policy terms of the basic plan because this product is attachable to all of the basic plan. It cannot become a stand-alone policy and only applicable if the participant buys one of the basic plans first.

10.4 Coverage

The Ikhlas Individual Hospital Benefit *Takaful* Rider Plan only offers hospital benefits to the participant where it is just to minimise the cost, but not to pay off all expenses. The benefit coverage should have an elimination period. The elimination period is the minimum number of days that entitles the participant to get benefit coverage. For this plan, the elimination period is three consecutive days. The elimination period is like the trigger point for the payment of benefits. The hospital benefit is valid in the event of hospitalisation of the participant due to any cause for more than three consecutive days; then the hospital benefit is payable from the first day of hospitalisation until the last day.

The maximum numbers of days are:

- 180 days per one case of hospitalisation;
- 365 days in aggregate arising from all causes of hospitalisation, after which the rider will be terminated.

This Hospital Benefits is a lifetime aggregate, where the participant only gets the benefits for 365 days in aggregate. After these 365 days have been used up by the participant, the benefit is no longer applicable. The participant only can apply this once in his/her life. The company will pay the benefit to the participant according to the plan that he/she takes out.

For example, if a participant is hospitalised for two consecutive days, in this case the benefit will not apply because the situation does not fulfil the elimination period of three days. In the case of participant who is warded for five days, the operator will pay the benefit. For example, a participant applies for the maximum benefit coverage plan; in this case, the benefit payment will be RM 1000.

Illustration:	RM 200 per days × 5 days = RM 1000

In order to receive benefit coverage, some other conditions need to be fulfilled to qualify for hospital benefit. First, no hospital benefit shall be payable to the participant unless the hospitalisation takes place at least three months after the inception date of this rider and, second, pre-existing conditions are excluded from this plan. If the participant wants to make any claim for the benefits, no claim should be made in the first three months.

10.5 Claim Procedures

General procedures for claiming benefit are shown in Fig. 10.3.

When a participant wants to make a claim, the participant should bring their hospital or medical bill to the operator immediately after hospitalisation. The bill will describe the time in, time out, date and also the duration. From the bill, the participant has to provide evidence to claim benefits. Once the bill is submitted and the relevant form is completed, the operator will issue payment. The payment is taken from the PRIA. Usually, the claim can be settled within three days if everything goes well.

As has been mentioned earlier, the benefit limits or a claim is:

- minimum coverage = RM 10 per day
- maximum coverage = RM 200 per day

General procedures to claim benefit can be shown below.

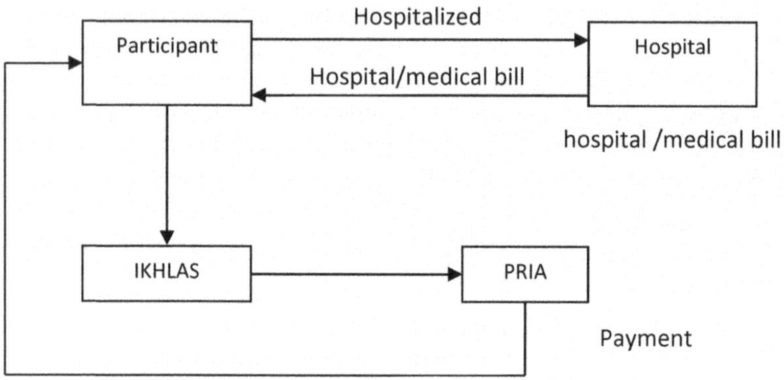

Fig. 10.3 Claim procedures. (Source: Author's own collection)

For instance, a participant who takes the minimum coverage plan suffers an accident and has been warded or hospitalised for a week. Therefore, the benefit payment is:

$$\text{Benefit coverage} = \text{Number of days} \times \text{coverage amount}$$
$$7\,\text{days} \times \text{RM}\,10$$
$$= \text{RM}\,70$$

In order to get the coverage, the participant must not yet have used up their total allocation of 365 days. In case there is any doubts about the bill, the operator can conduct an investigation and provide a report to the higher authority. If the suspected issue turns out to be true, the participant will not be accepted to join this plan and the agreement is terminated.

10.6 Fund Management

Fund management in *Takaful* Ikhlas is different from any *Takaful* company in Malaysia. It follows the concepts of *Tabarru'* and *Wakalah*.

10.7 The PRIA of Family *Takaful*

When participant pays a contribution or premium, first of all the company will deduct front-end charges. An agent's commission of 10% is deducted, as well as other costs associated with new business. Then, the balance will be put into investment account and TAP. The contribution in the investment account will be invested in ethical and moral businesses or investment. The profit will be shared between participant and operator on the concept of *Wakalah*. In TAP, the money will be divided into the three funds as discussed (Fig. 10.4).

10.7.1 Expenses Fund

The Expenses Fund consists of front-end charges and back-end charges. Participants will be charged expense associated with the establishment

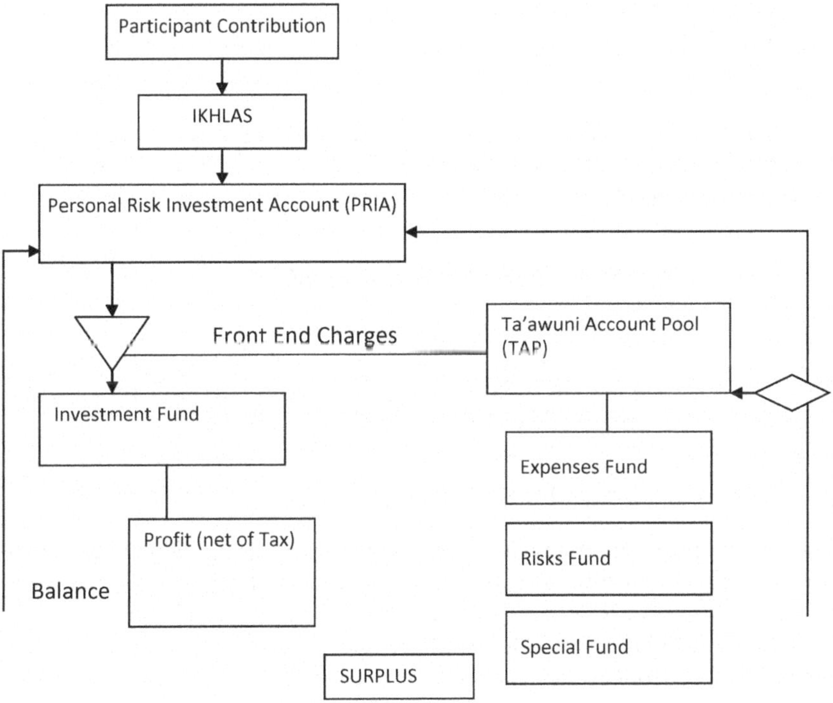

Fig. 10.4 PRIA of family *Takaful*. (Source: Author's own collection)

of new business, an agent's commission, transaction fees and other fees. It follows the *Wakalah* concept. The commission payable to operator must be:

- 3.5% of interest charged from participant's gross contributions;
- based on a sliding scale that represents risk charged in the first year being higher than for the second year;
- commensurate with the term;
- follow the policy term or be up to duration of the basic plan.

10.7.2 Risk Fund

The Risk Fund is a fund based on the concept of *Tabarru'* or donation. This fund will provide the participant with financial security and benefits payable. This fund includes:

- one year of risk premium
- Re-takaful
- reserves.

Through the concept of *hibah*, the surplus will be pooled back to participant's account. This will be done on a monthly basis in order to improve the account.

10.7.3 Special Fund

The Special Fund is based on the concept of *Tabarru'*. It serves as a contingency when there is loss or deficit in the Risk Fund. When the Risk Fund cannot support the special fund, the shareholder will provide the company with an interest-free loan known as *qard al-hasan*.

10.8 Conclusion

Practically speaking, many insurance companies and *Takaful* operators provide this sort of rider plan to attract customers. They will try their best to cater to the various needs of the customer. Ikhlas Hospital Benefit *Takaful* Rider Plan is suitable for all people, regardless of age. It lets the participant to concentrate on recovery from illness without worrying about finance. It gives the participant a facility that can reduce the burden of participant who has been hospitalised, based on the Shari'ah concept in Surah Al-Maidah verse two, which asks people to help one another in righteousness and piety.

References

1. Ali, A. Y. (n.d.), The Holy Qur'an, Text and Translation.
2. *Health Takaful Rider Plan*, *Takaful* Ikhlas, *Takaful* Nasional, *Takaful* Malaysia, and others.

CHAPTER 11

Group *Takaful* Plan

11.1 Introduction

Takaful Malaysia as part of BIMB Holdings was incorporated on 29 November 1984. On 2 August 1985, operations was commenced. The idea of founding *Takaful* Malaysia came from the Task Force on the Study of Establishing Islamic Insurance Company in Malaysia, which was formed in 1981. After the Cabinet approved the Task Force's report, *Takaful* Malaysia was formed. The report explained the general idea and about the characteristics of the company. These state that the company's capital must come from the legal sources that are in line with Shari'ah principles and no individuals hold company shares. Any rules and regulation regarding *Takaful* Malaysia are determined under The *Takaful* Act (Malaysia) 1984. The Shari'ah Supervisory Council (MPS—Majlis Pengawasan Shari'ah) will formed under this act. The act determines the company performs two types of business: General *Takaful* and Family *Takaful*. At first, *Takaful* Malaysia started its business with initial paid-up capital that amounted to only RM 10 million. But after capital was restricted in 1996, the results

It is acknowledged that, the idea of this chapter/product is significantly contributed by the practices/experiences/thoughts of Bank Negara, Takaful Malaysia, Takaful Ikhlas, Takaful Nasional, Etiqa Takaful, IBFIM, IIUM, MII and others (Malaysia).

Mohd Ma'Sum Billah, *Islamic Insurance Products*,
https://doi.org/10.1007/978-3-030-17681-5_11

were that it earned a profit of RM 55 million and the company was listed in Main Board of the Kuala Lumpur Stock Exchange on 31 July 1996 as publicly listed company.

11.2 Foundation of Group *Takaful*

Shari'ah approves of *Takaful* because the nature of the principles of *Takaful* are totally different from the principles of conventional insurance. *Takaful* practice is more concerned with the 'joint guarantee' or 'shared guarantee'. This means that participation in *Takaful* is a mutually agreed scheme, where every participant co-operates and helping one another from the defined fund (*Takaful*) to pay for a defined loss. Each participant also has the right to profit sharing.

According to Islamic Jurists, *Takaful* as the main concept of Islamic Insurance is permitted because of the following reasons:

- policyholders (participants) co-operate among themselves;
- every participant pays his 'subscription' (contribution) in order to assist those in need of assistance;
- it falls under the donation (*Tabarru'*) contract which is intended to divide losses and spread liability according to the community pooling system;
- it does not aim at deriving advantage at the cost of other participants.

11.3 Products

Under the Group *Takaful* Plan, there are three products available:

- Group Family *Takaful* Plan
- Group Medical Plan
- Group Family *Takaful* Plan (Credit)

11.3.1 Group Family Takaful *Plan*

This can be participated in by any group or organisation such as *badan khairat*, *qariah masjid*, employers and clubs. A number of shelves such products with some of the features mentioned is offered such as for badan khairat or masjid. This is an annual *Takaful* plan and has to be renewed on a yearly basis. The Group Family *Takaful* Plan standard scopes of cover are:

- natural death
- accidental death
- permanent total disability (due to accidental or natural causes)
- funeral expenses.

The cover also can be extended to include:

- permanent disablement (accidental)
- medical expenses benefit
- hospitalisation benefit.

Its participation quotation will be issued based on details forwarded to *Takaful* Malaysia. All quotations prepared are also based on the requirement of the proposer or client. Upon agreement of the quotation, a proposal and declaration form needs to be filled out. The minimum participation of 20 is required for acceptance of cover but if any less a health and declaration form needs to be filled out by each member. The age limit for this Group Family *Takaful* Plan should not be more than 55 years, unless stated in the quotation.

11.3.2 Group Medical Takaful *Plan*

A participation quotation will be issued based on details forwarded to *Takaful* Malaysia. Upon agreement of the quotation, a proposal and declaration form needs to be completed.

Proposal and Declaration Form

The proposer is required to fill out on of these or other relevant criteria that are required by *Takaful*. Among the necessary details are:

- name and address of employer or proposer
- name of persons to be covered
- date of birth

- position/occupation
- I/C number
- benefit class chosen.

Age Limit
The age limit for participation should not exceed 55 years, while those of dependants (children) are from 15 days to 18 years old or 25 if they are full-time students.

Exclusions
Among exclusions important to note are:

Pre-existing conditions: that is, disability that existed or has only newly developed symptoms or there existed some manifestation of the illness before the effective date of cover in respect to a person covered of which they were aware or should reasonably have been aware, or based on normal medically accepted pathological development of the illness or illnesses.

11.3.3 Group Family **Takaful** *Plan (Credit)*

Group Family *Takaful* Plan (Credit) is a group plan similar to the *Takaful* mortgage plan but with a small sum covered (less and equal than RM 50,000) and short-term financing. Proceeds from the plan will be used to redeem an outstanding balance in the event of the participant's death or permanent disablement. Therefore, the plan covers finances or loans either with financial institutions, employer or co-operative society. The plan is a contract between the financier and the company under the principle of *Al-Mudharabah*.

Benefits:

- peace of mind with assurance that the outstanding balance of your loan, credit or finance facility will be settled in full by Syarikat *Takaful* Malaysia Berhad in the event of death or permanent disability;
- the guarantor will be free of any liability from the participant's credit facility or loan;
- dependents or heirs will feel secure in inheriting the property without any encumbrances.

Scope of Cover

- Death
- Permanent total disability.

Eligibility
Any individual between ages of 18–55 years old with a financing/loan facility.

Takaful *Contributions*
The *Takaful* contribution payable will be based on:

- amount of financing/Loan
- repayment period
- age at next birthday
- rate of profit of facility or loan.

The *Takaful* contribution is payable in a single lump sum.

11.4 Payment of *Takaful* Benefits

Upon death or permanent total disability of participant.

11.4.1 How to Participate

No proposal and declaration Form needs to be filled out unless requested by the financier. The financier will forward any application to the company for processing.

11.4.2 Al-Mudharabah

If the Group Family *Takaful* Plan Account and Group Family *Takaful* Fund earn any profit, it will be distributed to the participant and *Takaful* company on *Al-Mudharabah* basis, with a ratio of 40% of the profit to the participant and another 60% to the *Takaful* company, with the condition that the participant will not receive any claim benefits.

11.5 Practicality

Other provision and participation conditions:

- *Takaful* protection is available 24 hours, all around the world;
- protection for children is available if the children are not married, aged 15 days to 19 years old and are a full-time student in higher educational institutions, which extends to 25 years old;
- if any claims occur, the participant or beneficiary must inform to the group in order to manage the appeal of the claim;
- free lower limit RM 16,500;
- each member is required to fill out the membership application form;
- each member is qualified to choose only one category of benefits for one participation. Nevertheless, members who have more than one spouse are allowed to choose more than one category of benefits according to the number of spouses;
- date of quotation was declared on 22 August 2002;
- quotation is valid within six months of the declaration date.

11.6 Shari'ah Ruling

11.6.1 Mutual Co-operation

Help ye one another in righteousness and piety. (Al-Maidah: 5:2)

As we can see, the *Takaful* scheme applies the *Tabarru'* fund whereby all participants will contribute a portion of their premium to that particular fund. And those who find themselves in need will receive financial assistance from the *Tabarru'* fund.

11.6.2 Misappropriation of Wealth

And do not eat up your property among yourselves for vanities, nor use it as bait for the judges, with intent that ye may eat up wrongfully and knowingly a little of (other) people's property. (Al-Baqarah: 2:188)

The wealth of the participants is managed by the Takaful agent in an appropriate way based on Shari'ah rulings. There will not be any charges of interest to the participants since that is against the rule of Allah (swt).

11.6.3 Flexibility

> God (Allah) intends every facility for you; He does not want to put to difficulties. (Al-Baqarah: 2:185)

Takaful seems to give benefits to all parties, for example the family of deceased will get the benefits from the *Takaful* Fund.

11.6.4 Contract

> O ye who believe! Fulfil (all) obligations. (Al-Maidah: 5:1)

The *Takaful* scheme involves agreement between two parties, the buyer and the operator. It contains the agreement in which the buyer can claim so long as they fulfil the terms and conditions in the contract.

Saving for Security

> Narrated by Amir bin Saad bin Abi Waqas (R), The Holy Prophet (saw) said: Verily it better for you to leave your offspring wealthy than to leave them poor asking others for help. (Sahih al-Bukhari)

It is better to someone to leave behind his/her wealth to his/her dependents rather that to the poor because otherwise it will encourage the poor to asking for help from others without doing anything to help themselves.

11.7 Conclusion

In conclusion, we can say that the Group *Takaful* Plan provides benefits not only to participants but also to their heirs or families since it is based on Shari'ah and the principal of *Al-Mudharabah.* The purpose is to provide long-term fund that will give benefits to participants and families if death happens before the maturity period. It is also to guarantee help to any participant facing the possibility of accident total permanent disability or to cover medical services. It is also designed to help a participant to have a proper budget based on his ability. Through this plan, the participant can save money during his chosen period. If the participant dies before or at maturity period, so *Takaful* Malaysia will have the authority to give amount of money to his representatives. Overall, the *Takaful* scheme seems to provide a lot of benefits not only to its participants but also to the participants' beneficiaries. It also functions as future material security and long-term financial fund in order to guarantee participants' safety and to protect them from any catastrophes or danger.

References

1. Ali, A. Y. (n.d.), The Holy Qur'an, Text and Translation.
2. *Group Takaful Plan*, *Takaful* Malaysia, *Takaful* Nasional, *Takaful* Ikhlas and others.

CHAPTER 12

Group *Takaful* Plan for Health Care

12.1 Introductions

In this era of globalisation, we see a lack of Islamic products. Thus, Islamic products are still new in our community and there is a challenge to convince people to take up these novel offerings. One such product is Islamic insurance, which operates throughout the world. Insurance is acceptable under Islam. This is because Prophet Muhammad (saw) approved the doctrine of *al-ʿaqila* that the ancient Arab tribes practiced. The concept of *al-ʿaqila* is a custom in which the members of the tribes were ready to make monetary contribution to compensate the family of the victim if one of their members killed the victim. This doctrine is believed to be the first form of insurance. In Malaysia, the Syarikat *Takaful* Malaysia Berhad was the first Islamic insurance policy and came into operation on 29 November 1984; this was followed by the *Takaful* Nasional Berhad. Both *Takaful* operators provide the financial benefit in order to reduce the risk of burden on the participants. *Takaful* Malaysia offers General *Takaful* and Family *Takaful*. In General *Takaful*, the operator will cover the participant if they have bought the product from the operator. The examples of the

It is acknowledged that, the idea of this chapter/product is significantly contributed by the practices/experiences/thoughts of Bank Negara, Takaful Malaysia, Takaful Ikhlas, Takaful Nasional, Etiqa Takaful, IBFIM, IIUM, MII and others (Malaysia).

Mohd Ma'Sum Billah, *Islamic Insurance Products*,
https://doi.org/10.1007/978-3-030-17681-5_12

products are Fire *Takaful*, Pilgrims *Takaful*, Engineering *Takaful*, Marine *Takaful* and so forth.

Takaful Malaysia Berhad provides Family *Takaful* for Education, *Takaful* Sihat, *Takaful* Ziarah, *Takaful* Wiladah, *Takaful* Siswa, *Takaful* Medical, *Takaful* Hawa and others. In this chapter, we focus on the Group Takaful plan for hospital and surgical costs. There are two products that relate to our topic: *Takaful* Medical and *Takaful* Hawa.

12.2 Central Idea

Takaful Malaysia provides two products under its hospital and surgical cover plans: *Takaful* Medical and *Takaful* Hawa. Both products deal with hospital and surgery expenses for the participants and family members. Through *Takaful* Medical, participants will be covered for hospital fees and surgery expenses. While in *Takaful* Hawa, participants also will be covered for hospital and surgery expenses but with a focus more on cancer and related diseases. As we know, nowadays women are easily infected by cancer, therefore *Takaful* Hawa is specially designed for women. These plans do not cover pre-existing illness (unless specifically mentioned otherwise) and those normally excluded under any health plan, such as maternity, related treatment, dental, mental illness, cosmetic surgery, alcohol or drug abuse, congenital abnormalities and all illnesses that commence within the waiting period of 30 days, except for accident-related injuries.

12.3 Medical *Takaful* Paradigm

12.3.1 Person Eligible for Takaful *Medical*

- All participant age under 70 years are qualified to partake of this product.
- The participant's spouse if aged under 70 years, unless legally separated from the participants.
- All unmarried and unemployed children who are aged between 15 days and below 19 years. For children who are still studying in an institution, the age limit will be extended to their 25th birthday.

12.3.2 Period of Cover and Renewal

Any person covered under this product who is confined in hospital as hereinafter defined, or receiving out-patient treatment as a result of injury or death, the company will, upon receipt and approval of proofs, pay reasonable and customary charges hereinafter provided in the Schedule of benefits attached to their certificate in respect of:

- illness occurring more than 30 days after the commencement of this *Takaful*;
- injury occurring after commencement of this *Takaful*.

Subject to provision, condition and limitation as contained herein or as may be endorsed hereon.

12.3.3 Benefits in Takaful *Medical*

- provides 24-hour worldwide coverage
- no need of medical check-up
- provide Special Catastrophe Disease Cover under the Ehsan Plan
- 10% discount given for more than one child covered
- higher protection amount
- Funeral expenses.

12.3.4 Description of Benefits

Hospital Room and Board
Charges for accommodation from the first day of hospital confinement, general nursing services and meals for each day of confinement as a patient in a properly constituted hospital licensed by the government.

Intensive Care Unit
Charges for intensive care unit rendered in lieu of normal accommodation charges but shall not exceed the maximum limit set forth in the Schedule of Benefits.

Miscellaneous Hospital Services
Hospital charges for x-rays, laboratory fees, drugs and medicines consumed on premises, dressings, physiotherapy and other customary services rendered or supplied during the confinement period.

Surgical Fees
Fees actually charged for the operation by the surgeon, anaesthetist and use of operating theatre, including the fee for the pre-surgical assessment and fee for the normal post-operative care up to a maximum of 31 days from the date of operation, provided that such treatment is received during hospitalisation. The maximum level payable benefits are assessed according to the amount provided by the chosen plan in relation to the Surgical Schedule of Fees, depending on the nature of operation performed. For any operation not listed in the Surgical Schedule of Fees, it shall be the sole discretion of the company to determine a maximum payment for such procedure which in the company's view is consistent with the procedures listed.

In-Hospital Physician's Visits
Fees charged by the physician for treatment or visits to a patient, for whom a full day's room charge is made by the hospital, except where a surgical procedure is performed.

Pre-Hospitalisation Diagnostic Services Specialist Consultation
Charges for diagnostic x-ray, laboratory examinations and for specialist consultation, opinion or advice, which are recommended by a licensed physician because of illness or injury, incurred within 90 days prior to hospital confinement or surgical operation. Payment will not be made for clinical treatment (including medications and subsequent consultations after illness is diagnosed), nor if the person covered is not subsequently hospitalised or surgically treated after such consultation or examination.

Ambulance Fees
Charges for ambulance services (inclusive of attendance) to and/or from the hospital. Payment will not be made if the person covered is not hospitalised.

Post-Hospitalisation Treatment
The expenses for follow-up treatment will be given to the participants immediately after she or he is discharged from hospital by the same physician, up to a period of 31 days.

Emergency Out-Patient Accidental Treatment
Charges for services and medical supplies provided by the hospital or clinic for emergency treatment of an injury as a result of an accident and received as an out-patient within 24 hours after the accident. Eligible expenses incurred thereafter for follow-up, up to 31 days from the date of the accident.

Government Hospital Daily Cash Allowance
Payment of a daily cash allowance for each full day of confinement at any government hospital in Malaysia.

Funeral Expenses
Payment of a fixed death benefit if the person covered dies within the period of *Takaful.*

12.3.5 Type of Package

There are two packages available under *Takaful* Medical, the Ehsan Package and the Bakti Package. Contributions for both packages are on yearly basis. The Ehsan Package consists of three plans, while the Bakti Package consists of four plans. The main difference concerns the annual contributions for the package. The Ehsan Package is more expensive than the Bakti package because it offers more benefits. For instance, there is the additional benefit of "Special Catastrophe Disease Cover" in the Ehsan Package (Table 12.1).

12.3.6 Termination of Cover

A person covered shall cease to be so:

(a) if the data in this certificate is terminated, or
(b) on the reaching of their 70th birthday, and for the children, on reaching of the age of 19 years and 25 years old for students.

12.3.7 Cancellation

Participants can cancel this certificate at any time they want by giving written notice to the company, including such notice to state when cancellation shall become effective. Participants who do not make any claim during

Table 12.1 Type of package

Ehsan package

	Plan 1	*Plan 2*	*Plan 3*
Hospital services and professional fees			
1. Hospital room and board (daily max. Up to 120 days)	350	250	150
2. Intensive care unit	15,000	10,000	6000
3. Miscellaneous services	5000	3500	2500
4. Surgical fees including anaesthetic fees and operating theatre	10,000	8000	6250
5. In-hospital physician's visit (daily max. up to 120 days)	150	120	90
6. Pre-hospitalisation diagnostic services and specialist consultation (within 90 days prior to hospitalisation)	1200	900	600
7. Ambulance fee	200	200	200
8. Post-hospitalisation treatment (within 31 days of discharge)	700	500	300
9. Out-patient accidental treatment (within 24 hours of the accident)	4000	3000	2000
10. Government hospital daily cash allowance (daily max. up to 60 days)	100	80	60
11. Funeral expenses	4000	4000	4000
Special catastrophe disease Cover/out-patient cancer treatment (limit per year)	30,000	20,000	10,000
1. Out-patient renal dialysis (limit per year)	30,000	20,000	10,000
2. Organ transplant for heart, lung, liver and kidney	50,000	30,000	20,000

Bakti package

	Plan 1	*Plan 2*	*Plan 3*	*Plan 4*
Hospital services and professional fees				
1. Hospital room and board (daily max. up to 120 days)	250	150	100	50
2. Intensive care	10,000	6000	4000	2000
3. Miscellaneous services	3500	2500	2000	1500
4. Surgical fees and including anaesthetic fees and operating theatre	8000	6250	5000	3750
5. In-hospital physician's visit (daily max. up to 120 days)	120	90	70	90
6. Pre-hospitalisation diagnostic services and specialist consultation (within 90 days prior to hospitalisation)	900	600	400	200
7. Ambulance fees	100	100	100	100
8. Post-hospitalisation treatment (within 31 days after discharge)	500	300	200	100
9. Out-patient accidental treatment (within 24 hours after the accident)	3000	2000	1500	1000

(*continued*)

Table 12.1 (continued)

Bakti package				
	Plan 1	*Plan 2*	*Plan 3*	*Plan 4*
10. Government hospital daily cash allowance (daily maximum up to 60 days)	80	60	40	20
11. Funeral expenses	4000	4000	4000	4000

Source: Author's collection from TMB

the current certificate year are entitle for the return of the Takaful contribution calculated on pro-rata basis in proportion to the period this Takaful has been enforce. The company also can cancel this certificate by giving written cancellation notice to participants, stating when, not less than 14 days thereafter, such cancellation shall become effective.

12.3.8 *Procedures*

In order to join the *Takaful* Medical Plan, the person should fill in a *Takaful* Medical form. This form is prepared to gather all personal details of the participants, the type of *Takaful* Medical he/she chooses, the person to be covered, health and medical statement, beneficiary declaration and also their own declaration.

12.4 Description of *Takaful* Hawa

12.4.1 *Eligibility*

People eligible to be covered by this product are those aged between 18 and 59 years old.

12.4.2 *Benefits*

- Medical contribution to cover the cost of cancer treatment
- Additional benefits if the participant is endorsed as infected by one of the
- cancer diseases
- Provide 'pap smear' test and breast cancer check every year
- Ward cash allowance until RM 150 per day and out-patient fees

- Funeral expenses of about RM 4000 given even if the death is not because of
- the cancer
- *Al-Mudharabah* profit sharing.

12.4.3 Period of Cover and Renewal

The policy anniversary shall be one year after the effective date and annually thereafter. On each anniversary, this policy is renewed at the contribution rates in effect at the time, as notified by the company.

12.4.4 Description of Benefits

Lump-Sum Benefit
This lump-sum benefit shall be payable not more than one time in the lifetime of the person covered. If the participants have made any claim, he or she cannot get another lump-sum benefit until she renews her policy. The total amount as specified in the benefit is RM 20,000 for Package A and RM 10,000 for Package B. A participant could claim this benefit when the doctor diagnoses that the she is infected by any cancer.

Additional Lump-Sum Benefit
The practice of offering an additional lump-sum benefit is just like the lump-sum benefit. However, it especially covers cancers of the breast, uterus, cervix, fallopian tube, ovary, and vulva or vagina.

Reconstructive Breast Surgery Benefit (Per Breast)
The amount covers for surgery expenses in order to reconstruct the breast are RM 10,000 for Package A and RM 5000 for Package B.

Daily Cash Allowance for Hospitalisation
Participants who are admitted to hospital will be provided with a cash allowance for a maximum of 30 days. The amount for Package A is RM 150 per day and under Package B it is RM 75 per day. Participants who are infected by breast, uterus, cervix, fallopian tube, ovary, and vulva or vagina cancers will be given an additional cash allowance for each day of hospitalisation for a maximum of 30 days. For Package A the amount is RM 150 per day and for Package B it is RM 75.

Annual Medical Check-Up for Cancer
Takaful Hawa provides reimbursement of the examination fees for the pap smear and breast medical check-up in which the amount covered are RM 100 for Package A and RM 50 for Package B. The payment will be made whether or not they are infected by the cancer.

Funeral Expenses
Takaful provides funeral expenses of RM 4000 in both packages. These benefits provide for any cause of death except death by suicide and due to any factors which are against Shari'ah teaching.

12.4.5 Termination

The termination of the policy is determined when the participants reach the age of 71. It also can be terminated on the date stated in the certificate.

12.4.6 Cancellation

The practice of cancellation of *Takaful* Hawa is same as with *Takaful* Medical.

12.5 Shari'ah Rulings

Islam allows the practice of *Takaful* Medical and *Takaful* Hawa. Both products are considered lawful according to Islam. In surah Al-Maidah, verse 2 states:

> help ye one another in righteousness and piety, but help ye not one another in sin and rancour (Abdullah Yusof 'Ali, n.d.)

This verse clearly refers to mutual help between Muslims. Thus, Allah encourages His *ummah* to co-operate in whatever permissible activities by Islam. In *Takaful* Medical and *Takaful* Hawa, the money that they collect is used to cover the participants. So, the policyholders help each other for their own benefit from the risk of unpredictable events. For *Takaful* Medical and *Takaful* Hawa, the participants share their responsibilities in helping other participants who are burdened by hospital and surgical fees. In addition, Allah also encourages His *ummah* to seek for medication to continue the life by any means. Allah said in His holy book:

> We ordained for the Children of Israel that if any one slew a person – unless it be for murder or for spreading mischief in the land – it would be as if he slew the whole people. ***And* if anyone saved a life, it would be as if he saved the life of the whole people.** (Qur'an 5:32) (http.www.freepctools.com/ethics.htm)

Therefore, both *Takaful* Hawa and *Takaful* Medical is permissible as Allah Has stressed the important of saving another's life. Medical treatment also one of the benefits that the participant receives in both products and this is also allowed by Islam. Hassan Hathout, at the Medical Ethics Symposium at the ISNA Convention in 1997, answered the question about medical treatment:

> Tell them that treatment is also God's will, that Jesus said, "I cure the sick with the leave of God"; That Mohammed said "your body has right on you, and said: seek treatment, servants of God, for every illness God created, he created a treatment for=2E (B.) The family should comply because the physician is one who knows best. But the decision is theirs." (http.www.freepctools.com/ethics.htm)

Thus, the benefits that these products offer in the form of cover for medical and surgical fees are considered permissible by Islam and the action of the Takaful operator in providing cover for participants is allowed too.

12.6 Practicalities

Takaful Hospital, surgical (*Takaful* Medical) and *Takaful* Hawa, are among the *Takaful* Family products. They have a one-year maturity period in which the participant has to renew whenever he wants to continue with the coverage. These Islamic insurance policies only cover the individual who buys the policy. The payment made by the participant will be put in a pool termed a fund. Here, the money will be credited into two accounts: *Al-Mudharabah* (profit sharing) and *At-Tabarru'* (donation).

Example (Fig. 12.1):
Under the *Al-Mudharabah* concept, the funds collected will be distributed into two accounts. Those are the Participant's Account, which shall be treated on the basis of *Al-Mudharabah*, and the Participants' Special Account, which shall be governed under the principle of *Tabarru'*. The

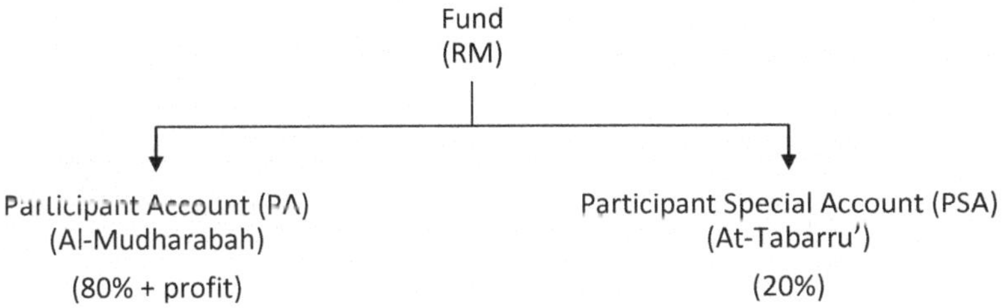

Fig. 12.1 Practicalities. (Source: Author's collection from TMB)

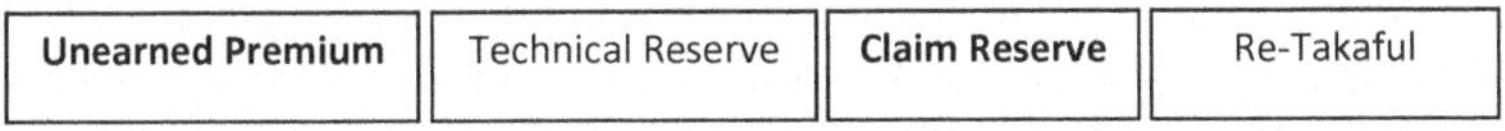

Fig. 12.2 Practicalities. (Source: Author's collection from TMB)

amount credited into the Participant's Account shall be invested by the operator in line with the principles of *Al-Mudharabah*. Then the profit will be shared between the operator and the participant according to the portion agreed for the month. The portion is not fixed and will change monthly according to the claim made by the participant in that month.

Further the amount segregated into the account of *Tabarru*' shall be subject to the allocation into the following avenues (Fig. 12.2).

But if there is no claim made by the participants, then the profit will be divided equally between the Takaful operator 60% and the participants 40%.

12.7 Experiences

Example 1
Mr Zaidi 30 years old, he bought a *Takaful* Medical policy. Then he made payment of RM 384 per annum as he chooses to participate in the Ehsan Package's plan 2. The payment will be put in the fund and the policy will only be renewed annually until Mr Zaidi arrives at the age of 70. The money will be separated into two accounts as outlined in the previous section. If he did not make any claim, he is entitled to get the profit according to the portion for that month. However, if he made any claim he cannot get any *Al-Mudharabah* profit from the investment.

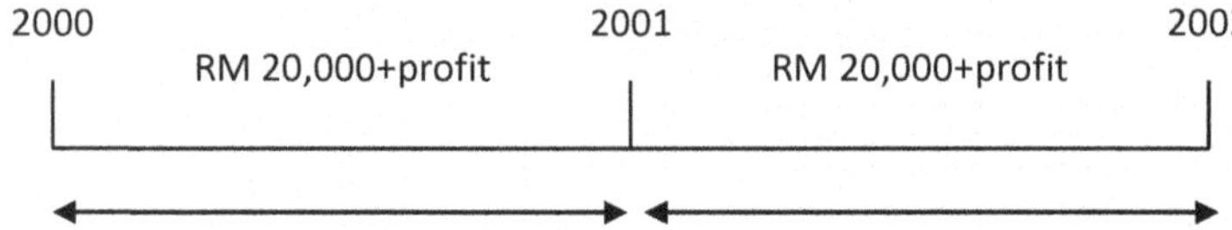

Fig. 12.3 Experiences. (Source: Author's collection from TMB)

Example 2
Mrs Safiah bought *Takaful* Hawa policy package A in January 2000. In July 2001 she suffered nerve cancer. So, after approval by the doctor she made a claim. She was entitled to get a lump-sum benefit of RM 20,000. She continued to renew the policy. However, in May 2002 she was infected by cervical cancer. Consequently, she made another claim for the additional lump-sum benefit. She managed to get RM 20,000 to cover her cancer treatment (Fig. 12.3).

12.8 Recommendations

The objective of both *Takaful* Medical and *Takaful* Hawa is to provide monetary benefit for participants. The individual as well as the community at large must grab the opportunity offered by the *Takaful* operator. Recently, these products have become a necessity in our life because we cannot foresee what will happen in the future. For instance, *Takaful* Hawa is specially designed for women. As we know, nowadays cancer frequently infects women. Treatment for cancer is costly and too expensive to afford by the patients. Moreover, the treatment also needs advanced medical technology with continuous use of expensive equipment. Therefore, with this product at least we have coverage to reduce the burden of hospital expenses faced by participants.

Nonetheless, through the observations we have made, we found that there are some issues that can be improved by the operator:

- Payment of hospital fees

The process of making claim for hospital expenses takes some time to be settled by the operator. The participants need to pay the expenses using their own money first, and then can only make the claim after receiving the bill. However, the benefits that that participants claim cannot be received immediately. They have to wait for one or two months. We suggest that the operator should back-date the procedure when making the claim, so that participants will not face difficulties in making a claim.

- Enhance promotion

Even though *Takaful* Malaysia (B) has been established for many years, people still lack information about *Takaful* products. The community still prefers to buy the conventional insurance rather than Islamic insurance. We recommend to the operator enhance promotion via media, both electronic and mass. In addition, the *Takaful* operator can sponsor any events such as charity work, motivation programmes and give scholarships to students. Thus, people will know more about the company.

- Limited coverage

Takaful Medical and *Takaful* Hawa only provide coverage for the individual who participates in the policy. These products do not cover the family members of the participants unless they also buy the products. Therefore, we propose that the operator can come out with new product that offers coverage for the participants and their family members.

12.9 Conclusion

Both *Takaful* Medical and *Takaful* Hawa are essential for the individual life. *Takaful* Medical provides financial benefits to the participants in order to pay medical fees such as ward, hospital fees and surgery expenses. While with *Takaful* Hawa the benefit will cover the medical costs for various cancer treatments. Allah the Almighty knows all the cures for disease. Thus, He creates the cure and leaves us to find it. Therefore, we should put some effort in order to seek out treatment. One of the ways is through participating in both products, which are *Takaful* Medical and *Takaful* Hawa. In addition, as vicegerents of Allah, we are responsible for our own health. In the knowledge of this, we have to take care of our soul and body to be accountable for what has been given to us.

References

1. Ali, A. Y. (n.d.), The Holy Qur'an, Text and Translation.
2. *Group Takaful Plan for Health Care*, *Takaful* Malaysia, *Takaful* Nasional, *Takaful* Ikhlas and others.
3. http.www.freepctools.com/ethics.htm
4. http.www.freepctools.com/ethics.htm

CHAPTER 13

Pilgrimage (Hajj) *Takaful*

13.1 Introduction

Takaful is an Islamic system of insurance which operates under the aegis of Shari'ah. It is defined as a policy of mutual co-operation, solidarity and brotherhood against unpredicted risk or catastrophes, in which the parties involved are expected to contribute genuinely. The purpose of this kind of co-operation is to protect participants against any burden, especially financial ones in case of accident, fire, death and so forth. In other words, the burden borne by someone due to any unpredicted risks will be alleviated through the contributions of the members. The practice of *Takaful* will not only assist the policyholder in a moment of hardship, but also instils and encourages the spirit of brotherhood among members. Every participant in the policy is indirectly responsible for helping and assisting one another. On top of that, *Takaful* insurance promotes the beauty of Islam to the outer world generally, and to non-Muslims specifically. *Takaful* for pilgrims is specially tailored to pilgrims and is only valid while they are performing pilgrimage. *Takaful* for pilgrims has been made compulsory for Malaysian pilgrims administered by Lembaga Tabung Haji, where

It is acknowledged that, the idea of this chapter/product is significantly contributed by the practices/experiences/thoughts of Bank Negara, Takaful Malaysia, Takaful Ikhlas, Takaful Nasional, Etiqa Takaful, IBFIM, IIUM, MII and others (Malaysia).

Mohd Ma'Sum Billah, *Islamic Insurance Products*,
https://doi.org/10.1007/978-3-030-17681-5_13

premium is included in the pilgrimage package payment. Different Takaful companies provide different packages and coverage for pilgrims. As for Bruneian pilgrims, Insurans Islam Taib (Brunei) provides a personal accident scheme for pilgrims. This scheme provides cover for pilgrims against personal accident resulting in death or permanent disability. Coverage includes compensation for any flight delay which exceed 12 consecutive hours in the course of the individual's pilgrimage.

13.2 Central Idea

No one in this world can run avoid all types of risk, disaster or catastrophe. Everyone's life, property or assets are subject to some sort of risk 24 hours a day, seven days a week. Thus, Shari'ah has provided a solution as precautionary steps against unpredicted risk. The practice recognised as *Takaful* is among the potential techniques which offer possible securities for someone who encounters risk. In case of pilgrimage, pilgrims are exposed to various kinds of risk, such as accident, delay of flight, loss of baggage and so forth. Such risks arise when huge numbers of Muslims worldwide gather to perform the Hajj. The place becomes so crowded and the possibility of incurring such risks as mentioned above is high.

In order to reduce the impact of such risks, one can apply for an insurance policy that offers protection against risks. For instance, among the *Takaful* operators that offer such policies are Tabung Haji, *Takaful* Malaysia, Insurans Taib, IBB, *Takaful* Nasional and so forth. Tabung Haji, in conjunction with Syarikat *Takaful* Malaysia, has created a *Takaful* policy for the pilgrims which covers the following risks:

- death due to accident
- death due to sunstroke
- theft or loss of money
- flight delay.

With the existence of such a policy, the pilgrimage activity appears to be more secure and Islamic. This kind of service may attract more Muslims around the globe to perform Hajj since the insurance provided is not against Shari'ah rules. Moreover, it is better for the Muslim to apply for Islamic insurance instead of using a conventional insurance policy.

13.3 Shari'ah Ruling

Takaful for pilgrimage is considered lawful as long as it does not contradict Shari'ah ruling. The purpose of this kind of policy is to provide assistance to the member against unpredicted risks while performing Hajj. Such co-operation is encouraged by Allah (swt), as stated in the Qur'an:

> Sustain a mutual co-operation among yourselves in righteousness and piety. (5:2)

In another part of Qur'an, Allah mentions that He has provided an easy life for believers and He does not want the believers to live in hardship. This statement can be applied in the practice of *Takaful* insurance for the pilgrimage. Insurance coverage will enable the pilgrims to be protected from unexpected risks while performing Hajj. As He mentioned in the Qur'an:

> Allah (swt) intends easy life for you while he does not want you to be in difficulties. (2:185)

The operations of *Takaful* must be in line with Shari'ah principles. This concept must be applied also in the practice of *Takaful* for pilgrimage. *Takaful* operations may be held void from the first place if any of its operations is proven to be opposing Shari'ah. For example, the *Takaful* practice must free from the element of *Riba* as mentioned by Allah (swt) in the Qur'an:

> Allah (swt) permitted trade while prohibiting *Riba*. (2:275)

The operation of *Takaful* also must be free from any element of fraud, for instance charging higher fees, being involved in bribery to increase profits, offering fake policies and so forth. Such deeds are prohibited by the Qur'an:

> O ye who believe! Do not consume your property among yourselves by way of unlawful means. (4:29)

By the above justification, *Takaful* for pilgrimage can be considered lawful and a necessity for pilgrims. This kind of policy offers both benefits for the *Takaful* operator and to the pilgrims against unpredicted risks.

13.4 Group *Takaful* Scheme for Pilgrimage Services

The *Takaful* Coverage Provided by Lembaga Tabung Haji in collaboration with *Takaful* National Pilgrims will be provided with the Takaful coverage 24 hours from checking in at Kompleks Haji, Tabung Haji or the last airport before they take off for Mecca. Cover will be automatically terminated 24 hours after they arrive at the last airport when returning home.

Personal Accident Group *Takaful* Scheme's benefits are coverage as follows:

1. Death or permanent disability caused by severe unintentional external accident which is free from other reasons which cause:
2. Death within 12 months from the accident (disability/physical injury)

   (a) Permanent handicap or disability (which is untreatable) within 12 months of the accident (disability/physical injury)
   (b) Death caused by heat stroke

3. Loss of money caused by theft or unintentional carelessness with evidence or witness
4. Flight delay caused by technical problems/damage and which is more than 12 hours. Maximum limit to be paid are only for three days or 72 hours only
5. Death khairat for burial expenses for death caused by accident or disease.

13.5 Distribution of Excess

If it happens that after the termination of Takaful coverage the scheme has some excess, it will be distributed among the participants and the company according to *Al-Mudharabah* principle as stated in the suggestion form and account according to agreed ratio of 50% to the participants and 50% to the company.

13.6 Compensation Category (Table 13.1)

Takaful benefit payment for physical disabilities is according to the percentages shown above. The maximum borne by the company for any transport accidents is RM 3,000,000 only.

13.7 Exception

The Takaful scheme does not give coverage/compensation for death or disabilities which are directly or indirectly caused by this event/accident:

- injury suffered from war
- self-inflicted injuries (intentionally), suicide (either felony or not), drunk, drugs, *sakit puan* (pregnancy-related illness) or any handicap or physical disability, giving birth or pregnancy
- travelling using flight other than ordinary licensed aircraft operated by airline services which use predetermined airport as a passenger who has paid for a ticket
- any disease
- Injuries related or caused by nuclear power, nuclear separation or nuclear weapon material (Table 13.2).

Table 13.1 Compensation category

	Scope	*Amount of* Takaful *Benefit (one person) (RM)*
i	Death caused by accident	10,000
ii	Death caused by heat stroke	3000
iii	Theft or loss of money	100
iv	Flight delay (a person on each delay)	50
v	Death khairat for burial expenses	1500

Source: Author's collection from TNB

Table 13.2 Benefits

Explanation of permanent disability	*Percentage of compensation paid (from the* Takaful *amount)*
Loss of both hands	100%
Loss of both legs	100%
Complete loss of eyesight in both eyes	100%
Complete loss of hearing in both ears	50%
Complete loss of sight in one eye	30%
Complete loss of hearing in one ear	10%
Loss of one arm from shoulder	60%
Loss of one arm between elbow and shoulder	50%
Loss of one arm below the elbow	45%
Loss of one arm between the elbow and wrist	40%
Loss of four fingers and a thumb of a hand	40%
Loss of four fingers of a hand	35%
Complete loss of a finger	25%
Complete loss of a forefinger	10%
Complete loss of a middle finger	6%
Complete loss of a finger (ring finger)	5%
Complete loss of a finger	4%
Loss of a leg from thigh	70%
Loss of a leg between knee and thigh	50%
Loss of a leg below the knee	35%
Loss of all fingers of a leg	15%
Loss of a toe (thumbnail)	5%
Loss of a toe	1%

Source: Author's collection from TNB

13.8 Conclusion

Takaful for pilgrimage has provided an alternative for pilgrims when choosing an insurance policy. Even though not all *Takaful* operators provides such a policy, at least it is a first positive step in developing and promoting the practice of *Takaful*. Moreover, *Takaful* operates within framework of Islamic law. Thus, it is far better for Muslims to select Islamic insurance rather than conventional policies. More Muslims might be impressed by such policies and may intend to perform a pilgrimage. Indirectly, the policy has led Muslims to good deeds. By this practice, it will promote the *Takaful* policy itself in the eyes of the world. This is because, during pilgrimage, Muslims from around the globe gather in one location to perform religious rites. The exchange of information between pilgrims will indirectly become a means of marketing *Takaful* policy. Thus, every *Takaful* operator should ensure excellent performance in order to give better picture of *Takaful* itself. *Takaful* for pilgrimage has provided a better service in terms of risk management for pilgrims. It is important for pilgrims since the possibility of incurring risk during pilgrimage is high. Thus by this service, the losses that might be borne resulting from these risks can be reduced.

References

1. Ali, A. Y. (n.d.), The Holy Qur'an, Text and Translation.
2. *Pilgrimage (Hajj) Takaful Plan*, *Takaful* Malaysia, *Takaful* Nasional, *Takaful* Ikhlas and others.

CHAPTER 14

Hajj Badal (Substitute Hajj) *Takaful*

14.1 Introduction

Tabung Haji is an elite organisation that co-ordinates all pilgrimage. It has been in the business for more than 40 years and has achieved world recognition in several areas for its competitive, comprehensive and quality services in Hajj management. This organisation has been recognised as a world-class model in other countries, which have been inspired to imitate its success. It has required huge effort to achieve such high value in positioning Lembaga Tabung Haji in the front line of successful corporate organisations in the country.

Among the facilities and services it offers are:

- providing passport for pilgrimage
- management of pilgrimage affairs
- health services
- courses on performing pilgrimage
- transport to and from the Holy Land
- protection, supervision, welfare and security to pilgrims at the Holy Land.

It is acknowledged that, the idea of this chapter/product is significantly contributed by the practices/experiences/thoughts of Bank Negara, Takaful Malaysia, Takaful Ikhlas, Takaful Nasional, Etiqa Takaful, IBFIM, IIUM, MII and others (Malaysia).

Mohd Ma'Sum Billah, *Islamic Insurance Products*,
https://doi.org/10.1007/978-3-030-17681-5_14

Hajj guidance is performed in many ways to help pilgrims have a full understanding of pilgrimage requirements, proper performance of compulsory and commendable religious rituals, forbidden practices during pilgrimage, healthcare and related matters, culture and lifestyle in the Holy Land, welfare and related matters, problem-solving, visits to historical sites and places of significance to Islam—thereby maximising their opportunity to perform a successful and fulfilling pilgrimage. The guidance is also aimed at minimising risks of being on the wrong side of the Saudi Arabian law and prevents untoward incidents due to pilgrim negligence and ignorance of safety matters. Tabung Haji organises preliminary and intensive courses on the Hajj nationwide. Such an approach helps pilgrims to have direct interaction with course facilitators, thus making information spread more effective and efficient. Dissemination of information is also done through mass media such as a series of articles in mainstream news outlets and on air (radio and television) guidance programmes.

To ensure effective and quality presentation of lectures, each course facilitator is sent for special training that covers comprehensive aspects, from content of courses to presentation of lectures, handling of enquiries and interacting with course participants. Guidelines for Performing Hajj for Weakness candidates. These guidelines are set out for every candidate that falls sick before they have reached Mecca and also for those who are going to perform the Hajj. If such undue circumstances occur, the performer has to make any necessary effort according to the sickness and the types of Hajj performed.

14.2 Conditions of Hajj Badal

In pilgrimage activities, there is the verb *Dharurat* (allowed by Shari'ah), which carries the meaning of something that prevents pilgrims from performing the pilgrimage courses. *Dharurat* is allowed in Islam and those who are infected by disease are exempted from paying *dam* and this is not a sinful thing. The law comprises all types of *ibadah* in either pilgrimage or *umrah*. *Dharurat* is a kind of *rukhsyah* (way to facilitate) that is given by Allah to each one of His subjects. For example, in a very bad situation (*musyaqqah*) every man has an opportunity either to proceed with the deeds according to the given solutions or follow the simple methods (*rukhsyah*), as has been posited by Prophet Muhammad (saw). The deeds are still valid under Islam. Another example is that while performing prayer, one of the pillars is to stand still but if he or she has a disease that prevents them from standing straight, they still can perform prayer by simply sitting on the floor or lying down facing the *kiblat*. Therefore, their prayer is still accepted by *syarak*. It is almost the same while fasting in Ramadhan. Those who are not able to abstain from taking the food or anything that would break the fast are allowed to move their fast to another day or just pay *fidyah* to the needy.

In performing pilgrimage and *umrah* there are many elements of *Dharurat*. For example, someone who is completely able in terms of his financial capabilities or healthy condition is encouraged and required to perform the pilgrimage. Those who are not able in the above matters or who are suffering from any disease that has no hope of recovery are allowed to seek someone who perform pilgrimage in their place. Pilgrimage is still valid in this scenario, especially for those who need someone to represent them by performing Hajj Badal. The conditions under which someone is allowed to perform Hajj Badal will be explained in detail below.

14.2.1 Sickness Rendering a Person Unable to Throw Jumrah

Throwing *Jumrah* is the only action that can be represented by others, instead performing *Wukuf*, *Tawaf*, *Saie*, shaving one's hair and stay overnight night in Mina or Muzdalifah. There are several ways to counter the problem, including:

If the pilgrim is badly injured so meaning that he or she is unable to throw *Jumrah* then they can be represented by other people within certain rules, as stated below.

- If the pilgrim is badly sick and with no chance of recovery for at least one to four days (from 10 Zulhijjah intil 13 Zuhijjah) and if the action could affect the life of performer.
- The representatives should be among those who are loyal and *amanah* with the right of others. The most important thing is that the representative should settle the throw for himself first before representing on behalf of others. Any child who has achieved puberty is also allowed to become the representative of a sick person.
- Pilgrims are reminded to look into themselves before representing the actions for others. It is because *Tahallul* is only accepted after the throwing of *Jumrah* is perfectly done. The representative should confirm that the pilgrims are truly not in a good condition. It is sug-

gested that throwing *Jumrah* is done day by day. The pilgrims should not perform the *Tahallul* until the representatives have settled the throwing of *Jumrah*.

- After the representative has finished performing the throw on behalf of another, he or she needs to inform the represented people so that the pilgrims will continue with other required obligations. It has to be known that the last day possible for throwing *Jumrah* is before the evening of 13 Zulhijjah.

14.3 Guidelines for Seeking Representatives

This duty could be given to any close relative such as to husband or adult children. If the family is not able to find someone to act on their behalf, the duty will be transferred to the Committee of Tabung Haji. The committee will find someone to be representative of that family. Basically, the family will be charged a certain amount of money as *diyah* to the representatives, with the consent and negotiation with both parties. Before the representatives take the place of the family member, there should be an agreement or *Ijab* and *Qabul* between these parties. The recitation of *Ijab* and *Qabul* is as follows:

> I want you to represent me to perform the *Jumrah* on behalf of myself.

It is followed by the representative by saying:

> I accept on your behalf to represent you to perform *Jumrah*.

14.3.1 Sickness Rendering Someone Unable to Carry Out Tawaf and Saie

Performing of *Tawaf* and *Saie* may not be represented by others even though the performers in question are not in good health. Therefore, in whatever conditions the performers are required perform these actions themselves because both *Tawaf* and *Saie* are the pillars of *ibadah*.

A common way to overcome these problems is by using a wheelchair to perform *Saie*. The charges imposed are different according to the size of our body. The minimum cost for the service is only RM 50. The safest way to use a wheelchair is by sitting properly and the hand holding the bars tightly. Those who are not able to sit can lay down with their legs facing the front. It is recommended that the family members follow the person in such a condition in order to ensure that the *Tawaf* is completed within seven rounds.

14.3.2 Sickness Rendering Someone Unable to Stay Overnight at Muzdalifah and Mina

Even though staying at Muzdalifah and Mina may not be carried out by others on someone's behalf, there are several groups who are allowed to do so:

- performers are afraid of their own safety or their wealth;
- those who are accompanying sick people;
- those who have difficulty staying overnight.

14.4 Guidelines of Hajj Badal

- The person who is representing others should complete the required obligations for himself.
- The representatives should only represent one person for one pilgrimage season.
- For a representative who is staying in Mecca, it is compulsory to be outside the Miqat pilgrims or closer to the Miqat.
- The representatives should perform for the pilgrims as they do for themselves. Prophet Muhammad (saw) said: From Laqit bin Amir: "My father is very old, not able to follow people to perform pilgrims and not even able to walk with others" and Prophet Muhammad (saw) replied "Perform the pilgrims for you and umrah for him." (*Sunan Abu Daud and Tarmizi*)

14.5 Health Examination

A full health examination is very important for every pilgrim in order to provide supplementary educational information at the Holy Land. Therefore, Tabung Haji has set up a proper health plan with the cooperation of the Health Ministry. The representatives of pilgrims are only allowed to represent someone after the pilgrims have been certified by doctors. The relevant pilgrims will receive proper medication in prevention of fatal diseases such as Meningococcol Meningitis Quadrivalent.

Furthermore, Hajj Badal can only be allowed after doctors confirm that prospective pilgrims suffer from chronic diseases that can be treated and their health condition is stable before their scheduled departure by identifying types of medication and treatments required. It is not easy for Tabung Haji to get a full overview of a pilgrim's health. With proper medical records and sufficient medical references it will be much easier to the Tabung Haji to perceive any problem. So, Tabung Haji will prepare for the sick pilgrims with the assistance to complete the pilgrimage including providing services for Hajj Badal.

Every year, there will be new cases that need proper attention by Tabung Haji. Health procedures are very important because some pilgrims have been identified as having mental disturbance, unsound minds that do not allow them to complete the pilgrimage. Tabung Haji also needs to properly identify all pilgrims because many of them are old and unfit to perform certain pillars of pilgrimage.

A health examination can only be conducted at government hospitals or panel clinics of Tabung Haji. The cost of the medical examination at the panel clinic will be borne by the pilgrims.

14.6 Methods of Examination

There are two stages of medical examination:

Prospective pilgrims age 60 years and over need to undergo medical examination between six months and ten months before departure to the Holy Land, to:

- identify their health status, including mental and physical fitness and dietary needs for early detection of ailments due to age factors. They need more time to adapt to today's healthcare practice and treatment as part of preparation for their pilgrimage;
- identify high-risk groups to enable early treatment;
- identify special treatment procedures, equipment and medications for those with chronic diseases.

Other pilgrims are required to undergo medical examination three months before their scheduled departure. Pilgrims are divided into three groups:

- all pilgrims selected for the coming Hajj season
- pilgrims on a stand-by list
- follow-up treatments for pilgrims aged 60 years and above.

Pilgrims who fail their medical examination and need follow-up treatments are required to undergo a final round of medical examinations. In some cases, pilgrims need to seek a specialist's opinion in determining their health status and fitness to perform the pilgrimage.

Those who are really determined to perform the pilgrimage despite failing their medical examination can submit their appeal to the Appeal Committee through Tabung Haji state office. The state office will call for the Appeal Committee to look into the appeal on a case by case basis. Decisions are made through discussion and not by the individual committee members.

If the appeal is turned down, the affected pilgrims will have no choice but to postpone their departure.

14.7 A Study on Pilgrims After Pilgrimage

Based on Table 14.1, those who have performed the pilgrimage more than once might have wider view, especially in terms of giving opinions, and their life was even well managed or perfect. Of them, 97.5% wanted to be a role model for society. Some of the pilgrims felt that their materialistic desires had reduced drastically after coming back from the Holy Land; 96.3% agreed with that statement. Meanwhile, 87.2% of pilgrims felt that their spending behaviour was slightly reduced after pilgrimage. Most of them thought that now is the perfect time to improve their *ibadah*. Besides, 99.3% of pilgrims are now giving full attention to the family needs, including food, clothing and better shelter in order to obtain perfection in life. Furthermore, from the responses given by the pilgrims it is evident that there are various positive reactions and improvements in their life afterwards. This statement is strongly supported by the evidence outlined in Table 14.2.

Table 14.1 A study on pilgrims after pilgrimage

No.	*Types of changes*	*Percentage (%)*
1.	To be a role model	97.5
2.	To attract others to make changes	87.6
3.	To protect family interests	99.3
4.	Reduction in seeking excessive materials	96.3
5.	Be more humble	98.8

Source: Author's collection from TMB and TH

Table 14.2 Changes between repeat pilgrimage and life improvement of pilgrims

No	*Type of changes*	*Percentage (%)*
1	Positive improvement	93.4
2	Remain unchanged	5.0
3	No feedback	1.6

Source: Author's collection from TMB

These data show that there is a close ship between those who have been to Mecca more than once and their enhancement in doing good deeds. Of pilgrims, 93.4% have a strong desire to be humbler, or put simply, they are totally different when compared to their life before. These improvements might come from good guidelines by the Tabung Haji in preparing the pilgrims before they go to Mecca. From the research it is also clear that in the cases of those who failed to change even after second time they went to the Holy Land, it is simply because their sources of income contained bad elements that could affect the pilgrimage. Only 1.6% of the pilgrims did not give feedback. Furthermore, other research regarding the changes of attitude after pilgrimage says that most of the repeat pilgrims are directly involved with the activities of local community, especially in attending congregational prayer at the mosque. In addition, some of them represent the community as the ***imam***, ***bilal*** or ***khatib***. After performing pilgrimage two or three times, pilgrims readily attend a ceremony which is held by their neighbours. Furthermore, 94.4% of them attend marriages frequently, followed by other activities such as the Nuzul Al Qur'an ceremony or Maulidur Rasul Celebration.

Following pilgrimage, the spirit of the neighbourhood is also enhanced among the community, which is required by Islamic teachings.

14.8 Conclusion

This chapter presents the implication of Tabung Haji plan for people who want to perform Hajj Badal. The issue can be treated from a social-economic perspective, in terms of family and the community and also from the economy perspective. From the social-economic perspective, Hajj Badal does not have any bad implications for pilgrims, their family and their society. In other ways, there are positive implications too, as there will be more savings from potential pilgrims that the main financial resources to perform Hajj, the improvement of the positive life value and involvement in society's activities. From the economic perspective, the amount of pilgrims that perform Hajj Badal is smaller and not worrying even though there are flow sign that it will be increase. The country's expenses from the cash outflow for the pilgrims who perform Hajj Badal are also very small.

References

1. Ali, A. Y. (n.d.), The Holy Qur'an, Text and Translation.
2. *Haj Badal Takaful Plan*, *Takaful* Malaysia, *Takaful* Nasional, *Takaful* Ikhlas and others.

CHAPTER 15

Ziarah (Visit) *Takaful*

15.1 Introduction

In our era, life is getting easier due to all the technological advances. People can manage their life in a more structured way, both economically and socially. With the infrastructure available, people can achieve things that it was once impossible to do. For example, long ago, people had to walk or sail from one continent to another in order to get there. But with the development of the human brain, they have managed to create a machine that can fly in the sky, known as an aeroplane. By aeroplane, people manage to travel to other places located far from their own country. Distance is getting less; time is saved if a person uses an aeroplane as their mode of transport. This facility has allowed people to go on vacation and spend their holiday time locally or abroad.

The purpose of vacation is to widen one's knowledge and experience in life. It is good practice for everyone because it can create consciousness about how wide this world is. For a Muslim, this practice will strengthen his/her faith and piety to Allah (swt). Moreover, Islam encourages its followers to perform *umrah* and visitations. In truth, performing *umrah* and

It is acknowledged that, the idea of this chapter/product is significantly contributed by the practices/experiences/thoughts of Bank Negara, Takaful Malaysia, Takaful Ikhlas, Takaful Nasional, Etiqa Takaful, IBFIM, IIUM, MII and others (Malaysia).

Mohd Ma'Sum Billah, *Islamic Insurance Products*,
https://doi.org/10.1007/978-3-030-17681-5_15

visitations is easy for those who are capable in terms of money, because it requires a person to spend quite a large amount. But with a structured and disciplined savings plan, everybody is able to perform these things.

In Malaysia, *Takaful* Malaysia Berhad has taken an initiative to help Malaysian citizens by offering them a product that is known as the Ziarah *Takaful* Plan or Tour *Takaful* Plan. The Ziarah *Takaful* Plan can help the participant to gather funds to pay their expenses on vacation or holidays and *umrah* for the whole family. This chapter will discuss in detail the Ziarah *Takaful* Plan and how it will benefit participants.

15.2 The Ziarah *Takaful* Plan

The Ziarah *Takaful* Plan is one of the products under Family *Takaful* that has been offered by Syarikat *Takaful* Malaysia Bhd. It has been available ever since *Takaful* Malaysia became operational. This plan is suitable for those who often travel or enjoy a relaxing domestic or overseas holiday. This plan also is offered to those who want to perform *umrah* or Hajj. Recently, *Takaful* Malaysia Berhad has come out with a new product that is known as the Hajj *Takaful* Plan. This plan is separate from the Ziarah *Takaful* Plan, which is a combination of Ziarah *Takaful* and Hajj *Takaful*. Therefore, those who want to go on pilgrimage do not have to deal directly with *Takaful* Malaysia. Instead, they will be represented by Lembaga Tabung Haji as their agent to deal with *Takaful* Malaysia.

Ziarah *Takaful* is a long-term savings programme with a purpose to help the participant to plan their savings by instalment for a period, until they are sufficient to cover the expenses for the holiday or vacation and visitation for the whole family. Even if this collective fund is not spent for the purpose of vacation, holiday or visitation, it is still considered the contributor's property as a future saving for themselves and their family.

The most important thing to note is that those who like to go on holiday or vacation and visitation should apply for the Ziarah *Takaful* Plan because all these activities require a lot of money, especially for those who want to bring their family together. Therefore, having savings in the Ziarah *Takaful* Plan is one of the solutions available to the participant in order to have the opportunity to travel locally or abroad. The Takaful fund is paid by instalments and it will be a collective fund that is enough to cover the expenses of the participant. They only have to choose the right package in accordance with their financial capacity.

15.3 Requirements of *Takaful* Ziarah

15.3.1 Participant

It must be understood that the party responsible for the arrangement of the plan is the participant himself. It is in accordance to the term 'invitation to treat' where the participant offer to *Takaful* operator whether they want to sell their product to them. This is shown in Fig. 15.1.

To ensure that all things are set out in the right way, the participant is responsible for making payments or the premiums to *Takaful* Malaysia Berhad or to any of its branches according to the date agreed.

15.3.2 Scope of Coverage

The scope of coverage under the Ziarah *Takaful* Plan is mentioned in the *Takaful* Malaysia Berhad brochures and handouts. This plan gives 24-hour coverage, whether it is within office hours or not, and no matter where we are in the world.

15.3.3 Participation in the Ziarah Takaful *Plan*

Takaful Ziarah can be participated in by all individuals between the ages of 18 and 55 years old at the date of entry. If the participant has reached more than 55 years old, they no longer are allowed to participate or renew the plan coverage period.

15.3.4 Information on the Participant

The participant must co-operate with the *Takaful* operator in order to give detailed information requested by the company. Participants have to follow the format that has been stated in the proposal for participation

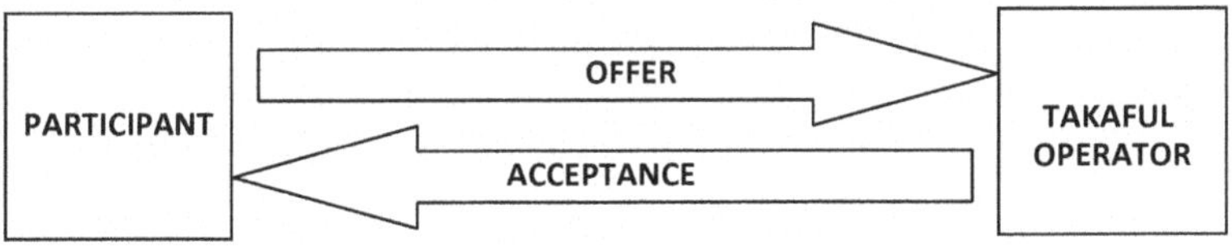

Fig. 15.1 Participant. (Source: Author's collection from TMB)

given by the *Takaful* company. Generally, the most important information that is required is as stated below:

- name of participant
- identity card no.
- date of birth
- occupation.

15.3.5 Specialities of the Ziarah Takaful *Plan*

The most apparent difference between the Ziarah *Takaful* Plan and other Takaful plans is that the Ziarah *Takaful* plan is the only product of *Takaful* Malaysia that covers the funeral expenses of the participant. In Life Takaful and Health *Takaful* Plan, there is coverage for any accident or the death of the participant, but it must be understood that those plans never provide any coverage for funeral expenses. Under the Ziarah *Takaful* Plan, if a participant is travelling or on vacation in another country, such as in United States of America, and encounter a tragic accident and happens to die, then the *Takaful* company will cover the expense of bringing back the body of the deceased and delivering it to their family. Even if a person never goes on holiday or travels to other places, they can still participate in the Ziarah *Takaful* Plan to get the benefit of the funeral expenses being covered. They can still get coverage if they happen to die in their home. The money will be used for funeral expenses and the balance will be given to the heirs.

In addition, by participating in the Ziarah *Takaful* Plan, a person can plan their holiday, vacation and visitation expenses through the facility of benefit withdrawal every five years. It also can guide the participant to have a disciplined saving account for a period of time in accordance with the participant's ability. Besides, as has been stated above, it prepares the benefit such as a death rider in event of the death of the participant or when the participant is handicapped in such a way that it stops him from performing his work. The Ziarah *Takaful* Plan also covers the medical expenses of a participant caused by an accident. Last but not least, the profits will be shared among the participants, following *Al-Mudharabah* principle.

15.4 Benefits of the Ziarah *Takaful* Plan

First, the participant must know the package amount of the premium that needs to be charged by the Takaful operator. All these depend on the financial capacity of the participant and the total amount that is needed by the participant for his interest on vacation, visitation, *umrah* and so on. If the participant wishes to pay the premium by monthly investment instead of by lump sum, the minimum amount to be paid by the participant to the Takaful operator is RM 50, and it can be increased to RM 100, RM 200, RM 150, RM 250, RM 300, RM 400 and RM 500. All these are by increments of RM 50, while RM 500 is the maximum monthly instalment. As with other products offered by the Syarikat *Takaful* Malaysia Berhad, under the Family Takaful plan, with the maturity period that already exists, all the premiums that have been paid by the participant will be divided into two accounts. The first account is the Participant Account (PA) and the other is the Participant Special Account (PSA). Most of the amount of the premiums will be credited to the PA, while the balance of the premium will be credited to the SPA as *Tabarru'* or donation that will be used by Takaful operator cover any claims for all Family Takaful participant.

All the benefits or amount of money that will be received by the participant are based on the package amount of Takaful instalment per month that has been chosen by them. The general benefits of Ziarah *Takaful* Plan are expenses to bring back the body, funeral expenses, medical expenses, accident, withdrawal and cumulative withdrawal.

15.4.1 Package at RM 50

If the participant chooses to pay RM 50 as his instalment package per month and if there is death during the period, the heirs of the participant will received the PA with the profit received from the investment or *Al-Mudharabah*, plus the balance of the premium that the participant should pay starting from the month he paid until the maturity date. Furthermore, the participant's heirs will get funeral expenses of RM 1000 and if the participant died outside the country while travelling, they will received RM 3000 and RM 1500 for Peninsular/Sabah, Sarawak.

If the participant did not die but is totally and permanently disabled, which means that he or she is unable to work, the participant will received the PA with the profit received from the investment or *Al-Mudharabah*, plus the balance of the premium that the participant paid until the maturity date.

If the participant is on his journey of vacation, holidays, visitation, ***umarah*** and so forth, and the participant needs any medical treatment due to an accident only, the Takaful operator covers the room charge and the treatment. In addition to this, the Takaful operator will cover the transport costs for the participant to return home either inside or outside the country. The amount that will be covered by the Takaful operator within the country is RM 1000 and RM 2000 for outside the country.

If the participant suffers any accident either while travelling or not, the participant will receive an amount of the total premium for a year multiplied by the number of maturity years. In case of withdrawal, the participant is allowed to withdraw his money and the amount of withdrawal is based on the maturity year that has been chosen by the participant. For five years, the maximum amount to be withdrawn is RM 2000, for 10 years it is RM 2500, for 15 years RM 3000 and for 20 years the participant can withdraw the maximum amount of the balance of the PA. The cumulative withdrawal for five years is RM 2000, for ten years it is RM 4500, for 15 years RM 7500. For 20 years, the participant can withdraw at the maximum amount of the balance of the PA.

15.4.2 Package at RM 100

If the participant chooses to pay RM 100 as his instalment package per month and if there is death during the period, the heirs of the participant will received the PA with the profit received from the investment or *Al-Mudharabah*, plus the balance of the premium that the participant should pay starting from the month he has not paid until the maturity date. Furthermore, the participant's heirs will receive funeral expenses of RM 1000 and if the participant died while travelling abroad, the heirs will receive RM 6000 and RM 3000 for Peninsular/Sabah, Sarawak.

As above, if the participant did not die but is totally and permanently disabled, which means that he or she is unable to work, the participant will received the PA with the profit received from the investment or *Al-Mudharabah*, plus the balance of the premium that the participant paid until the maturity date. If the participant is on vacation, holidays, visitation, ***umarah*** or the like, and the participant needs any medical treatment due to accident, the Takaful operator covers the room charge and treatment. In addition, the Takaful operator will cover transport costs for the participant to return home either from inside or outside the country. The amount covered by the Takaful operator within the country is RM 1500 and RM 3000 for outside the country. If the participant suffers any accident either while travelling or not, the participant will receive an amount of the total premium for a year times the maturity years.

In case of withdrawal, the participant is allowed to withdraw his money and the amount of withdrawal is based on the maturity year that has been chosen by the participant. For five years, the maximum amount to be withdrawn is RM 4000, for ten years it is RM 5000, for 15 years RM 6000 and for 20 years the participant can withdraw the maximum amount of the balance of the PA. The cumulative withdrawal for five years is RM 4000, for ten years it is RM 9000, for 15 years it is RM 15000. For 20 years, the participant can withdraw the maximum amount of the balance of the PA.

15.4.3 Package at RM 150

If the participant chooses to pay RM 150 as his instalment package per month and if there is a death during the period, the heirs of the participant will receive the PA with the profit received from the investment or *Al-Mudharabah*, plus the balance of the premium that the participant should pay starting from the month he has not paid until the maturity date. Further, the participant's heirs will get funeral expenses of RM 1000 and if the participant dies outside the country while travelling, the heirs will receive RM 9000 and RM 4500 for Peninsular/Sabah, Sarawak.

If the participant does not die but is permanently disabled, all arrangements are as with the previous two policies as outlined above. However, in this case the amount that will be covered by the Takaful operator within the country is RM 2000 and RM 4000 for outside the country.

If the participant suffers any accident either while travelling or not, the participant will receive an amount of the total premium for a year multiplied by the number of maturity years. In case of withdrawal, the participant is allowed to withdraw his money and the amount of withdrawal is based on the maturity year that has been chosen by the participant. For five years, the maximum amount that can be withdrawn is RM 6000, for ten years the figure is RM 7500, for 15 years it is RM 9000 and for 20 years the participant can withdraw the full balance of the PA. The cumulative withdrawal for five years is RM 2000, for ten years it is RM 4500, for 15 years it is RM 7500. For 20 years, the participant can withdraw the full amount of the balance of the PA.

15.4.4 *Package of RM 200*

If the participant chooses to pay RM 200 as his instalment package per month and if there is a death during the period, the heirs of the participant will receive the PA with the profit received from the investment or *Al-Mudharabah*, plus the balance of the premium that the participant should pay starting from the month he has not paid until the maturity date. Further, the participant's heirs will get funeral expenses of RM 1000 and if the participant dies outside the country while travelling, the heirs will receive RM 12,000 and RM 6000 for Peninsular/ Sabah, Sarawak.

If the participant does not die but is permanently disabled, all arrangements are as with the previous three policies as outlined above. However, in this case the amount that will be covered by the *Takaful* operator within the country is RM 2500 and RM 5000 for outside the country.

If the participant suffers any accident either while travelling or not, the participant will receive an amount of the total premium for a year multiplied by the number of maturity years. In case of withdrawal, the participant is allowed to withdraw his money and the amount of withdrawal is based on the maturity year that has been chosen by the participant. For five years the maximum amount that can be withdrawn is RM 8000, for ten years it is RM 10,000, for 15 years the figure is RM 120,000 and for 20 years the participant can withdraw the full balance of the PA. The cumulative withdrawal for five years is RM 8000, for ten years RM 18,000, for 15 years RM 30,000. For 20 years, the participant can withdraw the whole balance of the PA.

Packages at RM 300, 400 and 500 are similar.

15.5 Mode of Payment

There are five ways for the participants to pay the premium instalment every month:

15.5.1 *Salary Deduction*

Most of the companies have these facilities where they will deduct the amount of money and the money will be credited to the Participant Account. This kind of facility is usually offered by the big and established organisation.

15.5.2 Standing Instruction

This means is for the participant whose employer is not offering them salary deduction operation. The participant himself will ask the bank of his savings account to transfer the premium instalment to the *Takaful* operator. For example, the amount of the premium is RM 100. The bank will charge RM 3 for bank charges. Therefore, the amount to be debited from the participant account savings is RM 103.

15.5.3 GIRO or Any Other Bank

The participant has to mention and confirmed the savings account that they will use to the *Takaful* operator for example, BSN, BIMB or any other bank. For BSN and BIMB, these two banks will not charge anything to both parties.

15.5.4 Cheque and Cash

Credit card or charges.

15.6 Qur'anic Ayat and Hadith

There are many Qur'anic *ayat* and hadith related to this chapter. It explained the importance and the validity of Family *Takaful* including the Ziarah *Takaful* Plan. As we know, the purpose of Family *Takaful* is not to ensure an individual's life but it is one of the ways to provide financial security to our family.

Allah (swt) mentions in the Qur'an:

> Our Lord! Give us comfortable life in this world and comfortable in the hereafter.

Therefore, from this *ayat* we should understand that Allah S.W.T encourage us to lead a good life in whatever ways as long as it follows the rule of Shari'ah.

As stated in the Qur'an by Allah (swt):

> Sustain in mutual co-operation among yourselves in righteousness and piety. (5:2)

In terms of Family *Takaful* policy, it ensures joint co-operation among policyholders, and eventually will generate close feeling towards others, which will bring good impact onto each other. Offering the Ziarah *Takaful* Plan is one of the initiatives designed to make sure that a society or an individual does not have to face any difficulties or hardships alone. It will result in a comfortable and easy life. As mentioned in the Qur'an:

> Allah (swt) intends an easy life for all of you while he does not want you to be in difficulties. (al-Qu'ran)

15.7 Conclusion

From this chapter, we can see that the Ziarah *Takaful* Plan is focused on the welfare of the family as a whole rather than benefit for individuals only. We have shared our understanding of the details of the scope of coverage, its duration, the proposals and declaration needed from participants, the minimum numbers required for participation, age limit, contribution, mode of payment and so on.

The various products offered under Family Takaful are largely similar in terms of their characteristics and there are no significant differences among them. But we should note that only the Ziarah *Takaful* Plan provides the expenses for bringing back a body from anywhere and covers funeral costs. All these products are centred on giving priority to the family and giving them financial security, whenever something unexpected might happen.

This plan is well known among Malaysians. Some individuals have applied for it and it brings them many benefits. This plan is not limited to the Muslim community only, but it is also open to non-Muslims. Nowadays, non-Muslims also can distinguish the differences between conventional and Islamic insurance. They have found that there are many elements in conventional insurance which bring them many disadvantages. By using Islamic insurance, they can secure more benefits and advantages, not just in terms of money but also in terms of social relationships among the people.

We believe that by using the Ziarah *Takaful* Plan we will be more assured and have no doubt that this plan is one of the most important tools available to ensure good quality of life.

References

1. Ali, A. Y. (n.d.), The Holy Qur'an, Text and Translation.
2. *Ziarah Takaful Plan*, *Takaful* Malaysia, *Takaful* Nasional, *Takaful* Ikhlas and others.

CHAPTER 16

Group Islamic Cashline *Takaful*

16.1 Introduction

Insurance is one of the measures adopted in modern times for the organisation of economy and finance. It plays a key role in industrial development as well as in large-scale organisation of commerce, industry and agriculture. In some areas, it is considered to be more important than banking. Insurance is also a necessity for individuals to protect their dependants and family members. The term insurance, in its real sense, means community pooling, that is, to alleviate the burden of the individual. The simplest and most general conception of insurance is provision made by a group of persons, each singly in danger of loss, the incidence of which cannot be foreseen, that when such loss shall occur to any of them it shall be distributed over the whole group (Insurance, in EB (11th edition), Vol. 14, p. 656). The organisation of insurance under the Islamic system is called *Takaful*. The operation of *Takaful* is in line with the rules and regulations of Shari'ah. This insurance concept is grounded in Islamic *Muamalat*, and it has been practiced for over 1400 years.

It is acknowledged that, the idea of this chapter/product is significantly contributed by the practices/experiences/thoughts of Bank Negara, Takaful Malaysia, Takaful Ikhlas, Takaful Nasional, Etiqa Takaful, IBFIM, IIUM, MII and others (Malaysia).

Mohd Ma'Sum Billah, *Islamic Insurance Products*,
https://doi.org/10.1007/978-3-030-17681-5_16

Takaful is defined as a mutual arrangement between parties in which they agree to provide material assistance to one another or a group, in time of a misfortune. The agreement also stipulates that each party shall first agree on the form of contribution, which will be utilised later on the basis of mutual benefits (www.*Takaful*-ikhlas.com.my). The concepts of co-operation, protection and responsibility are merged and implemented together in the *Takaful* scheme. This illustrates that the scheme fulfils the spirit of Islamic Jurisprudence (Shari'ah), and this will certainly bring out the beauty of Islam, which is more practical than conventional insurance (not permitted in Islam). The next section will essentially discuss the Ikhlas Group Islamic Cashline *Takaful* Scheme, which is under family *Takaful* of *Takaful* Ikhlas. *Takaful* Ikhlas is one of the main *Takaful* operators in Malaysia. A subsidiary of the Malaysian National Reinsurance Bhd or Malaysian Re, *Takaful* Ikhlas is strongly capitalised to ensure its ability to meet its promises to customers, and to offer assurance of reliability to its business partners (www.*Takaful*-ikhlas.com.my).

16.2 Preview

Takaful Ikhlas operates its business to conform to the rules prescribed by Shari'ah. It exempts all elements that are not in accordance with the Islamic principles such as *Gharar*, which means there are unknown or uncertain factors, for instance the subject matter in the operation of a contract. The subject matter of a contract must be definite, clear and transparent so that the participant and the *Takaful* operator know this to be the case. The obligations and responsibilities under the contract also should be clear to both parties.

However, under conventional insurance, the participant has to pay certain amount of premiums and in turn the insurance company guarantees to pay a certain amount of protection to the participant in the event of misfortune, but how the amount of the coverage is derived is not known. The second element is *Maisir* or gambling, which arises as a consequence of the presence of *Gharar*. The element of gambling exists when the profitability of the policy is affected by the "underwriting" experience where the profits gained or the losses incurred are considered as a result of probability or chance. The last element that should not be incorporated in *Takaful* plans is *Riba* or interest, since it breaches the rules of the Shari'ah. Fundamentally, Muslim jurists have concluded that *Takaful* plans should be implemented based on mutual co-operation or *Ta'awun*, responsibility, assurance, common interest, protection, solidarity and assistance between groups of participants. Allah (swt) has mentioned in the Qur'an that Muslims should assist each other:

> Assist one another in the doing of good and righteousness. Assist not one another in sin and transgression, but keep your duty to Allah. (Al-Mai'dah: 2)

The *Takaful* system also should be practised based on the concept of *Takaful*, that is, a contract among a group of participants who agree to mutually guarantee among themselves against loss or damage that may happen to any of them. Besides that, the transactional aspect of the commercial activities of *Takaful* must also be based on the profit-sharing principle of *Al-Mudharabah*. Here, the *Takaful* operator will accept payment of the *Takaful* instalments from participants who act as *Sahibul Mal*. In order to eliminate the element of uncertainty in the *Takaful* plan, the concept of *Tabarru'* should be incorporated into the *Takaful* system. In essence therefore, the provision of insurance cover as a form of business in conformity with Shari'ah is based on the Islamic principles of *Takaful* and *Al-Mudharabah* (http://www.islamic-world.net/economic/*Takaful*/*Takaful*.html).

16.3 The Product

Under Ikhlas Group Islamic Cashline *Takaful* Scheme, the operator provides *Takaful* protection to settle the outstanding loan amount that the participant obtained from any financial institutions, banks or creditors company. Essentially, this scheme is designed to cover house financing, but the scheme also can be used to cover other financing. This scheme will be effective in the event of the participant's death, that is, the borrower. Cover will also be given in the event of the participant becoming totally and permanently disabled (www.*Takaful*-ikhlas.com.my).

The total and permanent disability benefit is payable subjected to the following conditions:

- The total permanent disability is based on "any occupation" definition.
- The disability benefit is payable after satisfying a qualifying period that such disability must last for a continuous period of not less than six months.

- Additional mortality and/or occupation loadings to be added as appropriate to group profile and totally and permanently disabled definition. Extra loadings shall be computed as a multiple factor to minimum net rate. No discount whatsoever will be given, as these are the minimum net rates.
- Pre-existing conditions are excluded from this benefit.

The participants are considered totally disabled if their disability prevents them from performing the essential duties of their regular occupations and if thus they are not working in any occupation. However, at the end of a specified period (not less than six months) after the disability has begun, participants are considered totally disabled only if their disabilities prevent them from working at any occupation for which they are reasonably fitted by education, training or experience. This definition of total disability usually specifies that whenever the participants are working in any gainful occupation, they are not considered to be totally disabled (Gene A. Morton 1984).

For this scheme, the range of age (eligibility) of participant to buy this scheme is between 18 and 60 years old. However, *Takaful* Ikhlas may extend this limit to a maximum age of 64 when it is applicable. Further, *Takaful* Ikhlas also sets the *Takaful* period for the scheme to be between one and five years. While its *Takaful* contribution depends on sum covered based on financial amount, contributions are based on financing period and age at next birthday. It follows that the older the age and the longer the term the riskier the plan is compared to those of younger age and taking out a shorter-term policy respectively. The minimum sum covered by *Takaful* Ikhlas for this scheme is RM 1000 and the maximum amount is subjected to the underwriting limit.

16.4 Model Structure: *Takaful* Ikhlas Experience

Ikhlas Group Islamic Cashline *Takaful* Scheme is a *Takaful* term for a group of participants of a financial institution (grantee), with different types of contribution payment methods. Typical plan designs may include single contribution and annual contribution (www.*Takaful*-ikhlas.com.my).

Generally, under a Family *Takaful* fund, each *Takaful* instalment paid by the participant should be divided and credited by the *Takaful* operator into two different accounts. A substantial proportion of the instalment is credited into personal investment account and would enable the participant to participate in a *Takaful* plan with certain objectives. These objectives may include saving a certain proportion of income monthly, to invest with an aim of earning profits in a manner not contravene to the teachings of Islam and to obtain a protection in the form of payment of *Takaful* benefits to heirs if a participant die before the maturity date of his *Takaful* plan (Ab. Aziz, A. R. 1987).

In line with the principle of *Al-Mudharabah* as stated in the contract, any profits generated from the investment shall be distributed between the participant and the *Takaful* operator in a ratio mutually agreed between the two parties. Regarding to the *Takaful* instalments, the participant shall decide the term of his *Takaful* plan. The instalments collected by *Takaful* Ikhlas will be invested in accordance with Shari'ah rules and requirements. Any profits gained from the investments will be credited into the participant's PRIA (personal risk investment account) with 100% contribution.

16.5 Contribution Treatment

Contributions will be allocated to the participant's PRIA account. There will be monthly dripping from the PRIA and there will be monthly charge made towards the *Takaful* Ta'awuni Account Pool (TTAP). TTAP will consist of an Expense Fee Fund, a Risk Charges Fund and a Contingency Loading Fund to cover expenses, risk and special fund reserves. The commission fees will be paid as a lump sum to the TTAP in the first month of coverage, while the expense fees and contingency loading charges will be paid monthly to the TTAP from the first month of coverage.

16.6 Profit

Takaful Ikhlas will charge a performance fee to any investment profit arising from the PRIA. The performance fee is charged at 10% of the investment income derived from the PRIA. The net investment income will be credited in full (100% contribution) to the Participant's Account.

16.7 Surplus (from the Risk Fund)

Takaful Ikhlas will also charge a Surplus Administration Charge (SAC) of 10% of the gross surplus arising every month. Any net surplus arising (after deducting SAC) from the Risk Fund is provisionally apportioned between the participant (through the PRIA) and the Stabilisation Fund.

Any deficit in the Risk Fund will first be paid from the Stabilisation Fund and, if necessary, the Contingency Fund. If such funds are not sufficient, then the deficit can be financed by an interest free loan (*Qard al-Hassan*) from the *Takaful* operator. Such loans would be a first charge against the surpluses arising from the Risk Fund. At year-end, the appointed actuary will assess the adequacy of the Stabilisation Fund. The appointed actuary will determine whether the amount in the Stabilisation Fund will be redistributed to the participant (via the PRIA as a final distribution of surplus) and/or Contingency Fund.

Example

To get a better idea of how profit is distributed, we should consider the example given below. This shows how profit is credited into the Participant's Account for different loan terms, between one and five years. After looking at the example, we will notice that the longer the loan term is, the higher the contribution.

Participant's age: 36 Loan amount: RM 21,000 Profit rate: 9%

- *Loan Term = 5 years* Single Contribution: RM 187.32 Monthly Contribution: RM 3.80
- *Loan Term = 4 years* Single Contribution: RM 149.31 Monthly Contribution: RM 3.70
- *Loan Term = 3 years* Single Contribution: RM 109.83 Monthly Contribution: RM 3.58
- *Loan Term = 2 years* Single Contribution: RM 72.03 Monthly Contribution: RM 3.32
- *Loan Term = 1 year* Single Contribution: RM 35.28 Monthly Contribution: RM 3.10

Generally, in case a participant wants to discontinue his participation in the *Takaful* plan before his plan matures, then he is entitled to the benefits all the same. The benefits given to him should be the proportion of his

Takaful instalments, which have been credited into his personal investment account plus his share of the profits from investment of instalments as credited into the personal account. The proportion of his *Takaful* instalments which have been credited into the PRIA in accordance with the Islamic concept of *Tabarru'* must not be given back to the participant (Ab. Aziz, A. R. 1987). However, in the case of *Takaful* Ikhlas, any participant who wishes to cease participating in the *Takaful* plan before his plan matures will not be entitled to any *Takaful* benefits. Unfortunately, *Takaful* Ikhlas does not provide any provision for such an event.

16.8 Claim Process

16.8.1 Types of Claim

Basically, there are three types of claim that can be made to *Takaful* Ikhlas by a participant if any misfortune happen. The participant can make a claim in the event of premature death, total permanent disablement and pre-total permanent disablement.

16.8.2 Claim Procedure

Takaful Ikhlas also has designed the claims process in three simple ways. A participant can make a claim easily by following the claims process as below.

First of all, the participant needs to submit the completed claim form to the head office or their nearest branch, with supporting documents to expedite the claim. For an accident case, a police report should be attached.

16.8.3 Supporting Documents (www.Takaful-ikhlas.com.my)

The documents required for funeral expenses comprise certificate number, participant and claimant names, death certificate or burial permit and bank's name and account number of claimant/named beneficiary. The documents required for a death claim include a claim form duly completed by claimant, physician's statement, certified copy of death certificate/burial permit, original certificate's contract, police report/post-mortem report (accident case only), proof of age (i.e. photocopy of identity card), proof of relationship between claimant and participant (i.e. marriage certificate), certification of salary confirmation from employer and certified true copy of the letter of appointment from an employer.

All claims must be supported by original documents/bills. However, in exceptional cases, certified copies of documents/bills are acceptable (any copy needs to be certified and endorsed by a registered Commissioner of Oath or staff of *Takaful* Ikhlas).

The documents required for pre-permanent total disablement benefit and total and permanent disability are a claim form duly completed by the participant, a medical attendant's report, a police report (in accident cases only), original certificate's contract, proof of relationship (i.e. marriage certificate), certified copy of letter of termination from employer, certified copy of letter of employment from employer and copy of attendance sheet certified by employer.

After that, the completed physician's statement must also be submitted to the head office or nearest branch *of Takaful* Ikhlas, with supporting documents to speed up the claims process (please refer to the above-listed supporting documents). Finally, after the *Takaful* operator receives and assesses the claim form and the physician's statement, the payment of claims will be credited directly to the participant's bank account or the beneficiary's bank account, or by cheque. As far as a claim for funeral expenses is concerned, payment will be payable within 24 hours of receipt of the documents mentioned (www.*Takaful*-ikhlas.com.my).

16.9 Benefits of the Scheme

This scheme is one of *Takaful* Ikhlas's products designed to cover the payment of debts, finances and facilities provided by Islamic and conventional banks, financing companies or investment houses for an individual borrower. The prime objective of Ikhlas Group Islamic Cashline *Takaful* Scheme is the full settlement of the debt by *Takaful* Ikhlas in the event of the untimely death or total disability due to illness or accident of the participant (debtor).

16.10 Responsibilities of *Takaful* Ikhlas

In the event of death of the participant within the term of the policy, *Takaful* Ikhlas will pay the sum covered in one lump sum to the grantee, while the balance in the participant's PRIA will be payable in one lump sum to the participant's beneficiary or next of kin. In the event of total permanent disablement of the participant within the term of the policy,

Takaful Ikhlas will pay the sum covered in one lump sum to the grantee, and the balance in the participant's PRIA will be payable in one lump sum to the participant.

16.11 With Ikhlas Group Islamic Cashline *Takaful* Scheme

- The bank or finance house providing the loan will be guaranteed full settlement of the debt in circumstances falling within the scheme's cover.
- The bank will relax its conditions for providing loans.
- The borrower is guaranteed that the outstanding balance of financing will be fully settled by *Takaful* Ikhlas in the case of untimely death in the period of the financing.
- In the case of borrower's (participant's) untimely death occurs when he is still in the period of financing, the burden of payment of the loan will not pass to the family of the participant (debtor) or to his guarantors.

16.12 Conclusion

In the modern economic environment insurance is a necessity, not only for individuals to care for their dependants and loved ones but also for institutions to protect their assets and other liabilities. However, conventional insurance practice is not in conformity with the requirements of Shari'ah. Therefore, a form of Islamic insurance based on the Qur'anic principle of *Ta'awun* or mutual assistance has been developed. Islamic Insurance (*Takaful*) is an alternative form of insurance based on the concept of trusteeship and co-operation inspired by the beliefs of the followers of Islamic teaching. Muslim societies all over the world are now practising *Takaful* schemes as their own way of sharing financial responsibilities to help each other.

Takaful Ikhlas is one of the *Takaful* operators in Malaysia; it offers several products based on Islamic concepts. One of them is Ikhlas Group Islamic Cashline *Takaful* Scheme. Overall, we believe the product is good, but there is one thing that needs to be clarified in the plan, which is the arrangement of the payment after the participant's plan has matured. Two questions that arise from this matter are: "If the participant dies after his plan matures, how does the *Takaful* operator arrange the payment of

Takaful benefits to his heirs?" and "If the participant becomes totally and permanently disabled after his plan matures, how does the *Takaful* operator arrange the payment of *Takaful* benefits to him?" We think that *Takaful* Ikhlas should include the answers to these questions in the plan. As the system for the product is currently being set out, and the products are not yet on sale, there is still room for improvement. Lastly, it is hoped that this scheme will get full support from the Muslim *ummah*, since it will bring many benefits to the participants and to society as a whole.

References

1. Ali, A. Y. (n.d.), The Holy Qur'an, Text and Translation.
2. *Group Islamic Cashline Takaful Plan*, *Takaful* Malaysia, *Takaful* Nasional, *Takaful* Ikhlas and others.
3. Insurance, in EB (11th edition), Vol.14, (n.d.), p. 656.
4. http://www.Takaful-ikhlas.com.my
5. http://www.islamic-world.net/economic/*Takaful*/*Takaful*.html
6. Gene A. Morton (1984), Principle of life and health insurance.
7. Ab. Aziz, A. R. (1987), "Conventional insurance (MNI)& Islamic insurance (STMSB) with special reference to their modus operandi", IIUM.

CHAPTER 17

Sukuk Takaful Plan

17.1 Introduction

An investment in *Sukuk* ignores risk of the danger to financial investors and the recovery of the capital market. Thus, risk analysis should be among the prime concerns before making this sort of investment. Therefore, we should analyse some economic sectors of primary markets, such as real estate or cars. Moreover, we must revitalise capital markets by providing new investment and financing tools, diversify the supply of financial products and stimulate the circulation of market instruments. This is because risk analysis may help to achieve transparency, improve the structure of the information in the market and the entry of many institutions in the financing process, which in turn provides more information on the market. The players shall impress a variety of segments of *Tawreeq* investors, which leads to the expansion of the size of capital markets and their recovery. There is also a need to facilitate foreign exchange to banks and financial institutions and creditors in the case of cross-border *Tawreeq*, since the buyer of the asset in this case is the bank or a foreign financial institution who will pay the local bank the value of the deal in foreign currency, which leads to an increase in domestic bank assets in foreign currency.

Mohd Ma'Sum Billah, *Islamic Insurance Products*,
https://doi.org/10.1007/978-3-030-17681-5_17

17.2 Risk Factors in *Sukuk*

There are various risks faced by the Sukuk industry, namely market risk, credit and counterparty risk, Shari'ah compliance risk, operational risk and institutional rigidity. This chapter will consider the challenges facing the management of financial risks of Sukuk for institutional reorganisation. In addition, it will look at the argument that most Sukuk implementation does not follow Shari'ah rules (AL-Maghlouth, A. K. 2009). Undesirable risks affect the competitiveness of the pricing of assets. Therefore, the innovation of *Sukuks* essentially involves a higher exposure to certain market and financial risks. A further illustration is as follows.

17.2.1 Market Risk

Market risks are of two classes, namely systematic and unsystematic. A systematic risk can arise due to public and economic policies, whereas unsystematic risk arises because of different firms' specific instruments are priced out by comparing with other firms' instruments. Market risk comprises profit rate risks, foreign exchange risks, equity price risks and commodity risks. The profit rate risk is rate of return risk where *Sukuk* is based on fixed rates that are exposed to this risk in the same manner as fixed rate bonds are exposed to profit rate risk. Moreover, an increase in market profit rates leads to a decrease in the fixed-income *Sukuk* values. However, all fixed-return assets, either from *Ijarah*, *Istisna*, *Salam*, *Al-Mudharabah*, *Qiradh* or any other origin, will face this risk. This also involves reinvestment risk and an opportunity cost of investing at the new rates, particularly if the asset is not liquid—as in case of the zero-coupon non-tradable *Sukuk*.

17.2.2 Credit Risk

This is the probability that a bad debt or an asset or loan becomes irrecoverable due to a default or delay in settlements while the counterparty risk is the probability that the counterparty retracts on the conditions of the contract if the relationship involves a contractual arrangement. The consequences can be severe, with a decline in the value of a bank's assets. The credit and counterparty risks inbuilt in Islamic finance are unique, owing to the nature of Islamic financial instruments that become the foundation of the *Sukuk* asset pools.

Unlike conventional financial institutions, Islamic banks do not have access to derivative instruments and other credit risk management mechanisms due to Shari'ah considerations (ibid.).

17.2.3 Risks to Shari'ah Compliance

The risk to Shari'ah compliance is the loss of asset value as a result of the issuer's breach of its fiduciary responsibilities with respect to compliance with Shari'ah. For example, if the *Sukuk* is based on a hybrid of *Ijarah* and *Istisna* assets, *Ijarah* must always be more than *Istisna* in the pool, otherwise the *Sukuk* deed will dissolve. Thus, broadly speaking Shari'ah compliance risk must be defined as a rate of return foregone in comparison to the market rates, as a result of complying with Shari'ah. Moreover, fixed-rate *Sukuk* faces serious market risks. So, to match the market requirements of *Sukuk* to be floating rate, and the Shari'ah requirements of rents to be fixed rate, the *Ijarah Sukuk* are based on a master *Ijarah* agreement with several subordinate *Ijarah* agreements. However, the investors could still face profit rate risk to a certain extent and since the originator can only guarantee the fixed return on the underlying asset pools, the issue of floating rate returns remains contentious, particularly in pooled or hybrid *Sukuk*. Therefore, the association of Shari'ah supervisors with *Sukuk* issuers will ensure investor confidence.

17.2.4 Management and Operational Risk

Management and operational risk are inherent to the structure of the issuances rather than the underlying Shari'ah principles. The risks specific to the operation mirror to those in conventional bond markets: default risk, coupon payment risk, asset redemption risk, investor-specific risks and risks related to the asset. Default risk is when each party has provisions for the termination of the certificate in the event of a default by the obligor. Coupon payment risk is when the obligor may fail to pay the required coupons on time. Asset redemption risk is when the originator has to buy back the underlying assets from the certificate holder. Investor-specific risks are when the certificate holder is exposed to several risks relevant to *Sukuk* structures, such as liquidity management issues in Islamic finance. Risks related to the asset are when the underlying assets of the *Sukuk* certificates are subject to numerous risks, such as the risk of loss of assets (ibid.).

17.2.5 Organisational Rigidity Risk

The banking and financial infrastructure is weak in most emerging economies' countries, despite a significant move observed in some, such as Bahrain, Saudi Arabia, Malaysia and Brunei, and Indonesia among others. However, *Sukuk* requires unique Shari'ah-compliant structures which create a state that can be termed as one of institutional rigidity and that cannot be removed in the short run and always increasing the risks of *Sukuk*. Furthermore, the features of this state are lack of hedging and financial engineering processes, non-existence of inter-bank money markets, lack of best practice uniform regulatory standards and regimes, weaknesses in litigation and legal framework support, particularly in the treatment of default, non-uniform accounting, auditing and income and loss recognition systems, non-robust investment appraisal, promotion and monitoring infrastructure, ineffective external assessment systems, the rudimentary state of financial markets and weak inter-segmental support and linkages (ibid.).

17.3 Managing *Sukuk* Risks

Sukuk serves to replicate the functions of conventional bonds and tradable securities in resources mobilisation from markets, while injecting liquidity into the enterprise or government and in providing a stable source of income for investors. Moreover, investing in *Sukuk* issuances involves the funding of trade or production of tangible assets. The next section will state the challenges facing the management of financial risks of *Sukuk* that are also the challenge of institutional reorganisation (ibid.).

17.3.1 Organisational Challenges

Government debt management, upon which the fixed-income markets in developing countries are based, is dominated by government bonds. Therefore, the single most important reorganisation of the markets will come from the reorganisation of public debt management. The introduction of derivative markets has further consequences for market and financing dynamics. Furthermore, markets stabilising role of futures and options markets depends on the speculator's information. Futures and options markets can also serve to stabilise the value of underlying assets by acting in an insuring role, and this can occur if these markets allow investors to pool risks more efficiently. Therefore, in short the evolutionary changes of financial innovation, deregulation, globalisation of financial services and introduction of novel financing instruments warrant the adoption of supporting risk management mechanisms, viable secondary markets and relevant regulatory bodies (ibid.).

The emergence of the market for asset-backed securities over the past two decades has permitted banks around the world to free their capital by repackaging and reselling portfolios of loans, assets and other receivables. This adjusts the criteria for lending by forcing financial institutions to meet the market's standards for loan quality and sufficient pricing for risk. It helps decrease funding risk by diversifying funding sources. Financial institutions also employ securitisation to purge profit rate mismatches. Moreover, this approach creates more complete markets by introducing formerly remote asset classes that better suit investor risk preferences and by increasing the potential for investors to achieve the benefits of diversification. Therefore, by meeting the needs of different market segments, securitisation transactions can generate gains for both originators and investors. The same benefits can be attributed to *Sukuk* certificates. They allow the institution to manage balance sheet mismatches to securitise longer-term assets. Moreover, investors are also given the option to invest in asset grades that are suitable for their investment needs. Financial markets are also more complete as previously untapped assets are now available for public-sector resource mobilisation.

The liquidity and secondary markets exhibit varying risk preferences and a secondary market should be developed to reflect this. *Sukuk* certificates are unique in that the investor becomes an asset holder and is directly tied in to the nature and functioning of the underlying asset pools, so *Sukuk* certificate holders carry the burden of these unique risks. The primary concern of an Islamic secondary market is its marketability (ibid.). All things being equal, a certificate holder would rather participate in a well-structured and well-regulated secondary market instead of trading in a poorly run market. However, the challenges remain to provide increased risk management mechanisms, increase market liquidity, create a truer bond yield benchmark as well as expanding the issuer and investor platform.

17.4 Conclusion

It is has been observed that the unfavourable risks faced by the *Sukuk* industry, such as market risk, credit and counterparty risk, Shari'ah compliance risk, operational risk and institutional rigidity, which affect the competitiveness of the pricing of assets, mean that the innovation of *Sukuk* essentially involves a higher exposure to certain market and financial risks. However, I believe that we should take care most about unsystematic market risk and Shari'ah compliance ri sk because they are related to each other in sense of that market risk will increase if Shari'ah compliance risk increases. The current *Sukuk* margin or profit based on LIBOR (the London Inter-bank Offered Rate) is an indictor only but still we depend on it, which leads us to violate Shari'ah compliance and this will cause market risk to increase because most *Sukuk* holders or investors are Muslims in search of Shari'ah-compliant products to invest in. They want to make sure they avoid investing in non-compliant or questionable products, and in our case the product could be questionable unless we try to avoid this risk.

This can be achieved through fixed percentages not related to anything, even if just as indicators. It is true that the *Sukuk* issuers in some periods will face problems due to crises of economy or complexities in their projects, but they accept the need for sacrifice in order to avoid violating in Shari'ah compliance (ibid.). Moreover, in order to develop the market of *Sukuk* and avoid risks to Shari'ah compliance, capital authorities of all Muslim countries should establish and create a *Sukuk* Authority Institution that reports to the Organisation of Islamic Cooperation and unifies the rules and regulations of *Sukuk* issuing, such as the price of *Sukuk* is among others.

References

1. AL-Maghlouth, A. K. (2009), *Sukuk*: An inside study of its background, structures, challenges & Cases, OUM, at pp. 38–47.
2. Products and System of Takaful Malaysia and Takaful Ikhlas.

CHAPTER 18

Online Takaful Business

18.1 Introduction

In essence, Takaful operations can be segregated into two principal activities. On the one hand, they act as the conduit for providing financial benefits in the event of misfortune through the various *Takaful* products and services that individuals and corporate bodies can participate in. Technically, the product is similar to insurance. From straightforward motor vehicle cover to the very complex requirements of the corporate sector, *Takaful* products are able to fulfil the demands of all. A long-term Family *Takaful* plan can satisfy the life insurance needs of an individual, while an industrial all-risks scheme can meet the insurance needs of a sophisticated manufacturing plant belonging to a huge conglomerate.

On the other hand, *Takaful* companies should provide products and services that are competitive enough to challenge conventional insurance. By adopting the latest technology, the *Takaful* industry could boost its growth and be accepted by everybody in the whole world. Therefore, the internet could help disseminate information on *Takaful* and sell *Takaful* products to everybody, anywhere in the world. This

It is acknowledged that, the idea of this chapter/product is significantly contributed by the practices/experiences/thoughts of Bank Negara, Takaful Malaysia, Takaful Ikhlas, Takaful Nasional, Etiqa Takaful, IBFIM, IIUM, MII and others (Malaysia).

Mohd Ma'Sum Billah, *Islamic Insurance Products*,
https://doi.org/10.1007/978-3-030-17681-5_18

would help to further accelerate the expansion of Islamic insurance at the international level. In the same manner, efforts towards converging and harmonising of various operations and practices would be more conducive to such results as well.

18.2 Central Idea

The idea of *Takaful* products online is basically to create a more competitive growth of the Islamic insurance industry and depends on *Takaful* companies' competence to survive in the highly developed insurance market. As with other industries that seek to expand, *Takaful* companies are also realising the potential of information technology, particularly the internet. Basically, *Takaful* products online are designed to educate visitors about *Takaful*. They offer information on the concept and the reasons behind the prohibition of conventional insurance and the importance of *Takaful* to Muslims. *Takaful* operators should also include the latest news about *Takaful*, views of the *Ulama'* and Shari'ah justification on *Takaful* products through their websites.

Through this concept, *Takaful* products online, *Takaful* operators could advertise their products and services on websites and customers could buy their products. This will definitely improve the relationship between *Takaful* operators and its customers. *Takaful* operators could reduce costs by using this application and customers, on the other hand, will not have the hassle of negotiating traffic jams just to arrive at the *Takaful* company office plus the queuing process, which can sometimes be tiring. Therefore, the concept of *Takaful* products online is to make life easier for everybody, giving essential information about *Takaful* to visitors as transactions for *Takaful* products—such as buying or renewal of policies by using hardware (a computer) and software (the internet)—can happen anywhere, anytime and anyplace.

18.3 Shari'ah Rulings

The implementation of *Takaful* products online generally is to give an understanding of *Takaful* products as an Islamic approach, counter to conventional insurance. Hence, the internet can play an important role in disseminating information on *Takaful*, its benefits and how this alternative model of insurance can be applied. The concept of the *Takaful* product online is design to educate people about *Takaful*, offering information on the concept, reasons behind the prohibition of conventional insurance and the importance of *Takaful* to Muslims. This concept, disseminating information for good reason to others is described in the Qur'an:

> Help you one another in righteousness and piety. (Al-Ma'idah: 2)

Selling *Takaful* products online can be an opportunity to consolidate and expand the market. By embracing and adopting the latest technology, it could anticipate a wider market access, improve quality and productivity and ultimately offer better services to both the principals and customers. The internet is thus an essential tool and a golden opportunity for relatively young *Takaful* industries to bridge the gap between well-established conventional insurance and their own offerings. On the other hand, *Takaful* companies should first make sure that their operations are in line with Shari'ah principles. They should avoid any element against the Shari'ah rules before introducing *Takaful* products online. *Takaful* operators should avoid elements not permitted under Islam, which include:

- uncertainty (*Gharar*), as encountered in conventional insurance practices. The *Takaful* operations are merely to provide financial security against defined risk.
- any elements based on *Riba* (interest), whether in investment of participants' contributions, any financing involving interest or borrowing from a conventional bank for *Takaful* operations. This is clearly stated in the Qur'anic verses:

> That is because they say, "Trade is like usury," But Allah permitted trade and has forbidden usury. (Al-Baqarah: 275)

- operations involving any element of gambling; this is strictly prohibited by the Shari'ah rules because gamblers are hoping for material gains. For example, *Takaful* operators should not invest participants' contributions in a company 5 involved in gambling. As stated in *Surah Al-Baqarah*:

> They ask thee concerning wine and gambling, "In them is great sin, and profit, for men; but the sin is greater than profit." (2: 219)

- activities involving the manufacturing or sale of prohibited (*haram*) goods such as liquor, pork and meat that has not been slaughtered according to Islamic custom. Lastly, any *Takaful* operator should not betray the trust placed in them by participants. *Takaful* companies should be honest and should bear the responsibility for holding and investing contribution money of participants.

And if one of you deposits a thing on trust with another, let the trustee (faithfully) discharge his trust, and let him fear his Lord. Conceal not evidence; for whoever conceals it, his heart is tainted with sin, and Allah knoweth all that ye do. (Qur'an 2: 283)

18.4 Functional Structure (18.1)

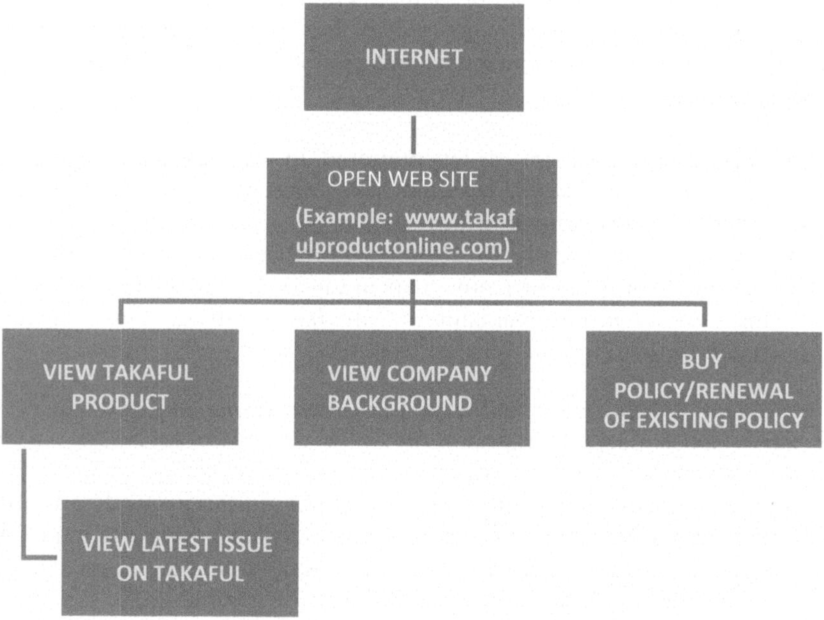

Fig. 18.1 Functional structure. (Source: Author's collection)

18.5 *Takaful* Products

Takaful products online are products and services specially packaged and managed strictly in accordance with Islamic principles. With *Takaful* products, participants will feel that their needs for insurance products are taken care of without compromising on their Islamic principles and practices. At the end of each year, after claims are made, the excess funds will be distributed between the participants. The *Takaful* online operations include the two common products that are the family *Takaful* and also general *Takaful*. Family *Takaful* consists of two accounts for the participant: the Participant Account (set up according to the profit-sharing principle of *Al-Mudharabah*) and the Participant Special Account (*Tabarru'*). General *Takaful* only consists of one account for the participants, that is the Participant Special Account. Both products could be divided as follows (Table 18.1):

18.5.1 Online Buying or Renewal of Takaful *Products*

Customers can register or renew their *Takaful* product policy through the internet. The form provided is for the renewal of motor vehicle *Takaful*. Other *Takaful* products could also be renewed using different forms provided in a *Takaful* company's website. This registering or renewal of *Takaful* product policies' is designed for customer who do not have time to visit the nearest *Takaful* company's office. It will definitely save time and hassle, and is simple—just by going on the internet a customer can

Table 18.1 *Takaful* products

General Takaful	
Fire *Takaful* scheme	Liability *Takaful* scheme
Motor vehicle *Takaful*	Marine *Takaful*
Accident *Takaful* scheme	House protection *Takaful* scheme
Family Takaful	
Family *Takaful* Plan	Group Family *Takaful* Plan
Family *Takaful* Plan for Education	Student *Takaful* scheme
Group Family *Takaful* Plan	Worker *Takaful* scheme
Group Medical *Takaful* Plan	Mortgage *Takaful*
Ziarah *Takaful*	Waqf *Takaful*
Health *Takaful*	Retirement *Takaful* scheme

Source: Author's collection

buy a policy and carry out other transactions. Payment can be made using any major credit card, such as VISA or MASTERCARD. Customers can also make payments using e-banking provided by banks such as Bank Islam, RHB Bank, Maybank, BCB Bank, Muamalat Bank and others.

After filling in the form, click 'send' and the information will be processed by the *Takaful* operator, while official receipt will be sent within three working days. If the official receipt does not arrive with the customer in three working days, the participant should call the *Takaful* company and ask for an explanation.

18.6 Recommendations

There are few adjustments and improvements that could be made to the existing application process. The *Takaful* operator should improve certain parts of their website to make *Takaful* product more competitive in the eyes of the people.

- The website should be designed to educate visitors about *Takaful*, offering information on the concept and the reasons behind the prohibition of conventional insurance and the importance of *Takaful* to Muslims. It should also be updated with the latest news about *Takaful*, views of the *Ulama'* and Shari'ah justification on *Takaful* products.
- The website should be attractive to visitors. Good website design plus a good combination of colours and icons could attract visitors to spend more time on the site.
- By embracing and adopting the latest technology, *Takaful* operators can anticipate wider market access, improve quality and productivity and ultimately offer better services to both the principals and customers.
- *Takaful* operators should develop a suggestion box on the websites for customers to give suggestions or ideas regarding any *Takaful* issues in order to improve the quality of the *Takaful* industry and able to be more competitive with conventional insurance. This will enable both customers and *Takaful* operators to exchange views and knowledge with each other, as mentioned in *Surah At-Taubah*: 122.

Preparing *Takaful* assistance online nowadays would be a big help and would be a marvellous boon to customers. With the prologue of online

Takaful service, *Takaful* operators could reach customers beyond the expected limit, thus giving a clear picture what *Takaful* and *Re-takaful* insurance is all about. As we all know, *Takaful* nowadays does not merely mean products that assist Muslims, but which also cover non-Muslims throughout the world. In order to improve services and particularly to widen the coverage, we have discussed some recommendations with Mr Shahrul Aman Zulkifli, Marketing Executive of *Takaful* Malaysia, Taiping, Perak Branch to be forwarded for public evaluation. The recommendations are as below.

- Online *Takaful* services should be implemented to aid the customers in joining the schemes offered more easily. It has been seen that online services could reach people beyond bounty. With the introduction of *Takaful* online service, people could get to know more about the schemes or products easily and have a clearer picture about the procedures and privileges of joining the schemes. With the introduction of online services, *Takaful* operators could prepare registration forms as well as report and claim forms. All data will be processed easily and so this will be time saving. According to our interview, at present a case would take about two months to be processed, but with online services the processing period could be reduced to a month or less. The faster the service, the more people would rely on it.
- Different types of form should be used for Muslim and non-Muslim participants.

Online or manual registration and claim forms should be separate for Muslims or non-Muslim participants. With this method, it would be easier for the person in charge to allocate other contribution to the unfortunate participants. For instance, a Muslim participant may have joined a Khairat Fund at his neighbourhood as well instead of just Life *Takaful* product. If any misfortune occurs to him within the *Takaful* cover period, *Takaful* would allocate a certain amount to him to cover his loss; but if the participant passes away, *Takaful* could arrange the funeral ceremony directly with the deceased participant's community. This would be easier for the deceased family as they have already been grieving for the loss of their loved one. In terms of non-Muslim participants, some of them may have taken out other life insurance policies too, with different beneficiaries in different schemes. If any tragedy happens, *Takaful* would arrange and allocate the provided amount for the beneficiaries as written in the agreement as above. *Takaful* will not breach the contract for some of the beneficiaries' interest. So, with the usage of different forms for Muslims and non-Muslims, it would be easier for both parties, the *Takaful* operator and the participants, in dealing with allocation of the fund due to unfortunate events insured against.

- The *Takaful* staff should be well trained in *Takaful* concepts, so as to be able to give clear information about the products provided to the customers. When of our group members went to a *Takaful* branch in Perak for assistance with a project, the staff in charge at the branch could barely explain the concept of *Tabarru'* and others. When it came to the matter of Shari'ah rulings, they could not even quote any verses from the Qur'an or the Hadith. This is viewed as a disappointment for us, as they mentioned that most customers do not really understand Qur'anic verses, even if they are translated for them.

It is thus, suggested that *Takaful* staff should be well trained in Islamic teachings so as to equip them in delivering the actual points about *Takaful* to the public, ranging from Muslims to non-Muslims, and thus promoting *Takaful* products to the market effectively.

- There should be an easy payment method for online registration and premium installation for the participants. Online services will not be efficient if payment still has to be done manually. In order to make online services more attractive, online payment method should be applied in order to comply with high-tech systems. Payment using credit card should be added. This way, participants or customers could easily reach their premium installations easily at any time. Just key in your credit or charge card numbers and other related information, then the system will process everything for you. This user-friendly system will also help to cultivate digital culture in our society. New participants can join *Takaful* schemes at any convenient time, where they can register through the online service and settle their related fees at once through the establishment of an online payment facility.

Other information should be added to the *Takaful* website for surfers. In order to make the *Takaful* website more attractive, we believe that adding other information would be a good idea. Summarisation of composite indexes, share market report and even gold price market are examples of some attractive information that would be considered useful to people nowadays. Instead of surfing through the *Takaful* website, surfers could even check the share market report easily from there. Some guidelines for investors could be added as well, and this would make the website more appealing. Indirectly, it would also attract servers to join the *Takaful*:

> Nor should the believers all go forth together: if a contingent from every expedition remained behind, they could devote themselves to study of religion and admonish the people when they return to them, that thus they (may learn) to guard themselves (against evil).

There are some other factors that will be affected by implementing the concept of *Takaful* products online. Information technology and the internet are being perceived as damaging to the co-operative human spirit, which is highly stressed in the *Takaful* theory, based on the *Ayah 2 in Surah Al-Maidah.*

The internet, although it may not completely eliminate the role of agents in the insurance business, could strip *Takaful* agents of the personal touch, which is often needed to provide a sense of comfort among customers and strengthen their credence in the efficiency of the business.

18.7 Conclusion

It is human nature that anything new is not normally easily and readily accepted simply as a matter of course. When *Takaful* was first introduced as an alternative to conventional insurance in the early 1980s, there were strong reservations that it would not be viable, and what is more profitable. But *Takaful* is highly recognisable nowadays. It is thus similar to the concept of *Takaful* products online being introduced, whcih will gradually be accepted by everyone. It will take some time for people to fully utilise the internet as a medium to gather information, transactions and businesses.

Therefore, *Takaful* products online are a concept for:

- disseminating information about *Takaful* and its products;
- providing the latest news about *Takaful*, it products, Shari'ah justification and the views of the *Ulama'*;

- advertising *Takaful* products;
- transactions between participants and *Takaful* operators;
- buying/renewal of policies;
- and the most important thing is to get the blessing from Allah for whatever we are doing.

References

1. Ali, A. Y. (n.d.), The Holy Qur'an, Text and Translation.
2. *On-line Takaful Services*, *Takaful* Malaysia, *Takaful* Nasional, *Takaful* Ikhlas and others.

CHAPTER 19

Digital Currency Takaful

19.1 Introduction

Digital currency is one of the fastest growing areas in today's financial environment. Despite this remarkably successful journey, it is not free from risk. These may arise in the form of technological catastrophe such as hacks, or manifest as technical failures, regulatory weakness, inadequate operational mechanisms, malpractice or lack of market confidence. A *Halal* alternative digital currency model is no exception and is exposed to similar risk factors. However, an attempt is made in this chapter to identify the risk factors in the *Halal* digital currency model and to offer further analysis of how those risks may be managed by a *Takaful* system.

Any commercial or financial activity is naturally exposed to numerous risks, be they financial or otherwise. Any commercial entity that carries out its activities without attempting to analyse unpredicted risks, is under threat in terms of its future. Therefore, the risk management component of any commercial entity should be among the prime concerns. And thus, different classes of insurance schemes are designed to facilitate such risk management. In the *Halal* digital currency model, the risk factors may be identified in the form of technological hazards or technical failure in the blockchain technology, system hazards which may occur in operations, moral hazards that may be anticipated in management in terms of malpractice, fraud or misappropriation, as well as natural disaster or acts of God (*Qada'* and *Qadar*). The tool of risk

Mohd Ma'Sum Billah, *Islamic Insurance Products*,
https://doi.org/10.1007/978-3-030-17681-5_19

minimisation under Shari'ah principles is a *Takaful* scheme; hence, a digital currency *Takaful* scheme may be a solution, minimising risk in *Halal* digital currency management.

19.2 Risk Factors in *Halal* Digital Currency

19.2.1 Legal

At present, in digital currency management there is no legal protection under standard law, policies or guidelines available to regulate digital currency activities fairly. As for the *Halal* digital currency model, there is no way for anyone to escape the legal or Shari'ah regulatory requirements, but if operations do take place in ignorance or with no proper regulatory compliance there is a regulatory risk.

19.2.2 Technical

In cryptocurrency management, technical risk may be catastrophe by hacking, technical failure, mistake, misrepresentation, loss of data, fraud and any form of careless malpractice. If any such catastrophe causes harm either to the receiver, user, system or technology then this may be seen as amounting to a technical risk.

19.2.3 Financial

Financial depreciation in any commercial or financial operation is common. Cryptocurrency management is no exception; thus, if any depreciation is realised in the capital of investors in cryptocurrency management due to unforeseeable occurrence this is a financial or capital risk.

19.2.4 Bankruptcy

Insolvency in any commercial activity, either individual or corporate or public, is not unusual or unforeseeable. In cryptocurrency management, thus far there is no record of any bankruptcy, but it is not impossible that this may occur due to many unforeseeable circumstances such as financial turmoil, price depreciation with huge losses or by regulatory sanction. Thus, these unforeseeable disasters are the risk here.

19.2.5 Management

In cryptocurrency management, if there is there is a dissolution of management by there being no proper replacement, if the management is sanctioned by law, if there is a disappearance of the management or failure of management responsibilities, then this amounts to a risk, which is likely to damage the total operations and activities of cryptocurrency platform.

19.2.6 Code Change

The HASH code is mandatory for any cryptocurrency platform to be maintained for recording and authentication. It is not common for a cryptocurrency to change its HASH code with no justifiable reason. But in case, due to an unforeseeable situation, the HASH code is changed either deliberately or otherwise, then there is a risk, which is likely to crash the whole system and its business activities.

19.2.7 Malpractice

In cryptocurrency management, the receiver has chances of malpractices in the total system and activities, which are likely to cause damage to users and the system, as well trying to defeat the law and the legitimate purposes of the currency. Fraud, misrepresentation or any deliberate violation of law leads to cryptocurrency risk through malpractice. Therefore, harmful malpractices in cryptocurrency are covered by an insurance scheme to create confidence in the market.

19.2.8 War Risk

War risk is a good excuse, because it is an unpredicted catastrophe, which diminishes the future not only of life and property, but also commercial activities—and cryptocurrency is no exception. If any war causes harm to any cryptocurrency management, particularly in its system, financial activities and/or management, then this is considered a war risk, which is likely to be a threat to cryptocurrency management overall.

19.3 A Cryptocurrency Risk Plan

No risk plan for digital currency management has been designed yet and the *Halal* alternative model is in the same position. Basically, there are two groups in digital currency management that are exposed to unpredicted risks. They are: the receiver or issuer and the user. In all situations, a risk must be defined and understood before it is underwritten. However, there are two schemes recommended here under Shari'ah principles to protect the victim ought to be suffered by either the receiver or the user due to unpredicted risk because of technical failure, natural disaster or another form of catastrophe. Hence, the schemes suggested are a digital currency receiver *Takaful* model and a digital currency user *Takaful* model. The following summarises both schemes (Fig. 19.1).

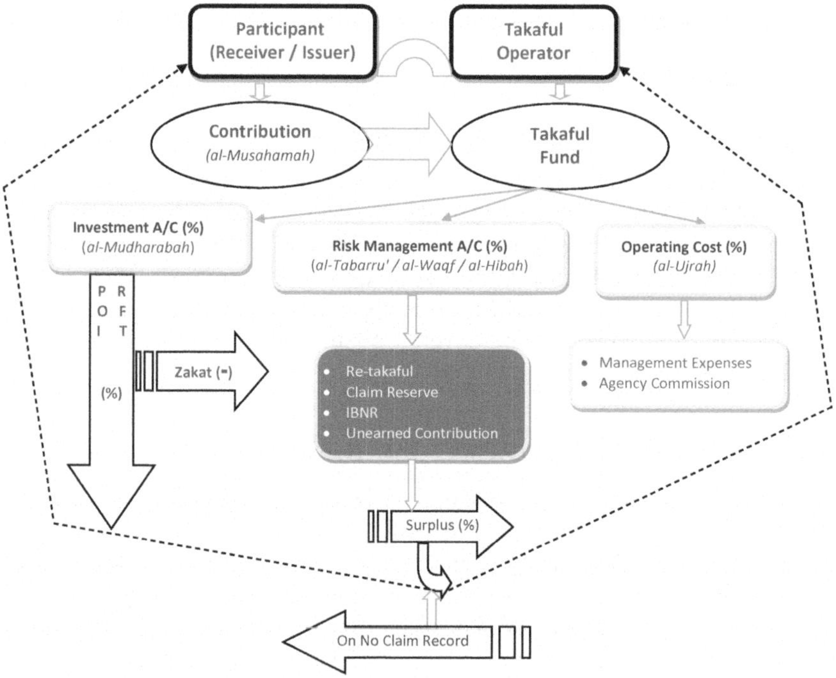

Fig. 19.1 Digital currency receiver *Takaful* model. (Source: Author's own)

In the above scheme, the participant (receiver) may hold a digital currency all-risk *Takaful* policy by agreement with a *Takaful* operator. This policy is suggested to be a short-term one depending on the policy of the receiver and the market phenomena. The risk shall be defined prior to underwriting.

The receiver shall be liable to pay the agreed contribution (premium) to the *Takaful* operator in view of managing their digital currency risk. The *Takaful* operator, in consideration of the received contribution, shall undertake to manage the risk and provide coverage (benefit) in favour of the receiver in case of any risk run over the agreed subject matter within the agreed policy period.

The *Takaful* operator shall distribute the received contribution i to three accounts by agreed proportion, complying with the operator's standard policy, and manage them accordingly. These three accounts are: first, the management account for the purpose of operating costs, which shall be treated on the basis of *al-Ujrah* (service charge) or *al-Ju'alah* (reward) or *al-Wakalah* (commission). The operating costs shall include total management expenses and the commission of the agents or brokers. Second, the risk management account, which shall be treated based on the principles of *al-Tabarru'* (donation), *al-Hibah* (gift) or *al-Waqf* (endowment). The purpose of this account is to maintain the *Re-takaful* requirement, claim reserve, incurred but not reported (IBNR) and unearned contributions. Third, the investment account, aimed at additionally saving a portion for the future benefit of the *Takaful* participant (receiver). This account shall be treated as *Al-Mudharabah* (profit- and loss-sharing technique).

The profit earned in the investment account shall be subject to the deduction of 2.5% as *Zakat* before the net income is distributed between the participant and the operator. In the risk management account, the *Re-takaful* contribution is a regulatory requirement. Similarly, the claim reserve is designed to meet the justifiable claims, IBNR and unearned contributions, which all are regulatory requirements. However, any surplus, if so realised in the risk management account, is suggested to be shared between the *Takaful* operator and the participants (on a no claims ground) in accordance with the terms of the policy agreement or the standard policy of the *Takaful* operator (Fig. 19.2).

The participant (user) in the above scheme may hold a digital currency all-risk *Takaful* policy with a *Takaful* operator by agreement. This policy

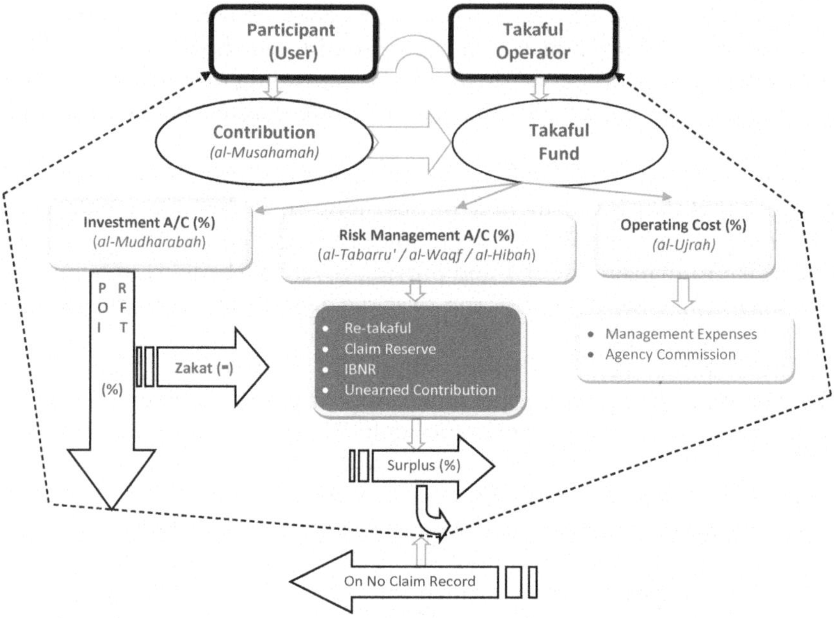

Fig. 19.2 Digital currency user *Takaful* model. (Source: Author's own)

is suggested to be a short term one depending on the plan of the user and the market phenomena. The risk shall be defined prior to underwriting or policy agreement.

The participant (user) shall be liable to pay the agreed contribution (premium) to the *Takaful* operator in view of managing their agreed digital currency risk. The *Takaful* operator, in consideration of the received contribution, shall undertake to manage the risk and provide coverage (benefit) in favour of the user in case of any risk run over the agreed subject matter within the agreed policy duration.

In this scheme, the *Takaful* operator shall distribute the received contribution into three accounts by agreed proportions, complying with the operator's standard policy, and manage them accordingly. These three accounts are set out in just the same manner as for the digital currency receiver *Takaful* model, as above.

In the digital currency user *Takaful* scheme, any profit earned in the investment account shall be subject to the deduction of 2.5% as *Zakat* before the net income is distributed between the participant and the operator. In the risk management account, the *Re-takaful* contribution is a regulatory requirement, as are the claim reserved to meet the justifiable claims, IBNR and unearned contributions. However, any surplus in the risk management account is suggested to be shared between the *Takaful* operator and the participants (on a no claims basis) in accordance with the terms of the policy agreement.

19.4 Conclusion

In digital currency management, there are numerous risks that may befall the user or the receiver due to capital risk, technical risk or moral hazard. In all situations, there is as yet no risk plan by any operator or provider or platform. Such weakness may hinder the sustainable growth of digital currency. For the *Halal* alternative digital currency model, to minimise risk, there are two categories of *Takaful* scheme recommended. First, the user *Takaful* model to provide protection against any defined risks. Second, the receiver *Takaful* scheme to provide protection from any unpredicted defined risk. To ensure the sustainable growth of digital currency, an effective risk plan shall be designed and thus *Takaful* may be an effective solution to such risk plan, particularly for *Halal* digital currency management.

Reference

1. Billah, M. M. (2019), (ed), *Halal Crypto currency Management*, Palgrave Macmillan (forthcoming).

PART III

Family *Takaful* Products

CHAPTER 20

Preview of Islamic Life Insurance Products

20.1 Introduction

The Sharī'ah model of life insurance does not mean to insure one's life, rather it is a financial transaction undertaking to protect widows, orphans and other dependants of the deceased (assured) against future unexpected financial risk. The conventional system, however, offers a life insurance policy, which may not be free from *Riba* (interest) or other elements not recognised by Islamic teaching. Based on observation of the practices of life insurance policies under the conventional system, many Muslims, and even some Islamic scholars, diametrically oppose the idea of life policies, but have not come up with an Islamic alternative model to the conventional one which would meet the expectations of contemporary Muslims and protect widows, orphans and other dependants in society from unpredicted future financial risk. Hence, the central idea of the model of Islamic life insurance is that it is not a policy to insure one's own life, but is a financial transaction relying on the principles of mutual co-operation to undertake a responsibility towards safeguarding widows, orphans and other dependants of the deceased (assured) from future financial risk, which does not involve *Riba* but operates following the principle of *Al-Mudharabah*, while neither clashing with the principles of *Mirath* or *Wasiyah*. In an Islamic model of life insurance policy, the nominee(s) is not

Mohd Ma'Sum Billah, *Islamic Insurance Products*,
https://doi.org/10.1007/978-3-030-17681-5_20

an absolute beneficiary(s) but a mere trustee,[1] who is under a duty to obtain benefits over the policy and distribute them among the heirs of the deceased (assured), according to the principles of *Mirath* and *Wasiyah* (Billah, M. Masum 1993).

This chapter attempts to come up with a solution to the operation of an Islamic model of life insurance policy in contemporary Muslim societies, refuting the misconceptions that some Muslims have placed against the validity of a life insurance policy.

20.2 The Problem

The central idea of life insurance under Islamic discipline is quite different from that which is practised under the conventional system. An Islamic model of a life insurance policy, however, is a financial transaction based on the principle of the *Al-Mudharabah* financing technique, relying on the principle of mutual co-operation, undertaking a responsibility towards safeguarding widows, orphans and other dependants of the deceased (assured/policyholder) from unexpected future material risk. The nominee(s) in the life insurance policy who is appointed by the assured, is not an absolute beneficiary(s) over the policy but a mere trustee who receives the benefits and distributes them among the heirs of the deceased (assured) according to the principles of *Mirath* (inheritance) and *Wasiyah* (bequest). Where the assured is still alive upon the maturity of the policy, he has the right to claim from the insurer the paid premiums, the share of profits made over the paid premiums, plus bonus and dividends according to the company policy. But if the assured dies at any time before the maturity of the policy, the claim of the nominee(s) includes the paid premiums, the share of profits made over the paid premiums, bonus and dividends according to company policy plus a donation from the company's charitable fund according to the financial condition of the beneficiary(s) of the assured. As for the claim for benefits over a life insurance policy, the death of the assured does not necessarily have to be natural or accidental, but any cause of the death (even an unlawful death like suicide or being killed in the act of a crime etc.) counts so long as the death of the assured is proved. This is because the death of any creature is determined by Allah (swt), as is stated in the Qur'an:

[1] *Fatwa* issued by the National Council for Muslims Religious Affairs in Malaysia, see in [1974] I MLJ at x.

> No soul can die except by the permission of Allah (swt), the term being fixed [by Allah (swt)]. (Qur'an, at ch. 3:145)

Moreover, as regards the act of suicide or any other crimes, the doer himself/herself is solely accountable to Allah (swt) for his/her own act. As Allah (swt) ruled in the Qur'an:

> They shall reap the fruit of what they did, and you what you do. (Id., at 2:134)

This does not mean that a criminal will simultaneously be accountable for his/her own wrongful act and also be deprived of other rights. It is a fundamental right of everyone in society to enjoy in business and other matters that they may require lawfully. Such personal rights should be exercised by everyone equally, regardless of whether one is innocent or a criminal as long as the rights within the lawful sphere. Hence, a life insurance policy is a transaction whereby the assured's beneficiary(s) should not be deprived due to the assured's criminal act (i.e. act of suicide or being killed for a wrongful act etc.). The agent in a life insurance policy is not supposed to be paid his salary out of the assured's premiums because they work for "The Company" and thus should be paid by "The Company." For example, since a life insurance policy is based on the principle of *Al-Mudharabah*, whereby the involved parties, that is, the insurer, assured and agents, share the profits of the business which is partly run by the assured's paid premiums, therefore the interest for the agent in a life insurance policy is a share of the profits made over the assured's paid premiums plus any dividend and bonus according to company policy. With regard to the insurable interest in a life policy under the Islamic model, the policyholder himself has an insurable interest if he is alive upon the expiry of the policy. If the assured dies at any time within the policy period, the insurable interest is to be vested only in the heirs of the assured according to the principles of *Mirath* and *Wasiyah*.

20.3 Objectives

Having an Islamic life insurance policy does not mean that one has insured one's own life, but it is a fair financial transaction catering for the benefits of certain helpless people in the society. The rationale behind having a Sharī'ah-justified life insurance policy could be summed up as follows:

- It is one of the means of providing a material safeguard for offspring and is thus in line with the saying of the Holy Prophet (saw). He (saw) spoke to this effect:

"it is better for you to leave you off-spring wealthy than to leave them poor, asking others for help." (Narrated by Saad b. Abi Waqqas (ra) (Dr Mohd. Muhsin Khan, n.d.))

- A life insurance policy provides future material security for widows and other dependants of the deceased (assured). The Holy Prophet (saw) in fact encouraged the providing of security for widows and poor persons as he highlighted in one of His traditions:

The one who looks after and works for a widow and for a poor person (dependant), is like a warrior fighting for the Cause of Allah (swt), or like a person who fasts during the day and prays throughout the night. [Narrated by Safwan bin Salim (ra)]. (Id., at no. 35)

- A life insurance policy guarantees future material protection for, inter alia, orphans, and it is again justified by the saying of the Holy Prophet (saw):

I and the person who looks after an orphan and provides for him will be in paradise like this, putting his index and middle finger together. [Narrated by Sahl bin Saad (ra)]. (Id., at No. 34)

- A life insurance policy provides certain persons (as widows, orphans and so on) with protection from unexpected future material difficulties, which may result a hardship for the life of these people. The Holy Prophet advised the *Ummah* to protect one from any form of hardship and difficulty when he said to the effect:

Whosoever removes a worldly grief from a believer Allah (swt) will remove from him one of the grieves of the day of Judgement. Whosoever alleviates a needy person Allah (swt) will alleviate from him in this world and the next... [Narrated by Abu Huraira (ra)]. (Ezzeddin Ibrahim, n.d.)

- Having a life insurance policy is like taking an initiative to reduce poverty and contribute towards a reasonable comfortable life without such difficulties. It is thus justified by the Qur'anic principle whereby Allah (swt) advised the creatures to seek from Him a comfortable life. He (swt) says:

> Our Lord! Give us comfortable life in this world and comfortable in the hereafter. (Qur'an, at ch. 2:201)

- A life insurance policy ensures mutual co-operation, a brotherly feeling towards others, which provides positive status and which can provide a feeling of brotherhood in society. For example, an assured pays the premium, which enables the insurer to invest and make a profit while the insurer ensures a financial protection for the assured's beneficiary(s). Such financial co-operation leads to a sense of brotherhood and economic progress. Moreover, having a life insurance policy is a positive initiative by the assured towards a positive material status of the widow, offspring and so on. Such mutual co-operation towards a positive goal is in fact ruled on by Allah (swt), where He (swt) says:

> Sustain in mutual co-operation among yourselves in righteousness and piety. (Qur'an, at ch. 5:2)

- Finally, having a life insurance policy is like taking an initiative towards ensuring a self-reliant society, without hardship and difficulties, and, of course, economic growth in society which may result in the elimination of hardship and bring about a comfortable standard of living more generally. It is thus in line with the Qur'anic principle where Allah (swt) Himself prefers an easy life for the creatures rather than them having difficulties. He (swt) says to the effect:

> Allah (swt) intends easy life for all of you while He does not want you to be in difficulties. (Id., at ch. 2:185)

20.4 Life Insurance: Conventional Versus Islamic

The purpose of scrutinising the differences in this area is to discover the basic contrast between the conventional system of life insurance and the Islamic model. This is because some *Ulama* and many Muslims are of the impression that a life insurance is totally prohibited in Islam. The argument has been raised from the scenario of life insurance policy practised under the conventional system. It is to be acknowledged here that even though in both the conventional system as well as in Islam a notion of the life insurance policy is being designed, there are undoubtedly several aspects whereby these systems are in conflict in terms of both principles and practices. I would therefore like to sum up the basic contrast between them which may enable us to grasp the nature of the Islamic model of a life insurance policy as an alternative to the one which is practised under the conventional system. The basic contrasts are as follows:

- A life insurance policy under the conventional system revolves around Riba, whereas an Islamic model of life insurance policy is totally free from this element for it operates based on the principle of *Al-Mudharabah* financing technique. (Anwar Ahmed Meenai 1995)

In a conventional life insurance system, the nominee(s) is an absolute beneficiary(s). Suffian J. (in *Re Man bin Mihat*, ((1965) 2, MLJ at 1)) gave a verdict that the nominee(s), inter alia, in a conventional life insurance policy takes absolutely and exclusively the benefits of the policy (Billah, M. Masum, n.d.). In contrast, the nominee(s) in a life policy under the Islamic model is not an absolute beneficiary(s) but a mere trustee who is in a position to receive the benefit of the policy on behalf of the assured's heirs and distribute it among them according to the principles of *Mirath* and *Wasiyah* (ibid.). In *Karim v. Hanifa* ([8] PLD 783), the High Court of Karachi ruled that the nominee(s) in a life insurance policy is nothing more than a mere agent (Billah, M. Masum, n.d.). The National Council of Muslim Religious Affairs in Malaysia also issued a *Fatwa* to the same effect in 1979, that the nominee(s) in a life insurance policy is a mere trustee who is supposed to receive the benefit over the policy and distribute it among the heirs according to the principles of *Mirath* and *Wasiyah*.[2]

The idea of a conventional life insurance policy is that if the assured person dies any time before the maturity of the policy, the nominee(s) is entitled to recover from the insurer the whole amount agreed in the policy; while if the assured is still alive upon the expiry of the policy period he is also entitled to the whole amount agreed in the policy plus the interest, dividends and any bonus, subject to company policy. On the contrary, the paradigm of an Islamic model of life insurance policy holds that if the assured dies before the policy matured the beneficiary(s) is

[2] The *Fatwa* was on succession and wills (1974) IMLJ at X.

entitled to the whole amount of paid premiums, the bonus and dividends according to company policy, a share of profits made over the paid premiums plus a donation from the company's charitable fund according to the financial status of the beneficiary(s) (i.e. if the beneficiary(s) is financially in a good condition, the amount will be small but if the beneficiary(s) is financially weak or unstable the amount could be bigger) (Billah, M. Masum, n.d.). Such transaction is considered as mutual co-operation towards the welfare of helpless people in society, and is thus in line with Qur'anic principles. Allah (swt) says to the effect:

> Co-operate among yourselves in righteousness and piety. (Qur'an, 5:2)

However, in a case where the assured is still alive at the maturity, he is entitled to the whole amount of paid premiums, a share of profit made over the paid premiums according to the principle of *Al-Mudharabah*, plus any bonus and dividends according to the company's policy.

In the operation of a life insurance policy under the conventional system, payments for the agents are to come out of the assured's premiums, whereas under the Islamic model, the agents work for the company and thus the company itself should pay them. This means that payment for agents could include a share of profits made over the paid premiums, plus any dividends and bonus.

With regard to the insurable interest under the conventional system, it is usually vested to the policyholder himself (Khuan, Lee Kam, n.d.) should he be alive upon the expiry of the policy. But, in the case of the death of the assured within the period, the insurable interest is to be vested in the husband or wife, parents or children, the benefactor or beneficiary or servant, company and director, trustee and employee, partners, mortgagor and mortgagee (Id., at 69f).

In contrast, under the Islamic model, the insurable interest is to be vested to the assured himself or to his heirs according to the principles of *Mirath* and *Wasiyah* (Billah 1970).

20.5 Shari'ah Rulings

It has been clearly established from the earlier discussion that a life insurance policy under the Islamic model is different from the one practised under the conventional system. Here I wish to propose the following basic governing principles for the Islamic model of life insurance.

Prior to entering into a life insurance agreement, the assured must have a sincere intention that the policy will not lead to gain but should look towards protection of their offspring, wife and the other dependants from unexpected future financial risk. Simultaneously, he also has to put his trust in Allah (swt) for the betterment of those dependants' future lives. Such initiative is thus in line with the advice of the Holy Prophet (saw):

> The Holy Prophet (saw) told a Bedouin Arab who left his camel untied trusting to the Will of Allah (swt): Tie the camel first then leave it to Allah (swt).[3]

A life insurance policy should not be involved in *Riba* but rather be based on the principles of the *Al-Mudharabah* financing technique, whereby the insurer as well as the assured or his beneficiaries share the profits, bonus and dividends accordingly.

In case of the assured's death at any time during the policy period, the beneficiary(s) of the assured should not fight for the whole amount but only for the paid premiums, a share of profits made over the paid premiums, bonus and dividends accordingly, plus a donation from the company's charitable fund according to the beneficiary(s) financial condition.

In a case where the assured is alive life upon the expiry of the policy period, the assured can only claim from the company the paid premiums, a share of profits (Adil Salahi, n.d.) made over the paid premiums, plus bonus and dividends according to the company's policy.

The nominee(s) in a life insurance policy does not necessarily have to be an absolute beneficiary(s) but a mere trustee who is under a duty to receive the benefits from the insurer and distribute them among the heirs of the assured according to the principles of *Mirath* and *Wasiyah*. Hence, should the nominee(s) fall into the category of heirs of the assured he/she is also entitled to a share accordingly.

The agents in a life insurance policy should not be paid out of the paid premiums by the assured but be paid out of the share of the profit made over the paid premiums by the company itself. This is because the agents are not working for the assured but for the company. Therefore, the agents should enjoy a share (a salary) of the profits according to the company's policy.

[3] *Sunan Al-Tirmidi*, Cagri Yayianlari, Istanbul Vol. 4, 1981, in *Kitabu Sifatul Qiyamat Wal-Raqaiq Al-Wara*, Bab 60, NO. 2517 at 668.

Regarding the investment of paid premiums, Adil Salahi suggested that the company (insurer) is under an obligation to invest the paid premiums in a lawful business which is free from *Riba* and other forms of unlawful transactions which are contrary to divine principles.

The insurable interest in a life policy should be presented either to the assured himself (should he be alive upon expiry of the policy period) or to the heirs of the assured (should the assured die at any time within the policy period) according to the principles of *Mirath* and *Wasiyah* (Billah, n.d.).

20.6 Misconceptions

Some Islamic scholars oppose the idea of contract of life insurance generally. They argue that a life insurance contract is contrary to divine principles and thus is not permissible in Islam. There is another group of *Ulama* who agree to the general insurance with certain conditions but they oppose the application of a life insurance policy (Billah, M. Masum, n.d.). In the following section, an attempt is made to highlight the opposing views of the *Ulama* against the validity of life insurance in today's society and possible refutation of this standpoint.

20.7 Negative Views

Among the opponents of the validity of life insurance are Mufti Mohd. Bakhit, Mohd. Abu Zuhra, Mohd. Musa, Ahmad Ibrahim, Al-Hanafi, Ibd Abdeen, Sheikh Shaukat, Khan Mohd. Yusuf Musa, Shaukat Alyan, Ahmad Fahmi, Ahmad Taha Sanusi, Abdur Rahman Isa, Ali Khaleef and a few others including Al-Sheikh Jad Al-Haq Ali Jad Al-Haq, all of whom vehemently oppose the idea as well as the operating of life insurance in light of divine sanctions. In their judgement, life insurance is absolutely opposed to the Shari'ah discipline and thus shall not be permissible in Islamic teachings.[4]

[4] See in Siddiqi, M.N., "Muslim Economic Thinking: A Survey of Contemporary Literature", (Ed.) Ahmad, Khurshid, in Studies in Islamic Economics, The Islamic Foundation, U.K. 1980 at 2116. Also see "Al-Tameen Alal Hayat Gaire jaizin Shar'an" in Al-Iqtasadul Islami, July 1995 at 60, and also see Hadagha, Refat Mohd., 'Insurance Contract and Its Provision in the Islamic Shari'ah', IIU Malaysia, (U.P.), 1995, at 17.

20.8 Grounds

The grounds for opposing the validity of life insurance are in fact based on many reasons. Here, I would like to sum up some of the principal grounds upon which the *Ulama* and many Muslims are reluctant to accept a life insurance policy under the aegis of Islamic teachings. Their arguments rely on the following grounds:

> It is a policy of insuring one's life. Sheikh Jad al-Haq issued a *Fatwa* against the validity of life insurance because it is a transaction, which ensures one's life, and insuring one's life by a creature is not permissible in the Shari'ah. (Al-Iqtisadul Islami, *loc. cit*)

A life insurance contract involves unlawful elements. A contract that involves such unlawful elements can never be binding, as the Holy Prophet (saw) says:

> Muslims are bound by the conditions except the condition which prohibits the permitted one or the one which permits the prohibited one. (Al-Sheikh Jad al-Haq, n.d.)

It contains the element of *Riba*. (Al-Sheikh Jad al-Haq, n.d.) Many *Ulama* oppose the validity of life insurance because it involves the elements of both kinds of *Riba*, that is, *Riba al-Fadhl'* and *Ribā al-Nasiah*. For example, if the insurer pays the insured or his beneficiary(s) in return of paid premiums more than what he paid, it becomes *'Ribā al-fadhl*, while the payments by the insurer to the assured after a particular period becomes *Riba al-Nasiah'*. Thus, both situations make a life insurance policy unlawful (Hadagha n.d.). This is because any transaction involving *Riba* does not have shelter in the Islamic Shari'ah, as Allah (swt) declared:

> Allah (swt) permitted trade while prohibited *Riba*. (Qur'an at ch. 2:275)

It supersedes the will of Allah (swt). In a life insurance policy, from the commencement of the contract between the insurer and the assured, the assured always aims that upon his death, his beneficiary(s) will gain a large amount of money. In such a situation the assured predetermines his own death as well as confirming the material gain for his beneficiary(s), whereas truly Allah (swt) is the one who determines one's death as well as future earnings. Allah (swt) reminds us of this:

> Nor does anyone know what it is that he will earn on the morrow, nor does anyone know in what land he is to die, verily Allah (swt) has full knowledge and He is acquainted (with all things). (Qur'an 31:34)

It contains an element of betting. In a betting the gambler always hopes for a chance to gain. Similarly, in a life insurance policy the assured upon the payment of premiums to the insurer always hopes for a chance of gaining a large amount of money. Hoping for such a chance is similar to gambling and thus Shari'ah never recognises it as a valid transaction.[5]

It has element of *Gharar* (uncertainty). Any contract whose *subject* matter or the object involves *Gharar'* the contract deemed to be null and void *ab initio*. In a life insurance contract, the subject matter is a death and it is not certain whether the assured's death will occur during the policy period. Thus, such uncertainty in a life insurance policy leads the policy being rendered invalid. Moreover, a transaction that involves *Gharar* is prohibited in the Islamic discipline, as the Hadith states:

> The Holy Prophet (saw) forbade the transaction through fraudulent means or *Gharar* sale. (Idoi, A. Rahman 1984)

If it contains the element of *Maisir* (gambling). A gambler pays a certain amount of money and subsequently hopes for a chance to gain an additional large amount of money (Musleh Uddin 1979). Any transaction involving such element of gambling is prohibited in the Shari'ah, as Allah (swt) says:

> They ask thee concerning wine and gambling say in the them is great sin. (Qur'an at ch. 2:219)

Similarly, in a life insurance policy the assured always hopes for a chance to gain, which is in the same vein as gambling and thus is prohibited in the Islamic 'Shari'ah.

There is no direct authority, which justifies life insurance. There are some who do not accept life insurance as a valid form of transaction. They claim that a life insurance policy is a transaction which cannot be justified by the injunctions from either the Qur'an or the Sunnah.

[5] It was deemed so in a Juridical Conference held in Mecca in Saban, 1398H.

It is contrary to the principles of *Tawakkul* (placing one's trust in Allah (swt). It is a fundamental obligation for believers, in conformity with their faith, to place their trust always on the Almighty Allah (swt). As Allah (swt) commands:

> but on Allah (swt) *Tawakkul* (put your trust) if you have faith. (Id., at ch. 14:12)

In a life insurance policy once the assured enters into an agreement and pays regular premiums, he hopes that when one day he dies the insurer will protect his beneficiary(s) financially. In this case, the assured puts his trust not in Allah (swt) but in the insurer, which is contrary to the Qur'anic principle of *Tawakkul*; therefore, a life insurance policy should be deemed unlawful.

It is contrary to the principles of *Mirath* and *Wasiyah*. It is a divine principle that one's property and wealth upon death are, *inter alia*, to be distributed according to the principles of both *Mirath* and *Wasiyah*. In light of this, the deceased has no jurisdiction to determine the beneficiary(s) upon his death. In a life insurance policy, however, the assured nominates the beneficiary(s) who are expected to enjoy the benefits of the policy. It seems that the assured determines the beneficiary(s). So, it is contrary to those principles as outlined (Billah, M. Masum, n.d.).

20.9 The *Fatwa* by Shaikh Al-Azhar

Sheikh al-Azhar, Al-Shaikh Jad-al-Haq Ali Jad al-Haq, responded in a *Fatwa* session on the position of life insurance in Islamic Shari'ah which has appeared in *al-Iqtisadul Islami* in July 1995, in the *Fatwa* column, at 60. In his *Fatwa* he established that a life insurance policy is prohibited in Islamic Sharī'ah (Al-Iqtisadl-Islami, *supra*). His claim was based on the following grounds:

> In the light of the principles of Islamic Shari'ah no one could ensure others' wealth or property unless there is a fear of unjust enrichment, losses or destruction. In a life insurance policy these three circumstances are not available; moreover, a life insurance policy involves the element of *Riba* and therefore it is not allowed in Islam. (Ibid.)

> Life insurance is a policy which insurers one's life and thus it is not permissible in Islam. (Ibid.)
>
> A life insurance policy involves the element of *Gharar* (uncertainty). A transaction which involves *Gharar* is not valid in the eyes of the Islamic Sharī'ah and therefore a life insurance is unlawful. (Ibid.)

Moreover, he went on to prolong his discussion by arguing that a life insurance contract revolves not around mutual co-operation but unlawful elements and thus if a contract revolves around such elements it is null and void relating on the following Hadith:

> Muslims are bound by the conditions except the of conditions which prohibit the permitted one or the one which permits the prohibited one. (As quoted in ibid.)

Finally, he advised Muslims that they should not get involved in a life insurance policy because anyone who obtains money from such a policy is *Haram*. (Al-Iqtisadul Islami, *supra*).

20.10 Justification

There are differences of grounds for relying on the divine authority, authenticating powers and analytical approaches put forward by distinguished Islamic scholars in opposing the operation of life insurance in the light of Sharī'ah discipline. I sincerely believe that if those scholars would spend some time deeply concentrating on the issue of life insurance policies without looking at the nature of how the conventional system operates but consider the material risk of unfortunate orphans, widows and other dependants who may unexpectedly lose their breadwinner, then surely they could come up with an alternative Islamic model of life insurance justified by the divine sanctions, which may protect these vulnerable persons from unexpected future material risks and ensure the elimination of poverty in society while guaranteeing an economic growth in the Muslim *ummah*. I would like to respond to the views put forward by the opponents against the validity of life insurance policies, which will enable us to understand the actual scenario of a life insurance policy under Islamic teaching, and be able to distinguish a life insurance policy under Islamic teaching from one which operate under the conventional system.

Aside from the various ways, outlined earlier in this chapter, in which we can see that *Takaful* does not contravene the adjurations of the Qur'an, to have a life insurance policy does not supersede the will of Allah (swt), nor is it contrary to the principles of *Taqdir* (fate), as some argue that the assured in a life insurance policy determines his own death, while ensuring a future financial gain for his beneficiary(s), and meanwhile places his trust in the insurer for the financial protection of his beneficiary(s). These situations would overrule the power of Allah (swt). In responding to this argument, in a life insurance policy the assured believes that he will surely die, which does not mean that he determines his own death, and such a believe is in line with the Qur'anic injunction:

> Every soul shall have a taste of death. (Id., at ch. 3:185)

The assured in a life policy does not determine the future financial condition of his beneficiary(s), but rather he takes an initiative towards rescuing his offspring and so on from future material risk. This is also in line with the tradition of the Holy Prophet (saw):

> Whosoever takes an initiative to alleviate one's [inter alia, material] difficulties, Allah (swt) will lighten his difficulties in the world and the next.[6]

Moreover, the assured does not place his trust in the insurer to protect his beneficiary(s) materially but he is in financial agreement with the insurer for a mutual co-operation to look after the future welfare of his beneficiary(s), and it is no doubt justified by the Qur'anic principle of mutual co-operation:

> Co-operate ye one another in righteousness and piety. (Qur'an, at ch. 5:2)

A life insurance policy does not involve elements of betting. Mustafa Al-Zarqa opined that in a bet the person always hopes for a chance and there is no element of co-operation in it (Al-Zarqa, Mustafa 1984), rather it is some sort of competition. In contrast, a life insurance policy is based on the principle of co-operation (the principle is set out at 5:2 of the Qur'an) in which the assured never hopes for a chance but works for the

[6] *Sahih al-Muslim*, as compiled in An Nawari, *Riyadus Saleheen*, Vol. No. 245.

welfare of orphans, widows and other dependants, which is in line with the saying of the Holy Prophet (saw).

A life insurance policy does not revolve around the element of gambling because a life insurance policy is for the purpose of the material welfare of orphans, widows and other dependants, whereas gambling is a game of chance whereby the gambler always hopes to gain. Therefore, a life insurance policy is contrary to gambling. *Al-Dareer* acknowledged that in the insurance policy there is safety against danger whereas gambling creates danger, so how could an insurance policy be equal to gambling? (Al-Dareer Sideeq 1990).

There is no element of uncertainty (*Gharar)* in a life insurance policy because the subject matter is the death of the assured; the assured believes that he will die one day, as ordained in the Qur'an, and thus it is not uncertain (*Gharar*). Moreover, sharing profits over the paid premiums are also not uncertain because a life insurance policy is based on the principle of *Al-Mudharabah*, whereby if the assured dies within the policy period, the beneficiary(s) will get the benefits. But if the assured is still alive upon the expiry of the policy period, he is also entitled to the claim according to the principles of *Al-Mudharabah*. In all these situations, the subject matter, the object and consideration (premiums) of the transaction are clear and not uncertain (*Gharar*).

Even though there is no express authority from the Qur'an or Sunnah highlighting the role and place of a life insurance policy, there are a number of moments in the Qur'an and Sunnah which impliedly justify a model of life insurance policy for the Muslim *Ummah* which is quite different from that which operates under the conventional system. For example, a life insurance policy is based on the principle of mutual co-operation, is justified by the Qur'anic injunction at 5:2, operates along the lines of *Al-Mudharabah* which is justified by the Sunnah of the Holy Prophet (saw) and there are many other authorities and authenticating statements which justify different aspects of life insurance policies, as mentioned earlier.

Some argue that a life insurance policy is contrary to the principles of *Tawakkul* (placing trust in Allah (swt)), because in a life insurance policy the assured puts his trust not in Allah (swt) but in the insurer who is expected to protect the beneficiary(s) financially. Responding to this argument, I would like to point out here that a life insurance policy is not contrary to the principle of *Tawakkul*, but it is a policy whereby the insured takes an initiative for the welfare of his offspring and so on, in which he mutually agrees with the insurer that the latter will undertake to provide a material assistance in consideration of the paid premiums. The assured simultaneously places his trust in Allah (swt) for the betterment of his beneficiaries' future life. Thus, the assured does not *Tawakkul* on the insurer but on Allah (swt). This is in line with the saying of the Holy Prophet (saw):

> The Holy Prophet (saw) told a Bedouin Arab who left his camel untied trusting to the will of Allah (swt): Tie the camel first then leave it to [put your trust in] Allah (swt). (Sunan At-Tirmidi, *supra*)

Nor is a life insurance policy contrary to the principles of *Mirath* and *Wasiyah* (Billah, M. Masum, n.d.). In a life insurance policy, the assured nominates a particular person(s) as a nominee(s) who is nothing more than a trustee,[7] who is under a responsibility to receive the benefits over the policy on behalf of the heirs of the assured[8] and distribute them amongst them according to the principles of *Mirath* and *Wasiyah*. Hence, the nominee(s) is entitled only to a portion of the benefits over the policy if he/she falls under the category of heirs of the assured.

20.11 Analysing the *Fatwa* of Sheikh Al-Azhar (Al-Iqtisadul Islami, Supra)

Sheikh Al-Azhar al-Sheikh Jad al-Haq Ali Jad al-Haq has submitted in a *Fatwa* session recently that a life insurance policy is unlawful in the light of Shari'ah (*Haram*). His claim for such a decision was based on various grounds (as mentioned earlier). I should like to respond to the grounds that the honourable Sheikh has put forward as a basis for opposing the validity of life insurance policies as follows.

> In Sharī'ah discipline, no one has the right to insure the other's property unless there is a fear of unjust enrichment, losses or destruction. In a life insurance policy, the insurer insures a benefit over the paid premiums (by the assured), for the welfare of the beneficiary(s) of the assured, for an unexpected event, the assured's death (loss of life) and also for the fear of the loss

[7] See the Judgement of the Supreme Court of Pakistan in *Amtul Habeeb v Musarrat Parveen*, [1974] PLD 185

[8] This principle has been laid down in a *Fatwa* issued by the National Council of Muslim Religious Affairs, Malaysia. See in [1974] IMLJ at X.

of the beneficiary's material stability upon the death of the assured. In all situations the life insurance policy contains an element of loss. Abu Jaib has pointed out that an insurance policy is a compensation for any loss incurred by the insured and it is neither a profit nor a gain as with betting (Abu Jaib, Saeed 1983). Hence, a life insurance policy is not contrary to Sharī'ah principles.

A life insurance policy does not involve elements of *Riba* but it is a financial transaction based on the principle of *Al-Mudharabah* financial technique relying on the principles of mutual co-operation which is justified by the Qur'anic sanction. Allah (swt) says:

> Co-operate ye one another in righteousness and piety. (Al-Qur'an at ch. 5:2)

A life insurance policy does not involve insuring one's own life, but it is a mutual financial transaction towards the welfare of orphans, widows and other dependants. Such an initiative is in fact well justified by the sayings of the Holy Prophet (saw). As He (saw) said in the following Hadith:

> Narrated by Sahal bin Sa'ad (r) the Holy Prophet (saw) said: I and the person who looks after an orphan and provides for him will be in paradise. (Sahih al-Bukhari, at no. 34)
>
> Narby Abu Huraira (ra) the Holy Prophet (saw) said ... whosoever takes an initiative (towards the welfare of) one's inter alia financial difficulties, Allah (swt) will lighten his difficulties in this world and in the hereafter. (Sahih al-Muslim, *supra*)
>
> Narrated by Safwan bin Salim (ra) the Holy Prophet (saw) said: the one who looks after and works for a widow and for a poor person is like a warrior fighting for the cause of Allah (swt) or like a person who fasts during the day and pray throughout the night. (Sahih al-Bukhari, at no. 35)
>
> Narrated by Saad bin Abi Waqqas (ra) ... the Holy Prophet (saw) said ... it is better for you to leave your off-spring wealthy than to leave them poor, asking others for help. (Id., at 725)

A life insurance policy does not contain any element of *Gharar*. The assured believes that the subject matter of life insurance is his death which is certain and not *Gharar*; moreover, the benefit from the policy in consideration of paid premiums is also available which is certain according to the principle of *Al-Mudharabah* and thus there is no element of *Gharar* at work. Hence, the misconception that life insurance involves *Gharar* is very much rebuttable.

A life insurance contract has been accused of involving unlawful elements such as *Gharar*, gambling, *Riba* and so on, which render the contract unlawful as claimed by Shaikh al-Azhar (Al-Iqtisadul Islami, *supra*). But it is a mutual financial contract that is free from the above unlawful elements (as proved in the earlier discussion) and therefore, it is binding, as justified by the saying of the Holy Prophet (saw):

> Muslims are bound by their contract except the one which prohibits the permitted one or permits the prohibited one. (Sunan al-Tirmidi, as quoted in ibid.)

Based on these responses, I would like to humbly remark that the idea that Shaikh al-Azhar put forward in conclusion of his *Fatwa*, advising Muslim *ummah* not to engage in a life insurance policy because it is *Haram* (unlawful) should be rebuttable. I sincerely expect that the Muslim *ummah* should not be confused but will clearly understand the concept that life insurance is valid if applied in the right way and that benefits can be rightly gained from it.

20.12 Further Justification

From the earlier debates and justifications based on various authorities and authenticities, it is quite clear that a life insurance policy designed under the Islamic model is an alternative to a conventional life insurance policy for the contemporary Muslim *ummah*. Nevertheless, I would also like to present a few other grounds here to justify the idea that a life insurance policy is not permissible for the purpose of luxury but that it *is* permissible and encouraged by Muslim *ummah* for *necessity*, in order to ensure economic growth and stability among the Muslim *ummah* of today. Further grounds for the justification of a life insurance policy are as follows:

> A life insurance policy is similar to a contract of *al-Wadiah* (deposit) whereby two parties in a financial transaction engage in an agreement that one party deposits money as an *Amanah* (trust) to the other party to be kept for the purpose of safety (Al-Zobydi, Mohammad 1967). *Al-Wadiah* is justified by the Qur'anic injunction where Allah (swt) commanded people to fulfil the trust (of, *inter alia, Wadiah*).

> Allah (swt) commands you to render back your trusts to those to whom they are due. (Qur'an, ch. 4:58)

A life policy is a financial transaction which has been dealt with by the people before Islam under the doctrine of *al-Aqila* as an *'Urf* (custom) which had been accepted by the Holy Prophet (saw), whereby the people of every tribe used to deposit money for a certain amount in order to pay blood money as a compensation on behalf of the killer of their own tribe to the heirs of the victim of other tribe. Such *'Urf* (custom) was deemed to bring benefit to society. A custom beneficial to society is permissible in Islam, as justified by the saying of the Holy Prophet (saw):

> Whatever Muslims see good, it is good in the eyes of Allah (swt). (Ibn Qudama, Rawdatul Nazir, n.d.)

A life insurance policy is based on the sanction of mutual co-operation so as the doctrine of *al-Aqila* practice was also based on mutual co-operation, therefore Zarqa and Alwan accepted the idea that there is great similarity between *Takaful* insurance and *al-Aqila* in the sense of them both being founded on co-operation (Al-Zarqa, Mustafa, n.d.).

Every transaction is basically acceptable, unless it involves unlawful elements. Relying on this principle, it is submitted here that in a life insurance policy the elements it contains are in line with the Sharī'ah principles (the life insurance policy which is based on the Islamic model), and therefore it is undoubtedly lawful.

A life insurance policy is for the purpose of sustaining public interest. For example, the purpose of a life insurance policy is to protect the orphans, widows and other dependants of the assured from future material risk and thus, it is a transaction to be justified by the doctrine of *Masaleh al-Mursalah* (public interest). A transaction which is in the public interest is lawful, because it eliminates hardship and assists a comfortable life for human beings, which in line with the Qur'anic injunction:

> Allah (swt) intends every facility [inter alia, a comfortable life] for you; He does not want to put you to difficulties. (Qur'an ch. 2:185)

A life insurance policy is not an attempt simply to gain profits or a way to gamble, rather it is a way to provide compensation for damage or loss. This is because the policy is an agreement between the insurer and the assured that, if the assured dies within the policy period, the insurer will pay an amount of money in consideration of paid premiums to the beneficiary(s) of the assured. Such a payment is like compensation for the loss of opportunity of future earnings by the breadwinner (assured) due to his death. To provide such compensation is a form of mutual co-operation, which is commanded by Allah (swt), thus:

> Co-operate one another in righteousness and piety. (Qur'an ch. 5:2)

A life insurance policy is similar to a retirement pension scheme. Al-Zarqa and al-Alwan apparently discovered that all contemporary scholars agreed on the validity of retirement pension scheme (Al-Zarqa, n.d.). Adil Salahi similarly acknowledged that

> all scholars and seats of Islamic learning approved of the concept of pension because it gives the subscriber security for himself and his Family in the difficult circumstances of his leaving work or in case of death. (Salahi, Adil, supra, n.d.)

Salahi, relying on his acknowledgement, poses the question:

> Why should Family security be lawful in one system and not in the other when the method of operation is practically the same? (Ibid.)

Relying on the above justifications it is admitted here that life insurance is like a pension scheme (which had been widely introduced during the period of Sayiidana Omar (ra)); therefore, it is not an unlawful transaction.

A life insurance policy is also justified based on the principle of necessity (*Darurah*). For instance, it is an important task for the guardian to work for the welfare of his own dependants. This is in line with the tradition of the Holy Prophet (saw) where he said:

> It is better for you to leave your offspring wealthy than to leave them poor, asking others for help. (Sahih al-Bukhari, at no 725)

It is also to be noted here that in the case of necessity that which is prohibited is also to be permitted in the Islamic discipline, as Ibn Nawjeem stated in his book *al-Ashbah Wa al-Nazaira*:

> Necessity permits an unlawful act. (Ibn Najeem, n.d.)

A life insurance policy of course does not allow for unlawful transaction, but why not if the principle of necessity allows it to be permissible.

A life insurance contract is a binding promise. In light of Islamic Jurisprudence, a promise either unilateral or bilateral is in both situations binding, as ordained in the Qur'an:

> O ye who believe? Fulfil all agreements. (Qur'an, Ch. 5:1)

According to Imam Malik (ra), the founder of the Maliki School of law, every binding promise is lawful; therefore, every insurance contract contains a binding promise and thus it is lawful. In other words, in a life insurance contract, there is an agreement between the assured and the insurer which is a binding promise towards the protection of widows, orphans and so on from future material risk, and therefore such a binding promise makes an insurance contract valid.

A life insurance contract involves elements of donation. This is because the assured pays regular premiums for the protection of his beneficiary(s); such payments of a premium are like a donation for needy people. Moreover, once the insurer pays an amount of money together with an additional amount from the charitable fund to the beneficiary(s) of the assured in consideration of the paid premiums, this also involves the element of donation. A donation is lawful in the Islamic jurisprudence as justified by the practices of the Prophet (saw):

> The Prophet (saw) used to accept gifts [donation]. (Al-Sanany, Mohammad 1987)

Relying on the above authenticity, this analysis admits that a life insurance policy does involve elements of donation and, therefore, such a policy is to be held lawful in the eyes of the Islamic discipline.

20.13 Conclusion

Our analysis concludes that conventional practice and Islam have designed different models of life insurance policy. There are many similarities in the two systems but both also diverge. In conclusion, I would like to summarise where the conventional and the Islamic model are in contrast. Finally, I wish to express a hope for the future application of the Islamic life insurance policy.

A life insurance policy under the conventional system involves, inter alia, *Riba*, which is opposed to the principles of *Mirath* and *Wasiyah*, payments of agents to be out of the paid premiums and so on. In contrast, a life insurance policy under the Islamic model is like a pension scheme, which operates based on the principles of *Al-Mudharabah* financing techniques, does not clash with the principles of *Mirath* and *Wasiyah*, as highlighted earlier, and also the payments for the agents are to be paid by the insurer out of the profit made over the paid premiums.

The insurable interest in life under the conventional system is to be vested to those who are not necessarily the heirs of the assured. In contrast, an insurable interest in life under the Islamic model should be vested only in those who are entitled to the property of the assured according to the principles of *Mirath* and *Wasiyah*.

The nominee(s) under the conventional system is an absolute beneficiary over the policy, whereas the nominee(s) under the Islamic model of a life insurance policy is nothing more than a trustee(s) who is responsible for receiving the benefits over the policy and distributing them among the heirs of the assured, according to the principles of *Mirath* and *Wasiyah*.

I would like to extend my humble request to the respectable *Ulama*, who oppose a life insurance policy generally, that they could oppose the conventional life insurance but not that which is designed under the Islamic model. It is my sincere hope that this chapter, and indeed the book as a whole, might enable the Muslim *ummah* to have no further doubt as to the application of an Islamic life insurance policy. Islamic scholars could come up with a better model as an alternative to the existing life insurance operating under the conventional system, for the noble purpose of ensuring further economic growth in contemporary Muslim society.

References

1. Ali, A. Y. (n.d.), *The Holy Qur'an*, Text and Translation.
2. *Fatwa*, issued by the National Council for Muslims Religious Affairs in Malaysia, see in [1974] I MLJ at x.
3. Billah, M. Masum (1993), "Life Insurance? An Islamic View", in *Arab Law Quarterly*, 8: 4, at 319.
4. *Sahih al-Bukhari* (trans. Eng.) Mohd. Muhsin Khan, Vol. 8, Kazi Publications, Lahore, Pakistan, 1979, no. 725, at p. 477.
5. *Sahih al-Muslim* as compiled in al-Nawawi, *Forty Hadith* (trans. Eng) Ezzeddin Ibrahim, *et al.* I.I.F.S.O., 1985 at no. 36.

6. Mufti Mawlana Mohd. Shafi, *Bima Zindegi*, (trans. Eng) Anwar Ahmed Meenai, *Life Insurance*, Darul Ishat, Karachi, 1995, at 36.
7. (1965) 2, MLJ at 1.
8. [1970] PLD 783.
9. The *Fatwa* on succession and wills, (1974) IMLJ at X.
10. Khuan, Lee Kam, *Life Insurance in Malaysia*, life insurance association of Malaysia, Kuala Lumpur, 1986 at 63.
11. *Sunan Al-Tirmidi*, Cagri Yayianlari, Istanbul Vol. 4, 1981, in *Kitabu Sifatul Qiyamat Wal-Raqaiq Al-Wara*, Bab 60, NO. 2517 at 668.
12. Adil Salahi, 'Is Life Insurance Haram?" in New Horizon, Islamic Banking and Insurance, Nov. 1995 no. 45 at 12.
13. Siddiqi, M.N., "Muslim Economic Thinking: A Survey of Contemporary Literature", (Ed.) Ahmad, Khurshid, in Studies in Islamic Economics, The Islamic Foundation, U.K. 1980 at 2116. Also see "Al-Tameen Alal Hayat Gaire jaizin Shar'an" in Al-Iqtasadul Islami, July 1995 at 60, and also see Hadagha, Refat Mohd., 'Insurance Contract and Its Provision in the Islamic Shari'ah', IIU Malaysia, (U.P.), 1995, at 17.
14. *The Juridical Conference* held in Mecca in Saban, 1398H.
15. Idoi, A. Rahman, *Shari'ah: The Islamic Law*, A.S. Noordeen, Kuala Lumpur, 1984 at 359.
16. Musleh Uddin, M. *Insurance and Islamic Law*, 3rd ed. Islamic Publications Ltd., Lahore, 1979 at 143.
17. *Sahih al-Muslim*, as compiled in An Nawari, Riyadus Saleheen, Vol. No. 245.
18. Al-Zarqa, Mustafa, *Nizam Al-Tameen*, Beirut, 1984.
19. Al-Dareer Sideeq, *Al-GhararWa al-atharohu fi al-Oqud*, Beirut, 1990 at 649.
20. The Judgement of the Supreme Court of Pakistan in *Amtul Habeeb v Musarrat Parveen*, [1974] PLD 185.
21. This principle has been laid down in a *Fatwa* issued by the *National Council of Muslim Religious Affairs*, Malaysia. See in [1974] IMLJ at X.
22. Abu Jaib, Saeed, *Al-Tameen binal Hazeer Wal Ebaha*, SyriaDarul Fikir, Syria 1983 at 36.
23. Al-Zobydi, Mohammad, *Tajul Aroos*, Vol. 2, Kuwait, 1967 at 591.
24. Ibn Qudama, *Rawdatul Nazir* (n.d.) at 85.
25. Al-Sanany, Mohammad, *Subul Al-Salam*, Vol. 1–3, 1987 at 90.

CHAPTER 21

Family *Takaful* Plan

21.1 Introduction

Life has its various ups and downs; we cannot be certain of what the future holds. In other words, we deal with uncertainties and risks all the time in our daily life. In order to minimise the risks we may face unexpectedly, people choose insurance policies as their future protection. Such a policy acts as a buffer against any misfortunes. That is, any loss incurred will be compensated according to the stipulations mentioned in the contract. Insurance policies are very popular among the non-Muslim community because they provide mutual financial assistance whenever people face loss due to accident, death, injuries or for other reasons. However, Muslims have a dilemma vis-à-vis whether to become a participant in such programs as they contradict Shari'ah rules and regulations. *Takaful* Malaysia provides the solution to this problem by offering similar products to the Muslim public. The obvious difference is that the products offered by *Takaful* conform to the Islamic teachings. However, to be specific, we will only discuss one particular product here: the Family *Takaful* scheme.

Protecting one's family is a very important fundamental in every person's life. This protection is crucial to make sure our family members will live in peace and harmony. There are many ways to protect our family. One is to insure our family with Family *Takaful* scheme. In this context, Family *Takaful* scheme is similar to Family *Takaful* fund. Thus, family members, that is, the descendants of a common ancestor, are provided with financial

Mohd Ma'Sum Billah, *Islamic Insurance Products*,
https://doi.org/10.1007/978-3-030-17681-5_21

resources for specific purposes. For instance, if the participant dies or acquires a permanent disability, then his family will be compensated. Therefore, this scheme is the perfect alternative to the conventional life insurance policy as it performs the same function but is based on the divine law.

Family *Takaful* scheme ensures some amount of money to lighten the financial burden of the people we love if something bad were to happen. The purpose is to save systematically to generate a long-term fund to cover the needs of our family in the future. It is as a guarantee or form of security to help us face the possibilities of accidents, permanent disabilities, to pay for hospital expenses or costs due to other unforeseen mishaps.

21.2 Central Idea

Family *Takaful* is a fixed-period, long-term savings and investment programme. The main idea of this scheme is to ensure that a certain sum of money will always be available to ease the financial burden of loved ones in times of need due to untimely death or other mishaps. It is a form of life insurance that is prescribed in the *Takaful* Act 1984. However, the Act only provides a few provisions concerning the implementation of the scheme. That is, it must conform to Islamic teachings and fundamentals. A family can enjoy investment profits and benefits from the Family *Takaful* plan and they will be provided with mutual financial assistance if the need arise.

There are three main purposes of Family *Takaful*. It is designed to enable participants to participate in a *Takaful* scheme with the aim to save regularly. This is because once a person participates in the programme, he is required to make monthly payment as agreed upon in the contract. The scheme also enables participants to invest and earn profits. However, there is no need to worry because all investments will be made and monitored by Bank of Islam. That is, the bank will only invest money in permissible activities. Another purpose of the scheme is to provide protection in the form of benefits to the family of participants who die before the maturity of their plans.

Family *Takaful* plans are based on certain criteria. First, the plan must be for a fixed period. A participant has the right to choose any plan offered by the company. Both the participant and the *Takaful* company will get into a long-term *Takaful* contract based on the principle of profit sharing (*Al-Mudharabah*). The contract clearly states the rights and obligations of the parties. Usually, the maturity date ranges from a minimum of five years to a maximum of 40 years. Although it is a fixed-period plan, the sum insured is not fixed. The amount of benefits that a participant receives from a Family *Takaful* plan depends on the maturity period. It also depends on the amount of contributions that the participant has agreed to make. The profits will be earned from the investment of his own contributions.

Upon deciding which plan he wants, the participant also agrees to pay a certain amount every month. Once again, he has the right to choose how much he wants to pay, provided the amount be more or at least equal to the minimum contribution set by the company. That is why Family *Takaful* is also described as a defined contribution plan. The participant can make their payment either in the form of monthly instalment, quarterly, half-yearly or by yearly instalment. From here, we can see that this is very different from the conventional method, in the sense that the amount of the premium that must be paid in such a policy is fixed regardless of the means of each participant.

The money paid to the *Takaful* company for the fund will go into two different accounts: the Participants' Account (PA) and the Participants' Special Account (PSA). The PA is actually a form of savings and investment account. The larger proportion of the money is paid into this account. On the other hand, the PSA represents a *Tabarru'* account. Money is paid into the PSA with the intention of helping fellow participants in times of hardship. So, a certain percentage from the payment received from each participant will be pooled in this account so that it can be used to provide mutual financial assistance for the needy due to certain circumstances such as death or other disasters. The money from the account will not be beneficial to all participants, but only to those who really need such funds. For instance, it will be paid to the families of participants who die before the maturity period of their plans. The company will determine the actual contribution of each participant to this account.

The *Takaful* company then invests the money obtained from both accounts on a profit- and loss-sharing basis (*Al-Mudharabah*). Such a basis is not contrary to Islam either in its operations or in the nature of the business. This is because it totally conforms to the rules and regulations of Islam. The *Takaful* company as *mudharib* will make investments according to the Shari'ah rules and the profit will then be pooled back into the account.

The profits generated from the investment will be divided between the participants and the *Takaful* company according to the agreed ratio. On the other hand, any loss made from the money invested in the accounts shall be borne by the *Takaful* company alone. This decision is recommended by the committee on the *Takaful* scheme, even though the Islamic principle of *Al-Mudharabah* requires that the participants should share the profits and losses of the company. This may be because the operators feel responsible for any loss that may have occurred due to their own error of judgment.

For instance, both the participant and *Takaful* operator agree on a monthly instalment of RM 100. The operator sets that 90% (RM 90) from the payment will go to the PA and another 10% (RM 10) is paid to the PSA. To get profit for the PA, the operator puts the money in an investment company on the ratio of 50:50. Let us say the profit is RM 20. Then 50% of the profit (equal to RM 10) will be paid back to the PA while the rest will be shared between the *Takaful* company and the investment company. The illustration in Fig. 21.1 explains the process of the Family *Takaful* scheme.

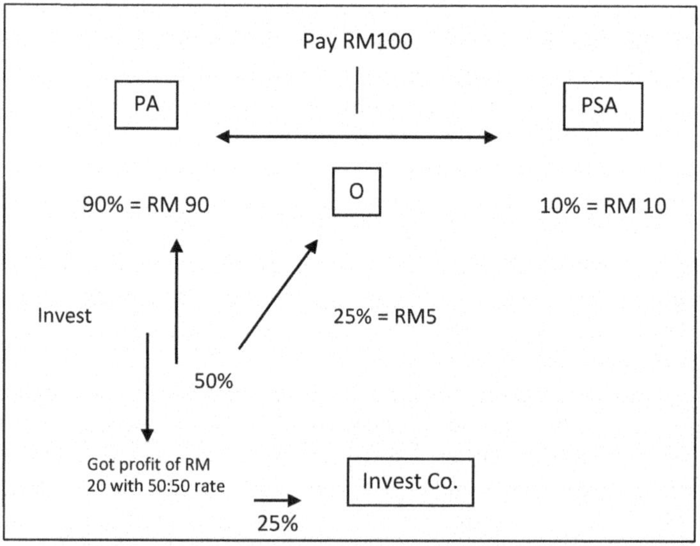

Fig. 21.1 Process of the Family *Takaful* scheme. (Source: Author's own)

The Family *Takaful* Plan is also open to non-Muslims. However, upon an application being received from a non-Muslim, the *Takaful* operator will investigate the source of the person's income first. If the source of income comes from the prohibited activities, then the application will be rejected. Otherwise, he will be granted permission to participate in the scheme. This is because the money received from all participants will be pooled into a single account for investment purposes. Therefore, if the money comes from *Haram* (prohibited) activities, then the profit that will be distributed later on will not be 100% free from prohibited elements.

Furthermore, the *Takaful* Act 1984 (*Islamic Financial Services Act* 2013) does not provide any provision concerning the recipient of the insurance benefits. Therefore, the Insurance Act 1996 is applicable here. Section 167 (Billah, M. M., 2003) of the Act provides that in a life insurance policy held by a Muslim who nominates someone in the policy, the nominee shall be a mere trustee, agent, manager or executor. He is the one who will receive the benefits from the policy and it will be his job to distribute it among legal heirs in line with the principles of *Faraid*. In other words, the benefits of a life insurance policy of a Muslim shall be treated as estate property. It must be divided accordingly among the heirs.

Section 166 (Billah, M. M., 2003) of the Insurance Act 1996, on the other hand, is applicable to non-Muslims but not to Muslims. It provides that if a non-Muslim who holds a life insurance policy and nominates someone as the beneficiary, then the nominee shall be an absolute beneficiary of the policy. In other words, the principle of *Faraid* will not be applicable to non-Muslims although he participates in the same policy as a Muslim.

Generally, benefits will be paid after the maturity date. However, there are circumstances that call for early payment. Some of these circumstances are as follows (Table 21.1):

21.3 Shari'ah Rulings

Every soul shall have a test on death. (Qur'an, 3:185)

In the above verse, Allah reminds us that everyone will die. Therefore, people must be well prepared not only to face the *akhirah*, but also to provide some security in form of materials to the remaining members of the family. Only then they will not face difficulties in going on with their lives. Life insurance or the Family *Takaful* scheme provides the partici-

Table 21.1 Special circumstances

Event	*Treatment*
The participant dies before maturity of the *Takaful* plan	Claims will include the total amount of *Takaful* instalment paid from the first day of inception to the due date of the instalment payment prior to his death plus his shares of profit from the investment credited into his PA. The outstanding *Takaful* instalment paid by the deceased calculated from the date of his death to the date of maturity. This amount will be paid from PSA according to *Takaful* contract as agreed by all the participants.
The participant is still alive at the date of maturity	He will get the total amount of instalments paid by him during the plan period plus his share of profits from the investment credited into his PA. However, he will not get back his contribution that go into the PSA.
The participant is involved in an accident but is still very much alive	He will get the total amount of instalments paid by him during the plan period plus his share of profit from the investment credited into his PA. He is also entitled to claim some amount from the PSA according to the *Takaful* contract as agreed by all the participants on the basis that he now is considered as a needy person.
The participant cannot continue paying the rest of his instalments due to personal injury (e.g. paralysis)	Claims will include the total amount of instalments paid prior to his inability to pay plus his share of profits from the investment credited to his PA. He will also get some amount from the PSA according to the *Takaful* contract as agreed by all participants. He will be treated as someone who has died before the maturity period.
If the participant withdraws the money before maturity	He is not required to pay back the money because the amount is his in the first place.
If the participant stops paying for some months, then continues his payment again after several months	For the period he missed paying his instalment, if anything happens, he will not get the coverage. Coverage is provided for as long as he continues to pay the instalment.

Source: Author's collection

pants with just that. Family *Takaful* scheme is not a policy that insures one's own life, but it is financial protection for the needy in our society. That is, in the event of unexpected death, the remaining heirs will receive benefits as a buffer to continue with their lives. The matter is further supported by a saying of the Prophet (saw):

> It is better to leave your offspring wealthy than to leave them poor, asking others for help. (Hadith narrated by Saad b. Abi Waqas)

According to the Qur'an, any deed done with a good intention is permissible as long as it does not contradict the teachings of Islam. The Family *Takaful* scheme is permitted because it helps society to be better financially, and the scheme is done collectively to enjoin the right—meaning that the scheme pools the resources from many individuals to develop a big collective account. This will spread the risks (systematic and unsystematic) over a large quantity that will help to reduce risk involved. Another example is the PSA, which is a collective fund where each participant must contribute. The money from the fund is considered as charitable donation, and will be used to help the needy. Therefore, the point of enjoining the right in the above verse is fulfilled.

> And cooperate ye one another in righteousness and piety. (Qur'an, 5:3)

In another verse, Muslims are encouraged to consult one another to come out with the best result. Allah said in the Qur'an,

> who conduct their affairs by mutual consultation. (Qur'an, 42:38)

The Family *Takaful* plan can be considered as a contract with a mutual agreement between two parties, whereby the parties are the participant and the *Takaful* operator. The parties express their consent, consult each other upon the agreed payment, ratio of profit and in the period of maturity of the plan.

The Family *Takaful* plan payment that goes to the PSA is considered as a charitable donation. This agrees with the teachings of Islam, in which people are encouraged to give charity. Unlike the Christian approach that stresses charity begins at home, the Islamic approach encourages extending kindness to all people no matter who they are. Thus, the plan conforms to the standards set by the Shari'ah in which the funds in the PSA will be used only by the needy, as stated by the Qur'an:

> to spend of your substance, out of love for Him, for your kin, for orphans, for the needy, for the wayfarer, for those who ask, and for the ransom of slaves. (Qur'an, 2:177)

The above verse is related to the saying of the Prophet, "Who is the best Muslim? He who fears Allah and has good relationship with his parents and relatives." That is to say, a Muslim should help another Muslim in the name of brotherhood in Islam. Therefore, using the PSA in the Family *Takaful* plan not only provides financial assistance to the needy but also strengthens the relationship among Muslim society at large.

Moreover, Family *Takaful* plan gives the freedom to participants to choose what they want to do with their contributions. That is, the *Takaful* operator asks for participants' consent first before making the contract binding. If after several years, the participant decides to withdraw from the policy regardless of the maturity period, it is his right to do so. Even the operator cannot force him to stay in the plan. And he should get all his due from the PA plus profits from the investment—as the Prophet said: "The whole Muslim to another Muslim is inviolable his blood, his property and his honour" (Narrated by Abu Hurairah).

However, upon the withdrawal, he will only get the amount from the PA and his share of profit but the amount from the *Tabarru'* account will not be refunded. It is supported by one of the Hadith, which goes, "Whoever gives something but take it back, he is like a dog that vomit and lick back its vomit again and again" (Takaful lecture, 2003).

21.4 Application

Today, people are gradually accepting Family *Takaful* and it is going to be in great demand soon. This is because there is a large untapped market, particularly among the Bumiputra Muslim population. Besides this, it is going to continue to be in demand as it is coupled with the increasing popularity and acceptability of the *Takaful* business as a whole. The participation of corporate bodies, including multinational corporations, in various types of *Takaful* product will also enhance the demand of Family *Takaful*. However, it is believed that the most important factor in the popularity of Family *Takaful* is its practicality and its applicability in our daily lives.

There are many products offered under Family *Takaful*. To name a few, there are *Pelan Takaful Keluarga*, *Pelan Takaful Sihat*, *Pelan Takaful Siswa*, *Pelan Takaful Ziarah* and *Pelan Takaful Hawa*. Looking at the products offered, these *Takaful* plans are suitable for all levels of people due to their practicability and applicability. Each Family *Takaful* plan is specifically designed to cater for the needs of all sorts of people. For instance, Pelan *Takaful* Hawa is specifically for women and Pelan *Takaful* Siswa is designed especially for students.

In terms of a practical scenario, the Family *Takaful* plan itself is a way to protect our loved ones from misfortunes, whereby a certain amount of money will be given to the family in order to help lighten its burden. We know that protecting our family is a very important and crucial thing in every person's life. This amount of money is generated from the contributions made by the participants themselves. Participants are actually saving money so that it can be used in the future. Practically, saving is a smart way of managing and budgeting for future expenses and revenues. Therefore, this is good conduct since we are actually preparing our families and ourselves in case anything will go wrong in the future.

With these kinds of savings, unfortunate people will have something to depend on and they will not be found begging along the street for food or money. Practically, this is something that people are taking into consideration because we surely do not want our family to beg and we ourselves do not like to see beggars on the streets (Billah, M.M., 2003). As the Holy Prophet (saw) said:

> Verily it is better for you to leave your offspring wealthy than to leave them poor asking others for help (Sahih al-Bukhay).

Family *Takaful* plan is a good means to protect our family. It is in accordance with Shari'ah, as nowadays people are more educated and they start to question whether it is *Halal* or *Haram*, especially among Muslims. It is suitable not only for Muslims but also for non-Muslims, as there are many religions in the world. Everyone could be a participant to the plan. It suits all because it is actually designed for people of all backgrounds.

The increase of the amount of contributions is proof that family *Takaful* is being accepted more widely. This is because it is related to daily life. For instance, we will look into one of the products offered in Family *Takaful*, Pelan *Takaful* Hawa. This Family *Takaful* scheme is a protection programme specifically designed for cancer that afflicts women. It can attack anybody—young, old, poor or rich. However, women are the most likely to be affected by this disease. People need a large amount of money to cure the disease. It is not just complicated, but patients need to use a modern machine that is very expensive and treatment must be done regularly. Although there are people who can afford such treatment, they still need a large amount of money. With this kind of *Takaful* plan, every woman can ensure that they get the best treatment if they suffer from cancer. This shows how practical and applicable Family *Takaful* is for women.

Another example is Education *Takaful* plan. We know that education is important in modern life. It helps people to get suitable jobs. More important is that an educated child or a child with knowledge could be easily taught to become a good person in the future. That is why Islam stresses the importance of education, as the Prophet proclaimed that:

> Seeking knowledge is compulsory for all Muslims.

This plan applies to parents who want the best education for their children. So, as a long-term investment effort, there are parents who could possibly mortgage or pawn their properties in order to provide a good education for their children. This Family *Takaful* plan provides financial planning for children and their parents to save and generate money to support education. This example shows the practically of Family *Takaful*, as seeking knowledge is a must for all.

21.5 Recommendations

Family *Takaful* plan is a great plan for society to hedge against unexpected risks and to provide security for participants. However, there is room for improvement as nothing is perfect, and there is no one best way to do anything. Here are some recommendations that we think appropriate to make the scheme more attractive and beneficial:

- Similar to an insurance policy, the Family *Takaful* plan requires two names as beneficiaries in case anything unfortunate happens to the participant. The benefits then will be paid straight to them. Therefore, it is up to them to divide the claims among the existing relatives as they see fit. However, we cannot be sure that these people will act according to Shari'ah rules. So, it is better for *Takaful* operators to investigate and divide the benefits accordingly based on the rule of *Faraid* in order that there will be no embezzlement or injustice later on.
- In case of the death or permanent disability of the participant, the named beneficiaries have the right to claim benefits from the plan. However, the claiming process can get very time consuming due to understaffing or too much job specialisation. It seems that the

headquarters control everything. Therefore, we suggest that the *Takaful* operators should be given the power to make their own decision (decentralisation), as it will speed up the process considerably. Thus, people will be more confident to participate in the scheme.

21.6 Conclusion

In conclusion, we can say that Family *Takaful* scheme is the best alternative for those who prefer Islamic insurance. Compared to conventional approaches, this type of insurance offers an absolutely Islamic practice where the participant will be assured that their money will be invested in the permissible way. Apart from that, the aims of the Family *Takaful* scheme are to encourage saving regularly, investment of the money according to Islamic principles, and to provide protection for the participant's heirs if he or she dies before the maturity period. There is also the diversification in *Takaful* such as the fact that it is not only for the sake of financial benefit due to unexpected death but also a way of saving for old age.

Family *Takaful* Scheme is long-term family product that is fixed in terms of financial planning programme and does not carry a fixed sum. And the benefits the participant will receive depends on the particular maturity period, the amount of contributions he agreed to make, and profits, if any are earned from the investments. Another important fact is that Family *Takaful* provides mutual assistance for the needy, meaning that it is actually a financial programme that pools efforts to help them dealing with the hardships of life once the breadwinner dies unexpectedly or in the event of other mishaps such as personal injury or disablement. For example, if such a thing happens, a mutual financial assistance such as *Takaful* death benefits is paid from the PSA account to fellow participants according to sound actuarial principles.

References

1. Ali, A. Y. (n.d.), The Holy Qur'an, Text and Translation.
2. *Family Takaful Models*, *Takaful* Malaysia, *Takaful* Nasional, *Takaful* Ikhlas and others.
3. The Islamic Financial Services Act 2013.
4. Billah, M. M., (2003), Principles and Practices of *Takaful* and Re-*Takaful*, IIUM.
5. *Takaful* lecture (2003), IIUM.

CHAPTER 22

Personal Accident *Takaful*

22.1 Introduction

Many people, specifically Malaysian citizens, lack any understanding of *Takaful*. Some find it difficult to differentiate between *Takaful* and conventional insurance practices. This means that many Malaysian citizens have readily accepted the latter, which has led to major hurdles for most of the *Takaful* operators in Malaysia. The *Takaful* concept has existed since the time of the Prophet, so there is no reason or excuse to reject the practice of *Takaful* in today's global business world. The concept of sharing and caring for each other should be a given. Allah mentioned and justified the practice of *Takaful* in *Surah al-Mai'dah, verse two:*

> Help one another in furthering virtue and God consciousness (T*aqwa*), and do not help one another in furthering evil and enmity. (Al-Qur'an, Surah Maidah: 2)

The word *Takaful* is derived from the Arabic verb *Kafala*, which means to join or to merge and includes the concept of shared responsibility. This indicates that insurance plays a role in supporting the needy, and thus

A significant contribution to this chapter has been made by the practices, experiences and thoughts of Bank Negara, Takaful Malaysia, Takaful Ikhlas, Takaful Nasional, Etiqa Takaful, IBFIM, IIUM, MII and others (Malaysia).

Mohd Ma'Sum Billah, *Islamic Insurance Products*,
https://doi.org/10.1007/978-3-030-17681-5_22

follows the principle of Islamic Shari'ah. The practice of *Takaful* in Malaysia can be divided into two types. The first is Family *Takaful*, which is Islamic life insurance. The second is General *Takaful*, or Islamic general insurance. The Personal Accident *Takaful* Scheme is one of the General *Takaful* products, which is also a type of short-term policy. In this chapter, we will be discussing the Personal Accident *Takaful* Scheme and highlighting some of its main points and concepts. This will help us to gain a clearer view of the concepts of *Takaful* and practices within the Malaysian insurance industry. In addition, some comparisons will be made between *Takaful* and conventional practices. This will help to educate Malaysian citizens about the benefits of *Takaful*.

22.2 Shari'ah Rulings

Shari'ah gives clear guidance in respect of what is lawful and unlawful based on the teachings of the Qur'an and the Sunnah (I. Doi, A. R. 1994). It is not human beings who decide what is lawful or unlawful. Everything is presumed to be lawful unless it is specifically prohibited by the Shari'ah rulings. This is based on the following verse of the Qur'an:

> It is He (Allah) who has created for you all things that are on earth. (Ali 1994)

It is lawful for a Muslim to practise Islamic insurance as long as it does not contravene the Shari'ah principles. There are some Islamic principles that make the *Takaful* scheme permissible. It is in agreement with the basic principle of *Takaful*, which encourages the practice of moral values and virtuous attitudes.

> Help you another in the righteous and piety, but help you not one another in sin and rancor; fear God; for God is strict in punishment. (*al-Qur'an* 5:2)

22.2.1 No Riba Culture

Takaful or Islamic insurance is a financing scheme that is based on Al-Qur'an and Sunnah and includes the concepts of brotherhood, solidarity and mutual co-operation. *Takaful* is free from *Riba* (usury), gambling, uncertainty, unlawful elements and many other things that are prohibited by Islam. Allah said in Al-Qur'an (Ali 1994):

> O ye who believe! Devour not usury, doubled and multiplied; but fear God; that ye may (really) prosper. (3: 130)
>
> O ye who believe! Intoxicants and gambling, (dedication of) stones, and (divination by) arrows, are an abomination, – of Satan's handwork: eschew such (abomination), that ye may prosper. (5: 90)

In these verses, Allah prohibited the practices of usury and gambling. *Takaful* is free from all Islam's prohibited elements.

- Islam encourages us to seek cures for illness.
- No *Gharar*.

In addition, *Takaful* is based on some of the Islamic practices.

22.2.2 Al-Tabarru'

Al-Tabarru' is a gift or donation, which is one of the main principles in *Takaful*. In the *Manual of Principles and Practices of Takaful and Re-Takaful*, the author defines Al-Tabarru' as "synonymous idea to and similar legal consequences with *al-Sadaqah* (charity), *al-Hiba* (gift), and *al-Khairat* (donation), wherein anything once given away as donation in favour of something or someone, the donated property cannot generally be retracted. The donor automatically loses title *over the donated property soon after it is made as al-Tabarru' or al-Sadaqah or al-Hiba* or *al-khairat*." In *Takaful*, the amount that is paid by the participant is divided into two accounts, which one of these accounts is based on this concept, which it is considered as *al-Sadaqah* and cannot be redeemed back by the participants. This amount is given to any other participants that deserve to receive the money.

22.2.3 Al-Mudharabah

Al-Mudharabah or profit and loss sharing is a widely used practice in *Takaful*. *Takaful* operators have adopted this practice, in which one party, called *Rabbul Mal*, provides money or fund to the other party, called *Darib*. *Darib* is the person or party who manages the money or fund by investing or doing business with the money, in the hope of generating profits. Based on *Al-Mudharabah* practice, both *Rabbul Mal* and *Darib* have to share the profits or losses from the money that has been invested.

22.2.4 *Al-Wakalah*

Al-Wakalah, or agency, is another Islamic principle that is used in *Takaful*. This is a kind of contract where a party delegates his business to another party. In *Takaful*, *al-Wakalah* means that participants ask the operator (*Wakil*) to use their skills to insure participants' property or anything else.

22.2.5 *Al-Musyarakah*

Al-Musyarakah is a principle that is based on partnership: in *Takaful* operations, both participants and the *Takaful* operator are considered to be partners, and their contracts are based on partnership. In *Al-Musyarakah*, both parties must contribute in order to form a partnership. In *Takaful*, participants contribute their money and the *Takaful* operator contributes their skills by ensuring financial security against a defined risk.

22.3 The Scheme Outlook

22.3.1 *Scope of Cover*

The Personal Accident *Takaful* Scheme can be categorized under three headings:

- Personal Accident *Takaful* (PA).
- Group Personal Accident *Takaful* (GPA).
- Group Personal Accident (Short Period).

The scheme covers personal accidents for individuals aged between 18 and 65. The scheme also compensates the person covered in the event of:

- Death.
- Permanent disablement.
- Medical expenses.

22.3.2 *Death*

There are two types of cover under this heading:

- Immediate death.
- Death up to six months from the date of the accident (caused by fire, lightning strike or underground fire).

22.3.3 Permanent Disablement

The scheme covers permanent disablement caused by accident. An accident can cause an individual to lose his or her job, and the victim might no longer be able to do anything at all. This permanent disablement should not be for less than six months. Temporary Total Disablement and Partial Disablement are also covered.

22.3.4 Medical Expenses

Takaful Malaysia pays medical expenses for an individual who is involved in an accident.

Additional cover can be provided under the scheme, but this is only valid if the policyholder pays an additional amount. The cover includes the following:

- Driver and passengers.
- Dangerous sports such as mountaineering, underwater activities, hunting.
- Use of woodworking machinery.
- Air travel other than that allowed by the standard cover.

22.4 Ratings

The ratings are further summarised and explained in Table 22.1.

22.4.1 Extra Loading to Be Charged for Additional Extension of Cover Requested

Hunting	10%
Polo and horse riding	10%
Water skiing	10%
Woodworking machinery	10%
SRCC	10%
Age > 65	75%
Mountaineering and scuba diving	30%

Table 22.1 Personal Accident *Takaful* (PA)

Benefits	*Class 1 (RM)*	*Class 2 (RM)*	*Class 3 (RM)*
Death and permanent disablement (per RM 10,000 cover)	14.50	18.00	25.00
Temporary total disablement inclusive of partial disablement subject to a maximum of 104 weeks only. (For every RM 100.00 cover)	20.00	32.50	42.50
Medical expenses cover: RM 500	10.00	13.00	16.00
RM 1000	15.00	18.00	22.00
RM 2000	22.00	26.00	–
RM 3000	27.00	34.00	–
RM 4000	32.00	–	–
RM 5000	36.00	–	–

Source: Author's collection

Table 22.2 Group Personal Accident *Takaful* Scheme (GPA)

Number of people	*Number of discount group*	
	Class 1	*Class 2*
11–15	10%	–
16–25	15%	–
26–25	20%	10%
36–50	25%	15%
51–100	30%	20%
101–200	35%	30%
More than 200	Refer Underwriting	

Source: Author's collection

22.4.2 *Group Personal Accident* Takaful *Scheme (GPA)*

In the Group Personal Accident Scheme, a group discount is allowed if the number of persons covered exceeds ten. The maximum discounts allowed are summarised in Table 22.2.

Should the majority of people covered belong to the named occupation class, such occupation shall be recognized as the occupation class of the group:

Table 22.3 Group Personal Accident *Takaful* (short period)

Sum covered	Takaful *contribution (per person)*		
Sum covered (RM) per person	*1–7 days (RM)*	*8–14 days (RM)*	*15–31 days (RM)*
5000.00	2.00	3.00	4.00
10,000.00	4.00	6.00	8.00
15,000.00	6.00	9.00	12.00
20,000.00	8.00	12.00	16.00

Source: Author's collection

Minimum *Takaful* contribution	
PA	RM 25.00 per certificate
GPA	RM 50.00 per certificate
GPA (short period)	RM 50.00 per certificate

22.4.3 Group Personal Accident Takaful *(Short Period)*

For a GPA *Takaful* scheme (Short Period), standard cover would be offered as noted in Table 22.3.

Notes:

- The age limit for GPAQ is 16–65 years (except for schools schemes). Group discount may be given after any personal discount.
- GPA is to be issued only if the full name of the people covered (including I/C number) has been submitted to the company. Cover based on position must be referred to the Underwriting Department.
- Limit for conveyance for known accumulation is RM 3000.
- There is a 5% service tax for company and a Stamp Duty rate of RM 10.00.

22.5 Occupation

The profession or occupation of an individual is a primary factor in determining the risk and probability of an accident. All of the cover schemes can be classified according to these classes, except for the Travel Personal Accident *Takaful*. The occupation classes follow.

22.5.1 *Class 1*

Individuals who work in professional, administrative or any personnel roles but are neither supervising nor engaged in manual labour. Examples include accountants, clerks, lawyers, doctors, nurses, dentists, surgeons, architects and teachers.

22.5.2 *Class 2*

Individual supervising but not actually engaging in manual labour, such as mine managers, foremen, planters, contractors (not working themselves), clerks of work, industrial clerks, printers, storekeepers, tailors and waiters.

22.5.3 *Class 3*

Those who are either engaged in or with manual labour, for example bus conductors, drivers, carpenters, electricians, farmers, fishmongers, hawkers, mechanics, plumbers, rubber estate workers and sales assistants. The maximum sum insured per person is RM 50,000.

22.6 Limitation to Benefits

- Death, Permanent Total or Permanent Partial Disablement must occur within twelve months of bodily injury.
- Weekly compensation may be considered for group participation by a corporate body.
- Compensation payable for the period of Temporary Total or Temporary Partial Disablement either separately or together shall not exceed 104 weeks, depending on the injury.
- Besides that, compensation payable under Temporary Total Disablement will not exceed 75% for Class 1 and 2 and 50% for Class 3 of the person's covered weekly earning.
- The sum of the cover payable under Temporary Partial Disablement should not exceed 50% of that payable under Temporary Total Disablement.
- Medical expenses (up to a maximum limit of RM 5000 for Class 1 and RM 3000 for Class 2 and RM 1000 for Class 3).

- All the sum-covered life (death) for all cover (PA/GPA) shall not exceed 60 times a person's covered monthly income (or five times annual income).
- Any compensation payable under Permanent Disablement Benefit shall be reduced by the amount of compensation already paid under Temporary Disablement Benefit in respect of the same injury.
- The aggregate of all percentages payable in respect of any one accident for any period of *Takaful* shall not exceed 100% of the capital sum covered.

22.7 Underwriting

22.7.1 Diseases and Physical Disabilities

A person who suffers from certain physical disabilities or who has a history of certain illnesses may be described as a poor risk. Extreme care must be taken in order to deal with a proposal that discloses any physical illness, especially when it is revealed that the individual has suffered from any infirmity or deformity that may affect agility or may increase the disability in the event of an accident.

22.7.2 Abnormal Risk

Abnormal risks that can be acceptable subject to special terms are listed below. In all cases, the clients must submit their proposal to the Underwriting Department for further inspection, together with a copy of medical reports that detail the extent of the disabilities.

22.7.3 Blindness in One Eye

If the condition is long standing and sight of the other eye is sound, the risk can be accepted subject to a loading of 25%, with an endorsement that in the event of loss of the remaining eye compensation will be paid to the client on the basis of loss of sight of one eye only, or 50% of the benefit available.

22.7.4 *Loss of One Arm*

For the loss of one arm the rate should be loaded by 25%, and with the endorsement that the loss of the other limb will comprise compensation on the basis of loss of one arm only, or 50%.

22.7.5 *Deafness in One Ear*

If the other ear is sound, acceptance is normally on normal terms, subject as usual to the endorsement that loss of the other ear will be covered on the basis of the loss of one ear.

22.7.6 *Ambiguous Occupation*

This occurs when the occupation stated is unclear (ambiguous). For example, the Director or Merchant, the subordinate must be determined from the prospective participant. In addition, the job description must be clear and accurate to ensure the correct rates are charged and to avoid any probability of rejecting a claim owing to misrepresentation.

22.8 Conclusion

To conclude, the Personal Accident *Takaful* Scheme gives many benefits to its participants, especially those who are in need or have been involved in an accident. It is indeed an alternative method by which society can shoulder the burden of unpredicted occurrences. Moreover, the scheme covers many aspects such as death, permanent disablement and medical expenses. It follows Shari'ah teachings and is free from elements that are forbidden. Takaful Malaysia still needs to improve its existing products in order to be able to compete with conventional insurance companies. More promotion should be done to attract more participants. The registration fees for the products should also be revised in order to stimulate higher demand. Currently, the main issue is to be able to educate society at large about *Takaful* products and how *Takaful* operates.

We believe that *Takaful* operators in Malaysia have a bright future. It may be possible to apply *Takaful* practices and thereby bring the principles of Islam more to the fore. *Takaful* is to ease people's lives and to take away their burdens and distress.

References

1. Ali, A. Y. (1994), *The holy Qur'an; Text and Translation*, Islamic Book Trust, Kuala Lumpur.
2. *Personal Accident Takaful Models*, Takaful Malaysia, Takaful Nasional, Takaful Ikhlas and others.
3. I.Doi, A. R. (1994), *Shari'ah the Islamic Law*, A.s. Nordeen, Malaysia, P. 407.
4. Product Application of Takaful Malaysia and Takaful Ikhlas.

CHAPTER 23

Critical Illness *Takaful*

23.1 Introduction

The implementation of *Takaful* is different from conventional insurance. Nowadays the practice is a combination of two *Aqad* (contracts), which are the *Tabarru'* (donation) contract and the *Mudharabah* (investment) contract. Both of these contracts are free from any elements of *Gharar* (uncertainty), *Maisir* (gambling) and *Riba* (interest). In the contract of *Tabarru'*, the participant agrees to donate a predetermined percentage of the contribution to the fund with a sincere intention to provide assistance to fellow participants if they face any hardship. Then, through the contract of *Mudharabah*, the participants contribute to the fund, which is managed by the authorized takaful operator, with whom they will share the profits from that investment. At Takaful Ikhlas, for example, they use the contract of *Tabarru'* and the contract of *Wakalah* as guidelines for conducting their business. For a *Wakalah* contract, the participant will authorize the Takaful operator to conduct affairs of the fund on his/her behalf. The Takaful Ikhlas allows the use of intermediaries in order to give a better service for its customers.

A significant contribution to this chapter/product has been made by the practices, experiences and thoughts of Bank Negara, Takaful Ikhlas, Takaful Malaysia, Takaful Nasional, Etiqa Takaful, IBFIM, IIUM, MII and others (Malaysia).

Mohd Ma'Sum Billah, *Islamic Insurance Products*,
https://doi.org/10.1007/978-3-030-17681-5_23

23.2 Product Preview

The Critical Illness Takaful Rider is one of the products that has been launched since 2010. This plan is not a stand-alone product; it is part of other contracts or basic plans. Therefore, the policyholder must have a basic plan if interested in the Critical Illness Takaful Rider. Usually the policyholder is encouraged to buy this extra cover alongside the basic plan. The Critical Illness Takaful Rider is a protection plan for individuals. It plan gives financial protection against any critical illness listed in the plan for the term of the plan. The Critical Illness Takaful Rider is created to give protection against financial loss resulting from a policyholder's critical illness. The policyholder can determine the duration or the term of the plan according to their preferences. However, this cannot be less than the minimum term outlined by the Takaful Ikhlas. The minimum length of this plan is five years. The policyholder can get many other benefits by choosing this plan.

Critical illness plans offered by other operators are quite similar to the Critical Illness Takaful Rider. The apparent difference is the number of critical illnesses covered by other operators.

23.3 Coverage from Different Operators

23.3.1 Takaful Ikhlas

- Takaful Ikhlas covers 40 types of critical illness.
- The waiting period before the coverage takes effect is 90 days, or three months.

23.3.2 Takaful Malaysia

- Takaful Malaysia covers 36 types of critical illness.
- The waiting period before the coverage takes effect is 30 days, or one month.

23.3.3 Takaful National

- Takaful National covers 28 types of critical illness.
- The waiting period before the coverage takes effect is 180 days, or six months.

Maybank Takaful does not offer this product yet.

23.3.4 Prerequisites for Buying the Policy

Generally anyone can buy the policy offered by Takaful Ikhlas as long as he/she fulfils the conditions required. However, the applicant must be aged between 18 and 55. If the policy is being bought for someone else, there must be a strong blood relationship with the person for whom the cover is being bought. The following are the relationships allowed by Takaful Ikhlas:

- Husband ←→ wife.
- Children ←→ parents.
- Debtor ←→ creditor (bank, etc.).

Relationships other than these are not allowed at all, such as grandparent ←→ grandchild, student ←→ teacher or best friend ←→ best friend.

23.3.5 Illnesses Covered by the Policy

There are 40 types of disease covered by Critical Illness Takaful. These are:

- Stroke.
- Heart attack.
- Coronary artery disease requiring surgery.
- Other serious coronary artery disease.
- Coronary artherectomy.
- Heart valve replacement.
- Aorta surgery.
- Coma.
- Primary pulmonary arterial hypertension.
- Benign brain tumour.
- Encephalitis.
- Bacterial meningitis.
- Kidney failure.
- Medullary cystic disease.
- Systematic lupus erythematosus with lupus nephritis (SLE).
- Chronic liver disease.
- Fulminant viral hepatitis.
- Chronic lung disease.
- Major organ transplant.

- Cancer.
- Aplastic anaemia.
- Motor neurone disease.
- Parkinson's disease.
- Alzheimer's disease/irreversible organic degenerative brain disorders.
- Apallic syndrome.
- Muscular dystrophy.
- Multiple sclerosis.
- Poliomyelitis.
- AIDS due to blood transfusion.
- Terminal illness.
- Blindness.
- Major burns.
- Loss of speech.
- Loss of hearing/deafness
- Loss of independent existence
- Paralysis/paraplegia
- Major head trauma
- Cardiomyopathy
- Brain surgery
- Total and permanent disability benefit.

23.3.6 Contribution

When the contract is made, it means that the policyholder agrees to pay a certain amount of money to the operator, which is the Takaful Ikhlas. This is for managing the risk. The participant can choose the payment schedule according to what is most convenient: it can be paid monthly, every three months, six months or yearly. As already mentioned, the policy can only be bought together with other basic plan or contract. Therefore, the contribution made by the policyholder will be deposited into two separate accounts. The first is the Personal Investment Account (PIA), which is for the basic plan. The second is the Personal Risk Investment Account (PRIA), under which the Critical Illness plan falls. We will focus on the PRIA.

After money has been deposited in the PRIA, some of it will be moved to the Ta'awuni Account Pool (TAP) and the Investment Dana. The money deposited in the TAP is to cover the charges involved in managing the money, such as *Wakalah*, management, administration, commission and also *Tabarru'*. The balance of the money will be deposited in the Investment Fund. The Takaful Ikhlas will then invest the money to make a profit. The profit from the investment (if any) will be placed in the policyholder's account. Usually this profit will be paid monthly.

Other Cases

If someone already has the basic plan and wants to add cover for critical illness later, then he or she will have to pay higher contributions than if the plan was bought along with the basic plan in the first place. The closer the basic plan is to maturity, the higher the contribution that will have to be paid. This is because the Critical Illness plan will mature after the basic plan.

If a policyholder already has a critical disease when he buys the plan, but the disease is not in its critical stage, the personal risk is higher than it is for other policyholders. In these circumstances, fairness demands that he might be required to pay a higher contribution than others to offset his higher risk.

23.3.7 The Product Structure

Regarding the contribution, as age increases, the level of risk will be higher; hence the contribution will increase too.

This is why, at Takaful Ikhlas, a flat rate payment method is used. This requires the policyholder to pay the same amount in contributions periodically until the maturity date. So, for example, even though latterly the participant should contribute more, they do not have to do so as this has already been covered earlier on (Fig. 23.1).

If the participant starts to contribute early, he will have to pay a lower amount. For example, X buys both the basic and the Rider plan at the same time, at the age of 20. X has to pay RM 60 for the basic plan and RM 40 for the Rider until maturity date. X will pay lower contributions for the Rider because the risk is lower: the plan durations are the same.

But if the policyholder joins the Rider plan later, he will have to pay a higher contribution than other participants. For example, X buys the basic plan at the age of 20 and the Rider at the age of 30. X therefore has to pay RM 60 for the basic plan and RM 55 for the Rider until maturity date. In this case, X will pay higher contributions for the Rider because the risk is higher: the duration of the Rider is shorter than it is for the basic plan.

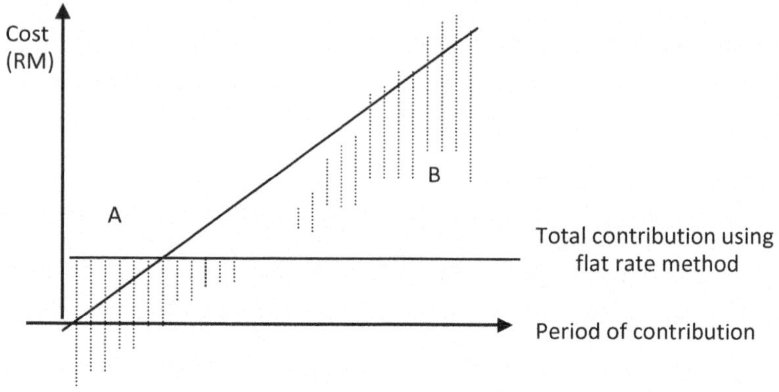

Fig. 23.1 The product structure. (Source: Author's collection TI)

23.3.8 Withdrawal

For the basic plan, it is permissible to withdraw some of the money up to three times throughout the duration of the certificate or until its maturity. Up to a maximum of 50% can also be withdrawn from the PIA, and this withdrawal can only begin after the fifth year. After the first withdrawal, the policyholder can only make a second withdrawal two years later. The third withdrawal can only be made two years after the second withdrawal.

With the Ikhlas Critical Illness Takaful Rider, the policyholder is not allowed to make any withdrawal from the PRIA until its maturity date. The purpose of this is to protect the policyholder in case they encounter one of the critical illnesses that is covered. If the policyholder wants to make a withdrawal before the maturity date, he can only withdraw from the basic plan. For example, X has contributed RM 80,000 to the basic plan and RM 30,000 to the Rider. From the basic plan he has received RM 7000 profit and for the Rider RM 2500. He wants to withdraw 50% of his contribution at the age of 40. But he cannot withdraw anything from the Rider as it must meet its maturity date before he can claim both contribution and profits.

23.3.9 Claim

When a policyholder encounters a disease that is covered by the Critical Illness plan, he can claim from the operator, the Takaful Ikhlas. The participant can claim up to 100% of the Critical Illness Sum Covered

(CISC) when proven to have one of the illnesses that is covered. Before payment is made, the policyholder has to complete a few forms and attach a doctor's medical report. This report is used to verify the statement made by the claimant. If Takaful Ikhlas doubts the validity of the report, the policyholder can be asked to have a second checkup with Takaful Ikhlas's panel doctor. When a claim is made, the following documents are required:

- Critical illness claimant's statement – form to be completed by the claimant.
- Critical illness medical report – form to be completed by the doctor.
- Policy certificate.

If the claim is made by the policy's beneficiary, the following documents are required:

- Death claimant statement – form to be completed by the beneficiary.
- Physician's statement – form to be completed by the doctor.
- Certified copy of death certificate.
- Post mortem/coroner's report.
- Police report (if any).
- Photocopy of beneficiary's NRIC/birth certificate.
- Policy certificate (if certificate is being issued to fund holder).

The policyholder can claim the money only 90 days after the contract is signed. In other words, for 90 days the policyholder must be free from any disease listed. The payment can only be made if the disease is at a critical stage. There are two types of payment plan offered by Takaful Ikhlas, as follows.

Accelerated Plan
As soon as the policyholder is proved to be suffering from the disease, Takaful Ikhlas gives the total payment of the CISC in a lump sum based on the basic plan. This means that the payment made is advanced from the basic plan. Any payment made in this way will reduce the amount covered by the basic plan.

Additional Plan
This plan provides a lump sum payment of the CISC as soon as the policyholder is diagnosed with one of the critical illnesses listed. Payment made in this way does not reduce the total covered by the basic plan.

If after the maturity date the policyholder is still healthy and has not encountered any critical illness, he can claim back his contribution to the fund. But the Takaful operator may not refund the total contribution since management costs are deducted. Although the participant will not be given back 100% of total contributions, he will still receive something. This is totally different from conventional Takaful where the participant will not be given back his contribution if he has not met with any critical illness until the end of the maturity date.

23.3.10 Conditions

As soon as the policyholder is diagnosed with one of the listed critical illnesses, the Takaful Ikhlas will pay the CISC to the participant according to the following:

- Total and Permanent Disability is based on the definition of the occupation.
- Disability benefit is to be paid after the qualification period (waiting period) whereby the disability will last not less than six months for a continuous period.
- The health of the policyholder before the contract is excluded from this benefit.
- Additional charge on mortality and/or occupation will be added as suitable for the policyholder's profile and the definition of Total and Permanent Disability. Extra charges will be computed as a multiple factor at the minimum net rate.
- Any critical illness diagnosed within three months of the date when the contract is issued is not covered by this plan.

23.3.11 Death of the Policyholder

When the policyholder agrees to buy this policy, they are required to name five beneficiaries in case the policyholder dies before the plan matures. Therefore, if the policyholder dies before the maturity of the plan or before the policyholder receives the claimed money, the first person named as beneficiary will receive the money. However, the first beneficiary merely functions as a trustee. When the policyholder dies, the beneficiary receives the money and must then distribute it to the other beneficiaries according to *Faraidh* law of Islam. Once the first beneficiary receives the money, he as a trustee passes the case to the Shari'ah court. The court then divides the money according to the *Faraidh* system. Thus, the policyholder should be careful in choosing a beneficiary, who should be a trustworthy. The policyholder should also educate the beneficiaries about their rights and obligations.

23.3.12 Benefits

The policyholder can receive many benefits from Ikhlas Critical Illness Takaful Rider. The most valuable is of course protection against the financial impact of critical illnesses. In addition, the Takaful Ikhlas invests the contribution made by the policyholder, and the profit from this goes directly to the policyholder. Another benefit is the maturity benefit, with a lump sum being paid and also the net surplus from the Risk Fund. Therefore, even if a policyholder is free from any critical illness throughout the term of the plan, he will still receive the total amount from PRIA, which compares favourably with conventional insurance practice.

Takaful is governed by two contracts, *Tabarru'* and *Wakalah*. In *Tabarru'*, the policyholder agrees to donate a percentage of his contribution to the charity fund. The benefit from this contract is therefore the reward given by Allah in the hereafter. In addition, by choosing to buy critical illness policy, the policyholder can have peace of mind and enjoy their life without worrying about financial requirements if something happens to them in the future.

23.4 Conclusion

Takaful is an insurance concept that is grounded in Islamic *Muammalat*, observing the rules and regulations of Shari'ah. In principle, the Takaful system is based on mutual co-operation, responsibility, assurance, protection and assistance between groups of participants and also the *Takaful* operator. These fundamentals are based on the sayings of the Prophet Muhammad. For co-operation, these include: "Help one another in al-Birr and in al-Taqwa (virtue, righteousness and piety): but do not help one another in sin and transgression" (Al-Qur'an, Surah Al-Maidah: 2); and "Allah will always help His servant for as long as he helps others" (Sunan Ahmad and Sunan Abu Daud). For the basis of responsibility, some Hadith are: "The place of relationships and feelings of people with faith, between each other, is just like the body; when one of its parts is afflicted with pain, then the rest of the body will be affected" (Sahih al-Bukhari and Sahih al-Muslim); and "One true Muslim (Mukmin) and another true Muslim (Mukmin) is just like a building whereby every part in it strengthens the other part" (Sahih al-Bukhari and Sahih al-Muslim). For the basis of mutual protection, the Prophet Muhammad stressed: "By my life, which is in Allah power, nobody will enter Paradise if he does not protect his neighbour who is in distress" (Sunan Ahmad). Based on these divine principles, Islamic scholars decided that there should be a concerted effort to implement the Takaful concept as the best way to resolve these needs.

References

1. Ali, A. Y. (n.d.), The Holy Qur'an, Text and Translation.
2. Sunan Ahmad and Sunan Abu Daud.
3. Sahih al-Bukhari and Sahih al-Muslim.
4. *Critical Illness Takaful Plan*, Takaful Malaysia, Takaful Nasional, Takaful Ikhlas and others.

CHAPTER 24

Group Students' Takaful Plan

24.1 Introduction

The world generally seems to realise that protection for the loved one after one's death is necessary. Financial stability is important for everyone. Therefore, the Malaysian government has imposed a charge on every worker in Malaysia, for his or her savings and to use when elderly. Insurance agencies have seemed to grow like mushrooms after rain. Some offer conventional insurance and some Islamic insurance. The main purpose and objective of the cover they offer is to protect the person, family or property. For example, if a man has a car accident and breaks his leg, with insurance he can be covered, and the insurance agency will pay him a particular amount for necessary treatment. Even in the USA, if you need any medical treatment in the hospital or clinic you need to have insurance. If not, the medical staff will not treat you. This shows that the importance of insurance nowadays. As well as life insurance products, many insurance agencies offer a variety of products, including property, health, education and investment, and of course much more.

In Islam, there are a number of views regarding Islamic insurance given by many ulama. They can be grouped into seven categories.

A significant contribution to this chapter has been made by the practices, experiences and thoughts of Bank Negara, Takaful Malaysia, Takaful Ikhlas, Takaful Nasional, Etiqa Takaful, IBFIM, IIUM, MII and others (Malaysia).

Mohd Ma'Sum Billah, *Islamic Insurance Products*,
https://doi.org/10.1007/978-3-030-17681-5_24

Group 1 claims that life insurance is entirely haram because it involves *Riba*, *Maisir* and *Gharar*. Group 2 says that they only accept general insurance and reject life insurance. Group 3 views insurance as lawful provided that it is free of *Riba* and other unlawful elements. Group 4 is made up of blind followers with negative attitudes, who make no effort to come up with alternative solutions. Group 5 claims to be confused, and states that no effort has been done to find the right solutions. They play a neutral role. Group 6 continues to seek an alternative model for insurance practices, finding that it is permissible as long as it is in line with Shari'ah principles. As a result, *Takaful* is Islamic insurance as an alternative to conventional practices. Group 7 claims that *Takaful* operations should be mandatory, to provide financial security for helpless people throughout society and ensure more economic stability for all.

In reality, *Takaful* does not involve any unlawful elements. It has been established to provide risk coverage for the participants. The *Takaful* operator is the person who manages the risk and gives cover to the policyholder. To fulfil the contract, there must be two parties, the operator and the policyholder. Whatever is insured must have commercial value (whether life, property, investment, for example); if not, the contract is invalid. The policyholder has to pay a certain amount of premium in order to fulfil the contract.

In Malaysia, the Islamic insurance agency Syarikat Takaful Malaysia Berhad (STMB) was incorporated on 29 November 1984. It was a subsidised company of Kumpulan BIMB Holdings Berhad, with 65.5% of its equity held by the bank. After some years, it was converted into a public quoted company, and its shares have been listed on the Main Board of the Kuala Lumpur Stock Exchange since 31 July 1996. Its corporate objective is to provide *Takaful* services at the highest level of efficiency and professionalism for all Muslims and the population of Malaysia in general.

Family Takaful is made up of Individual Takaful Plans and Group Takaful Plans. In individual Takaful Plans, there are fixed maturity periods, which are 10, 15, 20, 25, 30, 35 and 40 years. Individual Takaful Plans will cover key man Takaful Plan, family Takaful Plans for education, Family Takaful Mortgage Plan, Takaful Medical, Takaful Ma'asyi (Endowment), Takaful Siswa Plan and Takaful Waqf Plan. Group Takaful Plans include Group Family Plan, Group Takaful Medical and Group Family Takaful Plan. General Takaful Business includes Fire Takaful, Miscellaneous and Accident Takaful, Marine Takaful, Engineering Takaful and Motor Takaful.

Group Students Takaful Malaysia (GST) is categorised under Family Takaful. It is one of several education plans for all the students in Malaysia. Every school insured through the scheme have to insure all students, including non-Muslims. The contract is between the Ministry of Education and Takaful Malaysia. Every student who is registered in their first year at school will be covered by the Takaful Malaysia until form 6, the fee being RM 1.50 annually. A school is responsible for claiming an insurance pay-out within 30 days. Takaful Malaysia makes the payment as soon as possible.

24.2 Scope of Cover

GST benefits students who meet any kind of accident, these being determined by the *Takaful* operator. If a student dies, the benefits will be given to his or her beneficiaries, for example parents or siblings. The *Takaful* operator gives the benefits to any student or beneficiaries if the student meets with an accident that causes him to die or to be permanently paralysed, if some part of the body is severed, if any part of the body is lost, or if death occurs because of drowning, road accident, food poisoning, snake bite or other kinds of disaster. The *Takaful* operator will cover the student even if the accident happens outside school. The scheme provides 24-hour cover throughout the world. Recently, a secondary school student was drowned. STMB was informed and paid the benefits as stated in the contract. As long as a student is still studying and registered at the school, the Takaful operator will give them cover. But if the student does not continue studies up to form 6, the contract ends immediately. Students are also allowed to take out insurance using any product available in Takaful, for example Takaful Medical (Fig. 24.1).

24.3 Benefits Schedule

Table 24.1 shows the schedule of benefits from the *Takaful* scheme for school students in Malaysia. Members of the scheme can claim benefits in case of accident that causes breakage of bones or the loss of part of the body. In the case of death caused by normal sickness, family members get RM1000 from the Khairat Fund. In the case of broken bones or loss of a part of the body, the full payment will only be paid if both sides of the body are affected (i.e. both hands, feet or eyes). If only one side of the body is affected, then the total benefits are capped at 50%.

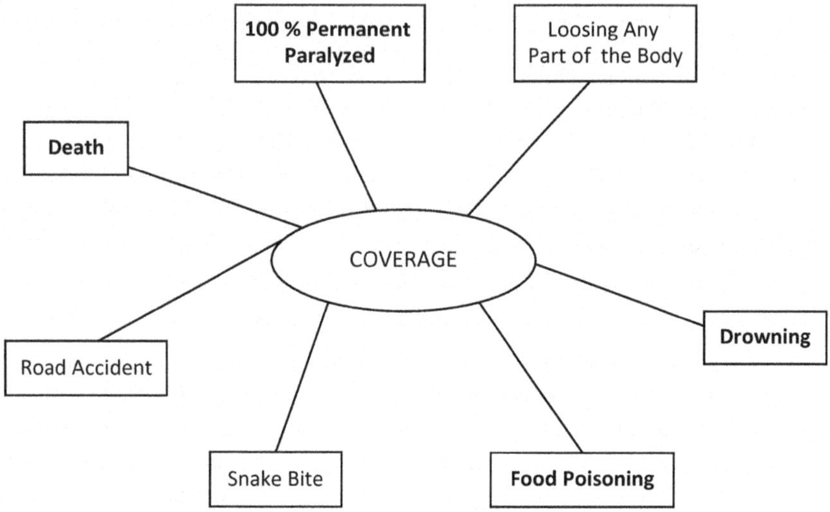

Fig. 24.1 Scope of coverage. (Source: Author's collection)

Table 24.1 Benefits schedule

Protection scope	*Benefits amount (RM)*
A) Death caused by accident	5000.00
B) Permanent **physical disability** to the whole body caused by accident	15,000.00
C) **Broken bone or blindness** caused by accident for[a]:	15,000.00
a) Both hands or	
b) Both feet or	
c) Permanent loss of eyesight	
D) **Death Khairat Fund**-death caused by normal sickness	1000.00
E) **Hospital Cash Allowance** for every day from the day the student enters the hospital until the day of departure; this is paid for either public or private hospitals. Admittance must be because of an accident and for not more than 60 days from the date of entering the ward.	25.00 Per day

Source: Author's collection

[a]If only one side of the body is affected or if there is loss of sight in one eye from b) and c), then the total benefits are 50% of RM15,000

Members also receive a hospital cash allowance if they are involved in a serious accident and need to get treatment either in a public or a private hospital. The allowance is given for not more than 60 days from the date of entering the ward. A further claim cannot be made for any more days. Neither can a claim be made for the total number of days in hospital if this is split into different periods, for example 20 days one month, 20 days the next and 20 days the one after.

This scheme only seems to give cover for risks that will be faced by students through accident, not through sickness caused by underlying health conditions. Therefore, students should take care of their own physical health and use the *Takaful* scheme to gain benefits for unexpected risks in the future, especially accidents.

Almost all education institutions, such as schools, colleges and universities, participate in GST in Malaysia because of the benefits.

24.4 Exception

Although the GST provides a considerable amount of cover, it has certain exceptions and does not provide any benefits payment in the following circumstances:

Death or unable physical body or injured body which formally or informally caused by;

- War, enmity, acts of warfare (whether declared or not), wars of brotherhood, the resolution of war, instigation of war, army rebellion or confiscation of power, army law governance, boycott, vigorous public protest, etc.
- Suicide or attempted suicide or any intentional injury, murder, crime or related activities.
- Disease or epidemic.
- Incapacity caused by alcohol, drugs or other chemicals.
- Pregnancy, giving birth or abortion.
- Racing, speed testing or generally testing a vehicle.
- Natural loss of ability in any part of the body.
- Any activity that is against Shari'ah or civil law.
- Death or loss of abilities caused by hunting.
- Death or loss of abilities caused by ice-skating, polo, motor racing, wrestling, parachuting, etc.

Conscious or occurs or caused by;

- Mengion ray, radiation, radioactive infection from any nuclear waste. This exception includes the process of burning should include every defence process of breaking nuclear.
- The materials of nuclear weapon;

This exception does not relate to the Death Khairat Fund.

Any intentional actions that bring about injury or death are not covered by this scheme. Neither does the scheme cover naturally occurring physical disabilities.

24.5 Claim Procedures

A school representative must issue a notice of claim and acknowledgement to the STMB no more than 30 days after the accident. The affected student's family can also make the claim direct. To make the process quicker and smoother, there are some documents that the insured should be aware of, and these depend on the type of accident.

If death is caused by road accident, the necessary documents are the completed claim form, police report, a copy of the burial permit and a valid death certificate.[1]

As well as the form used to claim death *Khairat*, a signed death certificate and a copy of the burial permit should be handed to the *Takaful* operator. Permanent paralysis or the loss of any part of the body requires the insured to enclose a complete claim form together with supporting documents and a police report.[2] To claim for hospital bills, the insured should present the completed claim report, a police report and treatment confirmation. The insured should always make sure that the required documents according to his or her category are correctly presented, so that claim procedures are smooth and quick. If one of the required documents is not handed in, the procedures may take longer.

[1] *Guidelines* for the distribution to the parents.

[2] These are to provide evidence that the participant is truly paralysed, and that this was caused by an unexpected accident.

Takaful operator has the right to ask for other documents if necessary to justify payments. All payment cheques are forwarded to the participating school; if parents want to receive cheques directly, they should inform STMB by letter.

Payment in the name of the student or his or her heir can only be made after written approval by the school authority has been received. If a student is an orphan, the payment will be given to whoever took care of the student, for example an orphanage. If the orphan has no family at all, the principal of the orphanage has the right to use the money for the benefit of the institution—not for his personal use. The *Takaful* operator will not make a payment if the student was not insured or did not pay the premium. An agent hired by the *Takaful* operator will check whether a student is qualified to receive payment or not. No forgery or intentional injury will be tolerated. As an example, a student who is pregnant will not be compensated.

24.6 Conclusion

The *Takaful* operator is one of the insurance agencies that has fully applied Islamic insurance in align with Shari'ah principles. During their time in school, students will be covered if any unexpected accident happens, and will therefore not face any difficulties or burdens in their future life—especially if they are poor. Hospital bills and other related expenses are often hard to bear. If the Takaful operator pays benefits, at least the victim's family will not suffer through having to pay the expenses incurred by an accident. The Takaful operator has determined the suitable level of benefits according to the type of coverage. Obviously, the highest benefits are given to the student who suffers permanent paralysis or loses any part of the body.[3] This is because this kind of disaster requires a lot of money to bear. The Takaful operator does not discriminate between student: this means Muslim and non-Muslim students alike can join this plan, and both are paid equally.

The Ministry of Education also encourages schools to insure with a *Takaful* operator because Malaysia is an Islamic country; therefore, this helps to promote Islamic practices.

[3] Refer to the benefits schedule.

We suggest that all students and schools in Malaysia should buy this insurance with Takaful Malaysia because the product has no kind of *Riba*, oppression, burden, *Gharar*, gambling or other unlawful or unethical element.

References

1. Group Students' Takaful Scheme, Takaful Malaysia.
2. Takaful Malaysia, *Guidelines* for the parents.
3. Takaful Malaysia, The benefits schedule.

CHAPTER 25

Education *Takaful*

25.1 Introduction

Family Takaful Plan for Education is one of the ways in which parents can create a fund to pay for higher education for their child. for the cost of higher education, whether in college or institute or university, is ever increasing. This allows parents to help even if they die before their child grows up. Parents are also entitled to a tax exemption for their monthly payments. This is a systematic way of providing a fund, whether as a saving plan or as a fund for the child if something happens to the parents. This plan is based on the concept of ***al-Mudharabah***, the Islamic ethical system that puts man in a central place in the universe: it shows the equilibrium among men. In Qur'anic Ayat:

> Verily all things we have created in proportion and measured. (Qur'an, 53: 54)

In the case of life insurance, upon maturity clients receive their premium plus interest earned. If the policyholder has passed away there will be an element of insurance coverage, which may partly be generated from non-permissible investment activities. The application of al-Mudharabah

A significant contribution to this chapter has been made by the practices, experiences and thoughts of Bank Negara, Takaful Malaysia, Takaful Ikhlas, Takaful Nasional, Etiqa Takaful, IBFIM, IIUM, MII and others (Malaysia).

Mohd Ma'Sum Billah, *Islamic Insurance Products*,
https://doi.org/10.1007/978-3-030-17681-5_25

may remove these doubts from Muslim clients (Islamic Insurance: Takaful 1996). The time of maturity is between 10 and 40 years. Extra protection is provided for the cost of hospitality, accidents and both mental and physical disability; there is also a khairat fund. It is open and easily joined by all people. The policyholder can withdraw up to 70% of the amount saved.

The importance from the contractual point of view is that the amount credited to the Participant's Special Account (PSA) is made as a Tabarru' or donation by the participant. The total aggregate of the Tabarru' paid by all clients into the PSA is the benevolent fund that provides certain benefits in the event of death of a policyholder. The death benefit from the PSA is calculated from the date of death to the date of maturity of the plan based on the contributions paid.

25.2 Product Outlook

Family Takaful Plan for Education encourages families or relatives to create a fund that will pay for their children's education. It is insurance in case the policyholder dies or begins to suffer from physical or mental disability before their certificate matures. The scheme also guarantees policyholders in the event of any accident or loss of ability, mental and physical, and as a guarantee to pay hospitalization cost. It is a saving programme that helps to accumulate a scholarship fund for children's future education. In addition, it enjoys income tax relief on the contributions.

25.2.1 Conditions

Policyholders can join the scheme when they are aged between 18 and 55 when they register. The policyholder is either the father or mother but the lump-sum payment is given to the children, including adopted children). The age of the child can be from 15 days to 18 years old.

25.2.2 Maturity Period

The certificate matures after 10, 15, 20, 25, 30, 35 or 40 years.

25.2.3 Payment

The minimum amount payable is RM 15.00 per month until the certificate matures as agreed. The predetermined interval for payments in to the

Family Takaful Plan for Education is every 3 months, every 6 months or every year until the certificate is matured.

25.2.4 Extra Protection

The other benefits are extra protection when the policyholder totally loses mental or physical ability, is involved in an accident or needs to pay hospital costs. IN addition there is a khairat fund.

25.2.5 Payment Procedure

Salary Deduction
The policyholder can request a salary deduction to be made from employer or bank. The benefit of making transactions direct with the *Takaful* operator is that all payments go directly to the Akauntan Negara. This is the organisation that manages participants' payments directly for the *Takaful* operator. In other words, all policyholders' payments are guaranteed. In the case of a conventional insurance company, the payment by the policyholder is processed by Biro Angkasa before it goes to the insurance company. This situation may lead to misunderstanding between policyholder and insurance company over payments.

Bank Standing Instruction
Participant also can make a payment via a bank that collaborates with Takaful Malaysia. These are Bank Islam Malaysia Berhad (BIMB Holding Berhad) and Bank Simpanan National (GIRO). The bank appointed will automatically make a deduction from the policyholder's account to make a payment. The payment is as in the agreement in terms of amount and interval. Payments can also be made by cash or cheque, or by credit or charge card.

Instalment Procedure
The policyholder agrees to pay the Takaful contribution in instalments monthly, quarterly, half-yearly or yearly as long as he or she is alive. To ensure that the policy is in force at all times and the benefits can be paid in the event of a misfortune, the contribution has to be paid on time, according to the schedule of payment. Once the policyholder has chosen Family Takaful Plan, the next decision he has to make is the size of contribution.

For most people this should not exceed 10% of their income. The operator, however, as a matter of policy sets the minimum amount.

When the policyholder pays the *Takaful* instalment, it is credited into a Family Takaful Fund that is segmented into two accounts: the Participant's Account (PA) and the PSA. Up to 98% of the instalment is credited into the PA, for saving and investment. The balance is credited into the PSA, as Tabarru', or a charitable donation, which allows Syarikat Takaful Malaysia (STM) to pay the *Takaful* benefits to fellow policyholders who are suffering from death or accident.

In order to facilitate investment, the Takaful instalment that is credited into the PA and PSA is pooled as a single unit. All the investment activities are permissible according to Shari'ah. Under the principle of al-Mudharabah, this product utilises an agreed ratio of 7:3, so that the policyholder shall be entitled to 70% of the profit; the balance is for the Takaful operator. The profit is credited into the PA.

Experience (Takaful Malaysia) (Table 25.1)

Individual A registered with the Family Takaful Plan for Education when he was 30 years old. The profit estimation was 6% a year with the instalment set at RM100.00 when his child was one year old. Individual A sets year of maturity for this certificate to 20 years. When this takes place, Individual A can receive almost RM40,000, and this amount allows his child to further his study. The Tabarru' rates above this, which are credited into the PSA, are for death and permanent total disability.

Table 25.1 Payment procedure: *Tabarru'* percentage into PSA (www.takafulmalaysia.com)

Age	*Year of maturity*						
	10	*15*	*20*	*25*	*30*	*35*	*40*
18–25	2.20%	3.90%	5.50%	6.10%	8.30%	10.50%	13.80%
26–30	2.20%	3.90%	5.50%	7.20%	9.90%	13.80%	
31–35	2.80%	5%	7.20%	9.90%	13.80%		
36–40	3.90%	6.60%	9.90%	13.80%			
41–45	5.50%	9.40%	13.80%				
46–50	7.70%	13.80%					
51–55	13.80%						

Source: Author's collection from TMB

Shari'ah Authority and Compliance

Underlying the Family Takaful Plan for Education is compliance with Shari'ah. The Memorandum and Articles of Association of STM prefaces that all investment activities engaged in by the Takaful operator will be transacted in accordance with Islamic principles, rules and practices.

Takaful was introduced in the early 1980s for Islamic insurance, at a time when it was strongly thought that it could not be viable or profitable. Takaful can help most to make a profit through the support of investment. As a system Takaful is steadily gaining popularity. It offers a variety of quality products and satisfies customers' needs at all levels of commodity, as well as at the corporate level.

Takaful is licensed and regulated by the Takaful Act 1984. Section 8 states that:

> The Director General shall also refuse to register an applicant unless he is satisfied…
>
> (b) that there is in Articles of Association of the takaful operator concerned provision for the establishment of a Shari'ah Supervisory Council to advise an operator on the operations of its takaful business in order to ensure that it does not involve any element which is not approved by the Shari'ah. (Takaful Act 1984 (repealed by the Islamic Financial Services Act 2013)

Accordingly, in the Articles of Association section 3(a) (Table 25.2):

> (a) A Religious Supervisory Council whose member would be made up to Muslim religious in the country, shall be established to advise STM on the

Table 25.2 Payment procedure: Fatwa complied by SAC (http://www.islamic-insurance.com/fatwa.html)

Fatwa issued by the State of Trengganu in 1974	Against the validity of conventional insurance
Fatwa issued by the State of Selangor in 1970	Against the validity of conventional insurance
Fatwa issued by the State of Negri Sembilan in 1972	Against the validity of conventional insurance
Fatwa issued by the State of Kelantan in 1975	Against the validity of conventional insurance
Fatwa issued by the State of Perak in 1974	Against the validity of conventional insurance

Source: Author's collection

operations of its takaful business in order to ensure that they do involve in any elements which are not approved by the religion of Islam. (Section 3(a), Articles of Association)

Analysis from the Articles

In the financial year ending 30 June 2003 it was announced by the Syarikat Takaful Malaysia Berhad (Takaful Malaysia) at the Eighteenth Annual General Meeting, which was held on 2 December 2003. Based on the report issued, at company level STM marked an increase in total profit of 30%, with the total RM18,364,416 before zakat and taxation for the year ended 30 June 2003 than previously RM14,103,430. Takaful Malaysia net profit for 2003 was RM 18,354,089, a jump from RM 6,691,906 in the previous year, an increase of 174%.

Takaful Malaysia has associate companies: ASEAN Re-takaful International (L) Limited, PT Syarikat Takaful Indonesia, Sharekat Takaful Al-Arabia Wal Malaysia (Arab Malaysia Takaful Co (AMTC) in Saudi Arabia and Amana Takaful Limited in Sri Lanka. At group level, improvement in the performance of these associate companies increased the net profit after zakat, taxation and minority interests to RM 18,976,562.

The Board of Directors recommended a dividend of 4.5% based on the share capital of 143,000,000 shares, equivalent to RM 4,633,200. There was also an increase in total net assets of the company of 22% or RM 1,750,744,309, the figure for the previous year being RM 1,439,902,661. After an accurate balance of provision for diminution in the value of quoted shares and unit trusts, the total net assets depreciated to RM 1, 699,000,579 but still higher by 23% than the previous year's figure of RM 1,382,916,395.

The cash accounting policy shows the total actual Takaful contribution collected increasing 26% for the year ended 30 June 2003, accumulating to RM 601,683,407. From here the Family Takaful Business took 58% of its total revenue.

The Takaful operator shows a profit of RM 11,662,183, with this increasing by 174% for net profit. Alternative taken by making association with other company shows the efficiency to increase a net profit for the year 2003. The Board of Dircctors announced a high dividend because of the increasing profit. The net profit still in high per cent than previous year for RM 316,084,175. Based on the promotion of products that are more beneficial to individuals, Family Takaful Business contributes more than 0.5% of the total collection.

25.3 Conclusion

Family Takaful Plan for Education provides Takaful services of the highest standard to all Muslims and the rest of the population in Malaysia. Like the other related products, it uses the concept of al-Mudharabah and Tabarru' to remove prohibited elements. The Islamic Takaful are encouraged by the government, since in 1974 the Malaysian Religious Council made a fatwa or legal injunction that conventional life insurance is void in Islam because it contains elements of gharar, riba and maisir ("Islam and Life Insurance," 1997). In 1985 the Family Takaful was introduced, including this product. Under Takaful, profits are distributed based on the two concepts as stated earlier. As we know, Tabarru' is a sharing and co-operation relationship among policyholders, and in the case of death the policyholder gets a benefit from the pool of funds (collective premium) and a dividend from the investment. The Takaful operator invests the premium in interest-free instruments and the profit is shared as the agreed profit-sharing ratio.

The Education Takaful introduced by STM makes improvements on the Family Takaful Plan for Education to give more benefits to clients. The characteristic added in Takaful Siswa is the issuance of a khairat fund if the policyholder dies, permanently loses mental or physical abilities, or is involved in an accident for RM1000+PA, according to the instalments paid by policyholders. This plan is for the children named in the agreement. For policyholders, the khairat fund, also according to instalments and calculations, is RM1000+RM amount of instalment x period before the child is 18 years old. In Malaysia, children further their studies in higher education from when they are 18 years old. The period of maturates when the children are 22 years old meanwhile the installment until the children is 18 years old. This is more efficient than making a fixed time for maturity, in 10,r 15 or 20 years, as stated in the Family Takaful Plan for Education. With this product the parents have to make their own plans for when their certificate will mature to ensure this policy can be used to support essential education.

Hence, the Family Takaful Plan for Education is the product that removes prohibited elements in order to help parents create a fund so that their children can further their studies in higher education. As an insurance system, this plan is confining the operation of Takaful within the Tijari (commercial) sector, popularly known as the private sector. Thus the transactional aspect of Takaful's commercial activity is subject to Islamic contractual laws in order to ensure its compliance with the Shari'ah. Within this fundamental framework, the contract of Tijari Takaful is therefore based on Islamic commercial profit.

References

1. Ali, A. Y. (n.d.), The Holy Qur'an, Text and Translation.
2. "Islamic Insurance: Takaful," (1996), *The Sun*, Friday March 15.
3. http://www.takaful-malaysia.com
4. Section 8, Takaful Act 1984 (repealed by the Islamic Financial Services Act 2013).
5. Section 3(a), *Articles of Association*, Takaful Malaysia.
6. *Fatawa* (Juristic Opinions) on *Different Issues of Takaful*, (Islamic Insurance) http://www.islamic-insurance.com/fatawa.html
7. Family Takaful Plan for Education, Takaful Malaysia.

CHAPTER 26

Senior Citizen Takaful

26.1 Introduction

Senior Citizen Takaful is an individual *Takaful* plan that provides protection against the financial impact arising from the untimely death of the policyholder. The plan is specially designed for those who are between 50 and 80 years of age to help them take better control of their life during their golden years. The policy certificate duration ranges from 5 to 35 years. Contributions are payable until the policy matures, upon which the maturity benefit, being the accumulated contribution (net of any charges) in the Personal Risk Investment Account (PRIA), is payable.

26.2 Scope of Coverage

This product is designed to provide the participant's beneficiary or next of kin with the comfort of a lump sum payment of the sum covered upon the demise of the participant within the term of certificate. There are two types of benefits, namely Accidental Death Benefit and Natural Death Benefit.

26.2.1 Accidental Death Benefit

In the event of death of the policyholder owing to accidental causes, a percentage of the sum covered plus the accumulated amount in the

Mohd Ma'Sum Billah, *Islamic Insurance Products*,
https://doi.org/10.1007/978-3-030-17681-5_26

PRIA are payable to the policyholder's beneficiary or next of kin. The percentages used depend on the policyholder's age at the time of death, as follows:

Age 50–65:	400% of natural death sum covered
Age 66–85:	250% of natural death sum covered
Age 81 and above:	100% of natural death sum covered

For example, if a male policyholder dies in a car accident at the age of 58, the total benefits would be (RM 8576) × (4) + (accumulated PRIA balance).

26.2.2 Natural Death Benefit

In the event of death of the participant owing to natural causes:

- If death occurs within the first two policy years, the Immediate Death Expenses benefit, which is equivalent to the total contributions paid up to the time of death, is payable to the policyholder's beneficiary or next of kin. In addition, the accumulated amount in the policyholder's PRIA is payable to the policyholder's beneficiary or next of kin. This is to protect the company's interests if a participant with a terminal disease buys a policy because he wants to gain the benefit.
- If death occurs within the third policy year and onward, the sum covered plus the accumulated amount in the participant's PRIA are payable to the policyholder's beneficiary or next of kin.

26.2.3 Special Feature

This policy has one fixed unit rate. The sum covered varies between the entry age of 50 and 80, with a minimum contribution of RM 50 a month per unit and a total maximum participation of five units per policyholder. This product requires minimum underwriting for easy and timely acceptance or rejection. No medical check-up is required. Pre-existing conditions are excluded from this benefit.

26.2.4 *Term and Age Limit*

The issue ages are 50–80 years old, with men and women both being covered. The sum covered varies between the sexes, with the amount of benefit for female policyholders being slightly higher than for female policyholders. The issuance per participant is 1 unit minimum with a contribution payment of RM 50 per month and a maximum of 5 units with a contribution payment of RM 250 per month. The expiry age is upon attaining policy anniversary and when the participant is 85 years old. The coverage terms are between 5 and 35 years, subject to a maximum expiry age of 85.

26.2.5 *Suggested and Treatment of Contributions*

The contributions are allocated to the Personal Risk Investment Account (PRIA). From the PRIA a monthly charge is made towards the Taawuni Account Pool (TAP). TAP consists of an Expense Fund, a Risk Fund and Contingency to cover expenses, risk and reserves respectively. The commission fees are paid to the TAP at each contribution due date and the Expense Fee and Contingency Loading charges are paid monthly to the TAP from the first month of coverage.

26.2.6 *Profit and Surplus Contribution*

The company charges a performance fee percentage to any investment profit arising from the PRIA. The performance fee percentage is charged at 10% of the investment income. The resulting net investment income is allocated in full to the policyholder. A Surplus Administration Charge (SAC) of 10% of the gross surplus arising every month is charged. Any net surplus arising (after deducting SAC) from the Risk Fund is provisionally apportioned between the participant (through the PRIA) and the Stabilisation Fund. The ratio of the net surplus (after deducting SAC) sharing is 50:50 or better, in favour of the participant. Any deficit in the Risk Fund will first be paid from the Stabilisation Fund and if necessary the Contingency Fund. If such funds are not sufficient it is met through an interest free loan (Qardul Hasan) from the shareholders' fund. Such loans are a first charge against the surpluses arising from the Risk Fund. At year end, the appointed actuary assesses the adequacy of the Stabilisation

Fund, and whether the amount in this fund will be redistributed to the participant (via the PRIA as a final distribution of surplus) and/or to the Contingency Fund.

26.3 Conclusion

Takaful Ikhkas, a new player in the *Takaful* and insurance industry, is trying to provide the best services by offering a wide choice of products that cater to the needs of the public regardless of age, sex and social status. The Senior Citizen Takaful Scheme is a good product that not only provides financial security but also is a mode of saving and investment. Older people now have the option to better manage their risk and savings. In Malaysia, there are two insurance companies that offer products for older people: AIA and Hong Leong Assueance. Takaful Ikhlas now offers better alternatives that suit the needs of its customers, in line with Shari'ah principles, both for Muslims and non-Muslims.

References

1. Ali, A. Y. (n.d.), The Holy Qur'an, Text and Translation.
2. Senior Citizen Takaful Scheme, Takaful Ikhlas.

CHAPTER 27

Endowment (Ma'asyi) Takaful

27.1 Introduction

Takaful means joint guarantee. Thus it can be visualised as a pact among a group of members or participants who agree to jointly guarantee among themselves against loss or damage that may be inflicted upon any of them as defined in the pact. Should any member or participant suffer a catastrophe or disaster, he receives a certain sum of money or financial benefit from a fund, as also defined in the pact, to help him meet the loss or damage. In other words, the basic objective of *Takaful* is to pay for a defined loss from a defined fund. Each member of the group pools efforts to support the needy. It means mutual help among the group.

27.2 The Product

Retirement is usually associated with the disruption of regular income. Although to some, such as civil servants, monthly pension benefits are available, the amount is usually not very large. Others perhaps enjoy a

A significant contribution to this chapter has been made by the practices, experiences and thoughts of Bank Negara, Takaful Malaysia, Takaful Ikhlas, Takaful Nasional, Etiqa Takaful, IBFIM, IIUM, MII and others (Malaysia).

Mohd Ma'Sum Billah, *Islamic Insurance Products*,
https://doi.org/10.1007/978-3-030-17681-5_27

lump sum benefit from savings on their EPF, but such an amount of money can disappear in a matter of days without proper care and planning. Now whilst you are still working you can plan your future retirement with the help of Takaful Malaysia. By participating in the Takaful Ma'asyi (Endowment) Plan, benefits in the form of a pension will be paid to you regularly.

27.3 Takaful Ma'asyi (Endowment) Plan

The practice of *Ma'asyi* (endowment) was known during the early period of Islam. It was reported that the second Caliph Saidina Umar Ibnu al Khattab, upon meeting an old, hungry and tired-looking Jew during one of his night rounds in Medina decided to provide him with food as a benefit from the *Baitulmal*. The practice was later developed and became a national system, under which *Ma'asyi* benefits were paid to those who had served the cause of Islam.

By this plan any individual intending to enjoy a fixed income after retirement may place his *Takaful* contribution either in a lump sum or on an instalment basis with Takaful Malaysia.

The company invests the contribution, and returns therefrom, if any, will be shared in accordance with the profit-sharing principle of *al-Mudharabah* in a ratio of 80% to the participant and 20% to the company.

27.3.1 Benefits

A participant in the Takaful Ma'asyi (Endowment) Plan enjoys the following unique benefits:

- A fixed income either monthly, quarterly or at any other interval of your choice during your life time until you attain 100 years old.
- A continuous act of good deeds through your contribution collectively towards the Waqf account, wherein *Ma'asyi* benefits will be payable to your fellow participants.
- Your entitlement to share profit, if any, on the investment income of the Ma'asyi Account in accordance with the principle of *al-Mudharabah*.

27.3.2 Participation

The plan is open to any individual. However, it is most suitable for those who are about to retire. It provides peace of mind with no financial worries even you survive into old age.

27.3.3 The Waqf *Period*

You may choose one of three *Waqf* periods:

- 10 years
- 15 years and
- 20 years.

The shorter the Waqf period, the more benefits you may receive.

27.3.4 Cessation of Benefits

The Takaful contribution either in lump sum or by instalments paid by the participant are credited into the Ma'asyi Account in the Family Takaful Fund. This account is in turn split into Participant's Account (PA) and the Waqf Ma'asyi Account (WMA). The proportion of the contribution credited into the WMA is fixed throughout the Waqf period. Ma'asyi benefits are paid to the participant from both the PA and the WMA.

The company invests both the PA and the WMA, and returns therefrom are subject to the profit-sharing principle of al Mudharabah between the participant as the provider of the contribution and the company as the entrepreneur.

27.3.5 Product Package

Depending upon the fixed income that a participant plans to receive, Takaful Malaysia offers two types of Ma'asyi Package.

Hasanah Package
Under the Hasanah Package a participant may choose the profits of the PA to be immediately paid out to him instead of being reinvested. By this method the participant ensures a higher amount of Ma'asyi during the Waqf period.

Ahsan Package
Under the Ahsan Package, instead of cashing the profit of the PA, a participant may choose that it be credited into the WMA. By this method the participant ensures a higher amount of Ma'asyi benefits not only throughout the period of participation but even after the Waqf period.

Table 27.1 shows the estimated *Ma'asyi* benefits payable under both the Hasanah Package and the Ahsan Package (Table 27.1).

27.3.6 Challenge

The basic challenges facing the Takaful industry are:

- Developing a practical and workable Takaful system.
- To leapfrog into the twenty-first century.
- To enhance collaboration between all Takaful operations worldwide.

Table 27.1 Product package

Estimated profit for Hasanah Package		
Year	*Balance in the participant's account (RM)*	*Total sum paid to participant/year (RM)*
1	50,000	2880
2	45,000	3230
3	42,800	3605
4	40,701	4005
5	36,751	4434
6	32,770	4893
7	28,051	5384
8	22,510	5909
9	16,057	6471
10	8590	7072
11	(1)	2880
15	0	2880
20	0	2880
30	0	2880
40	0	2880
45	0	2880
At maturity, participants will receive	5760	
Total Ma'asyi benefits paid during the Waqf period		47,883
Total Ma'asyi benefits paid until maturity		154,445

(*continued*)

Table 27.1 (continued)

Estimated profit for Ahsan Package		
Year	*Balance in the participant's account (RM)*	*Total sum paid to participant/year (RM)*
1	50,000	2880
2	45,000	3120
3	40,000	3338
4	35,000	3533
5	30,000	3703
6	25,000	3847
7	20,000	3966
8	15,000	4056
9	10,000	4118
10	5000	4150
11	0	4150
15	0	4150
20	0	4150
30	0	4150
40	0	4150
45	0	4150
On maturity, participants will receive	5760	
Total *Ma'asyi* benefits paid during the Waqf period		36,711
Total *Ma'asyi* benefits paid until maturity		187,726

Source: Author's collection from TMB

27.4 Conclusion

In Malaysia, the *Takaful* is still new compared to conventional insurance. But now there is a choice, and Muslims are able to stay away from conventional insurance and not worry about the elements of *Riba*, *Gharar* and *Maisir* that are prohibited in Islam. Perhaps communities will condemn Islamic insurance for not being perfect, but a first step is better than nothing. It is essential for Muslims to carry the responsibility of Islamic *Ummah*, doing good things and driving bad things away.

References

1. Ali, A. Y. (n.d.), The Holy Qur'an, Text and Translation.
2. Endowment Takaful Plan, Takaful Malaysia.

CHAPTER 28

Foreign Worker Takaful

28.1 Introduction

The Ministry of Human Resources in Malaysia appointed Takaful Nasional to provide protection for foreign workers against accidents, diseases, injuries or illness during work hours and off-work hours. The Foreign Worker Compensation Scheme is offered to the employer of a company to protect the foreign worker. The company must be legally operated and follow the rules and regulations stated by the Ministry of Human Resources. The scheme is applicable within Malaysia. The contract becomes invalid when the worker returns to his home country.

28.2 The Product

This scheme operates under General Takaful. The basis of this is the *Mudharabah* principle, where the funds are shared 50:50. In other words, when the contract reaches maturity and the person who is covered does not receive any benefit or make any claim, he receives 50% from the total funds. The operator receives the other 50%.

A significant contribution to this chapter has been made by the practices, experiences and thoughts of Bank Negara, Takaful Malaysia, Takaful Ikhlas, Takaful Nasional, Etiqa Takaful, IBFIM, IIUM, MII and others (Malaysia).

Mohd Ma'Sum Billah, *Islamic Insurance Products*,
https://doi.org/10.1007/978-3-030-17681-5_28

28.2.1 The Benefit Is Divided into Three Sections

- Section 1
  Workmen's Compensation Takaful.
- Section 2
  Repatriation Expenses.
- Section 3
  Personal Accident Takaful (Off-Work Hours).

See Table 28.1

28.2.2 Contract

The contract consists of three parties: the *Takaful* company, the employer and the foreign worker. An agent is involved in the contract to ensure the *Takaful* process runs smoothly.

- The *Takaful* company acts as an operator that offers the protection.
- The employer acts as participant, and is liable to pay the monthly premium of RM 72 for each foreign worker.
- The foreign worker receives the coverage.
- The agent acts as the intermediary who works on behalf of the operator, not only under law of contract but also under contract of *al-Wakalah*.

Table 28.1 Rational outlook

Benefits	*Contribution*	*Compensation*
Section 1	RM 72	The total amount that the employer should pay plus RM 7000 in the event of death
Section 2	RM 72	Less or equal to RM 4800
Section 3	RM 72	PTD: Less or equal to RM 23,000 PPD: Subject to the law TPD: Subject to the law Medical expenses: subject to the law

Source: Author's collection

28.2.3 General Condition

- The employer should ensure the foreign workers are legally registered and fulfil some conditions.
- The numbers of foreign workers are recognised in the proposal.
- The employer will pay the premium of RM 72 for each foreign worker.
- The event occurs within the period of *Takaful*.
- The claim is valid for the event within Malaysia.

28.2.4 General Exception (Foreign Worker Compensation Scheme, Takaful *Certificate, n.d.)*

The Foreign Worker Compensation Scheme is not valid, if the covered person:

- Makes a claim from outside Malaysia.
- Any loss, damage, injury by accident or disease caused by:
  - (a) War, invasion of a foreign enemy, hostilities (whether war be declared or not), civil war, mutiny, rebellion, revolution, insurrection or military or usurped power.
  - (b) Any action that is considered as terrorism or undertaken by government forces.
- Any loss, injury or liability that is caused by:
  - (c) Ionizing radiation or contamination by radioactivity from any nuclear fuel or nuclear waste.
  - (d) Nuclear weapons material.

28.2.5 Claim Procedure

When an accident occurs that may give rise to a claim under this certificate, the participant shall:

(i) Report the accident immediately to the Labour Department as provided under Section 13(1) and (2) of the Workmen's Compensation Act 1952.

(ii) Give immediate notice in writing within ten days of the accident to the company, stating the circumstances of the accident and the nature of the injury.

Compensation payable, as assessed by the Commissioner in accordance with the Act, shall be paid within seven days of receipt by the company of such assessment.

28.2.6 *Share of Net Surplus*

The participant and the operator share the net surplus of the Workmen's Compensation Takaful Account of the company's General Takaful Fund based on the Mudharabah principle. The proportion is agreed by the parties in the agreement. This is applied if the participant does not make any claim that exceeds contribution or does not receive any benefits.

28.2.7 *Benefits*

The Benefit is divided into three sections:

Section 1
Workmen's Compensation Takaful.

- Compensation will be provided to the covered person if he meets an accident or injury during the period of Takaful.
- The scheme is valid if the event occurs within working hours and at the workplace.
- Compensation is provided if the employer is liable to pay the compensation.
- The event occurs during the period of Takaful.

The employer can claim the total amount of compensation that he needs to pay his foreign workers from the *Takaful* company. The *Takaful* company does not limit the amount. The total amount is subjected to the following laws.

- Workmen's Compensation Act 1952.
- Workmen's Compensation (Amendment) Act 1956.
- Workmen's Compensation (Amendment) Act 1976.

- Modification Of Laws (Workmen's Compensation).
- (Extension and Modification) Order 1981.
- Workmen's Compensation (Amendment) Act 1996.
- Workmen's Compensation (Foreign Workers Compensation Scheme) (Insurance) Order 1998.

In the case of death caused by the injury or accident, the *Takaful* company will pay the extra amount of RM 7000.

Exception
The compensation does not cover foreign workers who are working under a contractor who is assigned by the employer. For example; Mr Gopal is working for Ladang FELDA Lapar Utara 05. He came from India and was to stay in Malaysia for three years. The employer registered all foreign workers for *Takaful* protection. He met with an accident within his work hours, and although he received medical treatment in hospital he died seven days later. The total cost of the medical treatment was RM 10000.

The employer has to pay the compensation for RM 10000. He can claim the payment from the *Takaful* company because the worker is bound by the contract of the Foreign Worker Compensation Scheme. The company also has to pay RM 7000 because death occurred.

Section 2

Repatriation Expenses
The employer who registers the foreign worker under the scheme can also claim compensation for repatriation expenses. The compensation is paid for foreign workers in the following circumstances:

- The company will pay according to the amount that the employer was liable to pay to the particular foreign worker.
- The foreign worker dies or suffers from permanent total disablement and is recognized to be unable to continue working.
- The foreign worker died within 12 months, caused by the accident or injuries.
- The event occurs within the period of *Takaful*.

The maximum amount payable is RM 4800. The employers can claim compensation based on the actual amount or less than RM 4800. The *Takaful* company will not be responsible to pay the excess amount.

If the particular person is willing to return to his/her country because of total permanent disablement, or in the case of death the family want the body repatriated, the employer is liable to pay the cost of transport and other expenses. Under the scheme, the employer can claim the actual cost equal to or less than RM 4800.

One of the foreign workers on the Sim Lian Sdn. Bhd died during the construction. His family was willing to receive the body. The total cost of transport and some other expenses was RM 3000.

The Takaful company will indemnify the employer for the compensation. Because the total cost of transport and other expenses is less than RM 4800, the company will only pay the actual amount of RM 3000.

Section 3

Personal Accident Takaful (Off-Work Hours).

The Takaful company will pay compensation to the foreign worker for accidents or injuries that occur outside working hours. The amount of payment will be based on:

- Permanent Total Disablement (PTD)

The foreign worker or his legal representatives will be paid a total of RM 23000 if the PTD occurs within 12 months of the accident.

- Permanent Partial Disablement (PPD)

The foreign worker will receive the amount of RM 23000 as calculated in the First Schedule of Workmen Compensation (Amendment) Act 1996.

- Temporary Disablement

The company will pay a total amount as stated in Section 8 (e) of Workmen Compensation Act 1952.

- Medical Expenses as mentioned in Workmen Compensation Act 1952.

The compensation in Section 3 will be provided according to the type of disablement. The maximum amount is subjected to the laws of Workmen

Compensation. If the foreign worker is only temporarily disabled, the Takaful company will provide coverage according to the amount stated by the law.

David Edward, manager of HP, is working in Malaysia, but within a year he meets with an accident when he is going back to his apartment. Unfortunately, he is crippled by this and the doctor recognises that he is unable to continue his job.

First, the employer will prepare a report and information about the accident and submit it to the Labour Department. Then the employer should submit an immediate notice in writing within ten days of the accident to the *Takaful* company. This appoints the qualified medical practitioner, who makes an examination to discover whether the victim was under the influence of alcohol or drugs. If this is not the case, then the operator will pay a total amount of RM 23000 to cover the permanent total disablement.

Special Provision to Section 3

- Loss of limb or member or part thereof means loss by actual physical severance or total and permanent loss of use.
- The total sum payable for Permanent Disablement in respect of injury to more than one portion of a limb or member or part thereof shall not exceed the sum payable in respect of such injury to the whole of that limb or member or part thereof.
- Payment shall only be made of either benefit (a) or (b) and not both.
- The maximum benefit payable under (a) and (b) shall be RM 23,000.00.

Special Conditions to Section 3

- This Takaful shall not apply to a foreign worker who has attained the age of 65 years.
- Notice in writing must be given to the company of any accident to which there may be a claim under this section within ten days of the accident.
- For the purpose of this scheme, General Condition 6 (other *Takaful* or insurances) shall not apply to (a), (b) and (c) of this section.
- This section shall not be assignable to any benefit; it can only be made to the foreign worker.

Exceptions to Section 3

No payment will be made under this section for bodily injury consequent upon:

- Any unlawful act of the foreign worker or wilful exposure to danger (other than in an attempt to save human life), suicide or attempted suicide or intentional self-injury.
- The effect or influence (temporary or otherwise) of alcohol or drugs not prescribed by a qualified medical practitioner, venereal disease, insanity or AIDS.
- Pregnancy or childbirth, miscarriage or abortion.
- Rock climbing, mountaineering (which requires the use of ropes or guides), skin diving, parachuting, polo, steeple-chasing, big game hunting or racing of any kind other than on foot.
- Flying as a member of an aircrew or in any aircraft for the purpose of any trade or technical operation therein or thereon or air travel other than as a fare-paying passenger in any properly certified or licensed power-driven aircraft constructed to carry passengers.
- Riding on motorcycle, motor scooter, moped or mechanically assisted pedal cycle (whether as driver or passenger) for sports, exhibition, competition or racing.
- Works carried out in relation to the foreign worker's employment with the participant.

28.3 The Experience of Takaful Nasional of the Product

See Fig. 28.1

28.4 Recommendation

1. The *Takaful* company should observe the foreign worker and give him some information.

The initial operation only highlights the participation of the employer and the *Takaful* company. The foreign worker only receives coverage or compensation without knowing his rights.

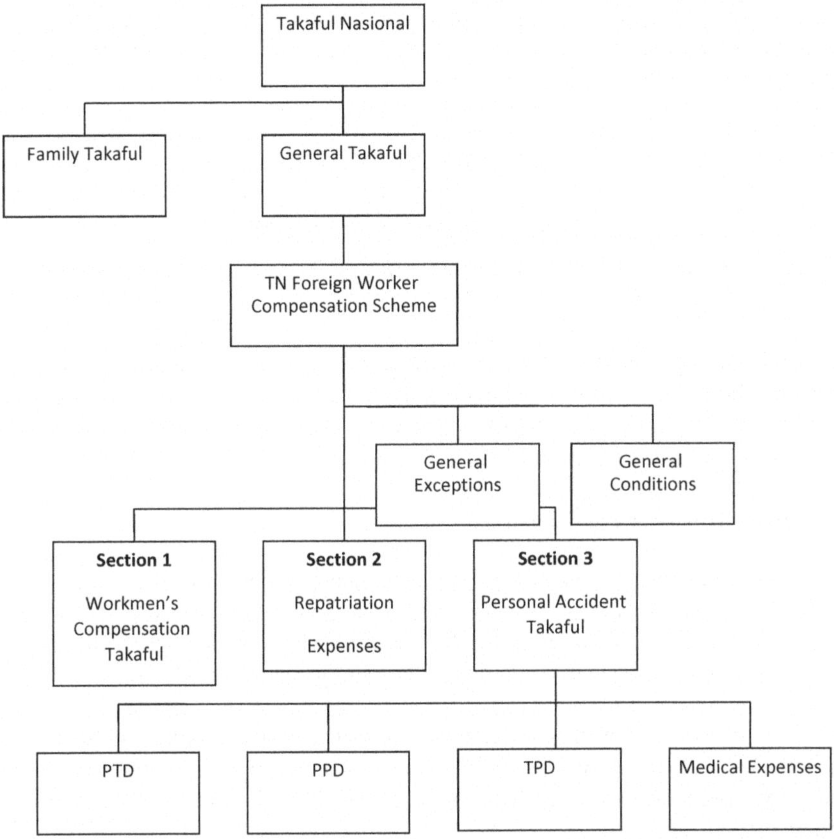

Fig. 28.1 The experience of Takaful Nasional of the product. (Source: Author's collection)

2. Delay the period of report submission according to the circumstances.

The Takaful company determined the due date of report submission to be within 10 days. This time might be too limited to compile the required information.

3. Pregnancy or Childbirth, Miscarriage or Abortion Should Be Included in the Conditions

For this issue, the *Takaful* company has rejected the cover in their conditions. In reality, a worker who is pregnant might be affected by either machinery or other equipment.

28.5 Shari'ah Ruling

28.5.1 Mutual Cooperation

> Help you one another in *Al-Birr* and *At-Taqwa* (virtue, righteousness and piety). (Qur'an 5: 2)

The Foreign Worker Compensation Scheme comes from the funds raised when the employer has to pay RM 72 for each worker. Such compensation provides financial assistant for a foreign worker's unexpected injuries or accidents that will cause death or permanent disablement.

Promotes Mutual Cooperation

> Narrated by Abu Huraira (r) from holy Prophet (saw) saying that: whosoever removes a worldly hardship from a believer Allah (swt) will remove from him one of the hardships of the hereafter, whoever alleviates the needy person, Allah (swt) will deviated from him in this world and the next.

The scheme promotes mutual cooperation and the spirit of brotherhood. The employer, as a participant, does not receive cover. However, he provides protection for his foreign workers. Thus he is trying to remove their difficulties.

28.5.2 Facilitates and Makes Life Easy

> Allah intends for you ease, and He does not want to make things difficult for you. (Qur'an 2: 185)

The scheme facilitates the covered person who suffers from injuries or accident. The compensation might cover some or the full amount of medical treatment. The victim's family might lose their source of income because of the total permanent disablement. The compensation might help them to pay for medical treatment. The employer also receives some benefits because he cannot pay the foreign workers the RM 23000 lump sum. The mutual fund from the scheme eases this difficulty.

28.5.3 Contract

O you who believe! Fulfill (your obligation). (Qur'an 5: 1)

The parties that participate in such a *Takaful* scheme are bound by the agreement. There are three parties: operator, participant and the person who is covered. There are also some conditions and restrictions that should be understood and agreed by all parties. Thus, whatever happens, the person who is covered should be able to claim successfully.

28.6 Conclusion

The Foreign Worker Compensation Scheme encourages employers to take care of foreign workers. This cover is provided only for those who are directly working for a particular employer, excluding his/her family. Next, the purpose is to give an amount of money to the participants as compensation if a death takes place or if injuries occur, with respect to Workmen's Compensation Takaful, Repatriation Expenses and Personal Accident Takaful. However, the participants can claim insurance after this has been agreed by the *Takaful* company. This must be according to the conditions that the operator has given when the agreement was made. Thus, any exceptions will be rejected by the *Takaful* company. This kind of insurance has been advantageous to foreign workers in Malaysia. It will help them become more secure and comfortable in a foreign country.

References

1. Ali, A. Y. (n.d.), The Holy Qur'an, Text and Translation.
2. Foreign Worker Takaful Scheme, Takaful Nasional.
3. Foreign Worker Compensation Scheme, Takaful Nasional Certificate.

CHAPTER 29

Mortgage Takaful

29.1 Introduction

It is a compulsory requirement that a mortgage against any loan should be provided by one of the authorized financial institutions in Malaysia. The research here specifically discusses mortgages in Islamic insurance (*Takaful*). These are different from conventional mortgages in the sense that they are implemented based on Shari'ah rulings and undeniably ensure justice, fairness and mutual co-operation amongst the parties involved. This chapter will discuss the basic idea of the Mortgage Takaful Plan and how it is applied in Malaysia, especially by the Takaful Nasional Berhad. The operations may be slightly different from one company to the next because of differing policies and rules. The discussion begins by introducing and defining the basic mortgage concept of *Rahn* and tries to define the term according to the *Takaful* plan. We have also extracted some verses from the Qur'an, Hadith and *Ijma'* of scholars as evidence for the legality of *Rahn*. Then we discuss important ideas such as benefits, scope of cover, amount and payment of contribution, and at the end of the chapter we highlight some major issues that are usually faced by the *Takaful* operator.

A significant contribution to this chapter has been made by the practices, experiences and thoughts of Bank Negara, Takaful Malaysia, Takaful Ikhlas, Takaful Nasional, Etiqa Takaful, IBFIM, IIUM, MII and others (Malaysia).

Mohd Ma'Sum Billah, *Islamic Insurance Products*,
https://doi.org/10.1007/978-3-030-17681-5_29

29.2 Mortgage *Takaful* Plan

The definitions of *Rahn* used here apply to the specific references in the Mortgage Takaful Plan. Under this plan, mortgage *Takaful* policy is a kind of protection on behalf of the policyholder as a borrower and as guarantor to the financier, such as the bank for providing credit or a loan facility for the purpose of purchasing assets such as shop premises, land, car and so on. This plan guarantees justice between both parties. It protects financial interests because if the borrower is unable to pay the remaining loan owing to his untimely death or permanent total disability, the Mortgage Takaful Plan will be held responsible to guarantee full repayment of the outstanding balance. On the borrower's side, this plan serves to guarantee the purchased assets will be forever his. The application of mortgage *Takaful* is justified by the technical meaning from the schools of Hanafi's thought as possessions (mortgage *Takaful* policy) offered as security (guaranteeing for repayment) for a debt (loan of borrower) than will be taken from the *Takaful* operator in the case the debtor (borrower) failed (due to unexpected defined risk either or permanent disability) to pay back the due money (outstanding loan).

29.3 Shari'ah Rulings on Application of Mortgage

The Holy Qur'an, the Prophetic Sunnah and *Ijma'* have directed the legality of *Rahn*. This serves as the basis for the implementation of the Mortgage Takaful Plan. The concept of *Rahn* is applied according to the evolution of changing dynamics in transactions today. So, in order to realize the beauty of muamalah in mortgage plans, the concept of *Rahn* should facilitate much economic activity today. The evidence for this is based on the following:

Allah says in the Qur'an:

> If you are on journey, and cannot find a scribe, a pledge with possession (may serve the purpose). (Qur'an 2: 283)

It is clear from the *Ayah* that a pledge is allowed when a traveller does not find a scribe during his journey. This does not mean that when he is not on a journey he cannot pledge because of the following hadith, which is also evidence of the legality of *Rahn*.

Hadith of the Holy Prophet:

It is reported also in the Sunnah and the biography of the Prophet (Pbuh) that, he has borrowed food from a Jew in Medina and offered his shield as pledge. (Sahih Muslim)

Abu Huraira reported that the Prophet said:

"A riding animal is used in return for its expenses, it the animal is pledged. He who rides the animal or drinks the milk has to pay the expenses". He (pbuh) said, "a pledge does not become the property of the mortgagee; it remains the property of its owner who mortgaged it: he is entitled to its benefits, and he is liable for its expenses". (Sahih Muslim)

The essence of the hadith is that the animal might be ridden provided that its maintenance is paid when it is pledged and the milk of the animal might be drunk provided that its maintenance is paid when it is pledged. For whoever rides and drinks is the payment of such maintenance. Then the foreclosure on the property is impossible, and neither pledger nor pledgee can sell, even after the expiry of the period named for payment, without express consent of both the parties of a judicial decree.

29.3.1 **Ijma'** ***of Scholars***

Muslim jurists agree on the legality of *Rahn*. The legality of *Rahn* is maintained as long as it is applied according to Shari'ah and it should promote goodness, justice and fairness to all parties involved without harming the others.

29.4 Rational Outlook of Mortgage

A mortgage policy under a Takaful plan signifies "a reflection to the creditor as financier and the debtor as borrower." This means that the Mortgage Takaful Policy is a certificate aside from requesting the payment from the financier. It also as the certificate in the side of guaranteeing and chapter of the right from the side of borrower.

The need for this certificate is strong from both sides (the borrower and the financier). The borrower must be aware that there is no easy loan without having the mortgage policy. The policy is absolutely needed when the person is intending to buy valuable assets by means of a loan. It is the trend that the financier will ask the borrower the authenticity by means of mortgage for his loan as a step for the caution in facing denial.

The wisdom behind the legalisation of *Rahn* is considerable, for the pledge ireleases the pledger (the financier) from a fear of bankruptcy. Someone may need money to fulfil and obtain their essential needs by means of a loan. But it is impossible to have as many loans as one may wish. The potential lender (the financier) may feel doubt about providing a loan owing to the probability of default (being unable to pay back owing to death or permanent disability) unless the loan is pledged with valuable items (Mortgage Takaful Policy).

Allah is all-knowing, and His knowledge is beyond human understanding. He legalised the pledge in order to give us a kind of confidence in His property. As for the benefits that might be derived by the legalisation of *Rahn*, it can bring about mutual love and kindness between people.

29.5 Benefits of the Plan

29.5.1 To the Borrower

- **Security:** the outstanding balance of the borrowers or participant's financing will be repaid in a lump sum upon untimely death or permanent total disability. The outstanding balance of the loan will be covered fully by the Mortgage Takaful Plan.
- **Relief:** The guarantor or beneficiary if any shall not be burdened with payment of the liability in the event of the death of the borrower or the participant. The guarantor is relieved from this responsibility.
- **Ownership:** because of the full payment and redemption of the facility, the fixed asset under the financing facility will be free to be inherited by rightful heirs. There is no risk that the asset will return to the seller.
- ***Al-Mudharabah*:** The participant in the Mortgage Takaful Plan shall be entitled to share the profits/surplus that arise from the actuarial valuation of the Participant Special Accounts of the Family Takaful Fund. In other words, they will gain a profit if there is a surplus in the fund.

29.5.2 To the Financier

- **Takaful Mortgage Plan will assure guarantee of settlement:** the full repayment of the outstanding balance of the financing facility in the event of the untimely death or permanent total disability of the borrower.

- **Cost-Saving:** since the Mortgage Takaful Plan will assure guarantee of settlement. The financier will not incur additional cost or expenses such as legal fees, reminders and litigation that are normally required to recover the unpaid outstanding balance of the financing facility.

29.6 Scope of the Cover

The Takaful Mortgage Plan offers the following cover:

- Death- (D).
- Permanent Total Disability- (PTD).

PTD is a supplementary benefit that may be endorsed to the basic cover for the benefit of borrower and financier. The Takaful Mortgage Plan will cover whatever outstanding balance is not paid by the participant. Borrower and financier will get benefits from this plan. Both do not in risky condition if apply this Takaful Mortgage Plan.

29.7 Terms of Participation

29.7.1 Proposal and Declaration Form

First of all an individual borrower proposing to participate in the Takaful Mortgage Plan shall be required to complete the proposal and declaration form provided by the company. These will include all the conditions that apply to the plan. If any information provided does not fulfil the conditions required, the application will be rejected.

29.7.2 Age

This is the same as for other plans. There is no difference between Islamic and conventional ways. At the time of the proposal the borrower must not be less than 18 years of age and not more than 65 at the time of maturity of the plan. However, subject to the authority limits, a borrower exceeding 65 years old at maturity may be accepted.

29.7.3 Period of Takaful

The period of Takaful should be equivalent to the period of financing. It will also include the interim period, if there is one.

29.7.4 *Limited* Wasi *Declaration Form*

The borrower shall also be required to complete and sign this form, which authorises the company to pay the outstanding balance of the facility to the financier from the proceeds under the plan. After the declaration form is signed the company will have authority to complete the outstanding balance if anything happens that causes death or permanent total disability to the borrower or participant.

29.8 Joint Financing/Loan

In case of joint financing, there are two options that are provided by the Mortgage Takaful Plan.

Option 1
Either the husband or wife participates in a single Takaful Mortgage Plan covering the total amount of financing; or

Option 2
Both the husband and wife participate in two separate Takaful Mortgage Plans based on the proportion of the repayment amount shared between the husband and the wife.

Example
Total amount of financing = RM100,000 monthly repayment = RM 1000.
Husband's contribution = RM 600. Wife's contribution = RM 400

Thus the amount of cover will be:

Husband = 60% of RM 100,000	RM 60,000
Wife = 40% of RM100,000	RM 40,000

For joint financing, the borrowers are recommended to participate under option 2. This is because both the husband and the wife may opt to cover 100% of the total financing, thus providing double coverage in the event both of them die.

29.9 Contribution

The Takaful contribution paid by the participant will be credited into the PSA as Tabarru'.

29.9.1 Rating the Contribution

- Amount of financing/loan to be covered.
- Age next birthday of the borrower. For example: the participant applies for a Takaful Mortgage Plan aged 25 on 12/09/2002, but the contribution amount will be calculated at the age of 26 on 12/09/2003.
- Rate of profit/interest per annum charged by the financier on the financing facility; the profit/interest will be based on the economic scenario. The bank will fix the profit/interest that will be charged.
- Period of financing including interim period if applicable;

It will be consistent with the loan period.

- Whether the Takaful contribution is incorporated as part of the total financing facility;
- Whether PTD benefit is opted.
- There is an option. The option will depend on the health of the participant. If the participant is already blind, he/she will be offered only death.

Payment by Instalments
As mentioned before, upon participating the participant shall be required to pay his *Takaful* contribution in one lump sum to the Takaful Mortgage Plan. However, the CEO and/or General Manager Family Division decided that the participant may be allowed to pay the contribution in instalments if it does not exceed a period of six months. However, the first instalment should be equivalent to 50% of the total contribution charged. For the balance of five instalments the participant is required to settle within a period of six months preferably through the issuance of a post-dated cheque.

Backdating the Age
Backdating the age based on the one declared in the proposal and declaration Form may be allowed if such backdating does not exceed a period of six months.

Difference of Contribution by a Margin of RM 50.00
If the amount of the contribution paid by the proposer differs within the margin of RM 50.00 from the actual contribution to be charged, such difference may be disregarded. Suppose the payment is RM 500.00, but the participant paid only RM 490.00, RM 10.00 will be covered by *Takaful.*

29.10 Underwriting

Please refer to the procedure and guidelines given under the Family Takaful Plan and Family Takaful Plan for Education. Insurance only covers certain risk, basically referring to a medical report. If a man aged 45 years old applies for a loan for RM 40,000.00, and is declared to have a serious illness, his application will be rejected because he has a bad risk and the risk is certain. The Mortgage Takaful Plan only can apply to uncertain risk.

29.11 Non-underwriting Procedure

Acceptance of a proposal without underwriting may be granted only to an employer of a financial institution provided that all employees or clients under the facility are required to participate only in the Takaful Mortgage Plan. They are not allowed to participate in other mortgage plans. Under the non-underwriting procedure, the company without submission of evidence of health will automatically cover all employees or borrowers. All employees will be accepted to participate in this plan, and for this purpose the employer or financier may be required to sign the proposal and declaration form on behalf of the client.

29.12 Covering Financing Period Less Than Five Years

The period of Takaful in respect of covering financing five years or less may be accepted for the following:

- Cost for medical examination, if required, shall be borne by the proposer.
- The minimum amount of a single *Takaful* contribution must be RM 150.00.
- Stamp duty shall be paid by the proposer.

29.12.1 Covering Amount

The amount of cover shown in the *Takaful* certificate shall be equivalent to the total amount of financing approved, inclusive of the *Takaful* single contribution if the contribution is financed and incorporated into the financing amount. In a case where the participant pays a single contribution, the amount of cover shall be the amount of financing approved. The amount of cover shall reduce annually (on the basis of reducing the sum at risk) as the borrower pays his regular monthly instalment, until the end of the financing period. If the amount paid by the participant is less than the amount of single contribution required, the amount of cover it shall be reduced in proportion to the amount paid after the expiry of the grace period, which is six months. Similarly, should the participant fail to undergo the medical examination required until expiry of the grace period, the amount of cover may be reduced to the amount of the non-medical limit.

29.12.2 Guarantee

As the party that provides the financing facility, the name of the financier shall be inserted in the *Takaful* Certificate as the grantee. In this regard, if claim is made under the certificate, the *Takaful* benefits shall be payable to the grantee to redeem the outstanding amount of the financing facility. After deducting the amount outstanding, the company shall remit the balance of the *Takaful* benefit, if any, to the proper claimant.

29.12.3 Effective Date of Cover

The effective date of cover for a proposal accepted may be determined as follows:

- The date when the financing facility is approved.
- The date when the first disbursement of the facility is made.

- The date as determined based on the underwriting guideline as stated in "Underwriting Guideline and Procedure" for Family Takaful Business.

Where backdating is required in respect of (a) and (b) above, such backdating shall not be more than six months.

29.12.4 Issuance of Certificate

Upon acceptance of the proposal and full payment of the total contribution, the certificate for Takaful Mortgage Plan shall be issued no more than two weeks later. A copy of the certificate will be extended to the financier.

29.12.5 Surrender

If the participant redeems his financing before the completion of the financing period, the participant may surrender his Takaful certificate and in return be entitled to the surrender value of the certificate. Upon surrender, the participant is required to submit the following documents to the company:

- Original copy of the Takaful Mortgage Certificate.
- Copy of identity card.
- Confirmation letter from the financier that the financing has been fully settled by the borrower, i.e. the participant.
- Surrender discharge form, duly completed and signed by parties, financier and the participant.

In compulsory cases, where the participant is compelled to participate in the Takaful Mortgage Plan, the financier may sign the discharge form on behalf of the participant.

A redemption letter issued by the financier to the company certifying that the participant has fully redeemed his financing facility may be accepted as discharged in place of the surrender discharge form.

- The company shall not accept surrender from the participant unless with prior consent from the financier.

- The effective date of the surrender for the purpose of calculation of refund shall be the date such notice is given to the company.

Where required, the date of surrender may be backdated to the date the full settlement was made with the financier. However, such backdating shall not exceed a period of three months.

- Certificate surrendered within a period less than twoyears shall be rendered with a service fee of RM 30.00 for non-medical cases or RM 60.00 for medical cases.

29.12.6 Payment of Benefit

- The participant will be entitled to receive his share of the surplus, if any, arising from the Participants' Special Accounts as shown in the last actuarial valuation of the company in accordance with the principle of al-Mudharabah. They will receive the profit or surplus upon the expiry of the period of Takaful, which corresponds to the expiry of the financing facility period.
- Upon maturity the participant is required to forward the following documents to the company:
  - Original copy of the Mortgage Takaful Certificate.
  - Copy of the Identity Card.

Payment of the surplus will be made direct to the participant, unless required otherwise by the financier.

29.13 Conclusion

The Takaful Mortgage Plan is one of the plans provided under the Family Takaful Business. It covers outstanding loan facilities either with financial institutions, employers or co-operative societies. Takaful Malaysia transacts its Takaful products in accordance with the Islamic principles of the *al-Takaful* and *al-Mudharabah.* The benefits of the plan are security, relief, ownership and *al-Mudharabah.* Meanwhile the benefits for the financier are guarantee of settlement and cost saving. The outstanding balance of the loan will be settled in full by Takaful Malaysia upon the untimely death or permanent total disability of the participant. Meanwhile, in line with the profit sharing principle of *al-Mudharabah* participants will be entitled to share profit or surplus of the operation, according to the PSA of the Family Takaful Fund. The scope of cover is death or permanent total disability and the eligibility for this plan is between the ages of 18 and 55, with financing or loan facility. This Takaful Mortgage Plan will ensure your asset is forever yours. Terms of participation of this plan are proposal and declaration form, age, limited Wasi declaration form and joint financing/loan. There are two options for joint financing/loan. There are a few factors that determine the contribution amount. These are the amount of financing to be covered, the age at next birthday of the borrower, the rate of profit, the period of financing, including interim period if applicable, and whether PTD benefit is opted for. The *Takaful* contribution is also determined by payment by instalments, backdating the age and the difference of contribution by a margin of RM 50.00. The Takaful Mortgage Plan also has two further considerations: underwriting consideration and proposal with non-underwriting procedure for covering financing period less than fiveyears. It will be accreted if the cost for medical examination is borne by the proposer, the minimum single *Takaful* contribution of RM 150.00 is made and the proposer is required to pay the stamp duty. Lastly, the Takaful Mortgage Plan will consider the amount of cover, the grantee, effective date of cover, issuance of certificate and payment of benefit at maturity. Shari'ah ruling on mortgage application is also included in this chapter.

References

1. Ali, A. Y. (n.d.), The Holy Qur'an, Text and Translation.
2. Mortgage Takaful Sceme, Takaful Nasional.

CHAPTER 30

Breast Cancer Takaful (Takaful Hawa)

30.1 Introduction

The social structure in Malaysia is changing. More women are going out to work, and are now not only responsible for work in the home that has traditionally been the woman's role but also are being given a chance to help with their family's economic situation. Usually, wives are given the responsibility of planning their family budget, which means their purchasing power is significant. Takaful Malaysia has seized the opportunity to provide a variety of plans and products that givefamiles financial benefits, protecting them from any risks that may occur in the future. For example, Mrs Rogayah has joined Takaful Siswa and Family Takaful in order to pay the potentially high costs of her children's education. Many women are realising that they will face further challenges and hardship if they do not invest and save for their future medical treatment. For those who have extra money, it is a good plan to buy Takaful products. Breast Cancer Takaful (Takaful Hawa) is among the solutions available that are designed especially for the protection of women.

A significant contribution to this chapter/product has been made by the practices, experiences and thoughts of Bank Negara, Takaful Malaysia, Takaful Ikhlas, Takaful Nasional, Etiqa Takaful, IBFIM, IIUM, MII and others (Malaysia).

Mohd Ma'Sum Billah, *Islamic Insurance Products*,
https://doi.org/10.1007/978-3-030-17681-5_30

30.2 Breast Cancer Takaful (Takaful Hawa) Plan

30.2.1 Product Brief

This plan was introduced for women, so they could protect themselves from unexpected risk, particularly the risk of breast cancer. The risk is that someone will need to pay an amount of money for cancer treatment when diagnosed during the agreed period. Cancer treatment can be costly, as it is difficult and involves very expensive modern equipment. Treatment is also repeated. Those who are able will choose private hospitals, for better treatment and more comfort, and these are very costly. Women who join Takaful Hawa will have special treatment in a better place without being worried about the financial cost. The plan also gives further benefits if cancer occurs in such places as the uterus, cervix, fallopian tubes, ovaries, vagina or vulva.

The policy cannot eliminate the risk of cancer, of course, but it provides a financial back-up through the payment of contributions to the Takaful operator. The operator is responsible for providing the policyholder with financial protection if cancer is diagnosed during the agreed period. The Takaful Hawa policyholder is required to pay contributions and al-Tabarru' (donation or charity). This is a similar idea to *al-Sadaqah* (charity), *al-Hibah* (gift) and *al-Khairat* (donation), and donations made in this way cannot be claimed back.

But if the policyholder is not diagnosed with cancer during the agreed time, she is entitled to the whole amount of paid premiums, based on the principles of *al-Mudharabah*, with the share profits coming from accumulated paid premiums based on *al-Mudharabah*, 50:50. Under Takaful Malaysia, the policyholder will agree the payment of premium into the Group Family Takaful Money for Group Family Takaful Account (GFTA) to be invested. If there is any profit, it will be split 60% for the policyholder and 40% for company.

30.2.2 Shari'ah Rulings

Allah says:

> Help ye another in righteousness and piety, but help ye not one another in sin and rancor. (Qur'an 5: 2)

In Takaful Hawa, mutual cooperation is involved through the sharing of risk between the participants through the principle of *al-Mudharabah* and by giving an amount of premium as *Tabarru'*. If one policyholder is diagnosed with cancer, through this donation others will help her. The Qur'anic doctrine of mutual cooperation, which Allah commanded, can be clearly seen.

The Holy Qur'an expressly forbids the Muslim from cooperating with or seeking help from unbelievers. Allah says:

> Let not the believers take for friend of helpers unbeliever rather than believers, if any do that, in nothing will there be help from Allah (swt), expect by way of precaution, that may guard yourself from them. But Allah (swt) cautions you (to remember) himself for the final goal is to Allah (swt) (Qur'an 4: 144)

The need of Takaful Hawa to help women, especially Muslims, is justified. Currently, the chance of being diagnosed with cancer is very high, which makes it all the more important to protect oneself from risk.

As-Sunnah

Abu Huraira from the Holy Prophet says that: "Whosoever removes a wordily hardship from a believer, Allah (swt) will remove from him one of hardship of the hereafter, whosoever alleviates the needy person, Allah (swt) will alleviate him in this world and the hereafter."

The hadith shows how important it is to help others, especially the needy. In Takaful Hawa the needy person is the one who has been diagnose with cancer. She will face the risk of expensive medical costs..

30.2.3 Eligiblity

Women who are under the age of 71 are eligible for the scheme (Tables 30.1 and 30.2).

Table 30.1 Contributions (p.a.)

Breast Cancer Takaful (Takaful Hawa)	*Package A (RM)*	*Package B (RM)*
	148	75
	252	132
	432	225

Source: Author's collection from TMB

Table 30.2 Additional payment

Age	*Package A (RM)*	*Package B (RM)*
18–34	40	20
35–49	110	55
50–59	230	115

Source: Author's collection from TMB

30.2.4 Policy Period and Renewal

This plan is effective for one year and can be renewed each year, the same as the Takaful Medical Plan. The certificate becomes effective on the date stated.

30.2.5 Geographical Territory

The benefits are worldwide.

30.2.6 Additional Persons Covered

Family members of the policyholder who are eligible to be covered are included under the Persons Covered if:

- The policyholder requests that particular family members should be included.
- Such members are insurable in accordance with the underwriting standards of the company.
- The required additional contribution is paid.

30.2.7 Benefits

There are two packages available. In choosing between Package A and Package B, the participant needs to look at her own financial position. Package A provides the policyholder with much greater benefits than Package B, and the difference between the two packages is summarised in Table 30.3.

Table 30.3 Benefits

Takaful benefits scope	*Package A*	*Package B*
On diagnosis of cancer	RM	RM
a. Lump sum on diagnosis of cancer	20,000	10,000
b. Additional lump sum benefits on diagnosis of any one of the following cancers:- (breast, uterus, cervix, fallopian tubes, ovaries or vagina/vulva)	20,000	10,000
c. Reconstructive surgery reimbursement (per breast)	10,000	5000
d. Daily cash benefit for hospitalisation due to Cancer (max: 30 days per confinement)	150	75
e. Additional daily cash benefits for hospitalisation due to Cancer of the-breast, uterus, cervix, fallopian tubes, ovaries or vagina/ vulva (max: 30 days per confinement)	150	75
Annual screening test		
a. Reimbursement for one annual screening test for women		
Smear test and breasts examination	100	50
Eligible after first year coverage	4000	4000
Death benefit		
a. Funeral expenses		
Reimbursement		
a. In-hospital expenses (cancer-related expenses only, per disability)	10,000	5000
b. Outpatient cancer treatment (per annum)	50,000	5000

Source: Author's collection from TMB

30.2.8 Description of Benefits

Lump Sum Benefit

On diagnosis, the policyholder will receive a lump sum, either RM20, 000 or RM10, 000 according to her selected package from Takaful Hawa. This is not payable more than once in the lifetime of the person covered; this includes all subsequent renewals.

Additional Lump Sum Benefit

If the policyholder is diagnosed with any cancer that has been stated in the certificate (breast, uterus, cervix, fallopian tubes, ovaries or vagina/vulva), an additional lump sum will be given to her. is payable just once in the lifetime of the person covered, with the same conditions applying as for the lump sum benefit.

Reconstructive Breast Surgery Benefit (Per Breast)
This is a payment of the amount actually charged for breast reconstruction that is performed in a hospital by a medical practitioner who is qualified to perform such a procedure. This benefit shall not exceed the limit per breast as given in Table 30.3.

Daily Cash Benefit for Hospitalisation
A daily cash benefit is specified. It is payable for every day spent in hospital, and does not exceed a maximum of 30 days per disability.

Additional Daily Cash Benefit for Hospitalisation
This is paid if the policyholder is suffering from cancer of the breast, uterus, cervix, fallopian tubes, ovaries or vagina/vulva. It is payable for every day spent in hospital, and does not exceed a maximum of 30 days per disability. After the first year of Takaful, the company shall provide benefits when the participant needs to undergo a smear test and clinical examination for both breasts.

Annual Cash Allowance for Cancer Screening
The charges incurred for one smear test and one clinical examination of both breasts per certificate year whether cancer is found or not.

Funeral Expenses
The policyholder is covered for funeral expenses if death has taken place for any cause, except suicide, AIDS and other prohibited causes underlined by Shari'ah.

30.2.9 *Exclusion*

- No benefits shall be payable with respect to any period of hospital confinement unless the entire confinement has been recommended and approved by a registered medical practitioner and in accordance with the diagnosis and treatment of the condition for which the hospital confinement was required.
- The certificate shall not pay any benefits or reimburse any expenses relating to:
    - Any cancer that existed or symptoms of which had developed or manifestation existed before the effective date of cover or the policyholder was aware of this or should have been aware based on normal medically accepted pathological development.

- Losses incurred within 30 days from the commencement of the certificate.
- Charges that are not reasonable expenses incurred in the treatment of the illness or treatment or surgery that is not necessary.
- Treatment for congenital conditions.
- Charges for private nursing, seeing a general practitioner, routine health checks, precautionary services, acupuncture and inoculation, and charges for telephone, television, newspapers and other ineligible non-medical items.
- Charges for services received in convalescent and nursing homes, natural cure clinics and similar establishments and for rest care.
- Any cancer directly or indirectly caused by ionizing, radiation or contamination by radioactivity from any nuclear fuel or any nuclear waste.
- Treatment directly or directly from or consequent upon war, invasion, acts of foreign enemies, hostilities (whether war has been declared or not), civil war, rebellion, revolution, insurrection or military or usurped power, or full-time service in any of the armed forces.
- Treatment arising from causes prohibited by Shari'ah.

30.2.10 Effect of Misstatement of Age

If the policyholder's age has been misstated and the payment made is insufficient, any claim will be based on the ratio of the actual Takaful contribution paid to the correct Takaful contribution that should have been charged. Any excess as a result of misstated age will be refunded without interest or profit. If anyone is proven to have provided an incorrect age, the participant will not have eligible for cover under the certificate and no benefits shall be payable.

30.2.11 Termination

A policyholder shall cease to be covered on:

- The attainment of her 71st birthday.
- The date of termination of the certificate or any person's coverage.

In any case the company's liability shall cease with the date of termination of the certificate or any person's coverage.

30.2.12 Alteration

The company reserves the right to amend the terms and provision of this certificate, and the amendment will be applicable from the renewal of the certificate.

Cancellation (Fig. 30.1)
The policy shall be void:

- If the declaration or written statement that is given by the policyholder is untrue in any aspect or if a material fact affecting the risk is incorrectly stated or represented in or omitted from the documents.
- If the policyholder makes any claim that is fraudulent or exaggerated, or there is a false declaration in support of any claim.

30.2.13 Applicable Law

All rights, obligations and liabilities will be construed according to the law of Malaysia.

Legal Proceedings
No action at law and in equity shall be brought with regard to this certificate prior to the expiration of 90 days after the proof of claim has been filed. Nor shall such action be brought unless it be brought within two years from expiry.

Currency Exchange Rate
If treatment takes place outside Malaysia, bills rendered in a foreign currency will be calculated on the basis of the quoted exchange rates in effect on the date of discharge from hospital.

Lodging Complaints with the Insurance Mediation Bureau
Policyholders who have made a claim against the company, which may either be rejected or where the settlement is not satisfactory for the policyholder, can appeal to senior management. If the policyholder is still

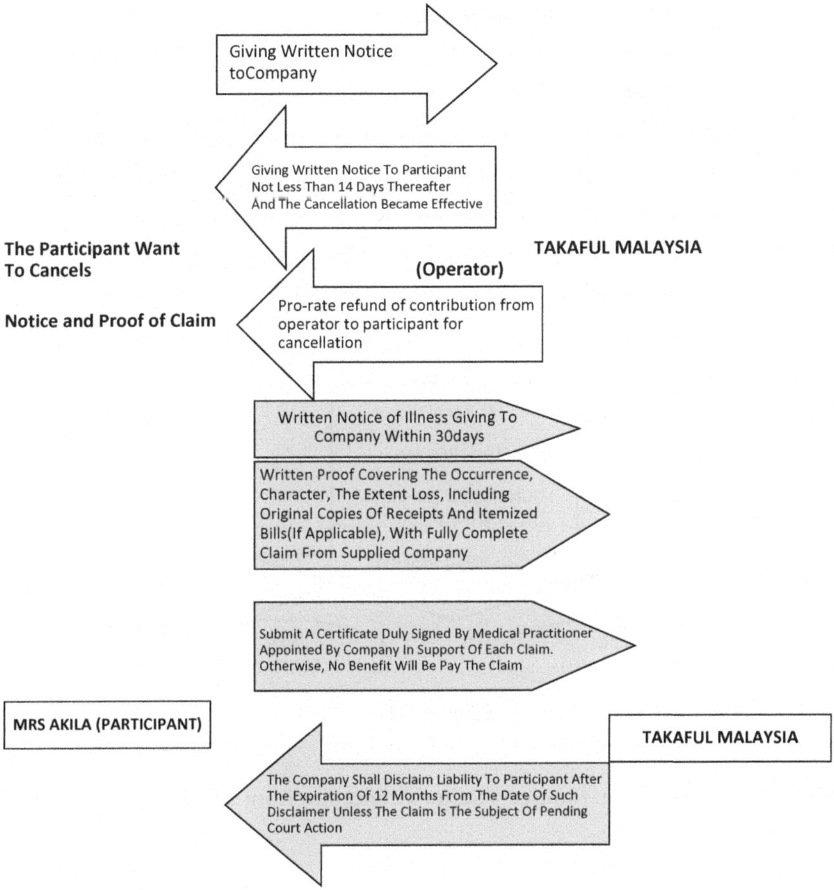

Fig. 30.1 Cancellation. (Source: Author's collection from TMB)

not satisfied, within six months she may ask the mediator to intervene by writing to the Insurance Mediation Bureau.

30.2.14 Experience (Fig. 30.2)

Example

Mrs Nurhaliza (54 years old) on diagnosis of cancer within the policy period. She registered with Takaful Hawa during February 2018 and

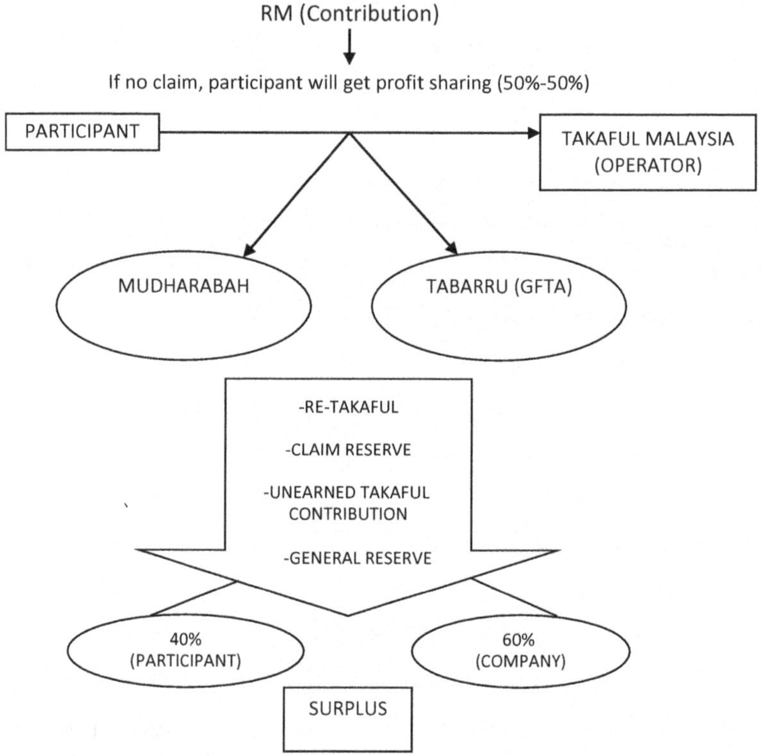

Fig. 30.2 Experience. (Source: Author's collection from TMB)

chose Package A (RM432 per month). Seven months later she was diagnosed with breast cancer. After giving all written proof and a certificate duly signed by a medical practitioner in support for each claim, she was entitled to claim a lump sum of RM 20,000 plus Rm20, 000 additional lump sum for having breast cancer plus profit (Fig. 30.3).

Mrs Zahrah (40 years old) who did not make a claim within policy period. She registered for Package B (RM252 annually) in September 2018, this ending in September 2019. She was entitled to receive a *Mudharabah* stated by the company to be a 50:50 profit share. If there is any surplus from the *Tabarru'* she will share this 40:60 with the operator.

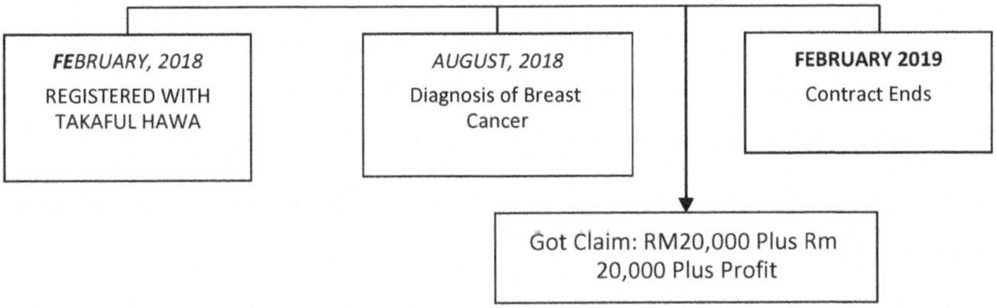

Fig. 30.3 Experience. (Source: Author's collection from TMB)

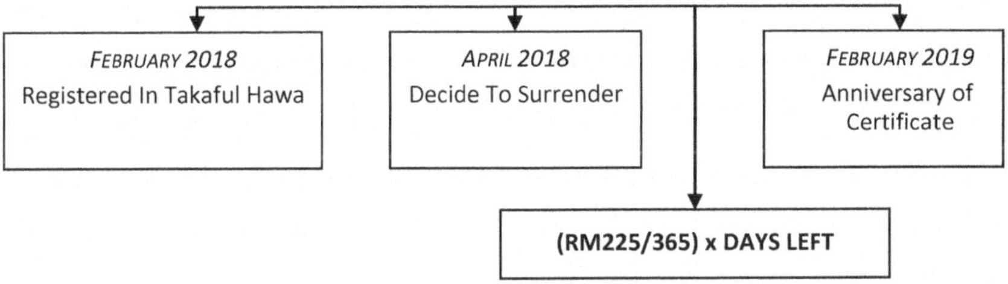

Fig. 30.4 Experience. (Source: Author's collection from TMB)

Miss Zainab (59 years old) surrendered before the anniversary of the certificate. She registered in Package B (RM225) in February 2018. Three months later she decided to surrender from the policy. She was entitled to get back the portion of RM225 that she had paid. The amount was divided by 365 days and multiplied by the number of days left (Fig. 30.4).

30.3 Recommendation

As more products come to market, more risks will occur. Most women, for example, use cosmetic products. There are positive effects, but also the possibility of negative effects, perhaps through using a product that isn't suitable. This might affect the skin. For those who use their personality and beauty in their work, in television or as a model, for example, it is really important to protect their assets (face and physical appearance). Providing cover for this could attract more users from these areas.

Women are in general responsible for many family the duties. These duties can include cooking, washing and cleaning. There are risks attached to all of these: for example, if you accidentally drop a pan of hot oil you may be very seriously burnt. The hospital and treatment costs will be very expensive, especially if plastic surgery is involved. If Takaful Hawa is able to provide cover for circumstances such as this, it would be beneficial for all parties.

30.4 Conclusion

The purpose of *Takaful* is to secure the risk that may occur when participants are facing any difficulties. Women should realise that one day they might be diagnosed with cancer. What are her feelings? What will she think? Where will she find the cost of treatment? These are among the questions to be answered. By having Takaful Hawa, women are not only provided with financial cover but also additional lump sum benefits. There is also potential profit based on *al-Mudharabah* principles..

No other insurance company offers this product. The benefits that it gives will allow women to be protected by good treatment against breast cancer.

References

1. Ali, A. Y. (n.d.), The Holy Qur'an, Text and Translation.
2. Takaful Hawa Scheme, Takaful Malaysia

CHAPTER 31

Pregnancy Takaful (Takaful Wiladah)

31.1 Introduction

In today's domestic environment, women are able to leave home and work in whatever area that interests them. Now, they not just responsible for a housewife's work but also have a chance to help provide for the family financially. In addition, the scope of what jobs they may do is widening day by day. Women are often given responsibility to plan their family budget by their husband and this development reveals that their purchasing power is significant. In considering this phenomenon, Takaful Malaysia has taken the chance to offer a variety of plans or products in order to provide financial benefits to the family. These also need to be protected from any risks that may possibility occur in the future. By having such a plan, the woman and the family are able to shore themselves against uncertain events through the provision of *Al-Mudharabah* and *Tabarru'*. For example, a certain Mrs Rogayah decides to participate in Takaful Siswa (education) and Family Takaful for education in order to cover her family with financial benefits so as to recover the high expenses of her children's education in the future.

It is acknowledged that the ideas in this chapter/product have been significantly contributed to by the practices/experiences/thoughts of Bank Negara, Takaful Malaysia, Takaful Ikhlas, Takaful Nasional, Etiqa Takaful, IBFIM, IIUM, MII and others (Malaysia).

Mohd Ma'Sum Billah, *Islamic Insurance Products*,
https://doi.org/10.1007/978-3-030-17681-5_31

Many women realise that they will face greater challenges and more hardships if they do not invest and save for their future survival and medical treatment. For those who have extra money, it is a good plan for them if they want to have savings by buying *Takaful* products. At present, there are many illnesses that may arise and we cannot know what will happen in future. By recognising that, the Pregnancy Takaful (Takaful Wiladah) Plan (TWP) might be a solution especially apt for the protection of women. TWP is a product that provides financial benefits to women against risk during pregnancy; it also provides financial benefits against risk during the maternity period. In the analysis supplied in this chapter, we will look at various aspects and examples pertaining to this product.

The scheme helps women in planning for their own savings against the risks of maternity. Important here is that the habit of saving will help to generate a happy family and bright future through better educational opportunities being available to their children and better medical treatment when they are in need of such. Thus, women can play an important role by understanding that to have savings will benefit not only themselves but also their other family members.

31.2 Product Brief

TWP was launched in 2001 and provides a long-term finance programme especially for women, acting as a fund for its participants to help them face any unexpected complications during pregnancy, newborn congenital anomalies or infant death. Participants are covered by this fund according to their contribution.

31.3 Shari'ah Rulings

Each couple (husband and wife) may feel that to have their own children is a special time that they have been waiting for. This honorable gift from Allah (swt) gives great dignity to a pregnant wife, as stated in the *Hadith* of Rasulullah (saw):

> Does not each of them (wives) feels happy if she is pregnant from her husband's sperm and her husband proud with her pregnancy, she will get reward, same as people fight to the way of Allah at the time they are fasting. And when she has a hard time during delivery, all the creation in the universe (sky and earth) do not know the happiness happiness hidden inside her heart (wife).

However, during pregnancy there are certain considerations that should be taken note of, especially the mother's health (physically and mentally). As is indicated in the Qur'an:

> In pain did his mother bear him, and in pain did she give in birth. The carrying of the (child) to his weaning is (a period of) 30 months. (Surah Alıqaf: 15)

This verse approves that the mother may face many difficulties or risks during pregnancy or in giving birth. In realising the need for plan like TWP, Takaful Malaysia has taken action to offer this plan to women. Through this plan, it provides coverage to secure against risks that may occur during pregnancy.

31.4 Terms and Conditions

This plan is for women aged between 18 years and 40 years at the date of participation. TWP provides three choices of maturity period: 10, 15 and 20 years. This plan should end before the age of participants reaches 50. In other words, a person who joins TWP at the age of 40 is allowed to take out a 10-year plan only. A participant can participate in one TWP and is entitled to only one certificate—a person may not have two TWP policies at the same time.

31.5 Contributions

The Takaful instalments payable under this certificate shall be divided and credited into the following accounts in the proportion determined by the company:

- Participant's Account (PA)
- Group Family Takaful Account (GFTA)

Participants shall agree to donate the portion of the Takaful instalments and the profits thereof as *Tabarru'* for the purpose of solidarity, brotherhood and cooperation among participants. A part of PA will be used to cover maternity and a portion of contributions will be given as stated in the certificate of the policy. The contribution that is credited to the GFTA will cover any complications during pregnancy or birth, and any other events upon which Takaful benefit shall be payable. The standing amount in GFTA (*Tabarru'*) is 9% of contributions and this proportion applies for participants at any age (18–40 years old) and for whatever maturity plan they take (10, 15 or 20 years). The participants of TWP shall pay instalments or contributions on a monthly basis. The minimum instalment for TWP is RM 50 per month, whereas maximum is RM 1000 per month. The participant can choose to pay RM 50, RM 100, or RM 150 up to RM 1000 as they wish.

31.6 Modes of Payment

- bank standing order
- GIRO
- cheque or cash
- credit or charge card
- salary deduction
- BIMB ATM smart card

Participants also can make payment to the payment counter at any branch of Takaful Malaysia.

31.6.1 Investment of the Contribution and Distribution of Profits

The company shall invest the Takaful instalments paid by the participant in conformity with the rulings of Shari'ah. Any profit generated from the investments of the PA shall be distributed in accordance with the principle of *Al-Mudharabah* to the following ratio:

- 70% shall be credited into the PA;
- 30% shall be paid to the company.

The net surplus, if any, from the operation of the GFTA shall be shared in the proportion of 40% to the participant, which shall be credited to the PA, and 60% to the company. If the participant is still alive at the time of the policy's maturity, all the accumulated contributions in PA and profits generated from it will be given back to her (Table 31.1).

Table 31.1 Schedule payment of *Takaful* benefits

The Contribution of RM 100 per month, the following schedule:

Scope of benefit	*Amount of benefit*
I Maternity—normal delivery or by caesarian procedure	70% of PA
II Pregnancy complications	RM 5000
(This benefit is payable only one time in the lifetime of the participant and shall only cover the following occurring during pregnancy):	
disseminated intravascular coagulation	
ectopic pregnancy	
still birth, Limited to the maximum one still birth per certificate per lifetime	
III Congenital anomalies	RM 5000
(This benefit is payable only one time per pregnancy irrespective of the number of congenital anomalies or number of children being delivered and shall only cover the following occurrences):	
Down syndrome	
spina bifida	
tetralogy of fallot	
missing limb(s)	
esophageal atresia	
IV Death (Due to any causes)	RM 5000
V Funeral expenses	RM 1000
participant	
child (death within 14 days of birth due to any cause)	RM 500

Source: Author's collection from TMB

31.7 *Takaful* Benefits Payable

Description of benefits.

31.7.1 Maternity

In the event that the participant shall deliver a child either through a normal delivery or by caesarian procedure, the participant shall be entitled to withdraw from the PA balance subject to the maximum limit.

Exceptions
The company shall not be liable for the following:

- pregnancy or birth of a child within a period of three hundred (300) days from the date of commencement of the certificate;
- pregnancy or birth of a child that is a consequence of treatment for infertility, including assisted reproduction technology.

31.7.2 Pregnancy Complications

In the event that the participant suffers complications during pregnancy, the company shall pay a lump sum benefit from the GFTA.

This benefit is payable only once in the lifetime of the participant and shall only cover the following occurring during pregnancy:

- disseminated intravascular coagulation
- ectopic pregnancy
- still birth, limited to a maximum of one still birth per certificate per lifetime.

Exceptions
The company shall not be liable under the certificate for the following:

- pregnancy or birth of a child within a period of three hundred (300) days from the date of commencement of the certificate;
- pregnancy or birth of a child that is a consequence of treatment for infertility, including assisted reproduction technology;
- any pre-existing conditions.

31.7.3 Congenital Anomalies

In the event that the participant delivers a child diagnosed with a congenital anomaly, the company shall pay a lump sum benefit from the GFTA. This benefit is payable only one time per pregnancy irrespective of the number of congenital anomalies or number of children delivered and shall only cover the following occurring:

- Down syndrome
- spina bifida

- tetralogy of fallot
- missing limb(s)
- esophageal atresia.

Exceptions
The company shall not be liable under the certificate for the following:

- pregnancy or birth of a child within a period of three hundred (300) days from the date of commencement of the certificate;
- pregnancy or birth of a child that is a consequence of treatment for infertility, including assisted reproduction technology;
- any pre-existing conditions.

31.7.4 Death

In the event that the participant should die due to any cause, the company shall pay Takaful benefits as follows:

- the balance from the PA, and
- the death benefit as shown in the Schedule 1.0 from the GFTA.

Exceptions
The company shall not be liable under the certificate for death due to or arising from suicide, AIDS or other causes prohibited by Shari'ah.

31.7.5 Funeral Expenses

In the event of death of the participant during the term of participation or death to the child within 14 days of birth due to any cause, the company shall pay the funeral expenses from the GFTA. This benefit is paid without exception (Fig. 31.1).

Example
Siti buys TWP with a five-year premium. Unfortunately, she faced complications during her first pregnancy, in her second she had a normal birth and the third time she bore a child with Down syndrome.

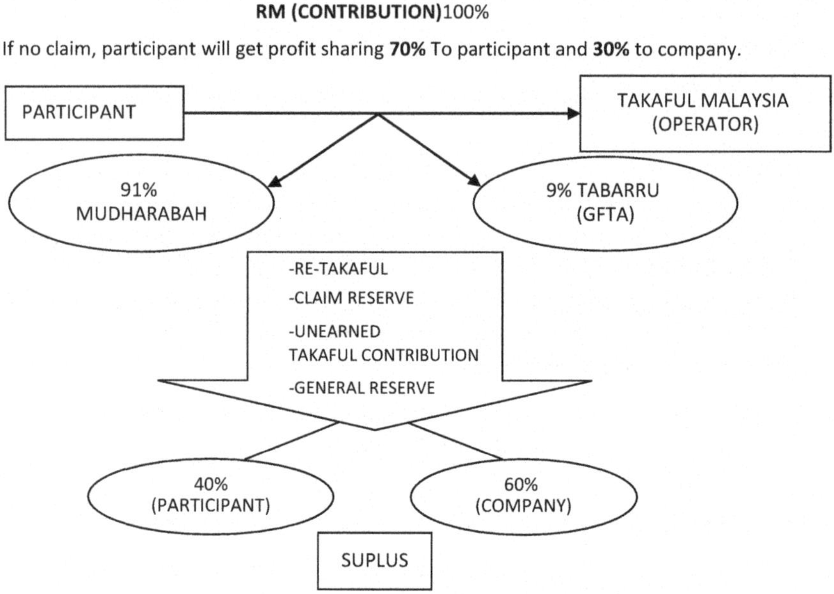

Fig. 31.1 Funeral expenses. (Source: Author's collection from TMB)

Solution
In this case, Siti will get RM 5000 from GFTA (*Tabarru'* account) for the first pregnancy (ectopic). Then the contract ends and she needs to renew it; if she does so, for a normal birth she can claim 70% from PA account and for having a Down syndrome baby she can claim once a lump-sum benefit payment for every birth (this will be paid only during the terms of the contract and depends on her payment of the premium every month) (Fig. 31.2).

In the event that Mrs Nora delivers a baby normally, she is entitled to withdraw 70% from the PA account after submitting these items:

- Family Takaful plan/mortgage claim—to ensure the claim reason is fully completed whether division A-illness or B-accident.
- Copy of identity card (participant—Mrs Nora).
- Copy of newborn's birth certificate
- Medical report—in general not required unless requested by operator.

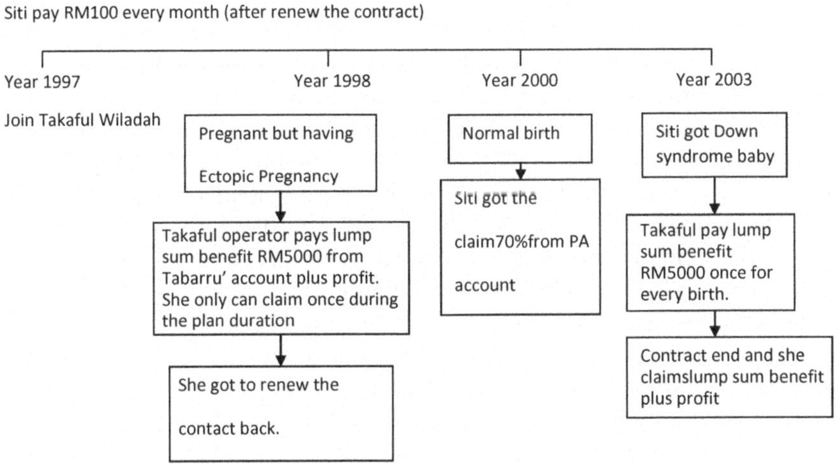

Fig. 31.2 Funeral expenses. (Source: Author's collection from TMB)

The claim process will take 14 days after submission of the above items. Unfortunately, her baby died and she had to submit together a copy of the death certificate and the burial permit. For this situation she can claim under funeral expenses for death of her son RM500 from a *Tabarru'* account.

31.8 Recommendations

The scope of TWP's benefits is even greater. There are many unexpected things that may occur in future and we can never realise what these will be. Therefore, we recommended several benefits that should be contained in this plan. In local news or international news, reports of Siamese twins often occur—the families affected need financial support from the public because they are unable to bear the cost of surgery. For example, Ahmad and Muhammad are local Siamese twins that just have been separated. Their surgery cost around RM 1 million but they were very fortunate because they were supported by a generous person. In order to separate them, surgeons had to wait several years and it was quite risky. It is recommended by having Siamese twins in benefits scope, it may attract those who have twins that unable to support surgery cost.

31.9 Conclusion

It is important to educate not only women on these matters but also men. By looking through the analysis, we hope that women will be able to understand more about their rights and the suitable products that should they choose in line with Shari'ah principles. The purpose of *Takaful* itself is to secure against risks that may occur when participants face any difficulties. Women should realise that they might one day have a diagnosis of cancer that they cannot imagine before. What are your feelings at that time? What will you think? Where will you find the money for treatment? These are among the questions that may be in your mind. By having TWP, women are not only provided with financial coverage but also the additional lump sum benefits for the following: cancer of the breast, uterus, ovaries, cervix, fallopian tubes or vagina/vulva. The claim also entitles a participant to any of the scope of benefits that the participant falls in plus profit based on *Al-Mudharabah* principles. This is makes Takaful products different from other conventional insurance products, which may contain elements of *Maisir*, *Riba*, *Gharar* and be contrary to *Faraid*.

TWP is unique: no other insurance company has ever offered such a product. As has been noted, pregnancy is a gift from Allah—it is natural risk that should have to be faced by productive and healthy women. Takaful Malaysia take positive slant in thinking on the *Maslahah* (welfare) of women that may face hardship during maternity and after giving birth. The benefits that will be claimed through the plan will make sure that the mother can successfully plan for any risk that she will face in future. TWP is still a new product and has not yet been promoted as well as Takaful Hawa. Since Takaful Wiladah and Takaful Hawa are only provided by Takaful Malaysia, there should be an increase in their marketing and promotion strategy. Takaful Malaysia can organise some educational programmes such as seminars and conventions at schools, higher learning institutions, hospitals, government situations or for any NGO.

References

1. Ali, A. Y. (n.d.), The Holy Qur'an, Text and Translation.
2. Takaful Wiladah Plan, Takaful Malaysia.

CHAPTER 32

Saving Takaful (Takaful Mesra)

32.1 Introduction

Saving Takaful (Takaful Mesra) is one of the products offered by Takaful Nasional. It works according to Shari'ah principles and was certified by the Shari'ah Supervisory Council of Takaful Nasional and the Shari'ah Advisory Council of Bank Negara Malaysia (central bank). The Takaful Mesra plan is a long-term savings and investment programme with a fixed maturity period. Apart from enjoying investment profits, the plan provides mutual financial assistance among its participants. The Takaful Mesra plan is a financial programme that pools efforts to help the needy in the event of untimely death or other mishaps resulting in personal injury or disablement.

32.2 The Product

Saving Takaful (Takaful Mesra) has been specially created for individuals who need risk management and savings benefits able to return cash value. Takaful Mesra also offers 24-hour worldwide protection, among other benefits. *Takaful* Mesra is based on *Al-Mudharabah* and *Tabarru'* through the operation of two accounts with a fixed ratio to assure distribution of

It is acknowledged that, the idea of this chapter/product is significantly contributed by the practices /experiences/thoughts of Bank Negara, *Takaful* Malaysia, *Takaful* Ikhlas, *Takaful* Nasional, Etiqa *Takaful*, IBFIM, IIUM, MII and others (Malaysia).

Mohd Ma'Sum Billah, *Islamic Insurance Products*,
https://doi.org/10.1007/978-3-030-17681-5_32

high profits, based on total contributions. Takaful Mesra practices flexible rules of participation by offering a minimum contribution plan of RM 50 per month or RM 600 annually, in accordance with affordability.

32.3 Takaful Mesra Niche

The management of this account is accordance with the concepts of *Al-Mudharabah* and *Tabarru'*. The Takaful Mesra plan is divided into two accounts, a Participant's Account (PA) (*Al-Mudharabah*) and Participant's Special Account (PSA) (*Tabarru'*). Payment of the Takaful contributions by the participant shall be credited into both accounts in the agreed ratio (Table 32.1). The ratio is:

The Takaful Mesra plan can reduce the financial burden of the participant or the family members/beneficiaries if the participant suffers from permanent total disability or if they die. The protection is 24 hours no matter where you are, day or night. The participant is also entitled to exemption from income tax through the certificate given. There are three major benefits of Takaful Mesra: death benefit, permanent total disability benefit and savings benefit. The death benefit shall be given in the event that the participant dies before the date of maturity of the certificate. The benefits given are from his saving in the PA account and also the additional sum of benefit from PSA account. The payments are subject to certain conditions: the information and particulars disclosed and declared by the participant in the application and declaration forms must be true and correct; the death of the participant must not be due to or arising from suicide or any other cause prohibited by Shari'ah; the participant also must not have made a request to surrender the certificate prior to the date of death; payment of all *Takaful* contributions due must be in order.

The permanent total disability benefit shall be given when the participant suffers from permanent total disability. Permanent total disability means disability caused by bodily injury or disease that wholly prevents the

Table 32.1 Niche of Takaful Mesra

Year	*PA (%)*	*PSA (%)*
1	10	90
2	10	90
3	50	50
4 and above	75	25

Source: Author's collection from TMB

participant from engaging in any business or occupation or performing any work for compensation or profit. However, in order to determine if the total disability has become permanent it must continue uninterruptedly for a period of at least six months.

Total disability also includes entire loss of sight in both eyes, amputation of both hands at or above the wrist, amputation of both feet at or above the ankle, irrecoverable loss of sight in one eye and the amputation of one entire limb at or above the wrist or ankle (Table 32.2). The payment of permanent total disability benefit will be in annual five-year instalment by the following percentages.

Takaful Mesra also includes saving benefits, whereby in the long term it will give higher and very great returns. In addition, the concept of *Al-Mudharabah* management is practised by Takaful Mesra where the division of profits is high, that is about 80% will be given to the participant and the remaining 20% will be taken by Takaful National for account management purposes (Fig. 32.1 and Table 32.3).

Table 32.2 Takaful Mesra Niche

Year	*Percentage from the benefits*
1	10
2	10
3	10
4	10
5	60

Source: Author's collection from TNB

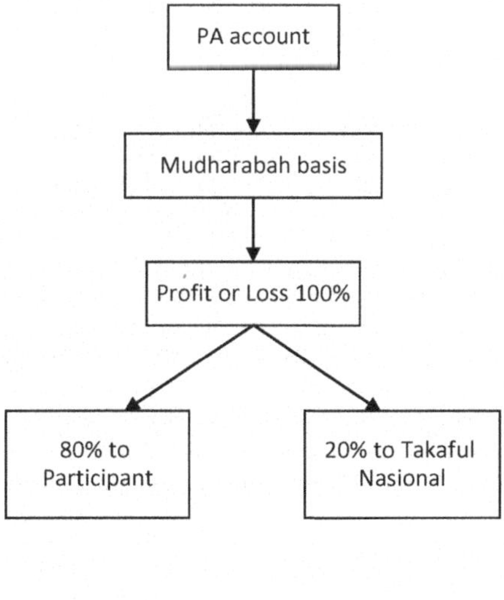

Fig. 32.1 Takaful Mesra Niche. (Source: Author's collection from TNB)

Table 32.3 Takaful Mesra Niche

Illustration of the Takaful Mesra Plan

Investment and savings according to Shari'ah principles are set out in the Takaful Act 1984. The operation of the *Takaful* business must under the supervision of the Shari'ah Supervisory Council of Takaful Nasional and the Shari'ah Advisory Council of Bank Negara Malaysia

			Example	
Year	**%PA**	**%PSA**	Participant age	25 years old
1	10	90	Term	20 year
2	10	90	Contribution	RM 1200 a year/RM 100 a month
3	50	50	Investment	7.6% (dividend in year 2000)
4–20	75	25		

Illustration of benefit

Years	*Annual contribution (RM)*	*Total contribution (RM)*	*PA annual savings (RM)*	*PSA death benefit (RM)*	*Total death benefit (RM)*	*Return total PA (RM)*	*Contribution return ratio*
1	1200	1200	129.12	93,600	93,728	127.80	10.65%
2	1200	2400	267.36	93,600	93,863	263.40	10.98%
3	1200	3600	881.04	93,600	94,475	875.10	24.31%
4	1200	4800	2054.64	93,600	95,609	2009.10	41.86%
5	1200	6000	3296.64	93,600	96,802	3201.60	53.36%
6	1200	7200	4607.04	93,600	98,053	4452.60	61.84%
7	1200	8400	5985.84	93,600	99,362	5762.10	68.60%
8	1200	9600	7433.04	93,600	100,730	7130.10	74.27%
9	1200	10,800	8948.64	93,600	102,157	8556.60	79.23%
10	1200	12,000	10,532.64	93,600	103,642	10,041.60	83.68%
11	1200	13,200	12,185.04	93,600	105,185	11,585.10	87.77%
12	1200	14,400	13,905.84	93,600	106,787	13,187.10	91.58%
13	1200	15,600	15,695.04	93,600	108,448	14,847.60	95.18%
14	1200	16,800	17,552.64	93,600	110,167	16,566.60	98.61%
15	1200	18,000	19,478.64	93,600	111,944	18,344.10	101.91%
16	1200	19,200	21,473.04	93,600	113,780	20,180.10	105.10%
17	1200	20,400	23,535.84	93,600	115,675	22,074.60	108.21%
18	1200	21,600	25,667.04	93,600	117,628	24,027.60	111.24%
19	1200	22,800	27,866.64	93,600	119,639	26,039.10	114.21%
20	1200	24,000	**30,134.64**	93,600	121,709	28,109.10	117.12%

Total minimum contribution is RM 50 a month or RM 600 a year. From the first year to the third year, 50% of your savings in the PA account can be withdrawn and the amount of protection is RM 93,600. Meanwhile, during the fourth year and onwards, 80% of your savings in PA account can be withdrawn and the amount of protection is RM 93,600. On the date of maturity, your savings in the PA account = RM 30,134.64. The participant can withdraw this amount. In the event that the participant dies before the date of maturity, *Takaful* Nasional shall pay the Takaful benefit to the nominee of RM 93,600. If the participant suffers from permanent total disability, the amount that the participant will receive is RM 93,600 and will be paid in five-year instalments (10%, 10%, 10%, 10%, 60%)

(*continued*)

Table 32.3 (continued)

Schedule of Takaful *benefit according to age for a contribution of RM 100 a month*

Age 25	**Age 26**	**Age 27**	**Age 28**	**Age 29**	**Age 30**	**Age 31**
93,600	91,200	88,800	86,400	82,800	79,200	75,600
Age 32	**Age 33**	**Age 34**	**Age 35**	**Age 36**	**Age 37**	**Age 38**
72,000	68,400	63,600	60,000	56,100	51,600	48,000
Age 39	**Age 40**	**Age 41**	**Age 42**	**Age 43**	**Age 44**	
44,400	40,800	38,400	34,800	32,400	30,000	

Source: Author's collection from TNB

32.4 Issues Related to the Takaful Mesra Plan

There are many issues that may arise regarding the Takaful Mesra plan, but the major issue as discussed from time to time among participants or policyholders is related to the division of premiums into the PA and PSA. As stated above, the general principal of Islamic insurance is that the payment by the participant must be divided into two accounts, that is, in an *Al-Mudharabah* account (PA) and a *Tabarru'* account (PSA). All people involved in the Takaful industry have agreed on this principle. Therefore, the major issue that usually arises in Takaful Mesra is about the ratio of the division of premium to the PA and PSA accounts. The common practice in other Takaful companies in Malaysia is that ratio between *Al-Mudharabah* account and the *Tabarru'* account is 90% or 80% in the former and 10% or 20% in the latter. This shows that the money contributed by the participant will be put more in the PA and less in the PSA.

However, the practice in Takaful Mesra plan introduced by Takaful National is different regarding the ratios. In Takaful Mesra, 10% of the contribution will be put in the PA account and 90% into the PSA account. People who are against the practice of this ratio in Takaful Mesra argue that Takaful Mesra still uses the element of *Maisir* because when the participant contributes RM 100, only RM 10 will be put in his *Al-Mudharabah* account. The criticism is that this amount is too little, so it seems similar to conventional insurance. This is an issue that has been raised by many people, especially those who work in other Takaful companies, as well as participants in *Takaful* Mesra. According to them, by imposing this ratio, their savings will be less and this is a loss to them. If they have to withdraw money from the PA in an emergency, they can only withdraw a small amount because 90% of their contribution is in the PSA account and, according to the Takaful concept, the money in the PSA account cannot be withdrawn because it is allocated to the needy.

The worry is that the ratio of the division of contributions practised in the Takaful Mesra plan will create injustice for policyholders. According to them, if the participant contributes RM 100 per month then after two years the amount of money will become RM 2400. Unfortunately, out of this RM 2400, the amount in PA is only 10%—that is, RM 240. The balance will be "disappeared" into the PSA.

The other issue in Takaful Mesra is the argument regarding the amount going into the PSA. As we know the PSA or *Tabarru'* account is only for helping those who are in need but unfortunately in Takaful Mesra the amount of money in the PSA has been used to pay the commission for agent of this Takaful Mesra plan. Thus, they have to increase the amount in the PSA up to 90% from total contribution in order to pay the agents.

32.5 Analysing the Issue

As far as we know that there are many opinions regarding Islamic insurance. Although there are many opinion, the Muslim scholars in Malaysia have reached a consensus that the basic principle in Islamic insurance are it must be free from the elements of *Riba*, *Gharar* and *Maisir*. The mechanism used to avoid these elements in the Islamic insurance is by dividing the amount of the contribution or premium into two accounts, PA and PSA. This mechanism was introduced in Islamic insurance and it is in line with the Shari'ah guideline. What about the issue of the ratio in the PA and PSA account? Is there any Shari'ah principle stated that the ratio in PA account must be greater than in PSA account?

In this survey we find out that the ratio practice in *Takaful* Mesra plan is not contrary with the Shari'ah. Because of that we oppose the opinion that said *Takaful* Mesra is not Islamic but more similar to conventional insurance. We support the ratio practice in *Takaful* Mesra because it gives benefit to the participants as a whole.

32.6 Shari'ah Rulings

The concept of *Takaful* itself is to help each other and create mutual co-operation. This co-operation will foster core brotherhood, as encouraged in Islam. It keeps Muslims close to each other in a fraternal relationship. As Allah (swt) said:

> And co-operate ye one another in righteousness and piety, and do not co-operate in sin and rancour. (Qur'an 5: 2)

A Muslim community based on true brotherhood is as a body that feels the pain when any of its parts suffer. Therefore, to ensure brotherhood, mutual co-operation should be applied. As Prophet Muhammad (saw) said:

> If one of you goes with your brother to help him fulfil his duty and then the Prophet made a sign with his finger added; that it is better for him than making *I'tikaf* [staying in mosque for worship] in my mosque for two months. (Hadith)

The main objective of participating the Takaful Mesra is protection. Investment and savings are only the second objective and also a part of long-term planning. That is why Takaful Mesra needs more money in the *Tabarru'* account, so that the pool will become bigger. And when the pool gets bigger, more money can be allocated to the beneficiaries if the participants dies or suffers permanent total disability.

> Narrated by Saad bin Abi Waqqas (R): The Holy Prophet (saw) said: It is better for you to leave your offspring wealthy than to leave them poor asking others for help.

> Narrated by Safwan bin Salim (r), the Holy Prophet (saw) Said: The one who looks after and works for a widow and for a poor person like a warrior fighting for the cause of Allah (swt) or like a person who fasts during the day and prays overnight. (Hadith)

32.7 Application

This is why protection is more important than savings. In Takaful Mesra, based on the illustration above, if the participant contributes RM 100 a month at the age of 25 years for 20 years, the Takaful benefit that the beneficiaries will get if something bad happens to the participant is RM 93,600. The amount of *Takaful* benefit in Takaful Mesra is higher compared to other products because the pool is big because the participants contribute more to the *Tabarru'* account. On the other hand, the *Al-Mudharabah* account at the date of maturity will stand at RM 30,134.64. Although at year two your savings in the PA are only RM 267.36 out of RM 2400 for two years, in the long term your savings will be greater (Fig. 32.2). This happens because, starting from year three, the ratio will be 50:50 and year four up to year 20 the ratio is 75% for PA and 25% for PSA. So, you can get more protection as well as bigger savings in the long term.

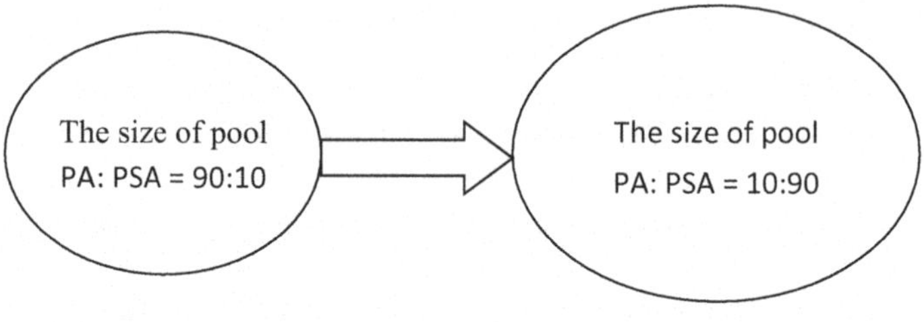

Fig. 32.2 Application. (Source: Author's collection from TNB)

The next point that we will discuss pertains to *Sadaqah Jariah*, or donation. Participants in Takaful Mesra must get the real picture about the concept of Takaful. In Takaful, the objective is not only to get profit in this world, but the most important is that your contribution is actually a good investment not only in this world but also in hereafter. This is because your contribution to the PSA is a kind of *Sadaqah Jariah* as long as your intention is to get blessings from Allah (swt).

> Narrated by Omar Ibn Khattab the Holy Prophet SAW said: The validity of the actions is depending on intention and therefore every man shall have but that which he intended.

After the participant has focused his intention of joining the Takaful to get the blessing from Allah through helping his Muslim brothers, Allah promises him good reward for his investment.

> Narrated by Abu Hurairah (ra) from the Prophet (saw) said that: whosoever removes worldly hardship from a believer, Allah (swt) will remove from him one of the hardships of the hereafter. Whosoever alleviates needy person, Allah (swt) will alleviate from him in this world and the next.

The last point that we want to share is that the Takaful Act 1984 stated that all *Takaful* operators must get the permission of the Shari'ah Supervisory Council and Shari'ah Advisory Council of Bank Negara Malaysia, in order to introduce a product to customers. We believe that these council members have expertise in the Shari'ah field. The council members are all Muslim scholars—so why claim that Takaful Mesra is not Islamic after the council has studied the plan and given a verdict that this plan is in line with Shari'ah?

32.8 Conclusion

The Islamic insurance industry in Malaysia is still new compared with conventional insurance. But the emergence of Islamic insurance is actually a *Rahmat* and relief to Muslims because now we have an alternative and so can avoid participating in conventional insurance, which clearly has the elements of *Riba*, *Gharar* and *Maisir*. We have to admit that maybe there are many imperfections in Islamic insurance. But to condemn the industry is not the solution to expanding the Islamic *Muamalah* in Malaysia. It is obligatory for Muslims to support the industry and give the suggested solutions if some problem exists, just talking and doing nothing will not suffice. Therefore, Takaful Nasional should put various initiatives in place so as to give explanations to the public regarding misunderstandings that happen nowadays. This body can provide the likes of forums, seminars, talks or it can come out with explanations on internet, in newspapers and magazines. By doing this it can open up the thinking of the public about the mechanism and concept applied in Saving Takaful (Takaful Mesra). Then the public can understand well and they will accept it as it is and not simply condemn the approach without knowing the facts behind it.

References

1. Ali, A. Y. (n.d.), The Holy Qur'an, Text and Translation.
2. *Takaful Mesra Plan*, *Takaful* Nasional.

CHAPTER 33

Unit Trust Takaful

33.1 Introduction

Takaful plays an important role in many people's lives: it provides financial protection for individuals, families as well as enterprises against risks (Manual peperiksaan asas wakil Takaful Nasional). In the business enterprise sector, insurance makes business more efficient and can ensure that a business will prevail in terms of its concepts. The insurance industry has grown tremendously since businesses and the public have realised the importance of *Takaful* and financial planning. In this chapter, several issues are analysed in terms of the role of *Takaful* in protecting the wealth of mutual fund holders or unit trust holders in Malaysia, which has a lot to do with risk and the return issue of an asset in the market. The success of the mutual fund industry, especially Shari'ah-related funds, in Malaysia is also reliant upon how fund managers manage the risks of any asset in their portfolio.

It is acknowledged that, the idea of this chapter/product is significantly contributed by the practices /experiences/thoughts of Bank Negara, Takaful Malaysia, Takaful Ikhlas, Takaful Nasional, Etiqa Takaful, IBFIM, IIUM, MII and others (Malaysia).

Mohd Ma'Sum Billah, *Islamic Insurance Products*,
https://doi.org/10.1007/978-3-030-17681-5_33

33.2 Risk Management

Although risk exists in almost any situation, there are ways to handle this risk by taking appropriate actions. One method is 'avoidance of risk' by not participating in any kind of activity that may cause harm. This approach is rather extreme, in the sense that in business one has to incorporate risk in order to expect return.

Managing risk by allowing small losses to the business is another technique for handling risk. In other words, minimising losses can be done when risks are managed accordingly. Other techniques, such as sharing the risk and transferring risk, are among those that can be adopted.

So, how can fund managers ensure high returns for the unit holder and at the same time minimise their losses. One of the answers is by managing the risk associated with the assets. Why is it so important to manage risk in the unit trust business? Maximising profit and minimising losses are the tenets in any business, and so the same holds true for the unit trust business.

33.2.1 Speculative and Pure Risk

It is always important to know what kind of risks we are dealing with so that we can handle these risks in the most appropriate manner. Business faces two sorts of risk: speculative and pure risk. Speculative risk involves three possibilities: gain, loss or no change (Manual Peperiksaan Asas wakil Takaful Nasional, p. 29). For example, investment in the stock market has the possibilities of capital gain, losses or no change. This type of risk cannot be insured due to the potential gain element inherent within it. Pure risk on the hand exists in situation whereby there is the possibility of losses and/or no losses incurred. For example, in the case of fire, the owner of the premises will suffer losses but does not lose anything if no fire occurs. This type of risk that has no element of potential gain is insurable.

Any type of risk that is either pure or speculative has the potential of losses and should be entitled to be insured, as the gain side will not harm the *Takaful* operator nor the *Takaful* participant as long as there are no elements that contravene Shari'ah law. Here the principle of insurable interest can be seen, whereby unit trust holder has financial interests in their assets or fund which are subject to losses which need to be minimised.

33.2.2 *Insuring Speculative Risk*

How do we use *Takaful* to protect the unit trust holder fund if this asset has the element of potential capital gain and so cannot be insured? For this aspect, I try to look at the elements that underpin the *Ta'awun* concept as applied in *Takaful*. It is a sort of mutual responsibility, co-operation and protection of unit trust fund by unit holder and fund manager to ensure the assets invested do not lose value. In the next section, I will discuss this idea in terms of mechanisms that can be used in order to hedge the assets of the unit trust holder using the underlying assets that evince the elements of mutual responsibility, co-operation and protection.

33.2.3 Ta'awun *Concept*

In the context of *Takaful*, *Ta'awun* (see bank Al Jazeera official website), meaning mutual help, allows participants to make donations with the intention of helping one another within the *Takaful* group. The elements underpinning the concept of *Ta'awun* as applied in *Takaful* can be broken down into the following:

- mutual responsibility
- mutual cooperation
- Mutual protection.

All these principles are in line with the Qur'an and the Sunnah.

Mutual Responsibility
The feeling of responsibility towards one another is the foundation of solidarity in the Islamic community. The poor feel safe being sheltered by the rich and the sick do not feel much hurt because they know the healthy will provide them with help. This principle is established through the following Hadith:

> The attitude of the believer and feeling of brotherhood to one another is like that of the single body. When one member of the body is hurt, it will have an effect on the whole body. (Sahih al-Bukhari and Muslim)
>
> The relationship between one believer and another [in a community] is like that of a building where one part of the building strengthens the other parts. (Sahih al-Bukhari and Muslim)

> Each one of you has a responsibility and each one of you is responsible towards those under your responsibility. (Sahih al-Bukhari and Muslim)
>
> One is not judged as righteous until he cares for his brother as much as he cares for himself. (Sahih al-Bukhari).
>
> If anyone does not have compassion towards others, then he does not get any compassion from God. (Sahih al-Bukhari and Muslim)

33.2.4 Mutual Co-operation

The principle of co-operation is established both through the Qur'an and the Sunnah. Some of the pertinent Qur'anic injunctions are:

> Help one another in furthering virtue and God-consciousness [*taqwa*], and do not help one another in furthering evil and enmity. (Qur'an 5:2)

It is not righteousness that you turn your faces towards east or west but righteousness is whoever believes in God and the Last Day and the angels and the Book and the messengers; and spending out of his wealth for His love towards kin, and orphans and the poor and the wayfarer and those who ask and the freeing of slaves and those in debt; to be steadfast in prayer and practice regular charity; to fulfil the contracts which you have made; and to be firm and patient in pain or suffering and adversity and throughout all periods of panic. Such are the people of the truth, the God-fearing. (Qur'an 2:177).

The Sunnah has also established the principles of co-operation. Some of the Hadiths that urge co-operation are:

> A Muslim is the brother of a fellow Muslim. He should neither commit oppression upon him nor ruin him; and he who meets the needs of a brother. God will meet his needs and he who relieves his brother from hardship Allah will relieve him from the hardness to which he could be put on the day of judgement. (Sahih Muslim)
>
> Whosoever fulfils the intention of a brother, God will fulfil his intentions. (Sunan Ahmad and Abu Daud)
>
> God always helps those who helps his brother. (Sunan Abu Daud)
>
> Help your brother either those oppressed or those who oppress. The companions ask "Oh Messenger of God, we understand about helping the oppressed how do we help those who oppress?" The Messenger replied "relieve them of their power." (Sahih al-Bukhari and Muslim)

33.2.5 Mutual Protection

This principle is established by both the Qur'an and the Sunnah. The Qur'an mentions protection from hunger and fear in several places. Allah (swt) says:

> [He] who has fed them against hunger and has made them safe from fear. (Qur'an, Surah Quraish: 4).
>
> And remember when Abraham said: "My Lord, make this city [Mecca] a place of security." (Qur'an, 2:126)

Sunnah on the issue:

> Indeed a believer is one who can give security and protection to the life and property of mankind. (Sunan Ibn Majah)
>
> By God in Whose power I am under, one will not enter paradise unless he provides protection to a neighbour in difficulty. (Sunan Ahmad)

Aishah reported that the Prophet of God (saw) said: "Jibrail impressed upon me the kind treatment towards neighbours so much that I thought as if he would confer upon them the rights of inheritance."

> A person is not a believer if he sleeps comfortably on a full stomach while his neighbour suffers from hunger. (Hadith Al Bazaar)

33.3 MECHANISMS OF UNIT TRUST TAKAFUL

In this section I will discuss a mechanism that can be used to hedge or protect the unit holder fund by way of *Takaful* involvement and basic hedging transactions.

In general, there are three parties involve in any insurance activity: operator, agent and participant. In hedging assets of the unit trust holder, the fund manager will act as an agent of *Takaful* to the unit trust holder or participant in the case of the *Takaful* model. The bilateral transaction between fund manager and unit holder can create a built-in *Takaful* mechanism to protect against such losses. In this model there will be no operator or supplier of *Takaful* services; instead, the markets themselves will provide a mechanism to protect the unit trust holder. The unit trust holder will be the participant whereby they need to buy a policy at a certain premium or contribution for protection against risks, both pure and speculative.

But does the whole framework work in terms of ensuring the downside potential risk can be minimised, if not eliminated? Here the role of the fund manager becomes crucial in managing assets as well as managing risk associated with these assets.

The parallel role and function of the fund manager are important in order to maximise return and minimise losses. In the portfolio of assets, the potential of an asset to increase and decrease in value are dependent on the fundamentals of that particular asset and its technical aspect. The fund manager needs to tackle both sides of the issue in order to anticipate price movement.

Anyhow, the lack of complete information will lead to diversion in targeting the optimal portfolio of assets. This will subsequently lead to gain or loss or unchanged net asset value of the unit trust holder fund. Here the role of the fund manager needs to be tailored in such a way that they can act as an agent and operator of *Takaful* for the unit holder.

Premium or contribution accounts need to be segregated from the portfolio account and placed in another financial instrument that contributes the most assets to the portfolio. For example, ABC asset management has a portfolio of RM 500,000,000 fund size. Suppose the assets are index fund assets. Most of the assets track the Kuala Lumpur composite index (KLCI). Since there is a futures market for KLCI, the fund manager can position themselves by short sell in the future market to protect against any losses due to the downside movement in the underlying KLCI. This offsetting position is called hedging.

33.3.1 Structure of the Scheme

In the diagram in Fig. 33.1, the unit holder-cum-participant of *Takaful* will invest a certain amount of money for the purpose of investment. On top of the investment that the unit trust holder places in the fund, a certain contribution is necessary for the purpose of protecting the assets from dilution. This premium will be placed in a separate *Takaful* fund and will be used to hedge any possibilities of downside speculative risk.

The *Takaful* agent, that is the fund manager, will manage the risk by way of placing the offsetting position in the futures market. This is to make sure that any movement of price in KLCI offsetting the predictions of the fund manager will be protected. By hedging the position, the fund manager will minimise downside losses. Here in the existence of the futures market there will be a built-in protection mechanism, whereby risk will be distributed or spread out among the market players in the futures and underlying market.

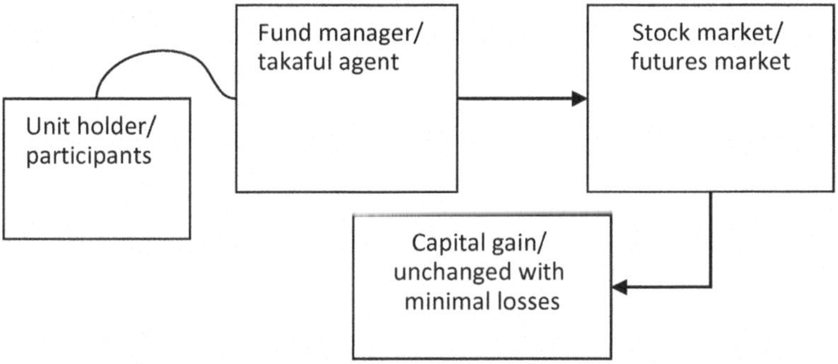

Fig. 33.1 Mechanisms of unit trust *Takaful*. (Source: Author's collection)

33.4 Conclusion

Both pure and speculative risks should be addressed in the unit trust assets, as the co-existence of the futures market and the underlying market will give an avenue for the fund manager to further accelerate capital gains to the unit holder while at the same time protecting the asset value at par with the initial investment. *Takaful* should play a greater role in managing risks which are not only subject to pure risk. If we can find an instrument or mechanism for managing speculative risk, then the role of *Takaful* should be expanded so that the Muslim *ummah* will advance in all areas and avenues. Even though people will argue about the mechanics of protecting assets by using a futures instrument while the Securities Commission of the Shari'ah Council is silent about the issue, it is in fact crucial for Islamic unit trust fund managers to be more competitive and efficient in sustaining high returns with low risk profiles. We should look at the issue of futures trading in a broader manner where we can apply *Maslahah Al Ammah* or *Masalih Al Mursalah* that can be highly beneficial to the *Ummah*.

References

1. Ali, A. Y. (n.d.), The Holy Qur'an, Text and Translation.
2. Unit Trust Takaful Plan, Takaful Nasional.

CHAPTER 34

Online Family *Takaful*

34.1 Introduction

In essence, *Takaful* operations can be separated into two principal activities. On the one hand, they act as the conduit for providing financial benefits in the event of a misfortune through the various types of *Takaful* products and services that may be participated in by both individuals as well as corporate bodies. Technically, the product is similar to insurance. From straightforward personal lines such as motor vehicle cover to the very complex requirements of the corporate sector, *Takaful* products can fulfil the demands of all. A long-term family *Takaful* plan would one way or another satisfy the life insurance need of an individual; whilst the industrial all-risks scheme would meet the insurance needs of a sophisticated manufacturing plant belonging to a huge conglomerate.

On the other hand, *Takaful* companies should provide products and services that are competitive enough to challenge conventional insurance. By adopting the latest technology, the *Takaful* industry could boost its growth and be accepted by everybody in the world. Therefore, the internet could help disseminate information on *Takaful* and sell *Takaful* products to everybody, anywhere in the world. This would help to further

It is acknowledged that, the idea of this chapter/product is significantly contributed by the practices/experiences/thoughts of Bank Negara, *Takaful* Malaysia, *Takaful* Ikhlas, *Takaful* Nasional, Etiqa *Takaful*, IBFIM, IIUM, MII and others (Malaysia).

Mohd Ma'Sum Billah, *Islamic Insurance Products*,
https://doi.org/10.1007/978-3-030-17681-5_34

accelerate the expansion of Islamic insurance at the international level. In the same manner, efforts towards converging and harmonising of various operations and practices would be more conducive to this aim.

34.2 The Product

The purpose of offering a *Takaful* product online is basically to create more competitive growth in the Islamic insurance industry and this depends on *Takaful* companies' competence to survive in the highly developed insurance market. As with other industries that are seeking to expand, *Takaful* companies are also realising the potential of information technology, particularly the internet. Basically, a *Takaful* product online is designed to educate visitors to a relevant website about *Takaful*. It offers information on the concept and the reasons behind the prohibition of conventional insurance and the importance of *Takaful* to Muslims. The *Takaful* operators should also include the latest news about *Takaful*, views of the *Ulama'* and Shari'ah justification of *Takaful* products through their websites.

Through this concept, the *Takaful* product online, *Takaful* operators could advertise their products and services on their websites, and customers could buy the product. This will definitely improve the relationship between *Takaful* operators and customers. *Takaful* operators could reduce costs by using this application and, by the same token, customers would not be up against traffic jams just to get to the *Takaful* company offices nor will they be required to queue once they arrive. Therefore, the concept of a *Takaful* product online makes life easier for everybody, giving essential information about *Takaful* to visitors and allowing transaction of *Takaful* products, such as buying or renewal of policies by using an internet-connected computer anywhere, anytime, anyplace.

34.3 Shari'ah Rulings

The implementation of *Takaful* products online generally is to give an understanding of *Takaful* product as an Islamic approach to counter the conventional insurance. Hence, the internet can play an important role to disseminate information on *Takaful*, its benefits and how this alternative model of insurance can be applied. The concept of the *Takaful* product online is designed to educate people about *Takaful*, offering information on the concept, reasons behind the prohibition of conventional insurance and the importance of *Takaful* to Muslims. This concept, that of disseminating information for a good reason to others, in reflected in the Qur'an (Al-Ma'idah: 2):

> Help ye one another in righteousness and piety.

Selling *Takaful* products online can be an opportunity to consolidate and expand the market. By embracing and adopting the latest technology, it could anticipate a wider market access, improve quality and productivity and ultimately offer better services to both the principals and customers. The internet is thus an essential tool and a golden opportunity for relatively young *Takaful* industries to bridge the gap between them and well-established conventional insurance.

On the other side, *Takaful* companies should first make sure that their operations are in line with Shari'ah principles. They should avoid any element that will lead to the principle against the Shari'ah rules before introducing the *Takaful* product online. *Takaful* operators should avoid non-permissible elements, which include:

- Uncertainty (*Gharar*), as found in conventional insurance practices. *Takaful* operations are merely to provide financial security against defined risk.
- Any elements based on *Riba* (interest) whether in investment of participants contribution, any financing involving interest or borrowing from a conventional bank for *Takaful* operations. This is clearly stated in the Qur'anic verses (Surah Al-Baqarah: 275):

> That is because they say, "Trade is like usury," But Allah permitted trade and forbidden usury.

- Operations involving any element of gambling, this is strictly prohibited by the Shari'ah rules because gamblers are out for material gain. For example, *Takaful* operators should not invest participants' contributions in a company which is involved in gambling.

> They ask thee concerning wine and gambling, "In them is great sin, and profit, for men; but the sin is greater than profit." (In Surah Al-Baqarah versus 219)

- Activities involving the manufacturing or sale of prohibited (*Haram*) goods such as alcohol, pork and meat that has not been slaughtered according to Islamic conventions.

Lastly, any *Takaful* operator should not betray the trust given by participants on them. *Takaful* companies should be honest and should bear the responsibility for holding and investing the contributions provided by participants.

> And if one of you deposits a thing on trust with another, let the trustee [faithfully] discharge his trust, and let him fear his Lord. Conceal not evidence; for whoever conceals it, his heart is tainted with sin, and Allah knoweth all that ye do. (Qur'an 2: 283)

34.4 Product Analysis

Takaful products online are products and services specially packaged and managed strictly in accordance with Islamic principles. With *Takaful* products, participants will feel that their needs for insurance products are taken care of without compromising on their Islamic principles and practices. At the end of each year, after claims are made, the excess funds will be distributed between the participants.

The *Takaful* online operation includes the two common products: Family *Takaful* and General *Takaful*. Family *Takaful* consists of two accounts for the participant: the Participant's Account (based on the profit-sharing principle of *AI-Mudharabah*) and the Participant's Special Account (*Tabarru'*). General *Takaful* only consists of one account for the participants, the Participant's Special Account (Tables 34.1 and 34.2). Both products could be divided into:

Table 34.1 Family *Takaful*

Family *Takaful* plan	Group family *Takaful* plan
Family *Takaful* plan for education	Students *Takaful* scheme
Group family *Takaful* plan	Worker *Takaful* scheme
Group medical *Takaful* plan	Mortgage *Takaful*
Ziarah *Takaful*	Waqf *Takaful*
Haelth *Takaful*	Retirement *Takaful* scheme

Table 34.2 General *Takaful*

Fire *Takaful* scheme	Liability *Takaful* scheme
Motor vehicle *Takaful*	Marine *Takaful*
Accident *Takaful* scheme	House protection *Takaful* scheme

Source: Author's collection

34.5 Underwriting Mechanism

Customers can register or renew their *Takaful* product policy using the internet. The form provided is for the renewal of motor vehicle *Takaful*. Other *Takaful* products could also be renewed using different forms provided in a *Takaful* company's website. This concept, the registering or renewal of *Takaful* product policies online, is designed for customers who do not have time to visit the nearest *Takaful* company's office.

Payment can be made by using any major credit cards such as VISA or Mastercard. Customers could also make payments by using e-banking provided by banks such as Bank Islam, RHB Bank, Maybank, BCB Bank, Muamalat Bank and others.

After filling in the information on the form, click 'send' and the information will be processed by the *Takaful* operator, while official receipt will be sent within three working days. If the official receipt does not arrive with the customer in this time, the participant should call the *Takaful* company and ask for an explanation.

34.6 Recommendations

There are few adjustments and improvements that could be made to the existing application. The *Takaful* operator should improve certain parts of their website to make *Takaful* product more competitive in the eyes of the people. The *Takaful* operator should include:

- The website should be designed to educate visitors about *Takaful*, offering information on the concept and the reasons behind the prohibition of conventional insurance and the importance of *Takaful* to Muslims. It should also update the latest news about *Takaful*, views of the *Ulama*' and Shari'ah justification on *Takaful* products.
- The website should be attractive to visitors. A good design plus a good combination of colours and icons could attract visitors to spend more time on the site.

- By embracing and adopting the latest technology, *Takaful* operators can anticipate wider market access, improve quality and productivity and ultimately offer better services to both the principals and customers.
- *Takaful* operators should develop a suggestion box on their website for customers to give suggestions or ideas regarding any *Takaful* issues in order to improve the quality of the *Takaful* industry and able to be more competitive against the conventional insurance. This will enable both customers and *Takaful* operators to exchange views and knowledge with each other, in line with Surah At-Taubah: 122.

Preparing *Takaful* assistance online nowadays would be a marvellous boom to customers. With the provision of online *Takaful* services, *Takaful* operators could reach customers beyond the expected limit thus giving a clear picture what *Takaful* and *Re-takaful* Insurance is all about. As we all know, *Takaful* nowadays are not merely a product that assists Muslims but also covers non-Muslims throughout the world. Our recommendations are as below.

- Online *Takaful* services should be implemented so as to aid the customers in joining the schemes provided easily.

It is clear that online services could reach far more people. With the introduction of *Takaful* online services, people could know more about the schemes or products more easily and have a clearer picture about the procedures and privileges of joining the schemes. With the introduction of online services, *Takaful* operators could prepare registration forms as well as the report and claim forms. All the data will be processed easily and this will be time saving. According to our interview, one case would take about two months to be processed at present—but with online services, the processing period could be reduced to one month or less. The faster the service, the more people would rely on it.

- Different types of forms should be used for Muslim and non-Muslim participants.

Online or manual registration and claim forms should be separate for Muslims and non-Muslim participants. With this method, it would be easier for the person in charge to allocate other contributions to the unfortunate participants. For instance, a Muslim participant may have joined a Khairat Fund at his neighbourhood as well as having a Life *Takaful* product. If any misfortune occurs to him within the *Takaful* cover period, *Takaful* would allocate certain amount to him as to cover his loss; but if the participant passes away due to the tragedy, *Takaful* could arrange the funeral ceremony directly with the deceased participant's neighbourhood. This would be easier for the deceased family as they are already grieving for the loss of their loved one.

For non-Muslim participants, some of them may have joined other life insurance schemes as well with different beneficiaries in different schemes. If any tragedy happens, *Takaful* would arrange and allocate the provided amount for the beneficiaries as written in the agreement. *Takaful* will not breach contract for any beneficiary's interest. So, with the usage of different forms for Muslims and non-Muslims, it would be easier for both parties, the *Takaful* operator and the participants, in terms of dealing with allocation of funds in light of unfortunate events.

- *Takaful* staff should be well trained in *Takaful* concepts, so as as to give a clear information about the products to customers.

We suggest that *Takaful* staff should be well trained in Islamic background in order to equip them for delivering key points about *Takaful* to the public, whether they be Muslim or non-Muslim, thus promoting the *Takaful* products to the market effectively.

- Easy payment methods should be set up for online registration and premium installation for participants.

Online services will not be efficient if payment still has to be done manually. So as to make online services more attractive, online payment method should be applied in order to comply with high-tech system. Payment using credit cards should be added to the system. This way, participants or customers could easily reach their premium installations easily at any time. Just key in your credit or charge card numbers and other related information then the system will process everything for you. This user-friendly system will also help to cultivate E-Comm culture in our society. New participants can join the *Takaful* schemes at any convenient time, where they can register through online services and settle their related fees immediately through the establishment of the online payment facility.

- Add other information to the *Takaful* website for surfers.

In order to make the *Takaful* website more attractive, we believe that adding other information would be a good idea. Summarisation of composite indexes, share market report and even gold price market are examples of some of the information considered useful to people nowadays. Instead of surfing through the *Takaful* website, surfers could even check the share market report while they are there. Some guidelines for investors could be added as well and this would make the website more attractive. Indirectly, this would also attract surfers to participate in *Takaful.*

> Nor should the believers all go forth together: if a contingent from every expedition remained behind, they could devote themselves to study of religion and admonish the people when they return to them, that thus they [may learn] to guard themselves [against evil]. (Qur'an 9: 122)

There are also some factors that will be affected by implementing the concept of *Takaful* products online. Information technology and the internet are being perceived as damaging to the co-operative human spirit, which is highly stressed in the *Takaful* theory, based on the Ayah 2 in Surah Al-Maidah.

The internet, although it may not completely eliminate the role of agents in the insurance business, could strip *Takaful* agents of the personal touch, which is often needed to provide a sense of comfort among customers and strengthens their credibility in terms of the efficiency of the business.

34.7 Conclusion

It is human nature that anything new is not readily accepted as a matter of course. When *Takaful* was first introduced as an alternative Islamic insurance in the early 1980s, there were strong reservations that it would not be viable, and what is more profitable. But *Takaful* is highly recognisable nowadays. In this way, it is similar to the concept of *Takaful* products online, which will gradually be accepted by everyone. It will take some time for people to fully utilise the internet as a medium to gather information, transaction and businesses.

Therefore, *Takaful* products online must aim at:

- disseminating information about *Takaful* and its products;
- providing the latest news about *Takaful*, its products, Shari'ah justification and the views of the *Ulama*';
- advertising *Takaful* products;
- facilitating easy transactions between participants and *Takaful* operators;
- buying and renewal of policies;
- and the most important thing is to get the blessing from Allah (swt) for whatever we are doing.

References

1. Ali, A. Y. (n.d.), The Holy Qur'an, Text and Translation.
2. *Online Takaful Services*, *Takaful* Malaysia, *Takaful* Nasional, *Takaful* Ikhlas and others.

PART IV

Re-takaful Products

CHAPTER 35

Re-takaful Products

35.1 Introduction

Re-takaful refers to the arrangement where the primary *Takaful* operators share risks among themselves. It is a process whereby the *Re-takaful* company agrees to bear all or part of the loss of the primary takaful companies. The development of *Re-takaful* companies was due to the need of *Takaful* companies to place a certain part of their risk with a reinsurance company. *Takaful* companies faced the dilemma of having to reinsure on a conventional basis, contrary to their customers' preference of seeking cover based on Islamic principles. *Takaful* companies, in general, started after the rediscovery of this concept in 1979 and have been steadily growing in size since then. In order to better understand the functions and legitimacy of *Re-takaful* products, we must first understand the concept of *Takaful* and the basis on which it is accepted as Shari'ah compliant. *Takaful* is an ethical system based on the concept of brotherhood, charity and mutual guarantee. It operates on self-sustaining principle as opposed to the profit maximisation evident in conventional insurance companies. Any surplus generated from the operations of *Takaful* is redistributed to the participants or donated to charity. In fact, *Takaful* is a mutual guarantee or security

It is acknowledged that, the idea of this chapter/product is significantly contributed by the practices/experiences/thoughts of Bank Negara, ARIL, MNRB, Takaful Malaysia, Takaful Ikhlas, Takaful Nasional, Etiqa Takaful, IBFIM, IIUM, MII and others (Malaysia).

Mohd Ma'Sum Billah, *Islamic Insurance Products*,
https://doi.org/10.1007/978-3-030-17681-5_35

provided by a group of people living in the same society, against a defined risk or catastrophe befalling on one's life, property or any form of valuable thing (Billah 2001).

The principle of providing mutual guarantee and sharing risks is equally valid and applicable for *Re-takaful*. *Re-takaful* is similar to conventional reinsurance in the sense that one party accepts a part of the risk or loss of the other. Most of the Takaful companies insure only part of the risk on any given policy while the remainder of the risk is covered by *Re-takaful* entity. The less risk a given *Takaful* company insures the more premium it has to pay to *Re-takaful* entity to cover the remaining risk. As evident from conventional practices, smaller companies are able to cover only a small portion of the insurance policy and therefore they join the pool of funds of a bigger reinsurance company by paying premiums depending on the proportion of coverage. Large companies, however, can safely cover larger portions of the policy, thus reducing the payments they give to the reinsurer.

The purpose of this chapter is to consider the *Re-takaful* industry by analysing its functions, legal aspects and performance. The first part will define *Re-takaful* and describe its functions, purpose and practicality. Next, the legal aspects of *Re-takaful* from the Shari'ah point of view will be examined. The last part will talk mainly about the performance and size of *Re-takaful* industry relative to the conventional reinsurance industry.

35.2 The *Re-takaful* Paradigm

Re-takaful is essentially about handling risk. It is a risk aversion mechanism in which the *Takaful* ceding company goes to either conventional reinsurer or a *Re-takaful* operator to reinsure original insured risks against an undesirable outcome if the risk insured were above the normal underwriting or claim. Thus, a *Takaful* ceding company may, with limited financial resources, hedge its risk against being incapable to meet all *Takaful* insurances if a number of damages occur at the same time. Therefore, it has to look for reinsurance protection from a financially capable reinsurer, which will be able to take over the coverage of a large proportion of the risk. *Re-takaful* is the process whereby the *Re-takaful* company agrees to bear all or part of the loss of the primary *Takaful* companies. It is quite similar to conventional reinsurance in terms of operations and handling.

Re-takaful is needed to remove hardship from a *Takaful* company when a number of damages occur at the same time. It is when the claims of insured may be more than the funds available. Removal of hardship is termed *Rafa al Harj* (Kamali 1989).

Among main objectives of Shar'iah is to make people's lives easier and to realise the benefit (*Maslahah*) of people. Therefore, *Re-takaful* is to remove hardship from *Takaful* companies, as *Takaful* companies are to remove hardship from people.

The Qur'an states:

> He hath chosen you and hath not laid upon you in religion any hardship. (Qur'an 22:78)

35.3 Objectives

Among the objectives of *Re-takaful* products are:

- To protect the *Takaful* operator from the threat of insolvency, underwriting the interest of the participants, to forge co-operation among the participants and investing the accumulated funds in accordance with Shari'ah.

As the Qur'an also reads:

> Help you one another in *Al-Birr* and *At-Taqwa* [virtue, righteousness and piety]. (Qur'an 5:2)

- To provide underwriting flexibility and to further consolidate the financial stability of the *Takaful* operator in order to compete with conventional insurance companies in accepting risk.
- It may allow the *Takaful* operator to use the retained deposit reserves of the *Re-takaful* fund in the interest of its clients without paying any interest.

35.4 Structure

Reinsurance contracts take place between the *Takaful* operator and the *Re-takaful* operator. It is thus a company-to-company relationship and a way to share risk. The original policyholders, people insured with a *Takaful* company, are not party to reinsurance contracts. The insured does not and cannot have any direct interest in the reinsurance contract. The contract of *Re-takaful* should remain between the *Takaful* and *Re-takaful* operators.

Compared to conventional reinsurance, a *Takaful* company reinsuring with a *Re-takaful* company would involve almost all methods used in conventional reinsurance. There are two methods in *Re-takaful* insurance. The first is the proportional basis of reinsurance, which can be written on a quota-share basis and surplus-share basis. The second method is non-proportional basis of reinsurance, which can be written in general reinsurance on excess of loss basis and stop loss basis.

Most of the primary *Takaful* companies, due to their relatively small size, can insure only part of the risk on their *Takaful* products. The rest of the policy is covered by *Re-takaful* entities. The size of the premium paid to the *Re-takaful* company depends on the proportion of the policy it covers. In general, the higher the portion covered by *Takaful* companies the lower the premiums they cede to *Re-takaful*, thus effectively reducing the cost to their policyholders (Fig. 35.1).

In Malaysia, the size of premiums and policy cover is of two types, facultative and treaty. The arrangement of treaty is imposed by the Central Bank and it compulsory for a *Re-takaful* company to reinsure with a *Re-takaful* company. Currently, there is a compulsory rate of reinsurance imposed by Bank Negara. The compulsory rate is ceded to the *Re-takaful* company while the amount risk taken is based on the same ratio. On the

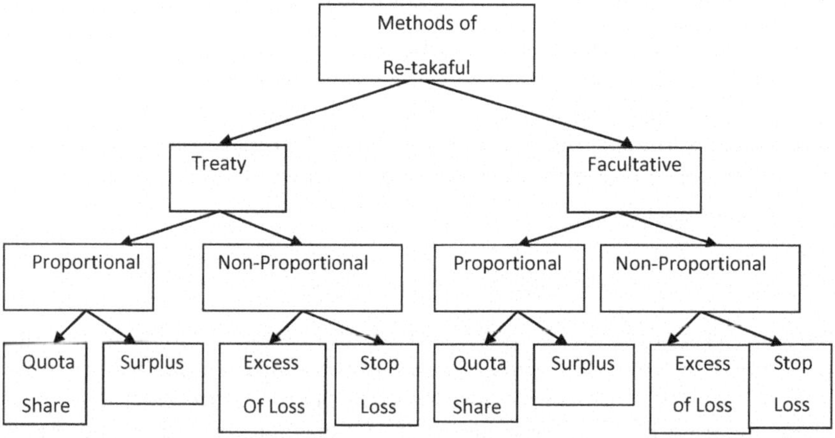

Fig. 35.1 Structure. (Source: Author's collection)

other hand, the facultative arrangement is determined by mutual agreement between the participants. In a facultative arrangement, the contract is made out on product-to-product basis. A *Takaful* company may make arrangements as to which ratio they are going to pay damages or profits.

The contracts in *Re-takaful* operations are based on the Islamic principle of profit and loss sharing and if there is a profit, the *Takaful* operators will get a share of the profit based on the predetermined ratio. The profits of *Takaful* from risk mitigation practices are guided back into the community for the well-being of the participants. The risk and profit sharing in *Takaful* and *Re-takaful*, according to Shari'ah principles, must be carefully observed (Fisher 1999). In other words, there must be a mutual agreement whereby the parties involved will share the profit and loss according to the pre-agreed guidelines.

35.5 Shari'ah Rulings

The practice of *Re-takaful*, as with all other *mu'amalat*, should primarily be guided by Shari'ah. Islam promotes fairness and justice in all spheres of life and it can be said that the practice of *Re-takaful* does not contradict the Shati'ah. As in all transaction in Shari'ah, the following should be avoided in *Re-takaful* transactions. There should be no element of *Riba* in the investments of *Re-takaful* companies. *Riba* is one of the biggest sins, as declared both by Qur'an and Holy prophet. It is the consensus of all schools of thought that if even an iota of *Riba* is present in a contract the contract and the transaction stands invalid. Nor should there be any *Gharar* present in the transaction. In the Qur'an the word *Gharar* has been used to describe Satan, the one who cheats, and also as expressing uncertainty about existence of God. In a transaction, all types of events and activities that can lead to fraud are included in the meaning. Hence, *Gharar* in its broadest sense includes all situations where the insurer may deceive the insured or creates an environment of uncertainty. There should be no element of gambling present in the transaction. Gambling has been prohibited in the Qur'an, which declares:

> O ye who believe! Intoxicants and gambling [dedication of] stones and [divination by] arrows are an abomination of Satan's handiwork: eschew such [abomination] that ye may prosper. Satan's plan is [but] to excite enmity and hatred between you with intoxicants and gambling and hinder you from the remembrance of Allah and from prayer: will ye not then abstain? (Qur'an 2:43)

The Islamic model of insurance and reinsurance, *Takaful* and *Re-takaful*, does not contain the above-mentioned elements. Generally, the characteristics of risk-sharing and mutual co-operation are applicable to *Re-takaful* in the same manner as in *Takaful*, as the latter is a system that allows participants to engage in mutual assistance whenever the need arises. It strengthens the social ties of the community, improves community morals and spurs economic self-help of the participants (*The Missing Link: Re-takaful and its Importance to Islamic Finance*). The profits of *Takaful* from risk mitigation practices are guided back into the community for the well-being of the participants.

35.6 Performance and Size of *Re-takaful* Industry

Conventional insurance was ruled to be unacceptable because it contained prohibited elements of *Gharar*, *Maisir* and *Riba*. For example, the National Religious Council of Malaysia issued a *fatwa* in 1974 that the conventional insurance is void in Islam due to above-mentioned reasons, with *Riba* as a major element of unacceptability (Rosly 2002). *Riba* is evident in conventional insurance because such businesses invest most of their funds in interest-based securities such as government bonds and private debt securities. Profits derived from interest-bearing securities, in turn, constitute one of the two components of total profit, namely investment profits and underwriting profits. The underwriting profits result when the premiums collected exceed the expenses of providing coverage.

As an alternative to conventional life insurance, the first *Takaful* insurance was introduced in 1985 and it has been growing fast and steadily since then. Today, there are two major *Takaful* companies in Malaysia, namely Syarikat Takaful Malaysia and Malaysian National Insurance Takaful. However, due to limited resources, *Takaful* companies had to seek protection from a financially capable reinsurer, which would take over the coverage of the large proportion of the risk.

Therefore, in the beginning, *Takaful* companies had to deal with conventional reinsurer since there was not any Shari'ah-compliant reinsurance entity. This raised doubts as to the permissibility of the *Takaful* company itself and there was a strong need to establish a *Re-takaful* company that would function according to Shari'ah principles. One such Shari'ah-compliant *Re-takaful* company is Asean Re-takaful International Limited, incorporated in 1997 and licensed under the Offshore Insurance

Table 35.1 Performance and size of *Re-takaful* industry

Re-takaful *operator/country*	*Capital USD*
IIRCO Saudi/Bahrain	25 million
Islamic Takaful & Re-takaful Bahamas	15 million
Sheikan Takaful Sudan	1 million
National Reinsurance Sudan	2 million
Takaful Islamic Ins. Reinsurance Bahrain/Saudi	10 million
Best Re # Tunisia	3–30 million
ASEAN Re-takaful Intl Labuan Malaysia	10–15 million
MNI # Malaysia	6.8–10 million

Source: Author's collection

Act 1990, in the International Offshore Financial Center of Labuan, Malaysia. A list of other *Re-takaful* companies is as follows in Table 35.1 (*The Missing Link: Re-takaful and its Importance to Islamic Finance*).

The growth in *Re-takaful* business depends on the performance and expansion of direct insurance (*Takaful*) operators (Arbouna 2000). With the projected rapid growth in *Takaful* operators (Fadzili 1996), we expect to observe significant growth in the *Re-takaful* industry as well. For example, Asean Re-takaful International Limited has shown a high and steady growth. The increase in general *Re-takaful* business of Asean Re-takaful International Limited was from USD 100,000 in 1998 to USD 1,700,000 in 2002, as shown in the data below:

Asean Re-takaful International Limited, growth of General *Re-takaful* business includes:

- Fire and Property *Re-takaful*
- Misc. Accident *Re-takaful*
- Marine *Re-takaful*
- Motor *Re-takaful*
- Engineering *Re-takaful*
- Special Risks *Re-takaful*

Growth in Family *Re-takaful* business of Asean Re-takaful International Limited was also increasing, although fell temporary in 2001. The increase is from USD 5000 in 1998 to USD 805,000 in 2002.

Under the family *Re-takaful* business are included the following categories:

Table 35.2 Performance and size of *Re-takaful* industry

Country	*(million)*	*Country*	*(million)*	*Country*	*(million)*
Malaysia	$ 1250	Iran	$ 800	Kuwait	$ 275
Indonesia	$ 1200	UAE	$ 500	Algeria	$ 200
USA	$ 900	Egypt	$ 475	Jordan	$ 175
Saudi Arabia	$ 850	UK	$ 300	China	$ 150

Source: Author's collection

- Individual Family *Re-takaful*
- Group Family *Re-takaful*
- Medical *Re-takaful*
- Group Hospitalisation *Re-takaful*
- Clinical Illness *Re-takaful*
- Mortgage *Re-takaful*
- Annuity *Re-takaful.*

The growth in the total pool of business for Asean Re-takaful International Limited was from USD 300,000 in 1998 to USD 2,100,000 in 2002, as shown above. In general, Asean Re-takaful International Limited has been growing steadily throughout the period considered. The high acceptability of *Takaful* and *Re-takaful* products and the shifting process of *Takaful* companies could explain such growth from the conventional reinsurance companies to *Re-takaful* entities.

The global *Takaful* premiums for Life and Non-Life were $500 million in 1998 (*The Missing Link: Re-takaful and its Importance to Islamic Finance*). Arab countries accounted for 60%; Malaysia accounted for 31%; the Far East and other countries 8%; while Europe/USA/other was 1% (Table 35.2). According to report by the CEO of Takaful International, Bahrain, the projected gross premiums written could amount to USD 7 billion by 2015. The 12 largest potential markets by country for Life and Non-Life combined would be as shown in Table 35.2.

35.7 Conclusion

Thus, we see that although a relatively a new industry, *Re-takaful* has a great potential to expand, especially in the wake of globalisation. The major aspect that can allow *Re-takaful* to expand is its acceptability to

Muslims has been its nature as Shari'ah compliant. Theoretically, *Re-takaful* has received little criticism from Shari'ah scholars. However, in practice there are a number of issues that must be addressed, such as avoiding investments in interest-based financial instruments and dealing with businesses that indulge in *Haram* activities. The benefits of *Re-takaful* together with *Takaful* institutions are mainly risk sharing among the participating parties. But far more welcome is the concept of brotherhood, charity and mutual guarantee that are enhanced by the *Takaful* industry.

References

1. Ali, A. Y. (n.d.), The Holy Qur'an, Text and Translation.
2. *Re-takaful* System & Model, ARIL and MNRB.
3. Billah, M. M. (2001), Shari'ah Model of Quantum of damages in Takaful & *Re-takaful*, IIUM.
4. Kamali, M. H. (1989), "Sources, nature and objectives of Shari'ah", *Islamic quarterly*, 4th Quarter.
5. Fisher, O. C. (1999), First Takaful[sm] Training Guide and Resource Manual.
6. The Missing Link: *Re-takaful* and its Importance to Islamic Finance.
7. Rosly, S. A. (2002), "Understanding Takaful", *Investors Digest*, March.
8. The Missing Link: *Re-takaful* and its Importance to Islamic Finance.
9. Arbouna, M. B. (2000), "The Operation of *Re-takaful* Protection", *Arab Law Quarterly*.
10. Fadzili, Y. M. (1996), The Concept and Operational System of Takaful Business.

CHAPTER 36

Structure of *Re-takaful* Products

36.1 Introduction

When it comes about conventional insurance, normally people will think of an operation which in its present form does not comply with the rules and requirement of the Shari'ah. Even if that is true in reality, it does not mean that insurance is totally prohibited for Muslims. The Muslim community should be aware that conventional insurance is forbidden only due to its operation that not comply with Shari'ah regulations, but not in terms of its concept. The pooling of common resources to help the needy itself is in line with the teaching of Islam, which is based on the spirit of solidarity, mutual help and Muslim brotherhood. Thus, Islam in addition to being guide for spiritual and moral obligations has its own rules of insurance, which is known as *Takaful*. The system of *Takaful* is not the same as the basis for the contract of sale, whereby there is an offer for protection, followed by the acceptance to buy the service on certain price. "It is actually a scheme whereby a group of people with common interest agreed to protect themselves from any misfortune or disaster through the creation of a pool contributed from their common resources" (Yusof n.d.).

It is acknowledged that, the idea of this chapter/product is significantly contributed by the practices /experiences/thoughts of Bank Negara, ARIL, MNRB, Takaful Malaysia, Takaful Ikhlas, Takaful Nasional, Etiqa Takaful, IBFIM, IIUM, MII and others (Malaysia).

Mohd Ma'Sum Billah, *Islamic Insurance Products*,
https://doi.org/10.1007/978-3-030-17681-5_36

Not many people realise the existence of *Re-takaful* business. Sometimes they only know the name, without understanding its operation and even its necessity for *Takaful* business. This might be due to the small number of *Re-takaful* companies and they fact that they are still inadequate for the needs of *Takaful* operators. *Re-takaful* is known as reinsurance in the conventional basis. Being the first time that this sort of product has been offered makes it quite difficult for us to interpret the real definition of *Re-takaful*. Because of this, we have interviewed Ms. Norfidah Abdullah, the senior manager, Re-takaful Division of Takaful Malaysia Berhad in order to get a clear understanding of *Re-takaful*. The application of *Re-takaful* is quite similar to conventional reinsurance, except that there are certain unallowable elements for Muslim society which must be be avoided by the *Re-takaful* operators.

The issue of *Re-takaful* or reinsurance in accordance with the requirements and practices [of Islam] will occupy the *Takaful* operators for some time. Although in a situation where *Re-takaful* is still inadequate to meet the needs of *Takaful* operators, Shari'ah allows them to deal with conventional reinsurers. (http://www.salaam.co.uk/themeofthemonth/november02_index.php?Ii9=8).

Re-takaful actually originated from the *Takaful* business. In other words, its operation is based on the *Takaful* fund. It emerged from the concomitant need to share the risks with other insurers. Ideally, *Re-takaful* should solely depend on the cession from *Takaful* operators. It plays an important role in ensuring that the operation of *Takaful* is fair. However, the operation of *Re-takaful* is actually beyond the knowledge of the insured. *Re-takaful* business can either be by treaty or by facultative. In case of certain exceptions, there will be no *Re-takaful* on treaty. This will be explained in the next section.

36.2 The *Re-takaful* Paradigm and Its Shari'ah Concern

The basic operational frameworks of *Re-takaful* and conventional reinsurance do not differ very much – they only contradict one another in certain conditions. Conventional reinsurance has always been in opposition with Shari'ah regulations, as it embodies three strictly prohibited fundamentals—*Gharar* (uncertainty), *Maisir* (gambling) and *Riba* (interest). These concepts will result in unfair contribution between different participants, including the possibility of a participant having an advantage over another participant. Another aspect that is strictly prohibited in *Re-takaful* business is the portion of profit commission that may be earnt from the *Re-takaful*, as it results in changes to *Re-takaful* fees.

The operation of *Takaful* generally starts from the process whereby the insured as well as the insurer agreed to pay a certain amount of premium as the contribution to the *Takaful* fund. Then it comes to *Re-takaful* business, when part of the contribution is being reinsured either by treaty or by facultative means or both. For example, let us say that KLCC becomes a client of Takaful Malaysia Berhad (TMB) for a $4 billion insurance. TMB might be able to cover the insurance up to $1 billion only. Therefore, it will reinsure part of the contribution to other company. In this case, TMB is the lead operation while other companies will be the followers. It is said to be the leader because when there is any problem related to contract, the clients will deal directly with the leading company. However, it does not mean that the TMB will have higher portion than the other companies, as there are no specific rules that require such proportions being allotted. We assume that the company will retain 40% of the amount and another 50% will be reinsuring under the treaty. Finally, the balance of 10% will go to the facultative, whereby the amount will be divided between the *Re-takaful* operators according to a certain rate. However, if there is an exceptional case, there will be no portion for treaty and all the 60% balance will go to the facultative. The exceptional case here refers to the *Takaful* contract whereby the insured person or company does not fulfil the requirements of the agreement.

In conventional reinsurance, "treaty refers to the transfer of liability from an insurer to the reinsurer on a portfolio of policies while the facultative reinsurance is refers to the transferation on a single policy of insurance which is also known as individual risk of reinsurance" (http://www.genre.com/page/0,,ref=ReinsProducts-en,00.html). For further operation, treaty can either be by surplus (case by case) or by excess of loss. The case-by-case treaty is actually based on the pre-agreement that a certain percentage or rate will be passed. For this *Re-takaful*, there will be an underwriter who is responsible to develop certain guidelines or policies, and also in determining the rate. Once the operators agree on the rates provided, then the agreement can proceed. The excess of loss is the relief from loss, including one that results from natural disaster.

Where there are not enough *Re-takaful* operators to continue the business, the *Takaful* company might deal with a conventional reinsurance company as long as the concept being applied is in accordance with

Shari'ah principles. However, the lead company must at first make an offer to *Takaful* operators. In choosing the operators, it must ensure that the company is from an 'A' list. What it meant by 'A' list is that the company listed is capable in terms of their financial position. In other words, it must be compliance with the requirements as stated in the agreement. The *Takaful* company also should avoid having *Re-takaful* business with any company that is not reliable in terms of the given condition. However, there are cases where the *Re-takaful* operators are unable to fulfil the obligation of the contract due to insufficient funds. As a result, the leading company might bring the case to the court for penalisation. Such a situation will only become a burden to the leading company, as the process always takes times to be settled. Thus, it is important for the leading company to learn in depth about the other operators before making a choice.

In the area of *Takaful* business, there is actually a fund known as General *Takaful* fund, which is earned from *Takaful* contributions paid by the participants. This fund will be invested and the returns will again be credited into the fund. However, the fund cannot be 'touched' by anyone except in the case where the participants suffer material loss, then the fund can be used to pay the claim. Other permissible expenditure regarding to the use of the fund is given to the costs that related to *Re-takaful*, which is in the basis of stabilising the fund and other related reserves. Even for the payment of the salaries of the operator's employees, they have to use the money received from the clients. If there is an excess profit on the fund then it will be distributed among the Takaful companies and the players.

The operation of *Re-takaful* might be suspicious in the eyes of the outsider as it is done without the knowledge of the insured. In explaining this, we can refer to the nature of the treaty itself. According to the senior manager of Re-takaful Division of TMB, the treaty is actually a blind agreement that does not have a specific written form. Besides, there is no definite condition related to the agreement. Thus, it is not necessary to involve clients with this kind of treatment. Furthermore, the objective of *Re-takaful* itself is for the benefit of the clients in ensuring that their rights are fulfilled.

36.3 Corporate Governance: The Shari'ah Supervisory Council

One of the important elements that differentiates conventional reinsurance and *Re-takaful* is the existence of the Shari'ah Supervisory Council. This council is vital in order to make sure that the operations of *Takaful* and *Re-takaful* is done according to the Shari'ah principles. Actually, the members of the Shari'ah Supervisory Council (SSC) for *Re-takaful* are the same as for *Takaful*. The main group refers to the SSC of Bank Negara and each *Takaful* operators has their own SSC. However, the members of SSC could be involved with not just one company. For example, Y Bhg Ustaz Mohd Bakir Haji Mansor who is the chairman of the SSC of TMB is also in position as the member of SSC for Bank Islam Malaysia Berhad (BIMB) and Asean Re-takaful International Ltd (ARIL). Meanwhile, Shahibul Al-Samahah Dato' Hj. Md HashimYahya, who is the committee member of Bank Negara Malaysia and the Security Commission, is also the member of the SSC of BIMB, MBB and some other institutions.

The main role of this council is to evaluate the form or statement provided by each *Takaful* operator. They must ensure that the stated conditions in the agreement are compliance with the Shari'ah requirements. However, we should realise that there is nothing perfect in this world. Where there is an advantage, there will always be a disadvantage too. We know that usually the members of the SSC are more theorists than practitioners. Consequently, there may be disagreement regarding to the opinion of SSC and the employees of the *Takaful* operators. In another case, sometimes the conditions provided in a *Takaful* company might vary from those of another company due to the different SSC. Nevertheless, these problems will not affect the clients, but it will give quite a bad impression about the company itself. In addition, there might be confusion among the clients regarding to the variety in terms of the policies of different *Takaful* operators. Nonetheless, the company still has to follow the words of the SSC as long as it is in accordance with the requirements of Shari'ah rules and regulations.

36.4 Experience of a *Re-takaful* Operator: Asean Re-takaful International Ltd (ARIL)

ARIL is the first *Re-takaful* company under Takaful Malaysia Berhad to have been established. The operation of this company is totally based on the Re-takaful business. It can be concluded that this company has its own methods and way in establishing the business and it obtains income from three main sources: the return on investment of the shareholders' fund, profit from the general *Re-takaful* fund and the profit from the family *Re-takaful* fund.

36.5 Conclusion

Re-takaful business is dissimilar to conventional insurance only in certain aspects. Both rely on the same concept, which is based on the intention to help the needy. Thus, the Islamic reinsurer might co-operate with the conventional insurer so long as the operation is within the boundaries of Islamic principles. However, this type of business is still new and the problem of lack of *Re-takaful* companies become the main point that needs to be considered. Therefore, the practical commitment from the various countries including their political willingness is needed in order to show their readiness in allowing *Takaful* operators to be incorporated in their respective countries. This will then cause the emergence of the necessary playing field for *Re-takaful* operations.

Another important element that should be of concern is the number of players. A sufficient number of players is needed in order for the *Re-takaful* operators to survive and increasing numbers will also promote the development of *Re-takaful* business. This is an important potential area of business, yet there is still no strictly Islamic reinsurance available globally. Therefore, Malaysia should take the opportunity to develop the global *Re-takaful* business in the longer term.

References

1. Ali, A. Y. (n.d.), The Holy Qur'an, Text and Translation.
2. Re-takaful Product Operation, ARIL and MNRB.
3. Yusof, M. F. (n.d.), Introduction to Takaful.
4. http://www.salaam.co.uk/themeofthemonth/november02_index.php?Ii9=8
5. http://www.genre.com/page/0,,ref=ReinsProducts-en,00.html

CHAPTER 37

Management of the *Re-takaful* Fund

37.1 Introduction

Nowadays, *Takaful* business is one of the most rapidly growing industries globally. Based on global statistics, there are about 30 *Takaful* companies in operation, with an estimated gross contribution of USD 500 million to the industry. On the other hand, we only have three *Re-takaful* or reinsurance companies globally, chalking up a total gross *Re-takaful* contribution of USD 30 million. This industry has a big potential market where the Muslim *ummah* is a large population spread all over the world. The *Takaful* operator has a great opportunity to penetrate this market. *Re-takaful* or the reinsurance business mainly undertakes to receive part of the liability or risk from *Takaful* companies. The idea behind this *Re-takaful* is that all *Takaful* operators are in the same boat in terms of risk and liability. Therefore, there is a need to manage and reduce the risk where they agree to transfer part of the risk to another party, namely the *Re-takaful* company, and where this is based on the concept that the losses of one shall be shared among the many.

It is acknowledged that, the idea of this chapter/product is significantly contributed by the practices/experiences/thoughts of Bank Negara, ARIL, MNRB, Takaful Malaysia, Takaful Ikhlas, Takaful Nasional, Etiqa Takaful, IBFIM, IIUM, MII and others (Malaysia).

Mohd Ma'Sum Billah, *Islamic Insurance Products*,
https://doi.org/10.1007/978-3-030-17681-5_37

37.2 SHARI'AH RULINGS

Insurance under Islamic law can be defined as a mutual financial transaction between two parties in which one provides material security for the other against a defined risk. In an insurance policy, the operator provides compensation against unexpected loss or damage, if any, but in case the risk does not happen to the subject matter of the policy within the agreed period, the insured participant, upon the maturity of the policy, should be entitled to the whole amount (in a life policy) of the paid contribution, together with a share of profits made over and above the paid contributions (Billah, M. M., 2003).

Today, various groups of Islamic scholars are in conflict in their views on Islamic insurance. This might be because of the nature of its operations, the principles used or the very term 'insurance' itself, which originated in the West. However, many scholars who are in favour of the product have proved that insurance can be Islamised if it is implemented using the underlying principles relevant in Islamic *mu'amalat*.

There is a Malay phrase, "malang tak berbau," which means that loss cannot be predicted. In light of this, most people who are risk averse try as far as possible to protect themselves against unfavourable risk. This is how *Takaful* (Islamic insurance) came into an existence. Many scholars rationalise the permissibility of *Takaful* based on the following perspectives:

> Our Lords, give us happiness in this world and happiness in the hereafter. (Qur'an, 2:201)

Every human being always hopes for the best in this world and in the hereafter. So, *Takaful* provides a wide and flexible policy to protect Muslims from harm. Life insurance, for example, provides material protection for unfortunate offspring in case of the death of policyholders (for example, a father). The prophet (saw) once advised people to leave their children with future material protection. He (saw) said:

> Narrated by Amir bin Saad bin Abi Waqas (r), the Holy Prophet (saw) said: Verily it is better for you to leave your offspring wealthy than to leave them poor asking others for help. (Muhammad Muhsin, 1979)

However, any *Takaful* operation is bound to certain rules in order to ensure that its operations are in line with Islamic teachings and principles. For example, Allah (swt) prohibits any kind of unjust accumulation of wealth and profit.

> O you who believe! Eat not up your property among yourselves unjustly except it be a trade amongst you, by mutual consent. And do not kill yourselves (nor kill one another). Surely, Allah is Most Merciful to you. (Qur'an, 4:29)

Insurance policy is operated based on the principles of *Al-Mudharabah*, whereby the insurer is a capital provider and the insurance company is the entrepreneur. They will share the agreed portion of profits and simultaneously could avoid the element of interest (*Riba*) which is strictly prohibited in Islam. As Allah says:

> Those who eat *Riba* [usury] will not stand [on the Day of Resurrection] except like the standing of a person beaten by Shaitân [Satan] leading him to insanity. That is because they say: "Trading is only like *Riba*," whereas Allah has permitted trading and forbidden *Riba*. So whosoever receives an admonition from his Lord and stops eating *Riba* shall not be punished for the past; his case is for Allah [to judge]; but whoever returns [to Riba], such are the dwellers of the Fire—they will abide therein. (Qur'an, 2:275)

Takaful as a policy is not only a medium through which to invest and protect one's wealth; the main purpose of it is to promote among the contractual parties mutual co-operation and not to take advantage or make profit at the expense of those who are in need or in difficulties. Allah (swt) says:

> and help you one another in righteousness and piety. (Qur'an, al-Maidah, 5:2)

The Prophet (swt) says:

> Narrated by Abu Huraira (ra) from the Holy Prophet (saw) saying that: whosoever removes a worldly hardship from a believer Allah (swt) will remove from him one of the hardships of the hereafter. Whosoever alleviates the needy person, Allah (swt) will alleviate from him in this world and the next. (Sahih Muslim (Arabic), Kitab al-Birr, 59)

Thus, we can say that the *Takaful* policy is designed not only to provide material protection to the policyholders. It is also a form of investment that can generate benefits to both contracting parties. The contractual relation between the contracting parties leads to strengthened brotherhood between Muslims and also non-Muslims within the society.

37.3 Unique Characteristics of *Re-takaful*

Re-takaful (Islamic reinsurance) is not that same as the conventional approaches. This is because Islamic reinsurance possesses a few particular characteristics to ensure that it operates in line with the teachings of Islam. Those characteristics can be categorised as in the following subsections (Billah 2002).

37.3.1 Sincerity

> Narrated by Omar bin al-Khattab (r) the Holy Prophet (saw) said: The reward of deeds depends upon the intentions and every person will get the reward according to what he has intended. (Khan, M.Mohsin, 1986)

By referring to the above hadith, every Islamic reinsurance contract should be based on the sincerity to lighten the burden of our Muslims brothers and sisters when they are in difficulties and not to take advantage of those who are in need. A reinsurance policy is only a mechanism to protect a person from any future unexpected loss and damages. However, Muslims should put the trust and faith only in Allah (swt), since He is the only one who knows the future and He is the absolute power of protection over the entire universe. Allah (swt) says in the Qur'an:

> To Him belongs the dominion of the heaven and the earth: to give life and death: And He has power over all things. (Qur'an, Surah al-Hadid 57: 2)

37.3.2 Absolute Shari'ah Principles

Islam is a way of life. Every Muslim is given two main resources to guide them in this world. Therefore, it is necessary for any *mu'amalat* to be in conformity with the divine sources of Holy Qur'an and Sunnah. Any practices against the teachings of both divine regulations will become invalid. As Allah (swt) says:

> If anyone desires any religion other than Islam never will it recognized by Allah (swt). (Qur'an, Surah Ali Imran 3: 85)

37.3.3 Moral Attributes

A *Re-takaful* contract should be bounded by the moral and spiritual elements. Any contract must be concluded with utmost good faith, honesty, disclosure and truthfulness (Billah 2003).

> O you who believe! Eat not up your property among yourselves unjustly except it be a trade amongst you, by mutual consent. And do not kill yourselves (nor kill one another). Surely, Allah is Most Merciful to you. (Qur'an, 4: 29)

37.4 Elements of a *Re-takaful* Contract

It is suggested that any *Re-takaful* contract should be concluded with the availability of the following elements: (Billah 2002)

- the parties of the contract must have legal capacity;
- the availability of insurable interest;
- indemnity clause: the insurer is unilaterally bound to compensate the insured for the loss to the agreed subject matter;
- the payments of premiums by the insured as a consideration to the contract;
- the presence of mutual consent by both parties;
- an offer and acceptance to be expressed in a formal agreement between the insurer and the insured, in which the terms and conditions are compliance with Shari'ah principles;
- specification of period for the agreed policies which are to be contained in the agreement.

37.5 Significance of *Al-Mudharabah* in *Re-takaful*

One of the critics of the impermissibility of conventional insurance is so minded due to the element of *Riba* that exists in its contract (Sa'id Abu Jaib 2000). As an alternative, *Re-takaful* operates using the principles of *Al-Mudharabah* financing techniques to ensure just and permissible transactions. This principle allows both contracting parties to share profits and dividends justly made over the paid premiums.

37.6 Governing Principles

37.6.1 Principles of Contract ('Aqd*)*

In Islam, '*Aqd* is very important element and must be present in business transactions. An offer and acceptance (*sighah*) will make the particular transaction valid and both parties who have entered into the contract are bound thereto. For reinsurance policy, a person who enters the contract must fulfil certain requirements, such as legal capacities of the parties, subject matters, insurable interest, *ijab* (offer) and *qabul* (acceptance), and *Uberrimae fidei* (Billah 2003). Once a person has entered into a mutual contract, is it an obligation for both parties to fulfil the contract as Allah (swt) has commanded:

> O ye believe! fulfil your agreement. (Qur'an 5: 1)

37.6.2 Principles of Liability

A person who buys an insurance policy from an insurance company is ready to transfer part of their risk to the insurer. The insurer is willing to undertake the risk and willing to compensate if any loss occurs to the policyholder. An insurance policy will mainly cover losses due to accident, fire, flood, death, disaster, business burglary, property and other losses.

In this situation, the concept of *al-Aqila* found among ancient Arab tribes and approved by the Prophet (saw) is pertinent: if a person was killed by another person from a different tribe either mistakenly or negligently, this would bring a liability to member of his tribe to pay blood money to the heirs of the slain.

37.6.3 Principles of Al-Wakalah *(Agencies)*

Application of *Al-Wakalah* principle in *Takaful* is also important where the insurer (*Takaful* operator) will appoint a designated agent to deal with the insured or customers. The main intention of this appointment is to ensure that the transactions and dealings between insurer and policyholder become more efficient and effective. The governing principles for the agents and brokers are laid down in the *Mejelle* as follows:

> *Wakalat* is for someone to put business of his on another and make him stand in his own place in respect of that business.

37.6.4 Principles of Daman *(Guarantee)*

The principle of *Daman* has been practised in *Takaful*, where the insurer is willing to undertake risk on behalf of the insured and where the insurer promises to provide material security against unexpected loss or disaster arising in the future and is willing to compensate for losses that may occur.

37.6.5 Principles of Al-Mudharabah

Al-Mudharabah concept is widely used in *Takaful* as an alternative to interest-based securities.[1] In practice, conventional insurance companies will invest in long-term bonds or stocks of companies which may or may not be involved in non-permissible activities such as gambling, production of alcoholic beverages and interest-based banking.

However, the operation of *Takaful* is carried out under Shari'ah principles. It is based on the principles of *Al-Mudharabah* and *Al-Musyarakah*. The *Takaful* operator acts as ***mudharib*** and will receive the sum of investments from ***sahib-ul-mal*** or ***rabb-ul-mal*** (capital provider) through premium payments. With this sum of investment, the ***mudharib*** will invest in productive industry using their skills and knowledge. At the end of the day, when the *Takaful* receives return (profit) on the investment, the *Takaful* operator will distribute the profit to the capital provider based on the agreed portion.

37.7 *Re-takaful* Fund

A Takaful company, with its limited financial resources, may want to hedge against possible inability to meet all *Takaful* indemnities if a number of damages occur simultaneously. Thus, a *Takaful* company may seek protection from the risks mentioned by putting some portion of money (called a premium) in a *Re-takaful* company, while in return the *Re-takaful* company provides security for the risk insured.

Conceptually and practically, the operational part of the *Takaful* company and *Re-takaful* company are almost the same. The difference between the only that the *Takaful* company receives premiums from individual participants instead of from corporations. In this discussion, the corporation is the *Takaful* company. This means that the insured party of a *Takaful*

[1] Rosly, S. A. (1996), *Islamic Insurance: Takaful*, Business-Focus. *The Sun*.

company is individual participants, whereas the insured party of the *Re-takaful* company is the *Takaful* operators themselves.

With regard to the requirements of Shari'ah and also financial prudence, the *Re-takaful* company should operate its funds separately. A full set of accounts for each fund comprising of the balance sheet, revenue, profits and loss and operational expenses are prepared on a monthly basis. The funds comprise (Billah, M. M., n.d.):

- shareholders' fund
- general *Re-takaful* fund
- family *Re-takaful* fund.

Basically, the sources of income for the *Re-takaful* company come from these funds. Investment income from the shareholders' fund contributes 100% of profits to the *Re-takaful* company. Distributable surplus from general *Re-takaful* fund is up to 60%. The distribution of income follows *Al-Mudharabah* principle and normally the profit ratio is 60:40, where 60% of profit goes to the *Re-takaful* company and another 40% goes to the *Takaful* company as a cedant. Distributable surplus from the family *Re-takaful* fund also contributes about 60% of profits to the company (Fig. 37.1). Fig. 37.1 best describes the sources of income for the *Re-takaful* company (www.sabah.com.my):

The profits raised by the *Re-takaful* company on the shareholders' fund, the general *Re-takaful* fund and family *Re-takaful* fund are basically garnered by putting *Re-takaful* funds (shareholder' fund, general *Re-takaful* fund and family *Re-takaful* fund) into investment portfolios. The graph in Fig. 37.2 illustrates how the *Re-takaful* company manages its funds (ibid.).

The *Re-takaful* fund will be invested into Shari'ah-approved companies. The entrusted commercial institutions will administer *Re-takaful* funds on the basis of *Al-Mudharabah* or *Ijarah*. The administration of *Re-takaful* funds by these institutions involves the following (Arbouna, M. B., n.d.):

- The *Takaful* operators mobilise contributions (*Re-takaful* premium) and the company then undertakes to manage the fund, settle claims and reimburse surplus, if any, to the *Takaful* operator's fund with fair and proportionate distribution (e.g. using the ratio of 60: 40).

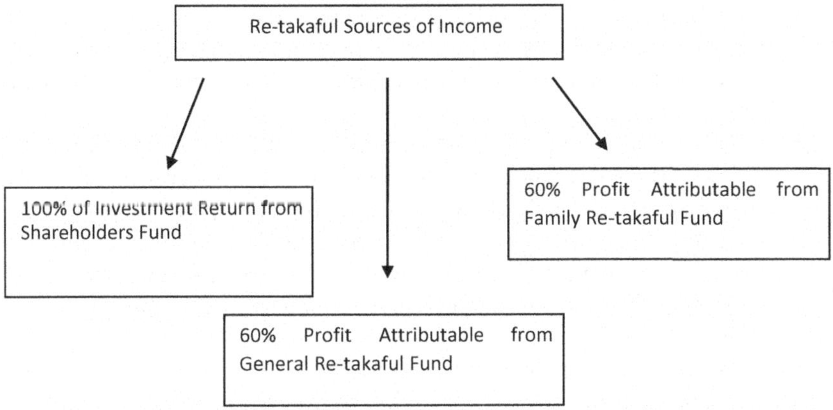

Fig. 37.1 *Re-Takaful* fund. (Source: Author's collection)

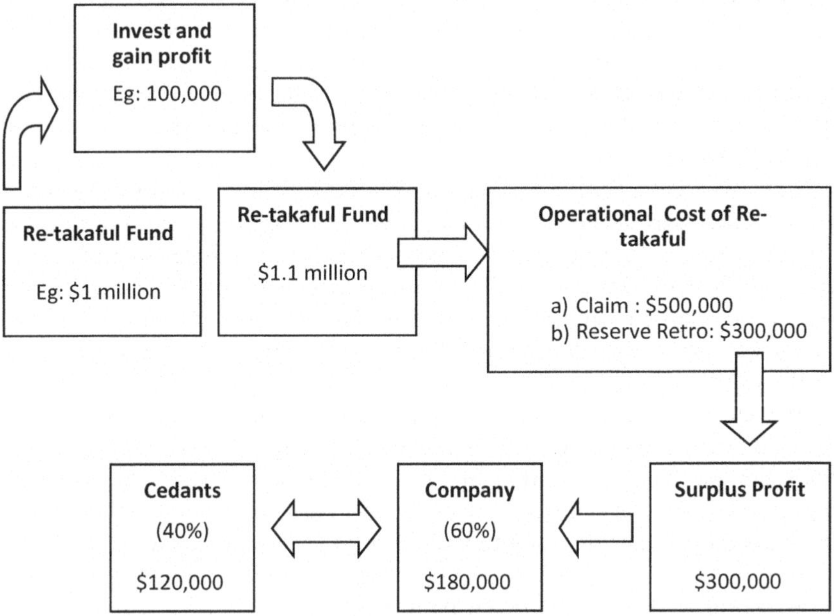

Fig. 37.2 *Re-Takaful* fund. (Source: Author's collection)

- The contribution (*Re-takaful* premium) may be deposited in an Islamic commercial bank in a current account, savings account or investment account until the need for the settlement of claims or indemnity arises.
- A shareholder company could administer the *Re-takaful* fund. In this case, the shareholder company will issue certificates or bonds of participation to *Takaful* operators, determine payable premiums according to standard methods of premium computation and settle the claims. The administrator may recoup costs of services rendered to the fund in two ways, namely, *Al-Mudharabah* and *Ijarah*.

In *Al-Mudharabah* instrument, the company will invest the accumulated *Re-takaful* fund to share profits to meet immediate operating expenses and costs of actual services rendered to the *Re-takaful* fund. The administrator's share of the profits can be predetermined in the agreement document in a percentage form. It must be noted that if the investment agreement is made on *Al-Mudharabah* instrument, the company is not responsible for investment losses provided there is no element of negligence or unprofessional investment decisions. The company will lose commission for its labour since the transaction was entered into on an *Al-Mudharabah* basis.

The *Re-takaful* fund may be administered and invested in by the company on the basis of the hire contract (*Ijarah*). The instrument entitles the company to earn a wage (*ujra*), whether the result of investment is positive or otherwise. Moreover, the administration costs of the administrator are commissioned on the basis of the *Ijarah* contract, which will be extracted from the *Re-takaful* fund, irrespective of the experience of the fund.

It is clear that if the bank or the company manages the Islamic reinsurance fund on the basis of *Al-Mudharabah*, the transaction appears unfavourable for having no adequate financial interest for its shareholders except the profit earned from the process of *Al-Mudharabah*. To earn this profit, it has to provide, as outlined above, three major services:

- administration of the investment process;
- administration of insurance activities as *wakil* (agent) or *mua'jar* (hired) without any financial return except the profit earned through the *Al-Mudharabah* contract, if any;
- underwriting financial stability (protecting insolvency) of the *Takaful* operators without return.

Thus, the company that has worked as *mudarib* undertakes to administer the reinsurance fund and underwrites the solvency of the *Takaful* operator without substantial financial return. It should be noted here that if the company or administrator chooses to invest the *Re-takaful* fund on *Al-Mudharabah* basis and the fund suffers losses it cannot claim any monetary benefit for its labour because the nature of *Al-Mudharabah* contract does not allow such claims. The administrator loses commission for its labours in such a case. However, the company's based on its reputation is not commissioned. It is thus argued that the *Re-takaful* administrator therefore has to be put in a favourable situation for the smooth running of operations. In this regard, it is suggested that the process should be considered as follows:

- As hinted at earlier, the process of administration and supervision of the *Re-takaful* fund should be conducted in lieu of financial consideration based on *Ijarah*. Hence, the company will receive remuneration irrespective of the experience of the *Re-takaful* business.
- The reinsurance administrator is regarded as a representative of the policyholders (the *Takaful* operator). Therefore, it could invest the accumulated *Takaful* premium/contributions according to *Al-Mudharabah* principles and share the proceeds with the *Takaful* operators as participants (Arbouna n.d.).

References

1. Ali, A. Y. (n.d.), The Holy Qur'an, Text and Translation.
2. Management of Re-takaful Funds, ARIL, MNRB and others.
3. Billah, M. M. (2003), Islamic and Modern Insurance: Principles and Practice. Ilmiah Publishers, Malaysia
4. Muhammad Muhsin (1979), *Sahih al-Bukhari*, *Kitab al-Faraif*, Kazi Publication, Lahore, Vol. 8, No. 725, p. 447.
5. Sahih Muslim (Arabic), Kitab al-Birr, 59.
6. Billah, M. Ma'sum (2002), *Manual of Principles and Practices of takaful and Re-Takaful*, International Islamic University, Malaysia p. 47.
7. Sahih al-Bukhari and Sahih al-Muslim, Kitab al-Wahi, Khan, M. Mohsin, op. cit. vol. 1, No. 1, p. 1.
8. Sa'id Abu Jaib, (2000), *Hukum Insurans Mengikut Perspektif Islam*, Percetakan Yayasan Islam Terengganu, at p. 26.
9. Rosly, S. A. (1996), *Islamic Insurance: Takaful*, Business-Focus. *The Sun*.

10. Billah, M. M. (n.d.), *Specific Analysis on Re-takaful, Manual of Principles & Practices of Takaful & Re-takaful*, Department of Business Administration, Kulliyyah of Economics & Management Sciences, Internatinal Islamic University Malaysia, P. 205.
11. Asean Re-takaful International, www.sabah.com.my
12. Arbouna, M. B. (n.d.), "The Operation of Re-takaful (Islamic Reinsurance) Protection", *Arab Law Quarterly*, Kluwer Law International, Netherlands, P. 354.
13. *Sahih al-Bukhari* (trans Eng.) Khan, M. Mohsin (1986), "The Book of Revelation", *Hadith* 1.

CHAPTER 38

Investment of *Re-takaful* Funds

38.1 Introduction

The *Takaful* brand of insurance is a classic example of consumer-driven response to needs. *Takaful* is a co-operative insurance with mutual agreement. Currently there are 40 takaful operators worldwide, mostly providing general business. It was estimated that the total assets and contribution of these operators amount to $1 billion and $500 million respectively. These figures are negligible if you compare them with the population of 1.2 billion Muslims. This is due to the fact that many issues are still unresolved. The key areas to be resolves are: the global standardisation of *Takaful* terminology, the development of acceptable form of life insurance (Family *Takaful*), especially for countries in the Middle East and a common consensus for a system to determine profits (or surplus) for distribution to participants and shareholders. Nevertheless, *Takaful* business has generally grown at high rate worldwide, which is a sign of its success.

It is acknowledged that, the idea of this chapter/product is significantly contributed by the practices /experiences/thoughts of Bank Negara, ARIL, MNRB, Takaful Malaysia, Takaful Ikhlas, Takaful Nasional, Etiqa Takaful, IBFIM, IIUM, MII and others (Malaysia).

Mohd Ma'Sum Billah, *Islamic Insurance Products*,
https://doi.org/10.1007/978-3-030-17681-5_38

38.2 Legality of *Takaful*

The idea to set up a *Takaful* system arose from the need of Muslims to conduct their affairs based on Islamic laws. The Muslim scholars of the nineteenth and twentieth centuries realised that Islam is not only restricted to set of rules and regulations concerning *Ibadah* and *Munakahat* but a complete way of life (*Nizamul Hayah*), including business transactions. There are disagreements among scholars on the permissibility of *Takaful*, which is a norm in the intellectual arena. The scholars who agree on the permissibility of *Takaful* argue that insurance is a modern contract and there is no injunction (*Nass*) regarding it, hence it is permissible (*Mubah*), as a legal maxim states:

> The original legal position on any matter is permissibility until there is evidence prohibiting it.

This maxim is in line with the Qu'ranic verse which says:

> We have subjugated to you all that is in the heaven and the earth. (45:13)

According to the scholars, this implies in principles that we are permitted to use the resources of the universe and acts that facilitate the use of it, such as transactions, are permissible. To reinforce this explanation, the Qur'an lays down the principles that explained Allah's prohibitions.

> He explained to you that which is forbidden to you, unless you are compelled thereto. (6:119)

Furthermore, the universe is described as an adornment of Allah (swt):

> Who has forbidden the adornment of Allah which He has brought forth for his bondsmen, and the good things of His providing. (Qur'an7:32)

Therefore, Muslim scholars asserted that any injunction that overruled this principle of permissibility must be decisive in meaning and transmission. (*Nass qati al thubut wal-dalah*).

According to the renowned scholars, the reasons for opting for *Takaful* are:

- A contract that brings *Maslahah* to the insured
- It is a custom (*'Urf*) that establishes insurance to protect public and individual interest is acceptable as a source of Islamic laws.

Takaful is not a contract of exchange, but falls under concepts of *Tabarru'* and as assistance and guarantee by the insurer to the insured.

38.3 *Re-takaful* Fund

After analysis of scholars' views on the permissibility of *Takaful*, another area of much debate is reinsurance of *Takaful* business on Islamic principles. *Re-takaful*/reinsurance comes from the desire of one party to share losses amongst many or of the insurer in turn to reinsure part of his risk with the reinsurer. The obstacle that made conventional reinsurance impermissible under Islam is the practice of paying a fixed periodic premium. With 40 takaful operators worldwide, *Re-takaful* has become a necessity in order for Muslim countries to benefit fully from the success of *Takaful*. The inadequacy of *Re-takaful* market to meet the needs of *Re-takaful* operators, and lack of commitment and political willingness among Muslim nations has delayed the establishment of a strong *Re-takaful* market, but Shari'ah does not allow *Takaful* operators to deal with conventional reinsurance, based on the maxim:

> Necessity makes forbidden things permissible.

However, some Muslim countries, for instance Malaysia, have made particular efforts in this area and now play leading roles in bringing *Takaful* to the international field. Malaysia established special *Re-takaful* operators such as Asean Re-takaful International Limited (ARIL), Asean Re-takaful Group (ARG), other Re-takaful company like Islamic takaful and Re-takaful Company in Saudi Arabia etc.

Takaful Malaysia has established joint ventures programs in Sri Lanka, Saudi Arabia and also provides technical assistant for *Takaful* in Australia. The International workshop on *Re-takaful* was held in Kuala Lumpur in June 1999, among other things, they agreed to transformed status of ARIL to *Re-takaful* operators for the D-8 countries; its capital shall be expanded and subscribed by member countries. Asean Re-takaful International Limited projected paid capital of US$50 million by 2006. Since there are not enough *Re-takaful* companies in the market, and demand is high, we shall look at a well-established and successful *Re-takaful* company among the few as our case study in analysing investment procedures of *Re-takaful* funds and return mechanisms to the *Takaful* operators.

38.4 Experience of ASEAN Re-takaful International Limited (ARIL)

ARIL was established on 17 May 1997 and was licensed under the Offshore Insurance Act 1999, in the international offshore financial center of Labuan. Its clients include various takaful operators, *Re-takaful* operators and brokers around the globe. The Syarikat takaful Malaysia Berhad (STMB) is the major shareholder, the pioneer and the largest *Takaful* operator in the region. ARIL has a religious supervisory council which comprise of renowned Shari'ah scholars with wide experience in Islamic financial services and *Takaful.*

38.4.1 The ARIL Offers

- to provide a variety of *Takaful* and *Re-takaful* services
- to ensure international-standard services
- to strictly fulfil Shari'ah requirements
- *Re-takaful* based on a contract of *Al-Mudharabah.*

38.4.2 Types of Business

The ARIL ventures into many different types of business, among them General *Re-takaful*, Family *Re-takaful* and *Takaful Lil-Istithmar.*

General Re-takaful *(General Reinsurance)*
The ARIL reinsures many types of *Takaful* business. It covers property/fire *Re-takaful*, miscellaneous accident *Re-takaful*, marine *Re-takaful*, motor *Re-takaful*, Engineering *Re-takaful* and special risk *Re-takaful.* These types of reinsurance have shown tremendous growth. It increased from US$1000,000 in 1998 to US$1.7 million in 2002.

Family Re-takaful
Life insurance remains one of the major unresolved issues in the *Takaful* industry in the Middle East and other parts of the Muslim world. Many Muslims still have it in their mind that life insurance is a taboo; they believe

that it contravenes some of the tenets of Islam. But on the legality of life insurance we can look at the hadith of the Prophet (saw). He said:

> Narrated by Amir been saad bin Waqqas (R) the holy prophet said: Verily it better for you to leave your offspring wealthy than to leave them poor asking others for help.

Furthermore, a life insurance policy guarantees future security for the deceased family.

> Narrated by Sahal bin Saad (r), the holy prophet said: I and the person who look after an orphan and provides for him security will be rewarded by Allah with paradise in hereafter.

However, the Malaysian case is different; Muslims have been increasingly sensitised to the permissibility of life insurance which is based on Islamic principles. In Family *Re-takaful*, it covers individual, group family, medical, group hospitalisation *Re-takaful*, and critical illness and mortgages *Re-takaful*. Family *Re-takaful* experience less response in 1998 because of the above problem but had achieves tremendous growth of US $ 805,000 in 2002, probably because of sensitisation.

Takaful Lil-Istithmar *(Investment Link)*

This represents the first offshore investment linked product globally that observes Shari'ah rules. This sector of business invests only in international Islamic funds through contracts based on *Al-Wakalah* and *Al-Ujrah*.

Benefits:

- Tax advantages—those who invest in this link are exempted from income tax and capital gains tax.
- Confidentiality—any investments are kept highly confidential under laws of Labuan IOFC.
- Flexibility—investors can switch easily to any portfolio he/she likes without incurring any extra costs.
- Liquidity—he can withdraw partially any time just by notifying the policy provider 30 days earlier.
- International investments are possible.

If investors choose invest via *Takaful Lil-Istithmar* in the international market, his investment risk can be minimized by diversifying his money in to variety of funds denominated in different currencies and in different parts of the world. In addition, he will face no complicated work or extra charges for buying and selling.

38.5 Portfolio Management

Takaful Lil-Istithmar manages portfolios of various types for different sorts of investors: risk averse, risk loving and risk neutral. This is achieved through the following strategies.

38.5.1 Istithmar Bil Awaid Al-Thaabitah *(Income Portfolio)*

This type of investment portfolio is low risk and offers low returns. It is designed mostly for investors who are risk averse. It ensures reasonable returns for medium- and long-term growth.

38.5.2 Istithmar Bil Awaid Al-Mutawassitah *(Balanced Portfolio)*

A portfolio for investors who are risk neutral, it offers reasonable and consistent returns in the medium and long term.

38.5.3 Istithmar Bil Awaid Al-Murtafiah *(Growth Portfolio)*

A type of portfolio for those who are risk lovers, it is a highly risky investment that offers high return on medium- and long-term growth.

38.6 Method of *Re-takaful*

As an example, ARIL operates by using facultative as well as treaty systems. For facultative it uses both local reinsurance which operates on conventional principles and other facultative which operates on a Shari'ah basis. The coverage on treaty system operates with the aid of the relevant brokers at international level from both conventional and Islamic companies. ARIL writes both proportional and non-proportional *Re-takaful*.

These mixed operations are still questionable by Shari'ah since the Qu'ran forbids us from covering truth with falsehood. Allah (swt) says:

> And cover not truth with falsehood, no conceal the truth when you know (what is). (Qur'an 2:42)

38.7 Sources of Income

The ARIL acquire it funds from three different types of sources:

- 100% from investment returns of shareholders' funds
- 60% profit of General *Re-takaful* fund
- 60% profit of Family *Re-takaful* fund

38.8 *Re-takaful* Fund Operation

The fact that ARIL operates on the basis of Shari'ah is a yardstick for its operations; ARIL uses contracts in *Al-Mudharabah* style and profit is distributed at a 60:40 ratio. From the discussion, we can analyse that RM 1 million comes from above three sources of funds. The ARIL invests this money and gains profits of RM 100,000. *Re-takaful* total funds including profit are thus RM 1.1 million. The operation costs of *Re-takaful*, such as claims cost RM 500,000, will be deducted from total fund. RM 300,000 will be reserved for reinvestment. The balance of RM 300,000 will be distributed according to the agreed ratio between *Rabb-al-Mal* (RM 180,000 company) and *Al-Mudharib* (RM 120,000).

38.9 Conclusion

Despite some limitations in *Takaful* and *Re-takaful*—such as technical issues which are still unresolved, capital problems, lack of awareness in some parts of Muslim countries about *Takaful*, lack of expertise and human resources with requisite knowledge of Shari'ah and the financial system, and the inadequacy of *Re-takaful* in market—the industry has achieved a lot in the less than three decades since its inception. To be fair to the industry, we cannot compare *Takaful* with conventional insurance, which was established more than 150 years ago. A difference in opinion among Muslim scholars and *Fuqaha* about *Takaful* and *Re-takaful* has proven that *Takaful* is going in the right direction of its final stage on the way to becoming a global competitor.

References

1. Ali, A. Y. (n.d.), The Holy Qur'an, Text and Translation.
2. Investment of *Re-takaful* Funds, ARIL, MNRB and others.
3. Billah, M. Ma'sum (2002), *Manual of Principles and Practices of takaful and Re-takaful*, International Islamic University, Malaysia p. 47.
4. Asean *Re-takaful* International, www.sabah.com.my

PART V

Claim and Quantum

CHAPTER 39

Claims Procedure in General *Takaful*

39.1 Introduction

Islamic scholars have accepted the importance and need for insurance and its legality. As discussed elsewhere in this book, the basic function of a *Takaful* company is to foster a spirit of co-operation among members of society. Everyone in this world is exposed to risk and uncertainty. Every Muslim believes that all disasters come from Allah (swt). These are known as *Qada'* and *Qadar*. Therefore, there should be a mechanism to provide protection from such risks. General *Takaful* offers coverage of both individuals and organisations in relation to material losses. The *Takaful* concept is in conformity with Shari'ah and is based on the Islamic principles of *Takaful* and *Al-Mudharabah*. There are several principles of *Takaful*, including utmost good faith, participant's interest, proximate cause and indemnity. Generally, Muslim jurists have noted three elements that need to be avoided in such agreements: *Gharar*, *Maisir* and *Riba*. If one of these elements exists in our agreement, the contract will be immediately invalidated.

It is acknowledged that, the idea of this chapter/product is significantly contributed by the practices/experiences/thoughts of Bank Negara, *Takaful* Malaysia, *Takaful* Ikhlas, *Takaful* Nasional, Etiqa *Takaful*, IBFIM, IIUM, MII and others (Malaysia).

Mohd Ma'Sum Billah, *Islamic Insurance Products*,
https://doi.org/10.1007/978-3-030-17681-5_39

39.2 General *Takaful* in Brief

General *Takaful* provides coverage against loss of properties due to various possible factors, including fire, accident and so forth. Basically, the participants of *Takaful* will become involved in a scheme on the basis of *Al-Mudharabah* contract. Payment will be saved by the *Takaful* fund for every instalment paid. This fund will be invested by the company according to Shari'ah principles and any profit generated from that investment will be returned to the fund. We should also note that the company will pay compensation or indemnity to participants who have suffered a loss of protected property.

39.3 Principles of General *Takaful*

39.3.1 Utmost Good Faith

The contract should uphold Islamic values as the main elements of any *Takaful* contract. Both participants and *Takaful* operators should apply good faith and intentions while under the contract. No one should expose others' confidential information, which will lead to the breach of contract.

39.3.2 Participant's Interest

The *Takaful* operators should clearly define the product offered to customers. It is important to avoid any attempt to defraud customers. The participant's interest should be aligned with the schemes provided. Any unclear information must be avoided in order to maintain the customer's confidence in the *Takaful* company.

39.3.3 Proximate Cause

Every participant should know that *Takaful* is an instrument to provide coverage against loss or risk to any valuable property. It is necessary to have a clear evaluation of any property to be covered and the reasons that the risk has occurred. There should be a distinction between any related incident and others that are similar.

39.3.4 Indemnity

The *Takaful* contract is a contract of indemnity, that is, a payment will be made to participants for any loss sustained. The *Takaful* company will provide financial assistance to each of its customer according to their policy.

39.4 General *Takaful* Schemes

General *Takaful* business in traditionally divided into five main classes: motor *Takaful*, marine *Takaful*, miscellaneous and accident *Takaful*, and engineering *Takaful*. The schemes afforded under the various divisions are as follows:

39.4.1 Fire Takaful

- Basic Fire
- Fire and Allied Perils
- Business Interruption
- House Owners
- Householders
- *Rumah Desa*
- Growing Trees
- All Industrial Risk.

39.4.2 Miscellaneous and Accident Takaful

- Personal Accident
- Group Personal Accident
- Employer's Liability
- Workmen's Compensation
- Burglary
- Public Liability
- Money
- Fidelity Guarantee
- All Risks
- Computer (Material Damage)
- Equipment All Risks
- Plate Glass

- Professional Indemnity/ Malpractice
- Personal Accident For Pilgrims
- Sprinkler Leakage.

39.4.3 Engineering Takaful

- Bonds
- Boilers and Pressure Vessel
- Contractor's All Risk
- Storage Tanks
- Machinery Breakdown
- Loss of Profit (Machinery)
- Erection All Risks.

39.4.4 Motor Takaful

- Private Car
- Motorcycles
- Commercial Vehicles
- Special Types.

39.5 Operation of General *Takaful* Business

General *Takaful* schemes are designed to meet the individual needs or organisation's purposes. The *Takaful* concept should be clearly aligned with Shari'ah and is based on the Islamic principles of *Takaful* and *Al-Mudharabah*. Any chance of fraud or uncertainty should be avoided in order to confirm its validity. In simple terms, the *Takaful* operator will collect the payments from the participant (*Shahib ul-Mal*) and function as fund manager on their behalf. The *Takaful* company as fund manager will invest the instalments and the profit resulting from the investment will be put back into the fund.

39.6 Examples of General *Takaful* Schemes

Everybody is exposed to risks, including the danger of fire especially to our house, office or business buildings. The implications of fire are huge. Fire not only damages our buildings but also endangers our lives.

And now the *Takaful* Fire Scheme enables everyone to protect our property against fire.

- Coverage: For any loss or damages caused by fire, explosion or lightning
- Additional Coverage: Earthquake, windstorm, aircraft damage, riot and explosion
- Assets covered: Buildings, stocks and householders
- Coverage amount: The coverage will be based on the current market value because the price is unstable overtime
- Information needed: Location of building, structure of building, occupation of building and total amount of property covered.

39.7 Claims Procedures

39.7.1 Duties

In the event of this risk becoming reality, there are certain procedures that need to be followed or upheld by the participant.

Implied Duties
It has to be known that the claim will not be easily transferred to the participant. The participant needs to take all possible steps in order to minimise the chance of loss of property. Their property should thus not be exposed to risk or any attempt at causing damage.

Express Duties
Almost all certificates require the company to be notified immediately of any event which could give rise to a claim under the certificate, and to provide full particulars within a stipulated period, say seven, 15 or 30 days. It is essential that the company is notified as soon as possible in order that a full investigation of the circumstances can be made.

39.7.2 Claim Forms

The participant should complete the form accordingly and clearly. The place of loss, the nature of loss and the time at which it occurred should be noted precisely. Any ambiguous information will result in the claim being rejected.

39.7.3 Proof of Loss

The important thing for every participant to prove and convince the *Takaful* operator is through doctor's certificate or any document that recognises the losses or damages of protected property. Besides, the evaluation of the total loss should be similar to the actual damages.

39.7.4 Claim Settlement

After all parties have followed the duties then a claim can be made. This is the stage where the transfer of money happens. The actual settlement depends on a number of factors, including the nature of the cover and so on.

39.8 Application

As noted above, a claim is an application by a participant to seek indemnity for losses provide for under a *Takaful* contract. This is the step needed to make a claim, which the participant is able to exercise as his rights under the contract, and all efforts must be taken to ensure that such rights are duly honoured. The *Takaful* company functions as fund manager on behalf of the participant. Thus, the *Takaful* operator possesses the great responsibility of managing the participant's money. They are the body that ensures that all applications made by participants are free from *Gharar* or any element of gambling, which are against Islamic principles and values. Any *Takaful* operator needs to minimise risks that will lead to failure in managing or upholding the trust of others. Therefore, processing claims is a key issue, one that requires further attention by the *Takaful* company in order to maintain its value to customers.

The handling of a claim is one of the most complicated procedures of the *Takaful* operation. It requires not only a wide and thorough knowledge of the various classes of *Takaful* schemes buts also a working knowledge of how to overcome each issue exists while exercising the claims. The general procedure for claims applicable to all classes of general *Takaful* schemes is as follows.

39.8.1 Notice of Claim

The participant may submit the claim either personally to the *Takaful* operator or the company or through the authorised representative acting on behalf such as his solicitor, broker or agent.

39.8.2 Proof of Loss

It is necessary to complete the claim form correctly because the *Takaful* operator will then justify the claim for further action. The information should be clearly justified, such as the total value of losses or cause of damages that will differentiate the true or fraudulent application. Usually, participants will use the approval from the recognised party in order to prove loss to the *Takaful* company.

39.8.3 Investigation

Sometimes it is crucial to determine the truth of the claim. The participants will use a variety of means to ensure the success of the claims application. Therefore, further investigation needs to be implemented to determine the validity of the information. All of the documents need to be examined thoroughly by the investigator. The *Takaful* operator must be fully satisfied with all of the documents presented by the participant. The investigation should not take a long time, because the delay of payment may affect the participant emotionally and mentally. It is suggested that an independent body investigate the document, so as to avoid any inconvenience or false evaluation of the claim application.

39.8.4 Settlement of Claim

If it is proven that the claim application is valid in accordance to the terms of the certificate, then arrangement for settlement of claim will be made immediately.

39.9 Procedure for Non-Claim *Takaful*

39.9.1 Notification

Any occurrence of event should be made to the *Takaful* operator. The *Takaful* operator will identify the claim for any further actions. Any unfulfilled or unclear information will be rejected or to be completed by the participant. All information should be precisely determined.

39.9.2 Preliminary Check

This the ambiguous step while having the evaluation of each claim made. The *Takaful* officer should have better guidelines for this process. Some participants have attempted to cheat the officer by providing unnecessary information to give full confidence to the claim officer. Once the notification is made, the officer needs to check the notification and immediate action must be taken.

39.9.3 Registration of Claim

While the notification file is open, the claim is immediately registered. There should no delay of registration because the participant needs financial assistance accordingly. Delay of payment will affect the participant in a negative way.

39.9.4 Documentation and Proof of Loss

This is the part where many participants fail to fulfil the obligations. Such participants take for granted the necessaries for completing all the documents. The entire claim form should be submitted before the claim is considered. The justification of loss or damage should be weighted more by the participants because any unclear information will affect the amount of claim that can be given to the claimant.

39.9.5 Claim Settlement

The offer of a claim must be made immediately. It must be within the limits of the operator.

39.10 Procedures for Claim *Takaful*

39.10.1 Types of Claim

If it is proven that the motor *Takaful* is appropriate, it may have arisen due to the following circumstances. Loss of own vehicle (applicable only to comprehensive cover):

- Partial Loss
- Total Loss
- Theft
- Windscreen.

39.10.2 Liability to Third Party

- Damage to property belonging to a third party and/or
- Death and/or bodily injury to third party.

39.10.3 Notification

A condition precedent to liability in accordance with the terms and conditions of the motor *Takaful* certificate, the participant must notify the *Takaful* operator of any event which may give rise to a claim. Notification to the claim must be made by the participant himself in order to avoid potential fraud.

39.10.4 Notification Form

Preliminary Loss Advice Form (PLA Form).

A preliminary interview will be conducted with the participant regarding the occurrence of the event giving rise to a claim. The objective of this interview is to solicit as much information about the event as possible. The initial information gathered will be entered into the PLA form. At the same time, proper advice would be given to the participant to enable him to take appropriate action and to prepare the necessary documents to support the claim.

39.10.5 Claim Form

If the claim application is straightforward and deemed that a claim form can be completed by the participant on the spot, then the completion of the PLA will not be necessary. The Motor Claim Form is a controlled document and therefore its insurance must be property registered and accounted for.

39.10.6 Registration of Claim

The information provided in the PLA Form or Claim Form would help the operator:

- to identify the type of potential liability;
- to verify the type of cover and liability of the operator in respect of the occurrence reported;
- to determine whether an investigation will be conducted.

However, the most important purpose of the information is to enable the setting up of a reserve. Motor *Takaful* is a "long-tail" business and as such adequate reserving would be crucial, particularly in relation to third-party liability. Inadequate provision of reserves will lead to situation of "paying today's claims from tomorrow's Takaful contribution."

39.11 Conclusion

The nature of insurance is such that it needs to be organised in a very Islamic way. In General *Takaful* claims, non-claim procedures, policies and renewal, we must be clear that the procedures are managed properly without creating doubt in the participant as well as the insurer. The insurer plays a vital role in convincing the participant that their products are in line with Islamic principles. Once there is any room for doubt in the operator and also the participant, either one of the parties will find some difficulties in implementing the rules governing the management of claim procedures, policies and renewal of general *Takaful*. It can be concluded that the claim, non-claim procedure, renewal and policies of general *Takaful* are bound up with the Shari'ah guidelines that contain the principle as set out in the Qur'an and hadith Rasullullah (saw). According to jurists' General *Takaful* claim, non-claim procedure, renewal and policies are based on a buying and selling contract according to Islam because of the presence of the following elements: *Gharar*, *Maisir*, *Riba*.

There is a need to make the *Takaful* a system that is capable of being accommodated in any Islamic jurisdiction, if it not in most jurisdictions of the world. There is a need to have a fresh approach to the application of concepts of claim, non-claim procedures, renewal policies for operation systems, to innovation and product development and the management of *Takaful* business. The *Takaful* system is a fair and ethical system for the consumer. For this reason, it appeals as a product for its good qualities and not just because it is Islamic. These fundamental qualities need to be properly explained, systematically and persistently, to increase awareness of *Takaful*.

References

1. Ali, A. Y. (n.d.), The Holy Qur'an, Text and Translation.
2. *Claim Procedures in General Takaful*, *Takaful* Malaysia, *Takaful* Ikhlas, *Takaful* Nasional and others.
3. Billah, M. M. (2003), Islamic and Modern Insurance: Principles and Practice. Ilmiah Publishers, Malaysia.
4. Billah, M. Ma'sum (2002), *Manual of Principles and Practices of Takaful and Re-Takaful*, International Islamic University, Malaysia p. 47

CHAPTER 40

Claims Procedure in Family *Takaful*

40.1 Introduction

As outlined earlier in this book, Family *Takaful* is a form of financial assurance that provides coverage against untimely death, accident and permanent disability. It is prescribed in the *Takaful* Act 1984. A participant would receive their benefits after going through the requisite claim procedures. These claim procedures are important to ensure that the benefits are distributed to the right parties. Whereas the distribution of benefits would determine the appropriate coverage received by participants due to their conditions. This chapter focuses on the claim procedures and the distribution of benefits.

40.2 Central Idea

In a Family *Takaful*, there are two different accounts:

- Participant's Account (PA)
- Participant's Special Account (PSA).

It is acknowledged that, the idea of this chapter/product is significantly contributed by the practices / experiences / thoughts of Bank Negara, *Takaful* Malaysia, *Takaful* Ikhlas, *Takaful* Nasional, Etiqa *Takaful*, IBFIM, IIUM, MII and others (Malaysia).

Mohd Ma'Sum Billah, *Islamic Insurance Products*,
https://doi.org/10.1007/978-3-030-17681-5_40

Table 40.1 Central idea

Takaful *Malaysia*	Takaful *Nasional*
Death claim	Death claim
Family rider supplementary claim	Permanent total disability claim
Permanent total disability claim	Accidental death benefit claim
Hospitalisation claim	Hospitalisation benefit claim
Permanent disablement arising from accident	Critical Illness claim

Source: Author's collection

PA is a form of savings and investment account. Normally, PA received a larger proportion of contributions than PSA. PSA is a fund utilised to pay *Takaful* compensation to participants who are entitled to a claim. In general, the participant will determine the proportion of each account. Under Family *Takaful*, there are two types of plans, that is, individual and group plans. In any case, a participant could receive a pay out from PA and PSA. However, a sum of the PSA is only claimable for certain circumstances. The Family *Takaful* Plan for *Takaful* Malaysia Berhad and *Takaful* National Malaysia Berhad consists of five types of plans (Table 40.1):

Generally, these are the procedures practiced by both *Takaful* companies:

Step 1: A participant or heirs has to inform about the type of claims to be made in written to the Family *Takaful* Section/Branch/*Takaful* agents.
Step 2: The claimant has to fill in the relevant claim forms.
Step 3: The claimant must provide the relevant documents as listed in required documents.
(Note: copies of death certificate, burial certificate and police report should be certified.)
Step 4: The completed form and the required documents must be submitted to Family *Takaful* Claims Section/ Branch/*Takaful* agents.
(Note: The claimant should keep copies of all documents submitted.)
Step 5: Family *Takaful* Claims Section will process the claim accordingly. If the claim is approved, it will be forwarded to Account Section.
Step 6: Account Section will issue cheque for the claim and sent it back to Claims Section for record updating.
Step 7: Then the Claims Section will send the cheque to Family *Takaful* Section/Branch/*Takaful* agents and the branch/section will inform the claimant to collect the cheque.

40.3 Death Claim

Claim notification: forward to the company within 90 days. Items required:

- Claim form under Family *Takaful* Plan/Mortgage—ensure that claim reason is completed, whether division A (illness) or B (accident)
- Copy of death certificate
- Copy of burial permit
- Copy of identity card
- Police report—compulsory if involved in road traffic accident and a participant in personal accident coverage
- Medical report—in general is not required unless requested by the company
- Original certificate of Family *Takaful* Plan for death of participant.

40.4 Family Rider Supplementary Claim

Claim notification: forward to the company within 90 days.

- Claim form under Family *Takaful* Plan/Mortgage—ensure that reason for claim is completed, whether division A (illness) or B (accident)
- Copy of identity card or birth certificate for children
- Copy of death certificate
- Copy of burial permit
- Medical report—in general is not required unless requested by company.

40.5 Permanent Total Disability Claim

Claim notification: forward to the company within 90 days.

- Claim form under Family *Takaful* Plan/Mortgage—ensure that reason for claim is completed, whether division A (illness) or B (accident)
- Copy of identity card
- Copy of termination letter from employer
- Medical board panel report
- Copy of police report, if disability occurs because of accident
- 'Medical attendant report' from specialist doctor—requested by company if the disability is not confirmed
- Original certificate of Family *Takaful* Plan.

40.6 Hospitalisation Claim

Claim notification: forward to the company within 10 days.

- Claim form Family *Takaful* Plan/Mortgage—ensure that reason for claim is completed, whether division A (illness) or B (accident)
- Copy of identity card
- Discharge note/ward chit or any statement produced by the hospital or clinic
- Copy of police report, if accidental
- Medical report from hospital or clinic.

40.7 Permanent Disablement Arising of Accident

Claim notification: forward to the company within 20 days.

- Claim form Family *Takaful* Plan/Mortgage—ensure that reason for claim is completed, whether division A (illness) or B (accident)
- Police report or industrial accident report—compulsory
- Medical report—compulsory and must be completed by the doctor who treated the participant
- Copy of identity card
- Photos, which show the disability—if requested by company.

Note: all copies must be certified.

Meanwhile, the required documents for *Takaful* National Malaysia Berhad claims are shown in the following table (Table 40.2):

40.8 Distribution of Benefits of Family *Takaful*

Generally, the participant in this sort of policy should nominate one or more person as a nominee. Under the *Takaful* scheme, the nominee shall be a mere trustee or executor (/executrix) or manager who will receive the benefits from the policy and distribute these among the legal heirs according to principle of *Faraid*. In other words, the benefit of Family *Takaful* shall be treated as estate. However, for non-Muslims, the benefits shall be distributed according to the Malaysia Distribution Act 1958, and the nominees shall not be the absolute beneficiaries. The distribution of benefits of Family *Takaful* depends upon certain circumstances. Under the Individual Plan, the benefits are as follows:

Table 40.2 Documents for *Takaful* National Malaysia Berhad claims

Documents/claims type	*AD*	*DI*	*PTDI*	*PTDA*	*ADB*	*CI*	*HB*
Individual family *Takaful* plan claim form	√	√	√	√	√	-	-
Individual family *Takaful* plan authorisation claim form	√	√	√	√	√	√	√
Medical report form	-	√	-	-	-	√	-
Medical attendant's report on permanent total disability form	-	-	√	√	-	-	-
Hospitalisation benefit claim form	-	-	-	-	-	-	√
Critical Illness rider claim form	-	-	-	-	-	√	-
Certified true copy of death/burial certificate	√	√	-	-	√	-	-
Certified true copy of police report	√	-	-	√	√	-	-
Certified true copy of post-mortem report (if any)	√	-	-	-	√	-	-
Copy of Attendance Record from Employer (if needed)	-	√	√	-	-	-	-
Original family *Takaful* plan certificate	√	√	√	√	√	-	-
Certified true copy of identity card	√	√	√	√	√	√	√
Copy of hospital's bill/discharge note	-	-	-	-	-	-	√

Source: Author's collection

Key: *AD* accidental death, *DI* Death due to illness, *PTDI* permanent total disability due to Illness, *PTDA* permanent total disability due to accident, *ADB* accidental death benefit, *CI* critical illness, *HB* hospitalisation benefit

In the event that the participant dies before the date of maturity, the *Takaful* company shall pay the benefits to the proper claimant, the administrator, executor or nominee of the participant as follows:

- From PA: They will receive all instalments that have been pooled into the PA from the date of the participation to the date of participant's death, including the profits from the investments of the instalments in the PA.
- From PSA: The beneficiaries will receive a portion of PSA account according to their financial status. A beneficiary of good financial condition will receive a smaller portion than needy people.

In the event that the participant is still alive upon maturity of the policy, the *Takaful* compensation shall be paid to the participant in the following manner:

- From PA: The participant will receive the total amount of contribution that been paid during the tenure of participation, plus profits from investments that are credited to the PA.
- From PSA: According to Shari'ah principles, the participant will not receive anything from the PSA account. Essentially, these *Takaful* funds belong to all participants. The basic function of the funds is to provide financial assistance, in the form of claim benefits, to any participant who suffers a loss due to a defined misfortune. In this sense, *Takaful* assumes the role of helping one another at times of need by participants. Proceeds from the claim benefits come from the collected contributions accumulated in the respective *Takaful* funds. However, some *Takaful* operators will pay a portion from the PSA to gain competitive advantage over conventional life insurance.

In the event that the participant is compelled to surrender or cancel their participation before the maturity date of the *Takaful* plan, the distribution of benefits are as follows:

- From PA: The participant shall be entitled to receive the amount of his contributions and profits from the investments credited into his PA. However, the management expenses would be charged to the participant.
- From PSA: The participant would not receive any amount from PSA accounts.

40.9 Shari'ah Ruling

40.9.1 Mutual Co-operation

Allah (swt) says:

> Help ye one another in righteousness and piety. (Al-Maidah: 5: 2)

The concept of *Takaful* is based on mutual co-operation and solidarity of people by participating in a *Takaful* scheme. Mutual co-operation is clearly applied in the family *Takaful* scheme, whereby all participants will contribute a portion of their premium into a *Tabarru'* fund (PSA). The participant who is in need will receive financial assistance from the *Tabarru'* fund.

40.9.2 Misappropriation of Wealth

Allah (swt) says:

> And do not eat up your property among yourselves for vanities, nor use it as bait for the judges, with intent that ye may eat up wrongfully and knowingly a little of [other] people's property. (Al-Baqarah, 2: 188)

The *Takaful* operator is responsible for managing the wealth (money) of the participants in an appropriate way. The premium paid is divided into two different accounts, PA and PSA. The *Takaful* operator does not charge any interest to the participants as Allah has prohibited all human-kind from taking one another's property and stresses the importance of respecting other people's rights.

40.9.3 Flexibility

Allah (swt) says:

> God (Allah) intends every facility for you; He does not want to put to difficulties. (Al-Baqarah, 2: 185)

Takaful operation is one of the facilities by which Muslims manage financial risk. For example, in the case of death, the family of the deceased will get the benefit. They will receive the benefit from both PA and PSA. So, the orphans can still manage to continue their studies by using the money. If their father is not a participant in a *Takaful* scheme, they may not able to do so.

40.9.4 Contract

Allah (swt) says:

> O ye who believe! Fulfil (all) obligations. (Al-Maidah, 5: 1)

Basically, participating in a *Takaful* scheme is one type of contract. The *Takaful* contract is based on the agreed terms and conditions signed by both the seller (*Takaful* operator) and the buyer (participants). So, a participant is eligible to receive claim benefits as long as they fulfil the terms and conditions as agreed before. Meanwhile, the *Takaful* operator is responsible for managing the contributions paid appropriately.

40.9.5 Gharar *in Family* Takaful

Allah (swt) says:

> Every soul shall have a taste of death. (Al-Imran, 3:185)

Some people have suggested that Islamic life insurance (Family *Takaful*) contains *Gharar* (uncertainty in either the object or the subject matter of a transaction). Some people claim that the subject matter (death) is not certain, which may indicate that the element of *Gharar* involved. Whereas in the real practices, the subject matter of a life insurance policy/Family *Takaful* is the life and the death of the assured person is not uncertain but definite. In this case, we can say that the element of *Gharar* does not exist in the Family *Takaful* scheme.

40.9.6 Charity

Allah (swt) says:

> Alms are for the poor and the needy. (Al-Tawbah, 9: 60)

A portion of premium paid by the participant would be contributed in PSA. The PSA is created on the principle of necessity by providing future material/financial protection for the society. Therefore, in Family *Takaful*, once the participant dies, his dependants are entitled to receive compensation from the PA plus a reasonable amount of donation from the PSA. This situation shows the social security (offering something valuable for the noble cause of the welfare of others) provided by family *Takaful*.

40.9.7 Saving for Security

> Narrated by Amir bin Saad bin Abi Waqas (r), The Holy Prophet (saw) said: "Verily it better for you to leave your offspring wealthy than to leave them poor asking others for help." (Sahih al-Bukhari)

40.9.8 Social Security

Narrated by Safwan bin Salim (r), the Holy Prophet (saw) said: "The one who looks after and works for a widow and for a poor person is like a warrior fighting for the cause of Allah (swt) or like a person who fasts during the day and prays overnight." (Sahih al-Bukhari)

Every person is encouraged to leave their dependants wealthy rather than poor. This is applied by the Family *Takaful* concept, which provides future material protection for unfortunate offspring upon the death of the assured.

40.9.9 Taking Back Donation/Gift

Ibn 'Abbas (ra) reported that the Messengers of Allah (swt) said: "He who takes his gift/donation back is like a dog, which eats its own vomit." But there is no such evil simile for us.

Ibn 'Umar and Ibn 'Abbas (ra) reported that the Messenger of Allah (swt) said: "It is not lawful for a man to give a gift and afterwards to take it back, except a father regarding what he gives his child. The parable of one who gives a gift and then takes it back is like the parable of a dog, which eats till it is satisfied, then vomits and then eats its vomit once again."

In the relationship to Family *Takaful*, it has been mentioned that the paid contributions from a participant may be divided into two portions. One portion may be regarded as partial capital to *Al-Mudharabah* financing arrangement (PA), while the remaining portion would be given away as the *Tabarru'*, that is, the PSA. The portion which is in PSA cannot be taken back because the account is a *Tabarru'* fund. The concept of *Tabarru'* is such that once a person has given away his/her possession, the ownership of the possession is not belongs to him/her anymore. In other words, for PSA account a participant who has donated is called a donor. And a donor cannot take back his/her gift/donation from the account.

40.10 Application

40.10.1 The Flow of Contribution

In the practices of *Takaful* Malaysia Bhd., the examples of the contribution paid are as follows.

A 25-year participant has participated in the Family *Takaful* Plan for ten years. He will pay the contribution of RM 1000 per annum with supplementary coverage of permanent total disability, personal accident of RM 15,000 and the hospitalisation benefits of RM 30 per day. Therefore, he should pay the additional contribution of RM 27 per annum for personal accident, RM 216 for hospitalisation benefits and family rider. Meanwhile, an RM 22 (RM 1,000 × 2.2%) from the total contribution will be credited to the PSA account, which covers permanent total disability.

The above example can be shown in the following diagram (Fig. 40.1).

Based on the previous example, the total *Takaful* benefit differs for each participant based on his/her conditions as shown below.

If the participant has passed away or suffers permanent disability, in the fifth year he/she would able to receive from his/her:

PA = RM 978 × 5 year (annual payment)	RM 4890
+ profit from 5 years investment (if any), say RM 400	RM 400
PSA = RM 1,000 × 5 year (risk period)	RM 5000
Total *Takaful* Benefit	RM 10,290

With *Takaful* Malaysia, the total benefit for the death claim will be paid in lump sum, whereas it will be paid in ten years of annual instalments for the claim of permanent total disability.

If a participant did not claim anything until the maturity, he/she is entitled to receive the benefit from:

PA = RM 978 × 10 years (the annual contribution) RM 9,780 + profit from the investment for 10 years (if any), say RM 1800	RM 1800
PSA, if there is any surplus the portion RM 1000 will be determined by the *Takaful* operator, say RM 1000	
Total *Takaful* Benefit	RM 12,580

If the participant had an accident within the period, the benefit will be distributed as below.

If the participant has passed away from the accident in the fifth year, the total benefits are:

PA = RM 978 × 5 year RM 4890 + profit from investment within 5 years (if any), say RM 400	RM 400
PSA = RM 1000 × 5 year RM 5000 (the remaining contribution that he/she should pay if he/she still alive upon the maturity date, i.e. the risk period).	
Group Family *Takaful* Fund	RM 15,000
Total *Takaful* Benefit	RM 25,290

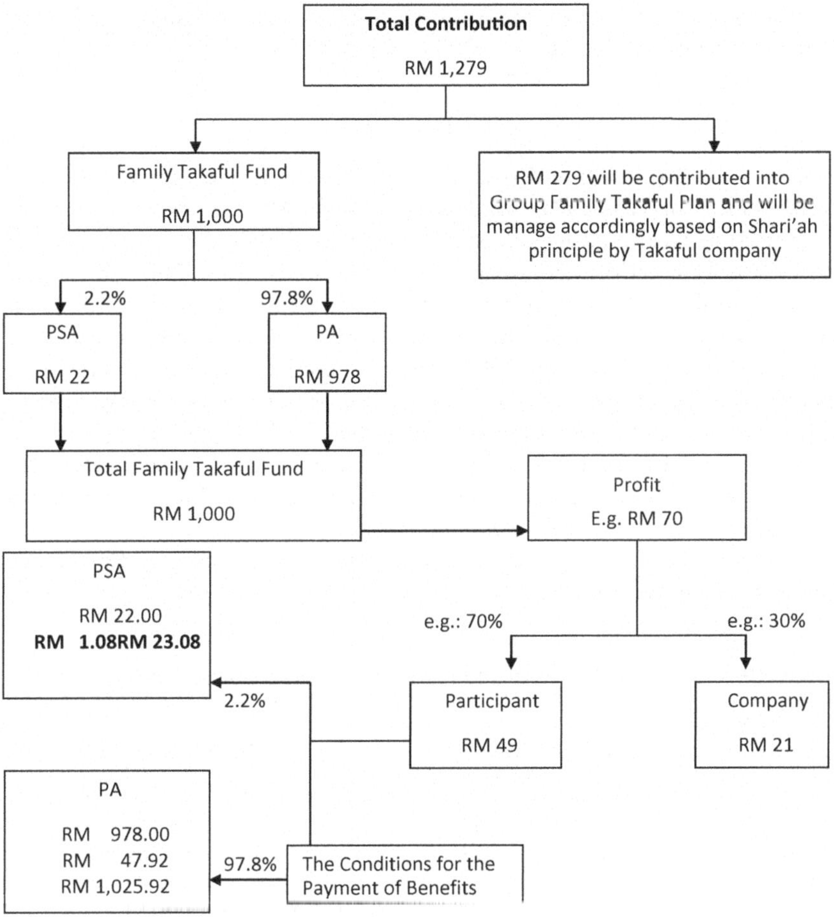

Fig. 40.1 The flow of contribution. (Source: Author's collection)

If the participant is disabled due to an accident, let us say he has lost a hand, so the benefit will be taken from the Group Family *Takaful* Fund, that is 50% from RM 15,000 = RM 7,500.

If a participant needs Hospitalisation Benefit and he has been hospitalised for five days, the claim for the benefit will be taken from the Group Family *Takaful* Fund, RM 30 × 5 days = RM 150.

If a spouse of the participant has passed away, the payment for Family Rider from Group Family *Takaful* Fund is RM 5,000.

40.11 Data

Statistics for the death and permanent total disability claims for *Takaful* Malaysia for the year 2001 can be seen in Table 40.3.

Referring to the above statistics, it is evident that the claim amounts differ based on various circumstances. For instance, June 2001 shows the largest number of death/permanent disability cases. However, the total claim amount captured for the month is only RM 107,143 compared to RM 245,651 in September 2001 which covered 14 cases only. This fluctuation may be due to certain factors such as participants' total contributions, maturity period, risk period and so on (Table 40.4).

Generally, the *Tabarru'* rate for participants is not fixed. The rate depends on participants' age and policy period. The longer the policy period, the higher the *Tabarru'* rate for them.

The flow chart in Fig. 40.2 shows the claim process practised by *Takaful* Malaysia as an example.

Table 40.3 Statistics for death and permanent total disability claims for *Takaful* Malaysia for 2001

Month	*Death/Ptd Number of Cases*	*Claims amounts (RM)*
January	18	118,053
February	11	68,760
March	7	18,405
April	7	86,419
May	20	4596
June	27	107,143
July	9	50,484
August	12	135,319
September	14	245,651
October	9	108,387
November	14	20,326
December	12	43,820
Total	**160**	**1,007,363**

Source: Author's collection

Table 40.4 *Tabarru'* Rates for PSA by *Takaful* Malaysia

Age group (years)	*Maturity period (years)*							
	10		*15*		*20*		*25*	
	D	*D+PTD*	*D*	*D+PTD*	*D*	*D+PTD*	*D*	*D+PTD*
18–25	2.0%	2.2%	3.5%	3.9%	5.0%	5.5%	5.5%	6.1%
26–30	2.0%	2.2%	3.5%	3.9%	5.0%	5.5%	6.5%	7.2%
31–35	2.5%	2.8%	4.5%	5.0%	6.5%	6.5%	9.0%	9.9%
36–40	3.5%	3.9%	6.0%	6.6%	9.0%	9.0%	12.5%	13.8%
41–45	5.0%	5.5%	8.5%	9.4%	12.5%	13.8%		
46–50	7.0%	7.7%	12.5%	13.8%				
51–55	12.5%	13.8%						

Source: Author's collection

Age Group (Years)	*Maturity Period (Years)*					
	30		*35*		*40*	
	D	*D+PTD*	*D*	*D+PTD*	*D*	*D+PTD*
18–25	7.5%	8.3%	9.5%	10.5%	12.5%	13.8%
26–30	9.0%	9.9%	12.5%	13.8%		
31–35	12.5%	13.8%				
36–40						
41–45						
46–50						
51–55						

Source: Author's collection

D Death only, *D+PTD* Death + Permanent Total Disability

40.12 Recommendations

Overall, *Takaful* Malaysia Berhad should proceed with its existing operations, which are aligned with Shari'ah principles. However, to remain competitive in the challenging insurance industry, the *Takaful* company should adopt new technology. For example, in terms of claim procedures, the *Takaful* company could design online claim forms, which would facilitate both parties in the process. Second, the *Takaful* company is suggested to implement the *Ta'awuni* model in the distribution of benefits. In real practice, the distribution of benefits by *Takaful* Malaysia is based on the

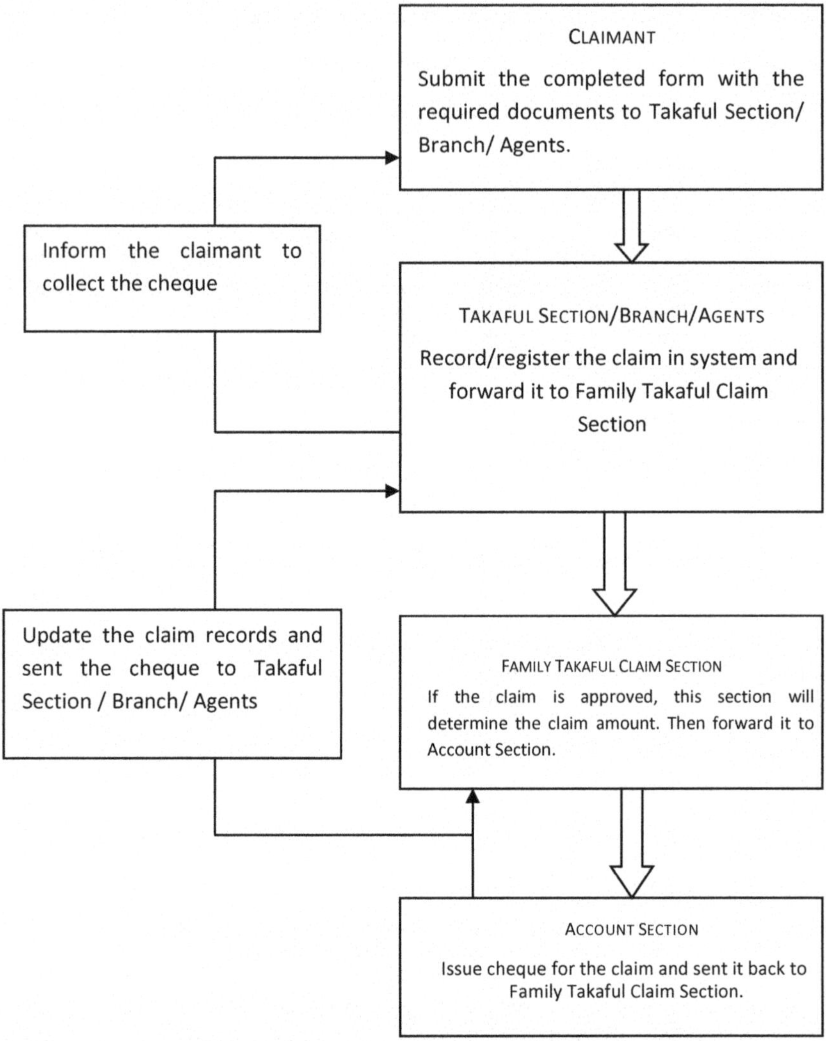

Fig. 40.2 Claim process practiced by *Takaful* Malaysia. (Source: Author's collection)

Tijari model, while the *Takaful* National Malaysia Berhad is based on *Wakalah* model where the participants receive the underwriting surplus. In the *Ta'awuni* model, the underwriting surplus should not be given to the participants in any condition. However, it must be taken by the company and be treated as service charge to the *Takaful* operator. The logic behind this is the service charges are essential for the financial stability of the company. From an Islamic point of view, there is no work without recompense. As Allah said in the Qur'anic verse:

> To them we shall pay the price of their works therein and they will not diminishingly. (Hud: 15)

The Prophet (saw) also said in his hadith:

> Pay the remuneration of the worker before his sweat dries up.

As a third suggestion, *Takaful* company also is recommended to promote their products effectively, especially in rural areas. This is because most Muslims, especially in Malaysia, lack awareness of *Takaful* concepts. Therefore, they should be exposed to the importance of *Takaful* in the welfare and development of Muslim society. Moreover, there are a number of Muslim societies who do not really understand about the importance of the differences between *Takaful* and conventional insurance. The main difference is that *Takaful* products are based on the *Tabarru'* concept, which provides sharing responsibility. If the concept is clearly understood by Muslim society, this would help them to generate a good Muslim *ummah*, who help each other when there is difficulty. Regarding this matter, Allah (swt) says:

> Help ye one another in righteousness and piety. (Qur'an 5: 2)

40.13 Conclusion

The Family *Takaful* Plan offers benefits to the participants and also *Takaful* operators. With the Family *Takaful* Plan, participants can be assured of a certain sum of money, which will go a long way to ease the financial burden of their family members in the event of untimely death. Normally, the claim procedures for *Takaful* products are quite similar to those of other companies. Furthermore, as mentioned, although the operations of the

Takaful companies in Malaysia are deemed successful and aligned with Islamic teachings, there are certain areas that need to be improved. The improvement is important in order to remain competitive in the insurance industry. For instance, they could design claim forms through their web pages, which would ease the claims process. In other words, the *Takaful* companies must provide a systematic claim procedures and transparent distribution of benefit for their customers.

References

1. Ali, A. Y. (n.d.), The Holy Qur'an, Text and Translation.
2. *Claim Procedures in Family Takaful*, *Takaful* Malaysia, *Takaful* Ikhlas, *Takaful* Nasional and others.
3. Billah, M. M. (2003), Islamic and Modern Insurance: Principles and Practice. Ilmiah Publishers, Malaysia.
4. Billah, M. Ma'sum (2002), *Manual of Principles and Practices of Takaful and Re-Takaful*, International Islamic University, Malaysia p. 47.

CHAPTER 41

Quantum of Damages in *Takaful*

41.1 Introduction

Takaful (Islamic insurance) is one of the most promising and fast developing areas in the contemporary world economy. It is a Sharī'ah-justified financing scheme adapted in the economy as an alternative to conventional insurance. Nevertheless, it is not impossible in practice that *Takaful* operations may have certain characteristics which might have some resemblance to conventional insurance. This does not mean that every mechanism of conventional insurance cannot be justified under Sharī'ah principles. The principles adapted in the quantum of damages against bodily injury or accidental death as indemnified by the *Takaful* operator is, inter alia, the phenomenon in question. It is quite clear that the indemnification provided for the victim of bodily injury or death under Islamic law is determined according to the principle of ***al-Damān*** (compensation) and ***al-Diyāh*** (bloodwit). But for the quantum of damages in *Takaful* practices today, whether the doctrine of ***al-Diyāh*** is adapted or not, it is useful to examine the possibilities for the *Takaful* operator to apply the doctrine of ***al-Diyāh*** and ***al-Damān*** in their quantum of damages. An attempt is, however, made in this chapter to arrive at a harmonisation of the doctrines of ***al-Diyāh*** and ***al-Damān*** in terms of the quantum of damages against accidental death or bodily injury.

Mohd Ma'Sum Billah, *Islamic Insurance Products*,
https://doi.org/10.1007/978-3-030-17681-5_41

41.2 Overview

Under Islamic law, damages are awarded to the victim of a bodily injury or death caused by an unintentional act mainly according to the principles of *al-Diyāh* (bloodwit) and *al-Damān* (compensation). The *Takaful* (Islamic insurance) practices in the contemporary world are one of the Sharī'ah-recognised financial schemes, adapted as an alternative to insurance practices under the conventional economy. Despite the fact that *Takaful* is an Islamic-based institution, in its operations it resembles certain aspects of existing common law principles, especially the rules relating to quantum of damages against bodily injury or death. Now, the question here is why do *Takaful* operators have to adopt the common law principles? Is it because common law influence is unavoidable or there is no solution given by the Sharī'ah principles or no model so far discovered by the *Ulamā* as to the principles relating to the question of damages? It is suggested that neither does the common law influence have an effect nor is there is no solution in the Sharī'ah for the above issue. The fact is that it is perhaps the *Ulamā* who have so far not come up with an Islamic applied model of principles for the quantum of damages appropriate in today's *Takaful* operations.

Therefore, this chapter examines the doctrines of *al-Diyāh* and *al-Damān* in the light of contemporary reality and outlines how to apply the doctrine of *al-Diyāh* as a solution to the quantum of damages in the *Takaful* industry, and as an apt alternative to principles applied under conventional insurance practices.

41.3 *Al-Diyāh* (Bloodwit)

The word *al-Diyāh* means bloodwit or monetary compensation imposed against a person accused of homicide and in favour of the victim or his or her legal beneficiaries. *Al-Diyāh* is also applied in cases of compensation for bodily injury. This doctrine is a pecuniary substitute for capital sentence *al-Qisās* (retaliation) against homicide or bodily injury. The doctrine of *Qisās* (retaliation) and its substitute *al-Diyāh* are ordained in the Qur'ān. The strict principle against homicide as ruled against as follows:

> We ordained therein for them: "Life for life, eye for eye, nose for nose, ear for ear, tooth for tooth, and wounds equal for equal." But if any one remits the retaliation by way of charity, it is an act of atonement for himself. (Qur'an, 5: 45)

But in the following *ayat* Allah (swt) provides a substitute to retaliation, which is *al-Diyāh*:

> O ye who believe! The law of equality is prescribed to you in cases of murder: The free for free, the slave for the slave, the woman for the woman. But if any remission is made by the brother of the slain, then grant any reasonable demand, and compensate him with handsome gratitude. This is a concession and a mercy from your Lord. After this, whoever exceeds the limits shall be in grave penalty. (Qur'an, 2: 178)

Furthermore, Allah (swt) ruled the extension of the application of *al-Diyāh* in the following *ayat*:

> Never should a believer kill a believer; but [if it happens] by mistake [compensation is due]; if one [so] kills a believer, it is ordained that he should free a believing slave, and pay compensation to the deceased's family, unless they remit it freely. If the deceased's belonged to a people at war with you, and he was a believer. The freeing of a believing slave [is enough]. If he belonged to a people with whom ye have a treaty of mutual alliance, compensation should be paid to his family, and believing slave be freed. For those who find this beyond their means, [what is prescribed is] a fast for two months running; by way of repentance to Allah; for Allah hath all knowledge and all wisdom. (Exodus, 21:23–25)

In the Bible an identical sanction appears for the penalty against a bodily injury or death as follows:

> And if any mischief follow, then thou shall give life for life, eye for eye, tooth for tooth, hand for hand, foot for foot, burning for burning, wound for wound, stripe for stripe. (Exodus, 21: 23–25)

From the above divine rulings, it is understood that for a homicide punishment is varied against the accused depending on the nature of the offence. The strict ruling for the homicide or bodily injury is the *Qisās*. However, the victim's family can select to eliminate the demand of *Qisās* and choose to substitute it with forgiveness or monetary compensation. The monetary compensation here was developed by the doctrine of *al-Diyāh*. In cases of homicide, with resemblance to intentional killing or homicide by mistake and indirect killing, the doctrine of *Qisās* shall not be applied as compensation. An alternative to this is blood-money and fasting for two consecutive months, or blood-money and freeing a slave. It is also understood by the above rulings that the doctrine of *al-Diyāh* is applicable only to awarding monetary compensation to the victim or his family, against the accused for the homicide or bodily injury, but not for the loss of property or any other form of damages or loss.

41.4 Governing Principles of *Al-Diyāh* (E.C. Howard, 1977)

The doctrine of *al-Diyāh* can be applied as monetary compensation for homicide or bodily injury in five basic situations:

Al-Qatl al-'Amd (intentional homicide), where the heirs of the deceased may exercise the right:

- to demand a retaliation be executed against the accused; or
- to demand that the accused should pay *al-Diyāh*; or
- to extend forgiveness to the accused.

The following hadith justifies this, as the Prophet (saw) said:

> He who commits wilful murder shall be handed over to the heirs of the deceased, and they may kill him if they like or may accept blood-money if they so choose. (Mishkat Al-Masabih, Book 15, (Diyāh) Chapter 1)

Al-Qalt Shibhu al-'Amd (culpable homicide): not amounting to murder. In this category of homicide, the accused is liable to free a believer. She slave or fasting for two consecutive months and also bloodwit, which is to be paid by the paternal relatives of the accused unless the deceased family remits it as alms (Qur'an, 4: 92).

Al-Qatl bi al-Khatā (manslaughter). The accused in this kind of offence is subject to the following sentences:

- to free a believer, a female slave;
- fast for two months, should the accused be unable to free a slave;
- blood-money to be paid by the paternal relatives of the accused, unless this blood-money is remitted by the heirs of the deceased as alms. (Ullah, M.W., 1982)

The author of *al-Hidāyah* views it that as far as the legal consequences are concerned *al-Qatl Shibhu al-'Amd* and *al-Qatl bi al-Khatā* are in the same platform (ibid.).

41.4.1 Al-Qatl bi al-Sabab (Indirect Homicide)

If someone brings about the death of another person indirectly, such as through digging a well and someone falls into it and dies as a result, then the legal consequence in this category of homicide is the payment of *al-Diyāh* by the *Āqilah* (paternal relatives of the accused) (*Shorter Encyclopaedia of Islam*, p. 229).

41.4.2 Al-Juruh *(Bodily Injury)*

This is a kind of offence caused intentionally by the accused, whereby the victim chooses to accept *al-Diyāh* instead of *al-Qisās*, or it could be an injury, which is caused by the accused accidentally. The above principle is further clarified and justified by the following rulings of the Holy Prophet (saw), he was quoted saying:

> Abu Bakr (r) reported that the messenger of Allah (swt) wrote to the inhabitants of Yemen and there was in his letter: who so kills a believer unjustly will suffer retaliation for what his hand has done unless the relatives of the murdered man consent otherwise. And there is it was: A man shall be killed for [the murder of] a woman. And therein it was: For the [murder of] a life there is bloodwit of 100 camels, 100 dinars on the owner of gold, for a nose which has been cut off from the root, its indemnity 100 camels and there is indemnity of murder in case of teeth, there is indemnity of murder in case of lips, there is indemnity of murder in case of testicles, there is indemnity of murder in case of penis, there is indemnity of murder in case of backbone, there is indemnity of murder in case of two eyes. There is half of the indemnity of murder in case of one foot, there is one third of bloodwit in case of wound in the head, there is one third of bloodwit in case of wound in stomach. In case of the fracture of a bone in head there is indemnity of 15 camels; in case of a finger out of the fingers of hand, each toe there are 10 camels, and in case of tooth there are five camels. (Mishkat al-Masabih, Kitab Al-Diyāh, Hadith 25)

From this prophetic sanction it is understood that for an intentional homicide the punishment is retaliation, but if the relatives of the deceased eliminate the sentence of retaliation and choose to demand *al-Diyāh* from the accused, then it is allowed. The bloodwit, therefore, is not necessarily awarded only against homicide but also applies in cases of bodily injury. For bodily injury the amount of *al-Diyāh* varies depending on the significance of the organ of the victim. To sum up, the principles of *al-Diyāh* can only be applied in accidental death or bodily injury but not against damage to property, economic loss, future earnings, medical expenses or any other form of damages. They may be compensated under the broad principles of *al-Damān*, which will be analysed later.

41.5 Application of *Al-Diyāh*

In the contemporary world, not only in secular states but also in most of the Islamic countries the application of the law relating to compensation imposed against personal injury or death resulting from negligence, is mainly based on the principles of modern law (common law, modern legislation, etc.). It is thus sad to note here that the institution of *al-Diyāh* survives in the contemporary world only just by name. Although the doctrine of *al-Diyāh* used to be the able institution, which ruled the aspect of compensation against accidental death or personal injury in the teachings of Islam. Despite this fact, there are some Islamic countries which apply the institution of *al-Diyāh* in today's world, which seemed to be in line with the customs of their respective states and are analogous to ancient Arabian customs, though they defer from tribe to tribe and often contradict the spirit of the *Qur'ān* and the rules of Islamic law (Amin, S.H., 1989). In this section an attempt is made to highlight the Islamic countries who somehow apply the doctrine of *al-Diyāh* in the contemporary practices of compensation against homicide or bodily injury resulting from one's negligence.

Among the Islamic countries that apply *al-Diyāh* principles in the early twenty-first century are Saudi Arabia, Pakistan, Syria, Egypt, Jordan and probably few other Arab states. Among the Arab tribes there is a practice of obligatory *al-Diyāh* in cases of homicide as well as in bodily injury cases, except in deliberate homicide. The composition of *al-Diyāh* varies from tribe to tribe, 40 male camels only, 40 male camels and a virgin girl, a sum of money for example in Egypt, £E400 or £E300 or £E150. The *al-Diyāh* of woman is markedly greater than of a man. In practice, in certain tribes the *al-Diyāh* of woman is four or eight times the amount of man's *al-Diyāh* (ibid.). In the Ottoman Empire, despite the modernisation in the middle of the nineteenth century, the law relating to compensation of loss suffered resulting from death or bodily injury was maintained based on the principles of *al-Qisās* and *al-Diyāh* under the terms of the Ottoman Penal Code of 1863. The amount of *al-Diyāh* was then officially fixed at *f*D224. Unfortunately, all this has now disappeared from positive legislative enactment (ibid.).

In Saudi Arabia, the institution of *al-Diyāh* is recognised in case of compensation for homicide or bodily injury. The amount of *al-Diyāh* was set in Saudi Arabia at 800 Maria Teresa dollars. In 1981, the *al-Diyāh* was set at 100,000 Saudi Riyals for accidental homicide, and 110,000 riyals for semi-intentional homicide (Kingdom of Saudi Arabia, Council of Ministers, resolution No. 734 (5/5/1396). The liability for personal injuries, a proportion of total *al-Diyāh*, will be payable by analogy and mathematical relationship. As *al-Diyāh* for fatal accidents is fixed at almost £18,200, an injury stopping short of death entails a proportionate amount compared with total destruction of the person. In other words, various losses and injuries to a person's body are assessed against the total damages for death of 100 camels. In practice, this means that the Sharī'ah court will award a percentage of 100 camels, which correspond to the proportionate depreciation in value that a 'slave' person would have suffered had he undergone the same injury. Accordingly, the injuries sustained by an injured party merit only a small portion of the total *al-Diyāh*. In addition to this, in Saudi Arabia moral injuries (pain and suffering) were not recognised under the principles of *al-Diyāh* (Amin S.H. n.d). However, Article 76 of the Labour and Workers Regulations of 1969 provides indemnity for moral injuries (pain and suffering) (Labour and Workers Regulations (Saudi Arabia), 1969).

In Pakistan, on the other hand, the government endorsed an ordinance called *Offences against human body (enforcement of Qisās and Diyāh)* draft ordinance, 1981, which provides an exclusive provision relating to *al-Diyāh* and *Qisās* against death and bodily injury to human beings. The law executed under this ordinance is based on the principles of *Hanāfi* schools of Islamic jurisprudence. The amount of *al-Diyāh* under this ordinance is awarded on a monetary calculation. From this country survey of the Arab states it has been observed that most adopt Islamic law more or less in some way, but as far as compensation against bodily injury or accidental death is concerned the doctrine of *al-Diyāh* is not generally applied—save in some states as highlighted earlier. However, states such as

Bahrain, Iran, Iraq, Kuwait, Lebanon, Oman, North Yemen, Qatar and the United Arab Emirates apply the law relating to compensation against bodily injury or death, which is based on their respective made legislations and not based on the institution of *al-Diyāh* (Id. pp. 320–380).

41.6 Beneficiaries of *Al-Diyāh* Against Bodily Injury or Death

Under Islamic law, for a bodily injury or homicide caused by negligence or intentional act the doctrine of *al-Diyāh* is applied as a monetary compensation imposed against the accused and also against his paternal relatives, to be repaid to the legal heirs or the beneficiaries of the deceased; or in case of bodily injury, the victim will be entitled to benefit under the institution of *al-Diyāh*.

In the light of Hadith 25, quoted above, the benefits available under the institution of *al-Diyāh* are itemised as follows:

- In the contemporary world it is not possible to provide a maximum compensation under the *al-Diyāh* principles by 100 camels. That is why Ibnu 'Ābidīn in *Raddu al-Muhtār* suggested that in this modern age the compensation for *Qatl* (wilful homicide) should be in money instead of camels. The proper (maximum) compensation in such case should be 1000 dinār (gold) or 10,000 dirhām (silver) (*Raddul Muhtar*, n.d.). Section 28 of the *Council of Islamic Ideology*, Pakistan, provides that one *al-Diyāh* is 12,000 dirhām, which are equivalent to 30.63 kg of silver or their value (Section 28 of the *Council of Islamic Ideology*, Pakistan) while 1000 dirhām are equivalent to 2.45 kg of gold (Dr. S. Sikandar, 1999). As for the monetary compensation against bodily injury or death caused by negligent act, it was determined first by the Holy Prophet (saw), but later the second Caliph Umar (r) ruled with slightly different accounting model on the above grounds, probably due to the diversed market phenomenon. Thus, the rules relating to the determined monetary assessment on (gold) can be observed in the following Hadith:

> Amr bin Shuaib (r) reported from his father (r) from his grandfather (r) that the value of bloodwit at the time of the Holy Prophet (saw) was 800 dinars or 8000 dirhams, and bloodwit of the people of the book at that time was half of the bloodwit of the Muslims. He (r) said that it continued thus, until

> Sayyedana Umar (r) when he (r) became Caliph. He (r) delivered a sermon and said: The camel have become dear. Then Umar (r) made it binding upon the owners of silver 12,000 dirhams and upon the owners of cattle, 200 cows and upon the owners of goat, 2000 goats, and upon the owners of clothes, 200 clothes. He left the bloodwit of the protected non-Muslims (as it was). He (r) did not increase it in proportion to the increase in blood-wit. (Mishkat al-Masabih, Diyāh, Hadith 31)

From this Hadith, it may be observed that the payment of *al-Diyāh* needs not necessarily be in 100 camels, but it could also be in currencies or other form of properties depending on the liable party's profession, business and custom. Thus, the payment of *al-Diyāh* can be accepted in any form which has commercial value, but should be assessed on the equivalent value as determined by the amount of *Dinār* or *Dirhām* in the Hadith.

- The amount of compensation in case of bodily injury or death resulting from negligence ruled out under the institution of *al-Diyāh* is as shown in Table 41.1.

41.7 *Al-Damān* (Compensation or Damages)

Under Islamic law, the law relating to compensation is more comprehensive than that of the common law principles. For bodily injury or death resulting from negligence, compensation is awarded under the doctrine of *al-Diyāh* as understood from the earlier discussion. But any other form of compensation awarded either against loss or damage to property, economy, reputation and so on, are ruled out under the broad doctrine of *al-Damān* (compensation). This section thus presents the conceptual framework of *al-Damān*.

The term *al-Damān* means compensation. Here compensation includes any form of monetary or material fine imposed against the fault party and in favour of the victim who suffers loss or damage to his reputation, economy or property. The doctrine of *al-Damān* originated from the Qur'anic sanction as follows:

> And remember Dawood and Sulaiman when they gave judgment concerning the field when the people's sheep pastured therein by night, and we were bearers of witness to their judgement. So we made Sulaiman to understand it, and to each one we gave wisdom and knowledge. (Qur'an, 21: 78–79)

Table 41.1 Beneficiaries of *al-Diyāh* (Bloodwit) against bodily injury or death

Particulars of damages		*Maximum compensation for one* al-Diyāh	*Percentage of* al-Diyāh *payable*	*Amount of actual compensation payable in RM*
Loss	Injury			
Life		30.63 kg of silver or 2.45 kg of gold (this is equivalent to 1000 dinār (gold) or 12,000 dirhām (silver)	100%	The value of 2.5 2.45 kg of gold in RM 98,000[a]
Nose from the root		- do -	100%	RM 98,000
Lips		- do -	100%	RM 98,000
Testicles		- do -	100%	RM 98,000
Penis		- do -	100%	RM 98,000
Backbone		- do -	- do -	RM 98,000
Both eyes		- do -	- do -	RM 98,000
One eye		- do -	50%	RM 49,000
One foot		½*al-Diyāh*	50%	RM 49,000
	Head	1/3 *al-Diyāh*	33.33%	RM 32,663.40
	Stomach	1/3 *al-Diyāh*	33.33%	RM 32,663.40
	Fracture of a bone in head	15/100 *al-Diyāh*	15%	RM 14,700
One finger		10/100 *al-Diyāh*	10%	RM 9800
One toe		- do -	10%	RM 9800
Tooth		5/100 *al-Diyāh*	5%	RM 4900
	Bone	- do -	5%	RM 4900

Source: Author's collection

[a]This figure has been obtained based on the market position at 5.25 p.m. on 30th April, 1999. [Ref. D.S. Jwellers, Ipoh, Perak, Malaysia]

According to leading commentators, the Qur'anic rule refers to sheep, which got into a vineyard by night and caused severe damage by eating the entire crop. Prophet Dāwūd (a.s) as king and judge, awarded the owner of the vineyard the sheep as compensation for damages. His son Sulaiman (a.s) suggested a better judgment, saying that corpus of the property was not lost. It was a loss of its fruits only. Therefore, the vineyard was to be given to the owner of the sheep to restore to its original condition. And in the meantime the owner of the vineyard should be allowed to detain the sheep long enough to benefit from their milk, wool and their young to make up for the time factor loss. Allah (swt) praised Sulaiman's insight in distinguishing in corpus and income (Muhammad Ata-Alsid, n.d.). It is again interesting to note that a similar well-reported case occurred during the time of the Prophet Muhammad (saw). Here, a she-camel belonging to Albara' b. 'Aazib (r), a famous companion of the Prophet (saw) strayed into an orchard and caused a lot of damage. The case was brought to the Prophet (saw) and he ruled that the owner of the field and cultivation was responsible for guarding them during the day, and the owner of animal was to be liable for any damage caused by their animal by night.[1] This ruling was accepted by *al-Jumhūr* comprising *al-Malikiyyah, al-Shafī'iyyah* and *al-Hanabilah* (ibid.).

From the above Qur'anic sanction, as well as the commentaries and the tradition of the Holy Prophet (saw), it notable that the doctrine of *al-Damān* does not only include the compensation relating to damage or loss caused to property only, but it also rules out compensation relating to any form of material damage or loss suffered except a bodily injury or death resulting from a negligent act, as they are compensated under the doctrine of *al-Diyāh*. It is therefore submitted that in the contemporary world, any form of monetary compensation or restitution—be it against one's life, body, property or income—may be awarded under the combined doctrines of *al-Diyāh* and *al-Damān* as an able or rather better alternative, than that of the theory of compensation set out under common law principles. This contention will further be justified in the subsequent analysis of this chapter.

41.8 Takaful

An alternative to the concept of insurance is the doctrine of *al Takaful* as adapted by the Islamic insurance operators of today as a Sharī'ah-justified model. The doctrine of *Takaful* is operated based on the Sharī'ah principles of shared responsibility, mutual cooperation, solidarity and brotherhood, (Ikram Shakeer, 1997) with a sincere view of safeguarding one against a defined risk, catastrophe, disaster, loss or damage, which is

[1] The incident was reported by Imam Shafii. See *Mukhtasar al Muzni*, Margin of *Kitab Al-Um*, Vol. 5, "*Kitabul Sha'b*", p. 174; This was also reported by Imam Malik in *al-Muwatta*, Imam Ahmad b. Hambal in *al-Masnad*, *Abu Daud*, *al-Nasai*, *Ibn Majah Dar Qutni*, *Ibn Hibban*, *al-Hakim*; and *al-Baihaqi*.

certainly opposed to the idea of unexpected gain. The term *al-Takaful* is *al-Masdar*, an infinite noun, which is derived from the root word *Kafl.* The word Kaflwhose chief characteristic is *al-Mushārakah*, which means 'Sharing'. Thus, the word *al-Takaful* means 'shared responsibility', 'shared guarantee' or 'assurance'. Technically, *al-Takaful* from the economic point of view means, mutual guarantee or security provided by a group of people living in the same society, against a defined risk or catastrophe befalling one's life, property or any form of valuable things. Hence, *Takaful* is better known as co-operative insurance (my doctorate thesis, (1998) IIUM, p. 26).

However, the concept of *Takaful* is acceptable in the Sharī'ah teachings for the following reasons:

- The policyholders would co-operate among themselves for their common goal of mutual security against risk.
- Every policyholder would pay his subscription in order to assist those among contributors who need assistance or financial security.
- It falls under the donation contract, which is intended to divide losses or damages and spread liability according to the community pooling system.
- The element of uncertainty *(Gharar)* is eliminated in so far subscription and compensation are concerned.
- It doesn't aim at deriving advantage, goal, gain or opportunity at the cost of other individuals. (*Takaful (Islamic Insurance)*, 1999)

Under Islamic law generally, any transaction that involves the elements like unjust enrichment, uncertainty and *Riba (usury)*, such kinds of elements will invalidate the contract. Hence, the contract of insurance under Islamic law could not be held valid unless it is free from these elements. Thus, in consonance with the above basic characteristics, the jurists resolved that the system of insurance, which falls within the confines of Islamic framework, should be founded on the concept of *Takaful.* An Islamic insurance transaction is a policy of mutual co-operation against tragedy in which the parties involved are expected to contribute genuinely. The nature of thc principles of *Takaful* is obviously different from the principles of conventional insurance. The general principles of *Takaful* are itemised as follows:

- The operation of *Takaful* must be in line with the Sharī'ah principles. A *Takaful* operation may be held ***void ab initio*** if any aspect of its operation is proven to be contrary to the Sharī'ah principles (Rules of the Shari'ah Supervisory Board, Faisal Islamic Bank, Sudan, n.d).
- The operation of *Takaful* generally based on the governing principles of *Al-Mudarabah* (profit- and loss-sharing financing technique) which is an alternative to the usury-based financing technique as adapted by the conventional practices.
- The operation of *Takaful* practices is generally supervised by an independent body called the Sharī'ah Supervisory Council. It is the duty of the council to advice the *Takaful* operators on their operations for the purpose of ensuring that no aspect of the company's operations involves any element which is not approved by the Sharī'ah principles. In other words, the establishment of Sharī'ah supervisory council for any individual *Takaful* operator is a prerequisite prior to the commencement of the *Takaful* operations.

It is also within the fundamental principles of *Takaful* operations to maintain utmost good faith or sincerity in *Takaful* operations. This is because a *Takaful* policy can at any time be called and questioned should either party (operator or participant) be able to prove the counters' breach of good faith in the material matters of facts of each respective policy. Therefore, the duty to disclose material facts or matters is not imposed only on the operator but on both the operator and the participants equally (Takaful (Islamic Insurance), 1999).

From this conceptual understanding, it is concluded that a *Takaful* is a unique doctrine which has been developed as an alternative to the conventional insurance. Thus, this doctrine of *Takaful* is a fully Sharī'ah-justified insurance model. In operation, however, all aspects of it are expected to be practiced in line with the absolute Sharī'ah principles. Furthermore, failure to comply with the Sharī'ah principles the doctrine cannot be said an absolute Sharī'ah-justified one. It is further clarified by the provision laid down under Section 2 of the Takaful Act 1984. The section reads to the effect.

> *Takaful* business means a *Takaful* whose aims and operations do not involve any element which is not approved by the Sharī'ah. (The Takaful Act, 1984, at S.2)

41.9 Damages: *Al-Diyāh* Versus *Takaful*

From the practical scenario it has been observed that the contemporary *Takaful* operators in their quantum of damages against personal injury or death generally apply the doctrine of *continental* skill, which is based on common law principles. It is quite clear that the *Takaful* business or operations in Malaysia by virtue of Section 2 of Takaful Act 1984 should be in line with Sharī'ah principles. But why in the issue of quantum of damages is the section not compliant with Sharī'ah? The reason is probably because of the strong influence of the common law, which became a common practice, as a result of which the *Takaful* operators might not yet have come up with an exclusive alternative model which can be justified under Sharī'ah. From the earlier analysis in this chapter it has been witnessed that under Islamic law as far as the quantum of damages against personal injury or death resulting from negligence are concerned, this can only be based on the doctrine of *al-Diyāh*, while the other forms of compensation against property or wealth, other than against life or body injury, should be based on the doctrine of *al-Damān*. Under both doctrines, there is no room for one to hope for an unlimited damage, but only a reasonable compensation can be awarded against genuine loss or damage against body or life or property or even wealth.

Hence, we now offer a closer examination via a comparative diagram of the quantum of damages as set out by the Holy Prophet (saw) in the doctrine of *al-Diyāh* against a personal injury and death resulting from negligence, and also the quantum of damages practised by the *Takaful* operators in today's Malaysian economy. All this may reveal the actual differences at play and subsequently may enable us to design an alternative framework of the quantum of damages, which is justified by the Sharī'ah principles for the *Takaful* operations in today's economy. The quantum of damages against bodily injury or culpable homicide set out under the doctrine of *al-Diyāh* is shown in (*Mishkatul Musabih*, *op. cit.*, n. 9.). (Tables 41.2 and 41.3).

From the tables of quantum as set out under both *Takaful* and also the institution of *al-Diyāh* it is clear that both institutions provide equitable provisions for pertinent damages, in terms of bodily injury or accidental death. The actual difference between them is the mechanism of operation and the basis of the law, which both institutions rely upon. The quantum under *al-Diyāh* was set out in the Hadith, whereas the quantum under the existing *Takaful* practices is based on the continental skill, which is set out

Table 41.2 Damages: *Al-Diyāh* versus *Takaful*

Particulars of damage		*Maximum compensation for one* al-Diyāh	*Percentage of* al-Diyāh *payable*	*Amount of actual compensation payable in RM*	*Payable by*
Loss	Injury				
Life		30.63 kg of silver or 2.45 kg of gold (this is equivalent to 1000 dinars (gold) or 12,000 dirham (silver) or 1000 camels	100%	The value of 2.45 kg of gold in RM 98,000[a]	Paternal relatives of the accused
Nose from the root		full *al-Diyāh*	100%	RM 98,000	- do -
All teeth		full *al-Diyāh*	100%	RM 98,000	- do -
Lip		full *al-Diyāh*	100%	RM 98,000	- do -
Testicles		full *al-Diyāh*	100%	RM 98,000	- do -
Penis		full *al-Diyāh*	100%	RM 98,000	- do -
Backbone		full *al-Diyāh*	100%	RM 98,000	- do -
Both eyes		full *al-Diyāh*	100%	RM 98,000	- do -
One eye		full *al-Diyāh*	50%	RM 49,000	- do -
One foot		full *al-Diyāh*	50%	RM 49,000	- do -
One finger		10/100 *al-Diyāh*	10%	RM 9800	- do -
One toe		10/100 *al-Diyāh*	10%	RM 9800	- do -
Tooth		5/100 *al-Diyāh*	5%	RM 4900	- do -
	Head	1/3 *al-Diyāh*	33.33%	RM 32,663.40	- do -
	Stomach	1/3 *al-Diyāh*	33.33%	RM 32,663.40	- do -
	Fracture of a bone in head	1/100 *al-Diyāh*	15%	RM 14,700	- do -
	Bone	5/100 *al-Diyāh*	5%	RM 4900	- do -

Source: Author's collection

[a]This value was determined based on the market position at 5.25 p.m. on 30 April 1999. [Ref.D.S. Jewellers, Ipoh, Perak, Malaysia]

in the light of common law principles. The other difference is the scope of coverage; for example, under the existing *Takaful* practices, the scope is explained in detail, unlike under *al-Diyāh*, where it provides only the general principles relating to scope of coverage, which are further required to

Table 41.3 Example of benefits for accidental death and permanent disablement in *Takaful*[a]

Particular of loss or damage	*Percentages of the covered*
A. Accidental death	100%
B. Permanent disablement:	
Loss of two limbs	100%
Loss of both hands, or of all fingers and both thumbs	100%
Total loss of sight of both eyes	100%
Total paralysis	100%
Injuries resulting in being permanently bedridden	100%
Any other injury causing permanent total disablement	100%
Loss of arm at shoulder	100%
Loss of arm between shoulder and elbow	100%
Loss of arm at elbow	100%
Loss of arm between elbow and wrist	100%
Loss of arm at wrist	100%
Loss of leg	100%
at hip	100%
between knee and hip	100%
below knee	100%
Eye: Loss of	100%
whole eye	100%
sight of	100%
sight of exception of light	50%
lens of	50%
Loss of four fingers and thumb of one hand	40%
Loss of thumb	
both phalanges	25%
one phalange	10%
Loss of index finger	
three phalanges	10%
two phalanges	8%
one phalange	2%
Loss of middle finger	
three phalanges	6%
two phalanges	4%
one phalange	2%
Loss of ring finger	
three phalanges	5%
two phalanges	3%
one phalange	2%
Loss of little finger	
three phalanges	4%

(*continued*)

Table 41.3 (continued)

Particular of loss or damage	*Percentages of the covered*
two phalanges	3%
one phalange	2%
Loss of metacarpal	
first or second (additional)	3%
third, fourth or fifth (additional)	2%
Loss of toes	
all	15%
great, both phalanges	5%
great, one phalange	2%
other than great, if more than one toe lost, each	1%
if more than one toe lost, each	1%
Loss of hearing	
both ears	75%
one ear	15%
Loss of speech	50%

Source: Author's collection from TMB

[a]The table has been extracted from *Certificate for Group Personal Accident Takaful*, TMB, at p. 2

be analysed relying on the doctrines of *al-Qiyās* and *al-Masalih al-Mursalah*. This analysis must be made until there is establishment of a reasonable compensation against loss, which shall be upon considering the degree or merit of damage suffered by the innocent party. And this again is justified by the Hadith:

> No harm is to be inflicted on another and no unjustifiable harm is to be inflicted in recompense. (Al-Muwatta)

41.10 *Al-Diyāh* and *Al-Damān* Can Be the Basis for Takaful in Its Quantum of Damages

It is undeniable that although a *Takaful* operator might adopt the existing quantum policy from the continental skill, which is based on the common law principles, it does not mean that this entire quantum policy is unlawful in the light of Sharī'ah. Some of the objections that may be raised against the existing quantum policy of *Takaful* is that this quantum is based on the conventional principles and thus may not be proper for *Takaful*, which is expected to be based on absolute Sharī'ah principles—and not only in terms of its principles but also in practice, as provided under Section 2 of The Takaful Act 1984. There may be another objection raised, for example, that the damages awarded by the *Takaful* operator against the loss of future earnings may not be justified by Sharī'ah principles. It may also be considered curious here that the damages awarded against accidental death should not be awarded by considering the status, position, sex or even age of the victim. Rather, they are awarded based on the degree of pain or loss suffered by the victim, since all human beings are equal as far as bodily pain, loss or suffering are concerned. For *Takaful* means to provide a security against pain, loss or suffering.

It has been observed that although the conventional policy of a quantum of damages may be not entirely rejected in view of Sharī'ah principles, there are some issues around the practices of a quantum of damages under common law which may not be justified Islamically. Thus, it might be appropriate for the *Takaful* operators to adopt a Sharī'ah-justified model for quantum of damages. But, the question arises here as to whether there is any justified Sharī'ah model for a quantum of damages that exists today which can be practised in the contemporary world of advanced technology? To solve this problem, we suggest that the doctrines of *al-Diyāh* and *al-Damān* may jointly be able to provide an alternative model of quantum of damages practised under today's common law principles. For instance, there are two categories of damages awarded for personal injury or accidental death. First, there is special damage, which is a pecuniary compensation, calculated from the accident until the trial. The second category is general damage, which itself falls into two categories:

- general damages (non-pecuniary)
- general damages (pecuniary).

General damages (non-pecuniary) are awarded only against bodily injury, permanent disablement or accidental death, while the general damage (pecuniary) are awarded against loss of future earnings, future medical expenses, and so forth (Rutter, Michael F., n.d.). To meet the scope of these two categories of damages, the doctrine of *al-Diyāh* and also of *al-Damān* jointly provide a proper alternative, except in the case of the damages against loss of future earnings, as this may involve the element of *Gharar*, which is not lawful. The doctrine of *al-Diyāh*, however, provides the damages, which are equivalent to that of general damages (non-pecuniary) under common law. The doctrine of *al-Damān*, meanwhile, may provide the quantum of damages as provided under the heading of special damages and also the general damages (pecuniary), save damages for the loss of future earnings. Hence, it is concluded that the doctrines of both *al-Diyāh* and *al-Damān* are jointly able to provide comprehensive damages against bodily injury or death resulting from any form of accident. So, there may not be any justification for the *Takaful* operators to adopt common law principles in the quantum of damages while there is a proper solution given under the doctrine of *al-Diyāh* and *al-Damān* in this regard. Furthermore, *Takaful* is a Sharī'ah-based financial technique whose aims and objectives and also the operational mechanisms should absolutely be based on the Sharī'ah principles as provided under the Section 2 of Takaful Act 1984. This fact shows that the *Takaful* operators may not have the opportunity to base its operation on common law principles, as this contravenes the Takaful Act 1984. Thus, it is submitted here that the doctrine of both *al-Diyāh* and *al-Damān* may be able to provide an alternative solution to quantum of damages as presently practised under *Takaful* operations.

41.11 Benefits May Be Awarded Under *Takaful* Against Bodily Injury or Accidental Death

From the earlier discussions and analysis it has been concluded that the *Takaful* operator in its quantum of damages against bodily injury or accidental death should adopt the Sharī'ah-justified doctrines *al-Diyāh* and *al-Damān* jointly, as a viable alternative to the structure of quantum of damages designed under the continental skill, which is based on common law principles. Thus, a structure is proposed for the quantum of damages of *Takaful* operations against bodily injury or accidental death, which may harmonise simultaneously the objectives of *Takaful* business with the Sharī'ah spirit and also the practical reality. The structure for such an approach may be set out as follows:

- The quantum of damages under *Takaful* operations against the bodily injury, accidental death and any related reasonable pecuniary loss may be awarded in the light of the combined doctrines of *al-Diyāh* and *al-Damān*.
- For accidental death, a full *al-Diyāh* should be the quantum of damage. A full *al-Diyāh* is 30.63 kg of silver or 2.45 kg of gold, which are equivalent to RM 98,000. It is also noted that the damages should be limited only up to the amount of a full *al-Diyāh*.

- As for bodily injury, the quantum of damage should also be based on the doctrine of *al-Diyāh*. The amount of compensation in bodily injury, however, should be awarded based on the degree or merit of damage caused to the body or organ.
- As for the loss of earning resulting from the accident and up to the final judgement should be reasonably calculated relying on the doctrine of *al-Damān*.
- As for the loss of future earning, this should not be awarded nor justified under the Islamic law as it involves *Gharar*. A transaction that involves the element of *Gharar* is unlawful, as the Holy Prophet (saw) prohibited it in the following Hadith:

> The holy Prophet (saw) prohibited transaction with *Gharar*. (Qur'an, 31: 34)

Furthermore, it is also contrary to the spirit of Sharī'ah to determine one's future earnings in advance. This is because future earnings are certainly determined by Almighty Allah (swt) as the following *ayah* reveals to us:

> Verily the knowledge of the hour is with Allah (swt). It is He who sends down rain, and He who knows what is in the wombs – nor does anyone know what it is that he will earn tomorrow … Verily with Allah (swt) is full knowledge and He is acquainted (with all things). (Qur'an, 31: 34)

- In the light of this Qur'anic *ayah* and Hadith it is concluded that there is no justification for the *Takaful* operator to include future earnings in its quantum of damage against bodily injury or accidental homicide. As for the medical expenses incurred from the moment of accident until the final judgment, and also from the final judgment until a fullest recovery, the reasonable expenses should be awarded under the doctrine of *al-Damān*, provided that the victim is not permanently disabled, in which case the victim shall be awarded under *al-Diyāh*, but not under *al-Damān*.
- The *Takaful* operator should also provide for the victim or his family a pecuniary compensation for any form of other reasonable expenses resulting from the bodily injury or accidental homicide. This category of compensation can be awarded based on the doctrine of *Al-Damān*. Regarding the medical expenses and also other forms of expenses, they are justified by the saying of the Holy Prophet (saw):

41.11.1 The Prophetic Ruling on damages

No harm is to be inflicted on another and no unjustifiable harm is to be inflicted in recompense. (Al-Muwatta.)

- Contributions may be made in favour of the dependants of the deceased or injured victim, who are affected by the accident of their breadwinner financially. This contribution can be made to the dependants of the victim for the loss of their breadwinner, based on the broad principles of *al-Damān*. It is also justified by the saying of the Holy Prophet (saw), which encourages believers to alleviate hardship be it financial or otherwise:

The Holy Prophet (saw) said: "Whosoever removes a worldly grief from a believer, Allah (swt) will remove from him one of the grieves of the day of judgment, whosoever alleviates (the lot of) a needy person, Allah (swt) will alleviate (his lot) in this world and the next." (Sahih al-Muslim)

The above-justified paradigm can further be witnessed in Fig. 41.1.

41.12 Possibilities for Adapting the Principles of *al-Diyāh* or *al-Damān* in *Takaful*

As has already been discussed, the doctrine of *al-Diyāh* is applicable only in cases of bodily injury or accidental death. The compensation under this doctrine is awarded based on the customs or practices of the people or tribe of the accused. The purpose of this doctrine is to provide compensation against loss or damage suffered by the victim or his family as a result. In human society, it is the Islamic teachings that no one should misappropriate others' property or cause any form of damage against another's life or body or property. This sanction was ruled in the saying of the holy Prophet (saw):

Narrated by Abu Huraira (may Allah be pleased with him), who said: The Messenger of Allah (May the blessings and peace of Allah be upon him) said: "Do not envy one another; do not inflate price one to another; do not hate one another; do not turn away from one another; and do not under cut one another, but be you, O servants of Allah (swt), brothers. A Muslim is a brother of a Muslim, he neither oppress him nor does he fail him, he neither lies to him nor does he hold him in contempt. Piety is right here and he pointed to his breast three times. It is evil enough for a

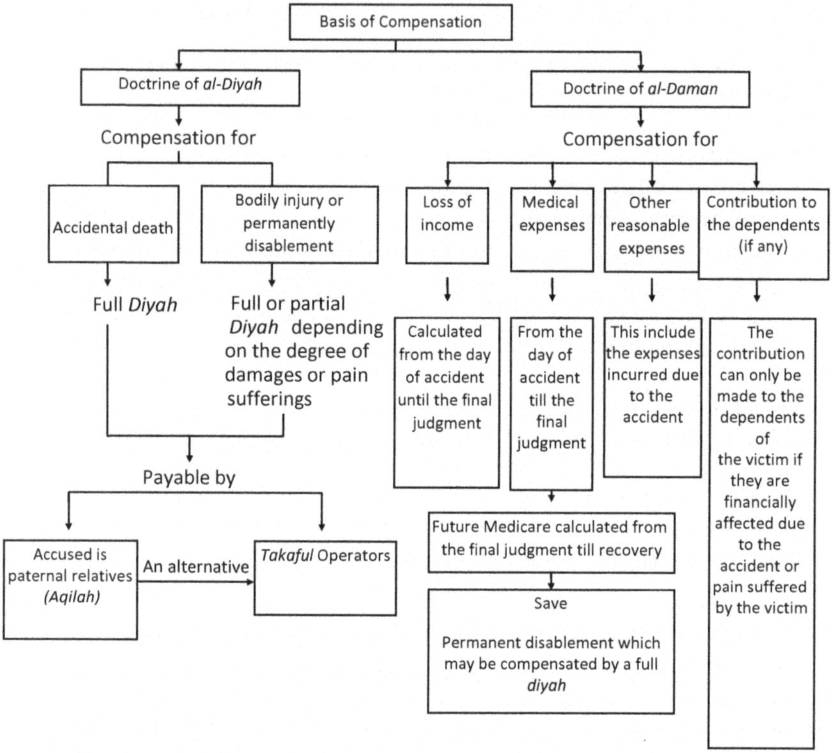

Fig. 41.1 Benefits may be awarded under *Takaful* against bodily injury or accidental death. (Source: Author's own)

man to held his brother. Muslim in contempt the whole of a Muslim for another Muslim is unlawful: his blood, his property and his honour" (Reported in Sahih al-Muslim).

In view of this Hadith it is understood that it is a violation of the law of Allah (swt) to cause any damage or loss to anybody's life body or property. If someone violates the rules of Allah (swt), the wrongdoer has to pay appropriate compensation against causing loss or damage to someone. As is stated in the following Hadith:

Reported by Abu Said Khudri (r), the Holy Prophet (saw) said: "No harm is to be inflicted on another and no unjustifiable harm is to be inflicted in recompense." (Al-Muwatta)

This Hadith lists the following basic principles:

- All harm to another's body or property is unlawful and must be avoided.
- The victim should not seek reparation by inflicting unnecessary harm in retribution.
- The Hadith and its totality established the primary liability of any wrongdoer to make up for the harm inflicted by him (Muhammad Ata-Al-Sid, n.d.).

From the above Hadith it is clear that it is a violation of the law of Allah (swt) should anyone cause harm, damage or loss to another's life, body or property. For such a violation, the law provides that appropriate compensation be imposed against the violator and in favour of the suffering party. Although compensation under ***al-Diyāh*** and ***al-Damān*** is available, it is the right of the injured party if they wish to compromise by reducing or eliminating partly or entirely the obligation of the wrongdoer; this is allowed in the Islamic *Sharī'ah*, as it is also a good deed to lessen the burden of others. Thus, the provision relating to compromise in compensation is justified by the following Hadith:

> Amr bin Shuaib (r) from his father from his grandfather reported that the messenger of Allah (swt) said: Whosoever kills intentionally shall be handed over to the relations of the killed. If they like, they may kill him, and if they like, they may take bloodwit; and that is 30 camels of four years old, 30 she-camels of five years old, 40 pregnant she-camels and there is for them. [This is] what they compromise upon. (Mishkatul Masabih; Kithab Al-Quisas, No. 18)

Agreeing to a compromise in compensation is like a contribution to lightening the burden of one's fellows, which is certainly in the sight of Allah (swt) a great and significant deed, as justified in the following Hadith:

> Narrated by Abu Huraira (may Allah be pleased with him) that the Holy Prophet (may the blessings and peace of Allah be upon him) said: Whosoever removes a worldly grief from a believer, Allah will remove from him one of the griefs of the day of judgment, whosoever alleviates [the lot of] a needy person, Allah (swt) will alleviate [his lot] in this world and the next. (Sahih al-Muslim)

The obligation of compensation upon the accused is like a debt, which may be compromised by the victim or his beneficiaries, as justified by the following *ayah*:

> If the debtor is in a difficulty, grant him time till it is easy for him to repay. But if you remit it by way of charity, that is best for you if you only know. (Qur'an, 2: 280)

41.13 No Discrimination in Quantum of Damages

The issue of quantum of damages under *Takaful* should always be determined based on Sharī'ah principles, as discussed earlier. The quantum of damages against bodily injury or accidental death is determined not based on the status or position of the victim, but should be determined upon considering the degree or merit of the pain or loss suffered by the victim. This can be justified by the prophetic ruling, which states that compensation for the loss or damage suffered by a person should be reasonable. The Hadith that determines the compensation considers only the aspect of loss or damage, but not the position nor the status of the victim. In other words, there is no discrimination or inequality in determining the quantum of damages under Islamic law. Thus, the relevant Hadith is as follows:

Narrated by Abu Said Khudri (ra), the Holy Prophet (saw) said: "No harm is to be inflicted on another and no unjustifiable harm is to be inflicted in recompense." (Al-Muwatta).

The Hadith lays down the following principles:

- All harm to another's body or property is unlawful and must be avoided.
- The victim should not seek reparation by inflicting unnecessary harm in retribution.
- The Hadith in its totality establishes liability of any wrongdoer to make up for the harm inflicted by him (Muhammad Ata Al-Sid, n.d.).

From this Hadith and its underlying principles, we may conclude that there is certainly compensation against loss or injuries provided for under Islamic teaching, but at the same time there is a limitation too as no one should set out in the hope for compensation, which is unreasonable and unjustifiable. This means that the victim can recover or claim for compensation only against the obvious loss or damage and he may not have the chance to claim unlimited damages. In other words, the victim cannot use his position or status in claiming damages. This is because in a personal accident that results in bodily injury or death, the sufferer suffers according to the degree of injury or loss and all human beings are equal as far as their pain and suffering are concerned—regardless whether one is a king or a labourer. Therefore, the quantum of damages under *Takaful* operations against bodily injury or accidental death should be determined without any discrimination considering the degree or merit of suffering and pain, and without looking at the position, status, sex or even age of the victim.

41.14 Conclusion

The quantum of damages against bodily injuries or accidental death is designed under both common law principles and also in view of Sharī'ah teaching. From this short survey it is understood that the provisions relating to the quantum of damages against bodily injuries or accidental death under Islamic law by virtue of the doctrines of *Al-Diyāh* and *Al-Damān* are quite comprehensive, compared to the structure practised under the common law principles. Under common law principles, compensation against the loss of future earnings is available, which may be unfair to the liable party as it is given on the basis of uncertainty. Furthermore, the quantum of damages determined under common law in some situations, considers the status, position age or sex of the victim, in which the notion of compensation is dominated by an unlimited or unjustified luxurious gain, rather than a reasonable and equitable indemnity against pain and suffering. Under Islamic law, on the other hand, in the light of the doctrine of *al-Diyāh* and *al-Daman*, compensation against the loss of future earnings may not be justified, on the grounds of *Gharar*. Furthermore, there is certainly no discrimination in determining the quantum of damages under Islamic law.

It is suggested *Takaful* operators consider the doctrines of *al-Diyāh* and *al-Damān* jointly in their quantum of damages for bodily injury or accidental death, so as to ensure that the rules set out under Section 2 of the Takaful Act are upheld in reality.

References

1. Ali, A. Y. (n.d.), The Holy Qur'an, Text and Translation.
2. *Techniques for the Quantum of Damages*, Takaful Malaysia, Takaful Nasional, Takaful Ikhlas and others.
3. *Exodus*, 21:23–25.
4. al-Nawawi, *Minhaj et-Talebeen* (Trans. Eng.By) E.C. Howard, Law Publishing Company, Lahore, 1977, at p. 413 ff.
5. Mishkat Al-Masabih, Book 15, (Diyāh) Chapter 1.
6. Ullah, M.W. *Muslim Jurisprudence and The Qur'anic Law of Crimes*, Islamic Book Service, Lahore, 1982, p. 154.
7. Shorter Encyclopaedia of Islam, P. 229.
8. Mishkat al-Masabih, Kitab Al-Diyāh, No.Hadith 25.
9. Amin, S.H., Islamic Law and Its Implications for Modern World, U.K., 1989, p. 319.
10. Kingdom of Saudi Arabia, *Council of Ministers*, resolution No. 734 (5/5/1396).
11. The Labour and Workers Regulations (Saudi Arabia) 1969, at Article 76.
12. Miskat al-masabih, Kitab al-Diyāh, no. Hadith 25.
13. *Raddul Muhtar*, Vol. V (Egypt), p. 504.
14. Section 28 of the *Council of Islamic Ideology*, Pakistan.
15. The information has been obtained from an expert @ Dr. S. Sikandar, IRKH, IIUM, in April, 1999.
16. Mishkat al-Masabih, Diyāh, No.Hadith 31.
17. The market position at 5.25 p.m. on 30 April, 1999. [Ref. D.S. Jwellers, Ipoh, Perak, Malaysia.]
18. Muhammad Ata-Alsid, "*Traffic Accidents in Islamic Law*" (paper) pp. 1–2.
19. Imam Shafii. See *Mukhtasar al Muzni*, Margin of *Kitab Al-Um*, Vol. 5, *"Kitabul Sha'b"*, p. 174; This was also reported by Imam Malik in *al-Muwatta*, Imam Ahmad b. Hambal in *al-Masnad*, *Abu Daud*, *al-Nasai*, *Ibn Majah Dar Qutni*, *Ibn Hibban*, *al-Hakim*; and *al-Baihaqi*.
20. *Mukhtasar al-Muzni*, *Ibid*. See also Ibn Hajar, *Fath al-Bari* Vol. 12, Dar Al Ma'rifah, Beirut, Lebanon, p. 258.
21. Ikram Shakeer, "Tomorrow's Takaful Products" in *New Horizon*, 66: 1997, p. 5; See also the *Takaful Act*, 1984 at S. 2.
22. Billah, M. M. (1998), *Doctorate thesis*, IIUM, p. 26.
23. "*Takaful* (Islamic Insurance)", in *New Horizon*, January 1999 at p. 3.
24. Rules of the Shari'ah Supervisory Board, Faisal Islamic Bank, Sudan, n.d. p. 12.
25. "Takaful (Islamic Insurance)", in New Horizon, January 1999, p. 3.

26. TheTakaful Act, 1984, at S.2. (Repealed by the Islamic Financial Services Act 2013).
27. The Certificate for Group Personal Accident Takaful, STMB, at p. 2.
28. Al-Muwatta al-Malek.
29. Rutter, Michael F. (n.d.), Handbook on Damages for Personal Injuries and Death, in Singapore and Malaysia, 2nd Ed.
30. The slamic Financial Services Act 2013.
31. Sahih al-Muslim.
32. Mishkat al-Masabih; Kithab Al-Quisas, No. 18.

Correction to: Islamic Insurance Products

Mohd Ma'Sum Billah

Correction to:

M. M. Billah, *Islamic Insurance Products*,
https://doi.org/10.1007/978-3-030-17681-5

The Front Matter has been revised to correct the 'Foreword' author signature to 'Tuanku Syed Faizuddin Putra'.

The updated original online version of this book can be found at
https://doi.org/10.1007/978-3-030-17681-5

M. M. Billah, *Islamic Insurance Products*,
https://doi.org/10.1007/978-3-030-17681-5_42

INDEX[1]

A
Accident, 76, 78, 79, 82, 85, 87–89, 91–93, 97–102, 283–292, 305–307, 309–311, 310n2, 314–316, 319
Account, 3, 215–218, 273–275, 277, 278, 281, 430, 432
Agreement, 124, 127, 129
Al-Rahnu, 343–346
Asean *Re-Takaful* International Ltd. (ARIL), 39, 43
Asset, 103, 105

B
Badal, 189–197
Benefits, 5, 6, 20, 25, 98, 101, 161–166, 183–186, 212–218, 220, 227, 228, 241, 242, 272, 273, 275, 276, 280, 281, 296, 298, 302, 303, 307–309, 311, 314–316, 319, 321–323, 331, 332, 334–338, 340, 343, 345–347, 349, 351, 353–356, 358–361, 366–368, 370–380, 382, 383, 395, 396, 409, 415, 420, 457, 460–463, 465, 466, 469, 471, 480, 483, 488–489, 491–494
Breast, 355–366

C
Cancer, 355–366
Care, 167–179
Cashline, 211–220
Ceding, 408
Citizen, 321–324
Claim, 68, 70, 78–84, 87–89, 94, 100, 101, 114, 116–119, 128, 133, 134, 137, 140, 145, 217, 241, 243, 280, 300–302, 305–312, 374–376, 398, 400, 408, 420, 441, 445–455, 457–472, 496, 497

[1] Note: Page numbers followed by 'n' refer to notes.

Mohd Ma'Sum Billah, *Islamic Insurance Products*,
https://doi.org/10.1007/978-3-030-17681-5

Contribution, 107, 114, 116, 119, 148, 151, 155, 156, 181, 208, 229, 230, 233, 241–243, 273, 278, 279, 281, 286, 314, 315, 318, 321–324, 326, 327, 334, 368–371, 378, 380–382, 384, 397, 398, 400, 493, 495
Coverage, 149, 151–154
Critical, 295–304
Cryptocurrency, 238–243

D
Damages, 98–100, 473–497
Death, 344, 346–349, 353, 354
Digital, 237–243
Disease, 125, 126, 129–133, 136–140, 143, 297–301
Documentations, 452

E
Education, 313–320
Employer, 331–338, 340, 341
Endowment, 325–329
Experience, 113–121

F
Facultative, 410, 411
Family, 23, 24, 148, 155–156, 266, 271–281, 284, 346, 349, 350, 352–354, 367, 368, 374, 378, 395–403, 457–472
Fatwa, 248n1, 252, 256, 258–259, 262–264, 262n8
Fire, 103–111, 113–121
Foreign, 331–341
Fund, 423–433, 435–441

G
General, 6, 13, 17, 23, 67–73, 76, 77, 82, 96, 445–455
Governing, 47–61
Group, 159–179, 211–220, 310–311, 439

H
Haj, 189–197
Hajj, 181–187
Hawa, 355–366
Health, 123–133, 141–145, 147–157, 167–179, 302
Hospital, 356, 360, 362, 366

I
Illness, 124–140, 142, 143, 295–304
Insured, 249, 256, 261, 263
Insurer, 248, 249, 251, 252, 254–262, 265–267
Investment, 411, 412, 415, 425, 429, 430, 432, 435–441
Islamic, 284–286

L
Law, 47–50, 48n1, 48n3, 56–59, 61
Life, 271, 272, 275, 276, 279, 281
Life insurance, 247–268

M
Management, 423–433
Medical, 123–145, 301
Mesra, 377–385
Misconception, 248, 255, 264
Mortgage, 343–354
Motor, 75–96
Mudharabah, 272–274

N
Nominee, 460, 461
Nutshell, 29–44

O
Old, 323
On-line, 227–236, 395–403
Operator, 67–69, 72, 73, 105, 109–111, 212–216, 218–220, 315–319, 396–401, 403, 418–424, 428–430, 432, 433, 462, 463, 471, 473, 474, 483, 485, 486, 489–492, 497
Overview, 3–25

P
Package, 200, 203–206, 231, 327–328
Parents, 307, 311, 313, 319
Participant, 68, 69, 72, 73, 104, 106, 107, 109–111, 160, 162–166, 181, 184, 397–401, 403, 424, 429, 430, 433, 457–468, 471
Period, 69, 449
Personal, 283–292
Pilgrimage, 181–187
Plan, 103–111, 123–145, 147–157, 167–179, 221–226, 271–281, 313, 350, 352–354
Policies, 47–52, 48n1, 48n2, 54–61, 57n9, 124, 127, 128, 131, 141, 144, 145, 205, 206, 208
Pregnancy, 367–376
Preview, 67–73
Principles, 47–61
Procedures, 445–455, 457–472
Products, 3–25, 29–44, 47–61, 407–415, 417–422
Property, 103–105, 108, 110
Protection, 368

Q
Qisās, 117, 474, 475, 479

R
Rating, 117
Receiver, 238–243
Refutation, 255
Reserve, 420
Re-takaful, 29–44, 47–61, 407–415, 417–433, 435–441
Return, 438, 440, 441
Rider, 147–157

S
Saving, 377–385
Scheme, 160, 164–166, 227, 233, 234, 324
School, 307, 309–312
Senior, 321–324
Shari'ah, 30–32, 34–35, 37, 38, 437–441
Structure, 417–422
Students, 305–312
Substitute, 189–197
Sukuk, 221–226

T
Tabarru, 76, 81, 273, 278
Takaful, 3–25, 47–61, 67–73, 75–111, 113–121, 123–145, 147–157, 159–179, 181–187, 189–197, 199–208, 211–243, 260, 265, 283–292, 295–304, 321–324, 331–341, 343–385, 387–393, 395–403, 417–425, 428, 429, 429n1, 445–455, 457–497
Treaty, 410
Trust, 387–393

U
Unit, 387–393
User, 238–240, 242, 243

V
Vehicle, 76–80, 82–96, 98, 100
Visit, 199–208

W
Waqf, 326–328
Wiladah, 367–376
Woman, 355
Worker, 331–341

Z
Ziarah, 199–208

The manufacturer's authorised representative in the EU is Springer Nature Customer Service Centre GmbH, Europaplatz 3, 69115 Heidelberg, Germany. If you have any concerns regarding our products, please contact ProductSafety@springernature.com

Printed and bound by CPI Group (UK) Ltd, Croydon, CR0 4YY
05/10/2026
02228125-0018